ARCHAEOLOGY:
THE KEY CONCEPTS

This invaluable resource provides an up-to-date and comprehensive survey of key ideas in archaeology and their impact on archaeological thinking and method.

Featuring over fifty detailed entries by international experts, the book offers definitions of key terms, explaining their origin and development. Entries also feature guides to further reading and extensive cross-referencing. Subjects covered include:

- Thinking about landscape
- Cultural evolution
- Social archaeology
- Gender archaeology
- Experimental archaeology
- Archaeology of cult and religion
- Concepts of time
- The Antiquity of Man
- Feminist archaeology
- Multiregional evolution

Archaeology: The Key Concepts is the ideal reference guide for students, teachers and anyone with an interest in archaeology.

Colin Renfrew is Emeritus Disney Professor of Archaeology and Fellow of the McDonald Institute for Archaeological Research, Cambridge.

Paul Bahn is a freelance writer, translator and broadcaster on archaeology.

YOU MAY ALSO BE INTERESTED IN THE FOLLOWING ROUTLEDGE STUDENT REFERENCE TITLES:

Archaeology: The Basics
Clive Gamble

Ancient History: Key Themes and Approaches
Neville Morley

Who's Who in Ancient Egypt
Michael Rice

Who's Who in the Ancient Near East
Gwendolyn Leick

Who's Who in the Greek World
John Hazel

Who's Who in the Roman World
John Hazel

ARCHAEOLOGY

The Key Concepts

Edited by
Colin Renfrew and Paul Bahn

Routledge
Taylor & Francis Group

LONDON AND NEW YORK

First published 2005
by Routledge
2 Park Square, Milton Park, Abingdon, Oxon OX14 4RN

Simultaneously published in the USA and Canada
by Routledge
270 Madison Ave., New York, NY 10016

Routledge is an imprint of the Taylor & Francis Group

© 2005 Colin Renfrew and Paul Bahn for selection and editorial matter; the
contributors for individual entries.

Typeset in Bembo by Taylor & Francis Books Ltd
Printed and bound in Great Britain by
TJ International Ltd, Padstow, Cornwall

British Library Cataloguing in Publication Data
A catalogue record for this book is available from the British Library

Library of Congress Cataloging in Publication Data
A catalog record for this title has been requested

ISBN 0–415–31757–6 (hbk)
ISBN 0–415–31758–4 (pbk)

CONTENTS

List of Key Concepts   vi
Contributors   viii
Introduction   xi

KEY CONCEPTS   1

Index   279

KEY CONCEPTS

Agency

The antiquity of man

Archaeoastronomy

Archaeogenetics

Catastrophist archaeology

The *chaîne opératoire*

Characterisation and exchange
theory

Childe's revolutions

Cognitive archaeology

Archaeology of cult and religion

Cultural evolution

'Dark Ages' in archaeology/
systems collapse

Darwinian archaeology

Ideas in relative and absolute dating

The descent of man

Theorising diffusion and
population movements

Ecological archaeology

Environmental archaeology

Epistemology

Ethnoarchaeology

The evolution of social complexity
and the state

Key ideas in excavation

Experimental archaeology

Feminist archaeology

Archaeological formation processes

Gender archaeology

Habitus

Historical archaeology and text

Holistic/contextual archaeology

Indigenous archaeologies

Innovation and invention –
independent event or historical
process?

Thinking about landscape

Material engagement and
materialisation

Materialism, Marxism and
archaeology

Mental modularity

Multiregional evolution

Non-linear processes and
archaeology

Notions of the person

Organisation of societies, including
chiefdoms

Peer polity interaction

Phenomenological archaeology

Post-processual and interpretive
archaeology

Processual archaeology

Public archaeology/museology/
conservation/heritage

Simulation

Site catchment analysis

Social archaeology

Theory of social practice

Principles of stratigraphic
succession

Survey

Symbolic and structuralist
   archaeology

Systems thinking

The Three Ages

Concepts of time

Uniformitarianism

CONTRIBUTORS

Leslie C. Aiello is at the Department of Anthropology, University College London, UK

Paul Bahn is a freelance writer, translator and broadcaster on Archaeology, UK

Geoff Bailey is at the Department of Archaeology, University of York, UK

John C. Barrett is at the Department of Archaeology and Prehistory, Sheffield University, UK

Richard Blanton is at the Department of Sociology and Anthropology, Purdue University, West Lafayette, Indiana, USA

Martin Carver is at the Department of Archaeology, University of York, UK

John F. Cherry is at the Kelsey Museum of Archaeology, University of Michigan, USA

Elizabeth DeMarrais is at the Department of Archaeology, University of Cambridge, UK

Kenneth L. Feder is at the Department of Anthropology, Central Connecticut State University, USA

Jonathan Friedman is at the Department of Anthropology, Lund University, Sweden

Peter Gathercole is an Emeritus Fellow, Darwin College, Cambridge, UK

Guy Gibbon is at the Department of Anthropology, University of Minnesota, USA

Chris Gosden is at the Pitt Rivers Museum, School of Anthropology and Museum Ethnography, University of Oxford, UK

Catherine Hills is at the Department of Archaeology, University of Cambridge, UK

Ian Hodder is at the Department of Cultural Anthropology, Stanford University, USA

Linda Hurcombe is at the Department of Archaeology, University of Exeter, UK

Timothy Insoll is at the School of Art History and Archaeology, University of Manchester, UK

Matthew Johnson is at the Department of Archaeology, University of Exeter, UK

Martin Jones is at the Department of Archaeology, University of Cambridge, UK

Kristian Kristiansen is at the Department of Archaeology, University of Gotëburg, Sweden

Vincent M. LaMotta is at the Department of Anthropology, University of Arizona, USA

Lynn Meskell is at the Department of Anthropology, University of New York, USA

Steven Mithen is at the Department of Archaeology, University of Reading, UK

Sarah Milledge Nelson is at the Department of Anthropology, University of Denver, USA

Paul B. Pettitt is at the Department of Archaeology and Prehistory, Sheffield University, UK

Colin Renfrew is at the McDonald Institute, University of Cambridge, UK

John Robb is at the Department of Archaeology, University of Cambridge, UK

Michael Rowlands is at the Department of Anthropology, University College London, UK

Clive Ruggles is at the School of Archaeology and Ancient History, University of Leicester, UK

Jeremy Sabloff is at the University of Pennsylvania Museum of Archaeology and Anthropology, USA

Michael B. Schiffer is at the Department of Anthropology, University of Arizona, USA

Nathan Schlanger is at the Institut national d'histoire de l'art, Paris, France

Michael Shanks is at the Department of Classics, Stanford University, USA

Stephen Shennan is at the Institute of Archaeology, University College London, UK

Marie Louise Stig Sørensen is at the Department of Archaeology, University of Cambridge, UK

Julie K. Stein is at the Department of Anthropology, University of Washington, Seattle, USA

Joseph A. Tainter is at the Rocky Mountain Research Station, Albuquerque, USA

Julian Thomas is at the School of Art History and Archaeology, University of Manchester, UK

Christopher Tilley is at the Department of Anthropology, University College London, UK

Sander E. van der Leeuw is at the Department of Anthropology, Arizona State University, USA

Milford H. Wolpoff is at the Museum of Anthropology, University of Michigan, USA

Ezra Zubrow is at the Department of Anthropology, University of Buffalo, USA

INTRODUCTION

Archaeological theory is itself something of a new concept. Until the 1960s it was widely assumed that archaeology was essentially a practical undertaking. The digger had of course to be experienced in the relevant craft skills, and to have a sense of problem. Sir Mortimer Wheeler set out the position well, with typically military metaphor, in his *Archaeology from the Earth* (Wheeler 1954), when he distinguished between the strategy and the tactics of a good archaeological field campaign. It is no coincidence that he was an admirer of the field techniques of that much earlier military field worker General Pitt-Rivers. During the twentieth century archaeological science gradually developed, not least with the invention of radiocarbon dating in 1949, and original thinkers such as Gordon Childe did indeed address the principles of archaeological reasoning in thoughtful works like *Piecing Together the Past* (Childe 1956). However, it was not until the 1960s that archaeologists became deeply concerned with the underlying logic of their discipline, with its epistemology (i.e. theory of knowledge) and with its rather curious status – according to some as a would-be science, yet undoubtedly directed towards the history and prehistory of humankind, and hence also to be situated among the humanities. Earlier thinkers such as Collingwood (1946) and the first historians of archaeology (Daniel 1950, 1962) had meditated upon these things. But it was not until the 1960s that questions of archaeological theory became acute, and that archaeology, to use David Clarke's famous phrase (Clarke 1973), underwent 'the loss of innocence'.

It was around that time that archaeological theory can be said to have become an explicit sub-discipline. In the early days of the New Archaeology, or processual archaeology as it came to be called, innovatory thinkers like Lewis Binford (Binford and Binford 1968) and David Clarke (1968) made explicit reference to such philosophers of science as Carl Hempel or Richard Bevan Braithwaite. Subsequently, with the developments of 'post-processual' archaeology, or interpretive archaeology as it is widely termed, the appeal to theorists in other disciplines became more numerous – archaeological texts (e.g. Bapty and Yates 1990; Tilley 1990; Hodder 1991) routinely made reference to Bourdieu, Derrida, Feyerabend, Foucault, Gadamer, Giddens, Heidegger, Husserl, Merleau-Ponty, Rorty, Searle, Waller-stein and a host of modern and post-modern philosophers and thinkers of bewildering diversity. Introductory books are now being published with titles like *Archaeological Theory, an Introduction* (e.g. Johnson 1999; Eggert and Veit 1998; Hodder 2001) which draw upon a wide range of traditions of thought including, but going well beyond, the philosophy of science.

It would seem then that the time is now ripe for a book which aims to set out in a clear and readable way some of the key concepts currently being used in archaeology and in what may be claimed as archaeological theory. Some of these concepts have their origins way back in the nineteenth century with the early developments of archaeology, such as the Three Age System, the Antiquity of Man or the principles of stratigraphic succession. Indeed, Darwinian evolution and Marxist materialism are still the focus of current debate, despite their early origins not long afterwards. Other approaches, such as archaeogenetics or the application of non-linear processes, are developments first systematically applied to archaeology over the past couple of decades and which have still to reach their full potential.

It has of course been difficult for us, as editors, to select some fifty or sixty key concepts which adequately encompass the scope of current archaeological thinking. No doubt we have made a number of serious omissions. But we have tried to embrace some of the main currents of current archaeological thought. The processual tradition is represented, for instance, by considerations of epistemology in archaeology, middle range theory, systems thinking, site catchment analysis, simulation and taphonomy. Recent developments in the interpretive archaeologies are well represented, for instance by discussions of phenomenology, habitus, notions of the person, structural archaeology and structuration theory. In each case we have tried to invite one of the leaders involved in the development of archaeological thought to give a clear and concise account of the kernel of their thinking. Contemporary social issues are also addressed, for instance in treatments of feminist archaeology, the archaeology of gender, and indigenous archaeologies.

As a work dealing with key concepts, this book does not set out to be a manual of archaeological method, nor an introduction to the application of scientific techniques in archaeology. But the editors are clearly aware that theory and method cannot be separated: they feed upon each other (Renfrew and Bahn 2004). So we have tried also to ensure that concepts underlying relevant archaeological methods are adequately addressed in such entries as those on characterisation, relative and absolute chronology, environmental archaeology, experimental archaeology, and excavation as analytical procedure. We are aware also that the concepts applicable in historical archaeology or to the formation of complex societies can differ from those applicable in deep prehistory to such topics as hominid evolution, evolutionary psychology or the notion of the *chaîne opératoire*.

Today the study of archaeology, including prehistory, has become a complex undertaking, drawing upon ideas as well as techniques derived from many adjacent disciplines. The very variety of the concepts used can sometimes give the impression that they are more difficult, more obscure even, than is in reality the case. Our hope is that the readers and users of this book will find that it helps them to cut through the verbiage and even the obscurity that can sometimes mar archaeological texts, and help them to get to the central point of the concepts employed, in a direct and straightforward way. We are grateful to the distinguished authors who have contributed, many of them innovators in the subject areas of which they write. Archaeology today, with its focus upon the origins of ourselves and of our society, is something of an intellectual adventure. We hope that the reader will come to feel the originality of the thinking which is today going into new initiatives in the construction of a coherent picture or series of pictures of the past. It is a construction built upon the basis of the material evidence. That is what modern archaeology is about.

References

Bapty, I. and Yates, T. (eds) 1990. *Archaeology after Structuralism: Post-Structuralism and the Practice of Archaeology*. London: Routledge.

Binford, L. R. and Binford, S. R (eds) 1968. *New Perspectives in Archaeology*. Chicago: Aldine.

Childe, V. G. 1956. *Piecing Together the Past, the Interpretation of Archaeological Data*. London: Routledge and Kegan Paul.

Clarke, D. L. 1968. *Analytical Archaeology*. London: Methuen.

—— 1973. Archaeology, the Loss of Innocence. *Antiquity* 47: 6–18.

Collingwood R. G. 1946. *The Idea of History*. Oxford: Oxford University Press.

Daniel, G. E. 1950. *A Hundred Years of Archaeology*. London: Duckworth.

—— 1962. *The Idea of Prehistory*. London: Watts.

Eggert, M. K. H. and Veit, V. (eds) 1998. *Theorie in der Archäologie: Zur englischsprachigen Diskussion* (Tübinger Archäologische Taschenbücher). Münster: Waxmann.

Hodder, I. 1991. *Archaeological Theory in Europe, the Last Three Decades*. London: Routledge.

—— (ed.) 2001. *Archaeological Theory Today*. Cambridge: Polity Press.

Johnson, M. 1999. *Archaeological Theory, an Introduction*. Oxford: Blackwell.

Renfrew, C. and Bahn, P. 2004. *Archaeology: Theories, Methods and Practice*, 4th edn. London: Thames and Hudson.

Tilley, C. (ed.) 1990. *Reading Material Culture*. Oxford: Blackwell.

Wheeler, R. E. M. 1954. *Archaeology from the Earth*. Oxford: Oxford University Press.

ARCHAEOLOGY:
THE KEY CONCEPTS

AGENCY

All theories of the past rely implicitly upon some concept of human nature: why humans behave the way we do, and how our behaviour relates to our social and physical environment. In culture historical views, for example, humans act primarily to reproduce their particular cultural traditions; in functionalist views humans act in response to environmental conditions to maximise their chances of survival. Such a concept is a necessary, though often unstated, bridge to understanding the past, as it allows us to interpret social relations and change in relation to cultural traditions, environmental changes, and so on.

In broadest terms, agency theory in archaeology is the attempt to state our model of the human agent explicitly and to trace out its implications for past societies systematically. Within this broad and varied rubric, the concept of agency has historically been invoked primarily within two distinct approaches, which build on contrasting views of symbols and of power.

Primarily within the American processualist tradition (*see* p. 212), scholars have explained social change as resulting from the strategies of ambitious political actors. Here, while it is acknowledged that actors live and act within particular world views and traditions, it is assumed that all humans are motivated by the desire to pursue prestige and power. Power is thought of as the personal control of other people's actions, and it is assumed that power and prestige provide cross-culturally recognisable motivations; symbols are manipulated ideologically to convince others. The political-strategising view of agency has underwritten much sophisticated understanding of how political and economic processes resulted from individual actions. However, it has a number of limitations. Theoretically, if we assume that intentional human action is conditioned by a particular historical and cultural framework, this approach has limited potential for explaining how that framework comes into being. If political actors are trying to win at a game, where do the rules they follow come from? How do they believe in their symbols while manipulating them strategically? Empirically, the unconscious and unintentional consequences of individual action may be more consequential in explaining social relations than what the actor thinks he or she is doing. Moreover, this approach has always been more successful at explaining would-be leaders, particularly male heads of households, than followers or the community as a whole, a limitation which reflects gendered assumptions in how agency is defined.

The second tradition of agency in archaeology comes from a deeper and more robust philosophical tradition, deriving originally from Marx's idea of 'praxis' – in Marx's view, human action in the world both has external physical consequences and shapes the actor: factory work creates both an economic product and a state of consciousness in the worker. This concept was developed in the work of post-structuralists such as Giddens and Bourdieu (*see* p. 134–5). According to Giddens, in human action, structures allow people to act and constrain how they can act, while at the same time individual actions perpetuate structures (a process termed the 'duality of structure'). One implication is that any action reproduces many beliefs and habits, of which the actors intend or are even conscious of only a few. A man opens a door for a woman: he may intend only 'normal' courtesy, but his action relies upon and perpetuates a particular view of enabled males and passive females. Bourdieu similarly postulates a relationship between the actor's 'habitus' (*see* p. 133) or deeply entrenched attitudes and values (for example, how being male in a particular society is understood) and the pragmatic strategies people use to pursue these values (for example, to gain male prestige or honour). As Bourdieu notes, the actor's deeply held values do not rigidly dictate specific actions, but rather provide a framework of practical logic through which actors understand situations and which underwrites their strategies. In both writers, power does not consist solely of controlling other people's behaviour, but is a more diffuse aspect of all social relations.

The work of Bourdieu, Giddens, Foucault, Sahlins and Ortner on agency began to influence archaeology in the early 1980s, particularly in the work of Barrett, though the basic concepts underwrite much of post-processual theory (*see* p. 207). Different post-processual theorists use agency in varying ways and with varying degrees of explicitness. The centre of gravity, to the extent there is one, covers the idea that humans are born into a world of meaningful structures. In acting, we not only carry out a particular action which we intend, but also reinforce and perpetuate these structures in ourselves and the social relations we act within. A funeral, for example, does not necessarily or only demonstrate the hierarchical status of the deceased; it may mask this status, emphasise the collective nature of the community, provide an emotional sense of belonging, reproduce cosmological notions (i.e. ideas about the nature of space, time and the universe) and a general sense of authority, and so on. Within this general approach, there has nonetheless been controversy. Some theorists have seen structures and meanings as relatively stable and even rigid, while others focus on humans' ability to redefine the meaning of symbols in the moment of action. Similarly, some have seen the individual as a necessary unit of action while others have inveighed against the modernist concept of personhood implied by the concept of a bounded, rational individual. The limits of the social-reproduction approach to agency generally complement that of the political-actor approach. Some reflect the choice of theoretical ground. Because interpretation has focused upon local scenarios, there has been little use of agency to explain long-term, large-scale or comparative patterns of change. A reaction against functionalist approaches has led to neglect of environmental, demographic and economic contexts, and a focus on meaningful human experience in a short-term present has sometimes led to interpretations lacking a developed politics and economics. More generally, relations between enduring structures and the actors' freedom to reconfigure or reinterpret them in action remain poorly explored (as indeed they are in social theorists such as Bourdieu, in spite of his post-structuralist polemic); Giddens' 'duality of structure' is sometimes invoked as a rather mystical mantra to cover this problem rather than a tool for probing it.

While these two theoretical traditions remain strong, such a survey overlooks much stimulating work by scholars not working within easily stereotyped camps. An increasing number of American scholars have adopted key points from both views in a convergence not easily described in terms of the processual/post-processual split. The core elements of agency theory within a broadly synthetic view include:

1   humans reproduce their being and their social relations through everyday practices;
2   practices take place in material conditions and through material culture;
3   practices happen within historical settings inherited from the past, including cultural beliefs, attitudes and habits; thus actors possess values which both help them to act and constrain their actions;
4   in action, humans do not simply reproduce their material conditions, inherited structures of meaning, and historical consciousness, but change, reinterpret and redefine them as well.

This is an abstract statement of first principles which requires intervening layers of theory before we can apply it to archaeological situations. To some extent, useful general theory is self-effacing: we know it is serving us well when we can get on to interesting interpretations. Here a broad research agenda based on these includes a number of key themes, among others:

- *the body, embodiment, and feminist archaeology* (*see* p. 116): the body is the principal physical locus of experience and the medium through which we act, understand our own identities and communicate them to others.
- *material culture studies*: like the body, material things are a medium through which we create ourselves and understand other people, and hence an inescapable element of social reproduction. Artefacts are a key to social relations and frames of mind. Indeed, there has been considerable debate among archaeological theorists about whether things can be considered as agents in the same way people can. Among the many ways in which material things relate to agency, we might note particularly technology as a system of social knowledge and embodied action, the use of everyday things to communicate subtle political meanings such as the authority of the state, the contextual use of material things to redefine or contest inherited meanings, and the question of the extent to which the archaeological record itself might be an intentional creation.
- *power*: if power is defined culturally, we can trace the development not only of ways in which agents tried to seize political control, but also the ways in which these attempts arose from specific culturally defined ways of thinking rather than 'universal' motivations such as power or prestige. We can also investigate how cultural beliefs relate to political structures and how people resist or contest political domination through cultural struggle.
- *long-term history*: through archaeology's time depth we can trace the trajectory of practices and institutions as each generation reproduces inherited cultural logics in new historical contexts.

Suggested reading

Barrett, J. 1994. *Fragments from Antiquity: An Archaeology of Social Life in Britain, 2900–1200 BC.* Oxford: Blackwell.
The classical source for an elegant use of post-structural agency theory in long-term archaeology.

Bourdieu, P. 1977. *Outline of a Theory of Practice.* New York: Cambridge University Press.
An important statement of practice theory.

Dobres, M.-A. 2000. *Technology and Social Agency: Outlining a Practice Framework for Archaeology.* Oxford: Blackwell.
An important recent synthesis and re-formulation of agency theory incorporating elements of phenemonology.

Dobres, M.-A. and Robb, J. (eds) 2000. *Agency in Archaeology.* London: Routledge.
An edited volume containing a wide variety of interpretations of agency in archaeology, illustrating most of the positions referred to above.

Giddens, A. 1979. *Central Problems in Social Theory: Action, Structure and Contradiction in Social Analysis.* Berkeley: University of California Press.
Lays out the theoretical basis of agency in sociology.

Johnson, M. 1989. Conceptions of Agency in Archaeological Interpretation. *Journal of Anthropological Archaeology* 8: 189–211.
A historical review of how agency has been used in archaeology.

Further reading

Barrett, J. C. 2001. Agency, the Duality of Structure, and the Problem of the Archaeological Record, pp. 140–64 in (I. Hodder, ed.) *Archaeological Theory Today.* Oxford: Polity Press.
Earle, T. 1997. *How Chiefs Come to Power.* Stanford: Stanford University Press.
Hegmon, M. 2003. Setting Theoretical Egos Aside: Issues and Theory in North American Archaeology. *American Antiquity* 68: 213–44.
Marcus, J. and Flannery, K. V. 1996. *Zapotec Civilization: How Urban Society Evolved in Mexico's Oaxaca Valley.* London: Thames and Hudson.
Pauketat, T. R. 2001. Practice and History in Archaeology: An Emerging Paradigm. *Anthropological Theory* 1: 73–98.
Price, T. D. and Feinman, G. (eds) 1995. *Foundations of Social Inequality.* New York: Plenum.
Sahlins, M. 1985. *Islands of History.* Chicago: University of Chicago Press.
Shackel, P. A. 1993. *Personal Discipline and Material Culture: An Archaeology of Annapolis, Maryland, 1695–1870.* Knoxville: University of Tennessee Press.
Tilley, C. (ed.) 1993. *Interpretative Archaeology.* Oxford: Berg.

JOHN ROBB

THE ANTIQUITY OF MAN

Although many ancient cultures – including the Greeks, Egyptians, Assyrians, Babylonians as well as ancient Mesoamerica – believed that humankind was tens of thousands of years old, such a notion does not seem to have existed in medieval Europe where the only framework for the origins of humanity lay in written documents, and, especially, the Bible. By the seventeenth century, attempts to develop a chronology for the whole of human history had culminated in the famous calculation by Archbishop Ussher that the world was created at noon on 23 October 4004 BC (see p. 65).

One of the most important factors which helped to alter this state of affairs was the work of the Danish naturalist Niels Stensen (Nicholas Steno) who, in 1669, drew the first known geological profile, and recognised that such profiles represented the process of sedimentation and stratigraphic superimposition (see p. 244) – i.e. the idea that later layers must lie on top of earlier ones.

One of the first archaeological applications of this principle came in 1797 when a British gentleman, John Frere, discovered worked stone tools, including Lower Palaeolithic handaxes, in a brick quarry at Hoxne in Suffolk. They were at a depth of 4 metres (13 feet), in an undisturbed deposit containing the bones of large extinct animals. Frere not only realised that the stones were artefacts, but also attributed them to 'a very remote period indeed; even beyond that of the present world'. But despite publication in *Archaeologia*, the journal of the Society of Antiquaries, Frere's discovery went unrecognised for decades.

Some years earlier, in 1771, a Bavarian pastor, Johann Friedrich Esper, had found human bones associated with remains of cave bear and other extinct animals in Gaillenreuth Cave, near Bayreuth in the German Jura. He speculated that the bones could be those of a Druid, an 'Antediluvian' (i.e. someone who lived before the biblical Flood), or someone more recent, but he concluded that they must be intrusive to the deposits containing the extinct animals – he did not dare presume that they could be of the same age.

Nevertheless, scholars were beginning to challenge – albeit very tentatively – the account of the Earth's formation as given in the Book of Genesis. The stratigraphic principle was applied to the study of fossils in geological layers, while palaeontologists such as France's Georges Cuvier were studying the differences between fossil animals and their modern equivalents, seeing the differences increase with the age of the layers. Yet Cuvier did not believe that fossil humans had coexisted with vanished animal species found in 'antediluvian' deposits that predated the Flood. He went by the Bible, and thought that humans appeared after the animals. Unlike his pupils and disciples, however, he did not categorically deny the possibility that fossil humans had ever existed – he simply denied that their bones had ever been found. So it was the establishment, by the mid-nineteenth century, that humans had indeed coexisted with extinct animals which was a major turning point in the history of archaeology.

In the early nineteenth century, scholars in various parts of western Europe were constantly finding crudely worked stone tools mixed with bones. For example, in 1823 William Buckland, an Anglican priest and Oxford professor of geology, published an account of his excavation of a male burial in Paviland Cave (south Wales) – we now know that it dates to c. 26,000 years ago. But despite the presence of elephant, rhinoceros and bear bones, he thought this burial was Romano-British (i.e. relatively modern). He simply did not believe in the contemporaneity of humans and fossil animals (though he later changed his mind in the face of overwhelming evidence). Another cleric, John MacEnery, in 1825 began exploring Kent's Cavern in southwest England, and here he too found flint tools mixed with bones of extinct fauna; unfortunately, he did not publish his findings in full until 1869 because orthodoxy was so clearly against him.

Paul Tournal, a French pharmacist, not only made similar finds in the 1820s in the Aude region, but also noticed marks of cutting tools on bones of 'lost species' recovered from the caves. But his real importance lies in the fact that he stressed geological evidence so much that he at last broke the tradition of linking ancient cave deposits with the Flood. By 1833 he was already dividing the last geological period – that of humans – into the historic (going back 7,000 years) and the 'antehistoric' (of unknown length). This was the first use of such a term (foreshadowing the word 'prehistory'), and the first real linkage of geology and history.

The real breakthrough came in Belgium. There had been sporadic reports of fossilised human bones being found in caves in Italy, France and Germany during the eighteenth century, but they had little impact. In 1833, however, Philippe-Charles Schmerling, a Dutch doctor, published an account of his work in caves around Liège. Here, in deep layers, he not only found the usual flint and bone tools, together with the remains of woolly rhinoceros, hyena and bear, but also uncovered human bones with archaic features – in fact, these were probably Neanderthal burials. He was surprised to find that the human and animal bones were of the same colour and condition, and in the same deposits. He was thus the first archaeologist to discover, save and investigate the potential age of such bones and their contemporaneity with extinct fauna. Another Neanderthal skull was found in Gibraltar in 1848, but then forgotten until after the discovery of the bones at Neanderthal itself in 1856 (see p. 71).

Despite the accumulating number of fossil human finds, however, and the serious claims being made by scholars all over western Europe, the scientific establishment remained unmoved. Cuvier went to his grave still dismissing all such finds as burials dug down from more recent levels, while his followers absolutely denied that people could have lived at the same time as extinct animals of the 'antediluvian' period. Others argued that stratigraphies in caves were always complex and could easily have been disturbed, and so insisted that an indisputable association of human bones and extinct fauna in an open-air site was required (of course, Frere had already provided this evidence, but his discovery had been forgotten).

The final milestones in the establishment of human antiquity came in France, and the man most responsible for providing the final proof was Jacques Boucher de Perthes, a customs officer whose excavations in the mid-nineteenth century at open-air sites in the Abbeville region of Picardy (northern France) demonstrated in a very influential manner that stone tools could be found well stratified in the same layers as bones of mammoth and woolly rhino.

The year 1859 saw not only visits by eminent British scholars to Boucher de Perthes' sites – visits which led to the official acceptance of the validity of his claims – but also the publication of Darwin's *On the Origin of Species*, in which man was seen not as a special object of divine creation but as the product of an evolution rooted among animals (*see* p. 70). After long doubts and vigorous opposition by the Church, within about eighteen months what had been a very doubtful idea was transformed into a widespread consensus. In the early 1860s, Edouard Lartet, a French scholar, unearthed some of the first examples of Ice Age portable art, including, at the French rock-shelter of La Madeleine, a depiction of a mammoth engraved on a piece of mammoth tusk. No clearer evidence could be desired of the contemporaneity of people and extinct animals; and in 1863 Charles Lyell's book *Geological Evidences of the Antiquity of Man* synthesised all of the information and laid the foundations for both prehistoric archaeology and palaeoanthropology. As Darwin wrote to him delightedly, 'It is great. What a fine long pedigree you have given the human race.'

Suggested reading

Bahn, P. G. (ed.) 1996. *The Cambridge Illustrated History of Archaeology.* Cambridge: Cambridge University Press.
Well-illustrated survey of the global history of archaeology.

Daniel, G. E. 1967. *The Origins and Growth of Archaeology.* Harmondsworth: Pelican.
Invaluable annotated collection of quotations from original sources important to the history of archaeology.

Daniel, G. E. 1975. *150 Years of Archaeology.* London: Duckworth.
Excellent history of archaeology by its foremost specialist.

Daniel, G. E. and Renfrew, C. 1988. *The Idea of Prehistory.* Edinburgh: Edinburgh
University Press.
Extremely useful survey which places emphasis on the history of ideas in
archaeology, rather than discoveries.

Lyell, C. 1863. *Geological Evidences of the Antiquity of Man.* London: Murray.
Lyell's hugely influential synthesis of the geological and archaeological evidence
for the existence of early humans.

Further reading

Grayson, D. K. 1983. *The Establishment of Human Antiquity.* New York: Academic
Press.
Schnapp, A. 1996. *Discovering the Past.* London: British Museum Press.
Trigger, B. G. 1989. *A History of Archaeological Thought.* Cambridge: Cambridge
University Press.
Van Riper, A. B. 1993. *Men Among the Mammoths, Victorian Science and the Discovery
of Human Prehistory.* Chicago: Chicago University Press.

PAUL BAHN

ARCHAEOASTRONOMY

Archaeoastronomy is generally defined as the study of beliefs and
practices concerning the sky in the past, particularly in the absence of
written records, and the uses to which people's understanding of the
sky was put. There can be no reasonable doubt that celestial objects
and events were of great importance to a wide range of human
societies in the past, as continues to be the case among many
indigenous communities in the world today. The central issue,
however, is why this topic should be of particular interest to
archaeologists.

The term 'archaeoastronomy' came into use in the 1970s, amid
efforts to resolve a long-running dispute between leading archaeologists and professionals from other disciplines, mostly astronomers.
The dispute concerned whether there existed intentional, high-
precision alignments upon the rising or setting positions of the sun,
moon and stars among later prehistoric British stone monuments, and
if so how they should be interpreted. Stonehenge had already achieved
notoriety in this respect through the work of an astronomer, Gerald
Hawkins, disseminated in a best-selling book, *Stonehenge Decoded*,
published in the 1960s. However, a more serious challenge to

conventional archaeological thought came from a retired engineer, Alexander Thom. Thom argued – with a large body of survey data and statistical analysis to back up his case – for the existence of sophisticated astronomical and calendrical knowledge in Neolithic and Bronze Age Britain. He also contended that a precisely defined unit of measurement, together with particular geometrical constructions, was used extensively in laying out what are loosely termed stone 'circles'. The ensuing debate over the social implications of this, which at times became highly contentious, began to be resolved only in the 1980s, following detailed reassessments of Thom's data which undermined many of his earlier conclusions.

This whole episode had the effect of colouring archaeologists' impressions of archaeoastronomy in a negative way that has proved remarkably persistent. Archaeoastronomers became characterised as people determined to fit an astronomical explanation to as many past human actions – and particularly monumental constructions – as possible, rather than sensibly assessing astronomical potentialities within a broader interpretative framework taking into account the full range of available archaeological evidence. For instance, there can be many reasons for a house, temple or tomb to be oriented in a particular direction, and there are evident dangers in presupposing an astronomical or, even worse, an exclusively astronomical, motivation. The very existence of archaeoastronomy as a self-declared 'sub-discipline' or 'interdiscipline' seemed to confirm this impression, and the use of terms such as 'observatory' to describe astronomically aligned monuments (and indeed, the very term 'archaeoastronomy' itself) became highly charged and seen by many as redolent of the same problem.

At around the same time, archaeoastronomy was progressing in a more productive direction among Mesoamericanists and particularly Mayanists. Here, in the New World, the existence of written data in the form of monumental inscriptions and documents (most importantly the Maya 'Dresden Codex'), together with ethnohistorical data in the form of accounts of indigenous practices by early Spanish chroniclers, provided a clearer motivation for studying monumental alignments and their possible astronomical significance, as well as a more secure context for interpreting the meaning of such alignments. Mesoamerican archaeoastronomers distanced themselves at an early stage from the debates going on in Britain, and in this region the term 'archaeoastronomy' rapidly became applied to wider, integrated studies involving a range of archaeological and historical data rather than simply to 'alignment studies'.

The wider acceptance of archaeoastronomy followed the rise of post-processual/interpretative archaeology in the 1980s (*see* p. 207). There is some irony here, since archaeoastronomy in the 1970s was strongly focused upon methodological problems concerning the objective selection of data and quantitative testing of hypotheses in a way that was very much in tune with the tenets of processual/New Archaeology (*see* p. 212). On the other hand (and this may help explain its lack of interest for many archaeologists at the time), it has no relevance if one's aim is to try to explain social process in terms of 'rational' exploitation of the natural environment, since the sky is immutable. Once we adopt a cognitive archaeology standpoint, however, and start to think about how people perceived and conceived the world that they inhabited, then we need to consider not only the land and sea (*see* p. 156) but the totality of the visible environment within which people lived.

People commonly identify direct connections between observed objects and events in the sky and many other aspects of their experience. Some of these connections make sense from a modern scientific, or 'rational', perspective, an obvious example being when the cycles of the sky are used to regulate seasonal activities. Thus, as we know from the historian Hesiod's works, Greek farmers as far back as the eighth century BC used the annual appearance of certain stars to identify the appropriate times for ploughing and harvesting, thereby overcoming the vicissitudes of the climate. Another example is the use of stars for long-distance navigation, as by the Polynesians when colonising widely scattered island groups in the Pacific. Other connections only make sense in terms of the system of thought in question, a good example being the Mesoamerican 260-day calendrical cycle (whose astronomical origins are the subject of continuing debate) and its associated prognostications.

Indigenous world views or 'cosmologies' – shared frameworks of understanding about the world – can be extremely localised, or can become dominant over wide areas. Aspects of world view may be reflected in various ways in the material record, and particularly in spatial patterning that may be recoverable archaeologically. Thus, various groups of native North Americans design dwelling houses or sacred buildings to reflect (among much else) the division into four principal directions that for them characterises the cosmos, so that (for example) entrances always face eastwards, towards sunrise. More generally, cosmological principles may influence the location, design and orientation of individual houses, temples or tombs, as well as the layouts of ceremonial sites, villages or even great cities. Perceptions of sky phenomena, and relationships involving celestial objects and events, invariably form an integral part of indigenous cosmologies. It follows that if we are investigating archaeologically how people's actions are shaped by, and enacted in accordance with, their perceptions of the world, then we cannot ignore the sky, any more than we can concentrate upon it to the exclusion of everything else.

This means that at one level, archaeoastronomy can be viewed as a set of ideas and methods relevant in studying concepts of space and time, calendars, cosmologies and world views, navigation, and many related topics. Archaeoastronomical field survey typically involves the measurement of the spatial configuration of some material remains (such as the orientation of a monument) in relation to the visible landscape and particularly the surrounding horizon. This is achieved using standard field survey equipment, but specialised data reduction techniques are then required in order to determine the rising and setting position of celestial bodies on the horizon, or to visualise the appearance of the night sky at different times of the night and year at the relevant epoch in the past.

There is good reason for going even further and singling out the sky for special attention. This is because our knowledge of the nature and appearance of the physical landscape at any particular place and time in the past is generally indirect and highly incomplete. On the other hand, thanks to modern astronomy we can determine, with remarkable accuracy, the actual appearance of the sun, moon, planets and stars at any place on Earth at any time in the past, and we can visualise their cycles of change on a computer or in a planetarium. This provides us with direct knowledge of the visual appearance of an integral part of the environment of a group of people in the past. Thus, for example, the alignment of a house, temple or tomb upon a sacred place in the landscape may not be evident to us because that sacred place may no longer be identifiable; however, we have some chance of identifying an alignment upon the rising or setting position of the sun, moon or a star, because we can identify that position with certainty.

There remains at the heart of archaeoastronomy a fundamental problem of methodology that has been recognised by archaeoastronomers from the outset. This is that the mere existence of an astronomical alignment does not mean that it was significant to anyone in the past. Many things may be identified as potential alignments and each one must point somewhere; there are many potential astronomical targets. It is possible to establish intentionality beyond any reasonable doubt where a similar alignment is observed repeatedly

– for example, among a group of similar monuments within a distinctive local tradition. This type of approach has been particularly successful in revealing solar, and in some cases lunar, associations among various groups of British and Irish stone circles and rows. It has also been very influential on a European scale, in demonstrating the importance of orientation in monument construction all over western Europe from the Early Neolithic onwards. With remarkably few exceptions, local groups of later prehistoric temples and tombs – sometimes numbering several hundred – show clear orientation preferences which, at the very least, can only have been achieved by reference to the daily rotation of the heavens. At the same time these traditions are localised, varying considerably from place to place and time to time.

The main limitations of this 'statistical' type of approach are that it can only reveal the most sweeping common traditions and that it goes no way towards revealing the social significance of the astronomical relationships that we observe. In order to take into account particular circumstances and individual actions, it is necessary to consider particular astronomical alignments and relationships in their broader archaeological context. Often, what one might call the 'statistical' and 'contextual' approaches can be in apparent conflict, and how they can best be reconciled still remains one of the fundamental methodological issues within archaeoastronomy. At the same time, questions of meaning can only be approached within a broader interpretative context. Here, the agenda of archaeoastronomy is necessarily bound to wider developments in archaeological theory as a whole.

Further reading

Aveni, A. F. 2001. *Skywatchers*. Austin: University of Texas Press.
This is an extensive revision of *Skywatchers of Ancient Mexico*, which was published in 1980, and provides a comprehensive and up-to-date survey of Mesoamerican archaeoastronomy.

Hawkins, G. 1965. *Stonehenge Decoded*. New York: Doubleday.
Hoskin, M. A. 2001. *Tombs, Temples and their Orientations*. Bognor Regis: Ocarina Books.
A synthesis of many years' fieldwork in southern Europe that epitomises the new direction taken by European archaeoastronomy in recent years.

Ruggles, C. L. N. 1999. *Astronomy in Prehistoric Britain and Ireland*. New Haven and London: Yale University Press.
This book, aimed at a cross-disciplinary audience, focuses on prehistoric Britain and Ireland but discusses a number of broader issues.

Ruggles, C. L. N. and Saunders, N. J. (eds) 1993. *Astronomies and Cultures*. Niwot, Col.: University Press of Colorado.

A collection of papers covering theory, method and practice that gives a good insight into the scope of archaeoastronomy as well as some of the main issues of contention.

CLIVE RUGGLES

ARCHAEOGENETICS

Archaeogenetics may be defined as the study of the human past using the techniques of molecular genetics. This is a rapidly evolving field in which some of the key ideas are still being worked out. It has been powered by developments in the field of genetics, starting with the study of human blood groups as early as 1919, which was well advanced by the 1950s. As the field of biochemistry developed, more data became available, and much information was available from what are sometimes called 'classical' genetic markers: blood groups, enzymes, etc.

But it was the cracking of the genetic code of DNA in 1953 which opened the way to the range of methods which are based upon DNA sequencing. This involves the determination of the sequences of bases (adenine (A), cytosine (C), guanine (G) and thyamine (T)) which make up the long strands of the 'double helix' of DNA, and whose order constitutes the basic genetic information. It is these which make up the genes themselves, although long stretches of the chain of bases seem to be of lesser significance.

Since the mid–1990s great progress has been made using what may be described as lineage methods. It was realised already in the 1980s that the mitochondrial DNA in each of us – the DNA present not in the nucleus of the cell but in small components within the cell termed the mitochondria – is inherited from the mother. For each human, whether man or woman, the DNA sequence of the mitchondrial DNA is normally identical to that of the mother, the maternal grandmother, her mother and so on back through the generations. It differs only if a mutation has occurred, changing one of the bases along the sequence. People who are closely related on the mother's side usually have identical mitochondrial DNA. But those much more distantly related, for instance populations living on different continents, may differ significantly because of the mutations which have occurred over the generations in their mitochondrial DNA. The resulting diversity can be studied, and different human populations classified, in terms of their similarities or differences. One approach to classification allows the construction of a tree, a taxonomic (i.e.

classificatory) tree, which can be regarded as a kind of family tree, operating back over the millennia. In a pioneering paper in 1987, Cann *et al.*, using samples taken from living individuals in different continents, were able to construct a tree tracing human ancestry back to a notional female ancestor something like 100,000 years ago, who, they were able to infer, must have lived in Africa. This ancestral female was colloquially called the 'African Eve' (*see* p. 178) or the 'mitochondrial mother'.

Subsequently it has been possible to carry out analogous studies, this time in the male line, using that part of the Y chromosome which does not recombine in the fertilisation process but is passed on unchanged from the father. Thus the genetic information is passed on unchanged from father to son. So it has been possible, in a similar way, to construct descent trees, where all the different human varieties (or haplotypes), as determined in terms of the Y-chromosomal DNA, are classified in terms of their inferred descent from their early male ancestor, who is again believed to have lived in Africa.

It seems remarkable that one of our most important sources of information about the early human past resides in our own DNA – our past within us. Yet it is the case that we have learnt more in recent years about human origins and early human dispersals from the study of the diversity of DNA samples from living populations than from new archaeological discoveries of the actual remains of our early ancestors. At the same time, however, it should be stressed that it is possible, in favourable circumstances, to recover ancient DNA from the bone, hair or other organic remains of long-dead individuals. Often such ancient DNA is much degraded, and there are many problems of contamination, so that the study of ancient DNA has not progressed as rapidly as was at first hoped. However, there have been some remarkable successes. Perhaps the most notable of these has been the recovery of ancient DNA from the bones of a Neanderthal hominid (one of the very early finds from the Neanderthal site itself). The analysis showed that *Homo sapiens neanderthalensis* was less closely related to our own species *Homo sapiens sapiens* than had been expected, the common ancestor living as much as 600,000 years ago. That is a highly significant result, which takes one beyond the inferences which can be made from the anthropological study of the fossil bones themselves.

Turning back now to the earlier development of archaeogenetics, the study of blood groups showed as early as 1994 that there was a high frequency of the Rhesus Negative blood group in the Basque country of Spain. Since the Basque language has no known relatives, and is certainly unrelated to the Indo-European languages found over most of Europe, it was natural to suggest that the Basque language was a survivor of the languages spoken in the area before the arrival of the Indo-European languages, and therefore that the special genetic features of the living Basque population might be inherited from these very early indigenous inhabitants.

The first major synthesis in the field of archaeogenetics, relying mainly upon classical genetic markers, was *The History and Geography of Human Genes*, published in 1994 by Luca Cavalli-Sforza and his colleagues. This proceeded through a study of the geographical distributions of gene frequencies for each continent, using statistical methods (mainly principal components analysis) to clarify the spatial patterning. In Europe, for instance, synthetic maps were obtained where the first principal component showed a strong directionality from Anatolia in a north-westerly direction towards Britain and north-western Europe. The proposed explanation was that this reflected the spread of a farming population from Anatolia at the onset of the Neolithic period.

That landmark survey marks the culmination of the first phase of archaeogenetic research.

The second phase begins with the development of the lineage methods, discussed above, by which mitochondrial DNA and the DNA of the non-recombinant portion of the Y chromosome give information respectively about the female and male descent lines. The interpretive methods used have not been without controversy, and involve a number of assumptions. When the various DNA analyses have been obtained from the various individuals providing samples, it is always possible to classify these in different ways, using the classificatory techniques of what is called 'numerical taxonomy'. These have been used in one form or another for 150 years in evolutionary biology to produce, on the basis of the degree of similarity or difference between each pair of the various units being classified, descent trees like those which Charles Darwin used to outline the origin of species (*see* p. 58). This field of study is termed 'phylogenesis'. As noted earlier, one of the standard phylogenetic methods is to use a form of taxonomic analysis to arrange the data into the form of a tree diagram (dendrogram). If one is willing to assume that all the individuals or populations involved are descendants of a single individual or population, and that the mutations occurring do so at a roughly constant rate, then these classificatory trees may be regarded as genuine descent trees, offering a reasonable approximation to the phylogenetic processes which have occurred. Estimating the rate of change, the mutation rate, is one of the long-standing problems of molecular genetics. If one is willing to assume an approximately constant mutation rate, then one has the basis for a 'genetic clock' by which the various changes in the past (the nodes in the tree) can be dated. Recently other analytical approaches to the data, known as median-joining network methods, have been developed which more accurately trace the mutational pathways involved.

So far the principal results of archaeogenetics have been to establish a clear outline for the place and date of origin of our species and of the subsequent dispersals by which it has populated the globe, dispersals (and reversals) much influenced by climatic factors. The approach is also helping to resolve some of the problems in the origins and history of world linguistic diversity. Ancient DNA studies are increasingly informative about specific populations, for instance about the diversity revealed in a single cemetery. Moreover the domestication and use-histories of plant and animal species can also be approached in this way, thereby contributing to the study of the human past.

Suggested reading

Cavalli-Sforza, L. L. 2000. *Genes, People and Languages*. London: Allen Lane.
A popular account by one of the pioneers of molecular genetics, with some interesting speculations.

Jobling, M. A., Hurles, M. E. and Tyler-Smith, C. 2004. *Human Evolutionary Genetics*. Abingdon: Garland Science.
A textbook with good, up-to-date discussions of many related topics.

Jones, M. 2001. *The Molecule Hunt, Archaeology and the Search for Ancient DNA*. London: Allen Lane.
Covers a range of biochemical methods in a clear and readable way.

Renfrew, C. 2002. Genetics and Language in Contemporary Archaeology, pp. 43 66 in (B. Cunliffe, W. Davies and C. Renfrew, eds) *Archaeology, the Widening Debate*. London: British Academy.
A concise survey, dealing also with linguistic problems.

Renfrew, C. and Boyle, K. (eds) 2000. *Archaeogenetics: DNA and the Population Prehistory of Europe*. Cambridge: McDonald Institute of Archaeological Research.
A collection of technical papers which gives a good overview of the scope of the subject.

Sykes, B. (ed.) 1999. *The Human Inheritance*. Oxford: Oxford University Press.
A readable account, focusing on mitochondrial DNA, but restricted in its scope mainly to Europe.

Wells, S. 2002. *The Journey of Man, a Genetic Odyssey*. London: Penguin Books.
Probably the best readable introduction to the subject.

Further reading

Bandelt, H.-J., Forster, P. and Röhl, A. 1999. Median-Joining Networks for Inferring Specific Phylogenies. *Molecular Biology and Evolution* 16: 37–48.

Cann, R., Stoneking, M. and Wilson, A. C. 1987. Mitochondrial DNA and Human Evolution. *Nature* 325: 31–6.

Cavalli-Sforza, L., Menozzi, P. and Piazza, A. 1994. *The History and Geography of Human Genes*. Princeton: Princeton University Press.

Forster, P. 2004. Ice Ages and the Mitochondrial DNA Chronology of Human Dispersals, a Review. *Philosophical Transactions of the Royal Society of London*, Series B, 359 (1442): 255–64.

Krings, M., Stone, A., Schmitz, R.-W., Krainitzki, H., Stoneking, M. and Pääbo, S. 1997. Neanderthal DNA Sequences and the Origin of Modern Humans. *Cell* 90: 19–30.

Underhill, P. A., Shen, P., Lin, A. A. *et al.* 2000. Y-chromosome Sequence Variations and the History of Human Populations. *Nature Genetics* 26: 358–61.

COLIN RENFREW

CATASTROPHIST ARCHAEOLOGY

The catastrophist paradigm, in which Earth history was interpreted as a saga punctuated by a series of devastating natural cataclysms, held sway among European thinkers until the cusp of the nineteenth century. The controversy among these thinkers was not whether our planet had been regularly ravaged by catastrophes on a planetary scale, but focused, instead, on which natural process had been the primary agency of such catastrophes: specifically, flooding or volcanism.

The Scottish geologist James Hutton was an early proponent of a different perspective. In his seminal publication, *Theory of the Earth*, published in 1795, Hutton suggested that 'the operations of nature are equable and steady', not unpredictable and catastrophic (1795: 19). Hutton's work gave rise to the uniformitarian perspective (*see* p. 274) that viewed the current state of the planet as having resulted from the application of mundane, already recognised and observed, gradual processes of weathering and erosion over vast periods of time. Hutton's intellectual heir, Charles Lyell, was to carry the banner of uniformitarianism into the nineteenth century, championing the perspective of a natural history of the Earth best understood as having resulted from 'the slow agency of existing causes', applied uniformly over a heretofore unimaginable 'immensity of time' (1830: 63).

The uniformitarian paradigm has dominated geology ever since Lyell. His view of an ancient Earth characterised by gradual, accretional change was to inform prehistorians attempting to interpret the trajectory of the human past within the context of Earth's natural history. As uniformitarian geologists interpreted Earth history as slow and steady through the mechanism of known, observable causes, archaeologists came to view the pathway of human change as the result of slow-acting cultural evolutionary processes. The tripartite division of human antiquity into a stone, bronze and iron age as developed by Danish museum curator Christian Jurgensen Thomsen in 1836 (see p. 266) was predicated on a historical trajectory characterised by slow and uniform progression of human technological prowess. Thomsen's view was expanded by Edward Tylor (1865) in his book *Researches into the Early History of Mankind and the Development of Civilization*, in which he viewed human history as a slow progression of technological achievement. American anthropologist Lewis Henry Morgan (1877) followed with his cultural stages of savagery, barbarism and civilisation reflecting the gradual development of human technology and behaviour. Whatever the particular sequence or stages proposed by various thinkers, the belief was that culture progresses gradually and steadily, and that civilisations were born, evolved and then collapsed at a measured pace.

Geological catastrophism regained more than just a measure of respectability in the late twentieth century as a result of geologist Walter Alvarez's (1998) hypothesis that a cataclysmic collision between an extraterrestrial object and Earth resulted in a massive extinction event some sixty-five million years ago. Suggestions of other great natural catastrophes have been proposed, the result especially of extraterrestrial collisions whose direct footprint can be seen today in eroded impact craters scattered across our planet.

Though the planetary-wide catastrophes suggested by modern earth scientists have been limited to deep time, in a period far too early to have had an effect on the development of civilisation, there have been some suggestions that natural catastrophes beset the planet in time periods recent enough to have affected the course of human history. This argument is bolstered, however slightly, by evidence of an extraterrestrial impact in Siberia in 1908. The so-called 'Tunguska bolide' represents a major impact event between Earth and a meteor or cometary nucleus perhaps 50 metres across, resulting in an explosion that was the equivalent of between 15 and 30 megatons of TNT. Modern catastrophist archaeology is rooted in the notion that a natural disaster − or series of disasters − on the scale of Tunguska, or far greater, afflicted the Earth in the geologically recent past, radically altering human history.

Both directly and indirectly, explicitly and implicitly, modern archaeological catastrophism is rooted in the story of the destruction of a highly advanced ancient civilisation, Atlantis, as told by the Greek philosopher Plato (427–347 BC). In Plato's dialogues *Timaeus* and *Critias*, after the valiant warriors of ancient Athens have defeated in battle the far more powerful Atlanteans, the gods destroy the island continent utterly (Hutchins 1952). 'Violent earthquakes and floods' decimated Atlantis, which 'disappeared in the depths of the sea' in 'a single day and night' (p. 446). All of this happened, in Plato's telling, 9,000 years before Egyptian priests related the tale to the Greek sage Solon who, in turn, lived some three hundred years before Plato. The destruction of Atlantis, therefore, can be dated to approximately 11,700 years ago if we interpret *Timaeus* and *Critias* literally.

Whether they explicitly embrace the Atlantean dialogues as historically valid or carefully tiptoe around the connection to Plato's tale, catastrophist archaeologists tell a story remarkably similar, at least in its general theme and chronology. Though the advanced ancient civilisation proposed by the catastrophists may be located in an area different from that indicated by Plato, its level of technological development, the time period of its ascendance, its cultural impacts on the rest of the world, and the catastrophic nature and dating of its fall are all quite similar to Plato's Atlantis.

One of the most popular of the catastrophist scenarios has been proposed by writers Rand and Rose Flem-Ath (1997) who claim that a highly sophisticated, enormously ancient civilisation developed on an Earth vastly differently configured from the planet with which we are familiar. In the Flem-Ath scenario, the home base of this civilisation – which they explicitly label Atlantis – is located on the continent of Antarctica, during a period when the climate there was considerably more benign than it is today. Following Charles Hapgood (1999) and his scenario of a catastrophic shift in the location of the Earth's poles, the Flem-Aths propose that a displacement of the Earth's crust, and a resulting shift in the location of the poles, caused a nearly unimaginable series of floods and climatic displacements, including the blanketing of the southernmost continent with a permanent ice field. The great Antarctic civilisation was destroyed, and the ripple effects of first its evolution and then its rapid destruction are marked by ostensible archaeological evidence throughout the rest of the world. This all occurred 11,600 years ago, almost precisely the date for the destruction of Atlantis in Plato's dialogues.

Catastrophists base much of their argument on the presence in the archaeological record of claimed evidence of a technologically advanced, extraordinarily ancient civilisation that, they assert, developed long before those cultures believed by traditional prehistorians to have been the earliest, i.e. long before the appearance of the first Mesopotamian city-states and long before the well-documented Old Kingdom of Egypt (Hancock 1996). For the most part, the evidence marshalled by the catastrophists consists not of newly discovered archaeological sites but, instead, the reinterpretation and re-dating of already well-known archaeological features. This is a key point; the ancient monuments ascribed to the Atlanteans (or whatever they choose to call them) by the catastrophists have already been dated and firmly ensconced by prehistorians and archaeologists in chronological sequences that do not reflect any substantial disconti-nuities. The catastrophists, however, reject the dates on which these sequences are based. For example, the Great Sphinx located in the pyramid complex at Giza, in Egypt, has been confidently dated by Egyptologists to about 2500 BC, during the reign of the pharaoh Khafre. The catastrophists assert that the Great Sphinx must be much older, basing this claim on the work of geologist Robert Schoch (1999), dating to a time before the destruction of the most ancient civilisation which is, in their reality, actually responsible for its construction.

It is no coincidence that Plato situated his mythical continent in the middle of the Atlantic Ocean and at a time 9,300 years before his own. There simply was no way for his readership to test the historicity of the place, and that suited Plato's purpose (Jordan 2001). Herein lies another commonality between the Atlantis of Plato and that of the modern catastrophists. The most popular version of catastrophist archaeology places its great lost civilisation and, by implication, any archaeological evidence of its existence, at the base of the southern ice sheet, thoroughly inaccessible to any kind of direct archaeological testing.

The great Atlantis populariser of the nineteenth century, Ignatius Donnelley, closed his book, *Atlantis: The Antediluvian World* (1881) by asserting hopefully that in one hundred years hence, the world's great museums would be filled with fabulous treasures recovered from the lost continent, indisputably documenting its existence. Though it turned out to be wrong, at least Donnelley's prediction was informed by an understanding that material evidence resides at the core of archaeological reasoning. Today's catastrophist archae-ologists may or may not recognise that without such direct evidence, their Atlantis and the cataclysm that destroyed it are as ephemeral as Plato's.

Suggested reading

Alvarez, W. 1998. *T-Rex and the Crater of Doom*. New York: Vintage Books.
Walter Alvarez's popular treatment of his hypothesis, now roundly supported by geologists and paleontologists alike, that an impact with an extraterrestrial body, probably a meteor, resulted in an enormous cataclysm that led to the extinction of the dinosaurs.

Donnelley, I. [1881] 1971. *Atlantis: The Antediluvian World*. Harper: New York.
Because most of the modern catastrophists promulgate what is essentially an updated version of the Atlantis story, Ignatius Donnelley's nineteenth-century popular book is an important source. Donnelley bases his belief in the historicity of Plato's Atlantis on historical and archaeological evidence that he interprets as indicating connections between the ancient civilisations in the Old and New Worlds, positing a common source for both: Atlantis. The archaeological evidence that Donnelley predicted in 1881 would prove his argument has not been forthcoming.

Flem-Ath, R. and Flem-Ath, R. 1997. *When the Sky Fell: In Search of Atlantis*. New York: St Martin's Press.
The Flem-Ath hypothesis that a great civilisation, which they in fact call 'Atlantis', was located on the continent of Antarctica and was destroyed when the Earth's crust slipped, causing a fundamental change in world-wide climate, is articulated in this book.

Jordan, P. 2001. *The Atlantis Syndrome*, Phoenix Mill, England: Sutton Publishing.
The definitive work on Atlantis, Jordan explores Plato's purpose in the Timaeus and *Critias* dialogues, showing that the works are philosophical explorations and not based on historical realities. Jordan shows that Plato hoped to exemplify how a hypothetical 'perfect society' would respond when threatened by an economically and militarily far more powerful nation. Atlantis was not a real place but the foil in Plato's historical morality tale.

Lyell, C. [1830] 1990. *Principles of Geology; Being an Attempt to Explain the Former Changes of the Earth's Surface, By Reference to Causes Now in Operation*, 2 vols. Chicago: University of Chicago Press.
This work arguably caused a sea-change in how natural scientists viewed Earth history. In it Lyell presented a stunning argument for an ancient planet, marked by consistent and uniform change through time. Lyell based his uniformitarian perspective on a firm understanding that geological processes currently in operation were sufficient to explain the physical state of the planet; in his words. 'the present is the key to the past'.

Schoch, R. 1999. Erosion Processes on the Great Sphinx and its Dating. *Society for Interdisciplinary Studies, Internet Digest* 2: 8–9.
The work of geologist Robert Schoch in re-dating the Great Sphinx is often cited by the modern catastrophists. This article presents his argument for the Great Sphinx being thousands of years older than traditional Egyptology allows. Many catastrophists interpret Schoch's dating of the Sphinx as indicating the existence of a civilisation, far older than any recognised by archaeologists, that may have been destroyed in a natural cataclysm, as yet unrecognised by most geologists.

Further reading

Hancock, G. 1996. *Fingerprints of the Gods.* New York: Crown Publishing Group.
Hapgood, C. 1999. *The Path of the Pole.* Illinois: Adventures Unlimited Press.
Hutchins, R. M. 1952. *The Dialogues of Plato.* Translated by B. Jowett. Chicago: William Benton/Encyclopedia Britannica.
Hutton, J. [1795] 1959. *Theory of the Earth: With Proofs and Illustrations,* 2 vols. Weinheim, Germany: H. R. Engelmann (J. Cramer) and Wheldon & Wesley.
Morgan, L. H. [1877] 1964. *Ancient Society.* Cambridge, Mass.: Belknap Press.
Tylor, E. 1865. *Researches into the Early History of Mankind and the Development of Civilization.* London: J. Murray.
Velikovsky, I. 1950. *Worlds in Collision.* London: Macmillan.

KENNETH L. FEDER

THE *CHAÎNE OPÉRATOIRE*

Exotic as this French notion may sound, the *chaîne opératoire* is really a straightforward and stimulating concept for both archaeological and anthropological research. In its basic definition, the *chaîne opératoire* (literally 'operational chain' or 'sequence') refers to the range of processes by which naturally occurring raw materials are selected, shaped and transformed into usable cultural products. The extraction of a flint nodule from an outcrop (to give an obvious example), and its testing, transport, knapping and reduction into a handaxe for butchering meat is one such process, and so is the mining of clay, its mixing with temper, shaping into a vessel, decorating and firing. The material traces and by-products left by these processes can in principle be identified and retrieved in the archaeological record. Their analysis makes it possible to document the steps and sequences of bygone material operations, and then reconstruct the dynamic links between these stages, their interlocking causes and effects, their attending equipment and settings, their temporal and spatial unfolding, and so on. This in turn opens the way for addressing some of the complex social, ecological and cognitive dimensions surrounding ancient technical activities. As used in the recent French and Anglo-Saxon literature, the notion of *chaîne opératoire* can designate a concrete occurrence of some particular technical process (e.g. observed in ethno-archaeological research (*see* p. 95), and also a generalised model or pattern of technical behaviour inferred from archaeological and experimental studies (e.g. the 'Acheulean handaxe *chaîne opératoire*'). However, most relevant for us here are the broader connotations of this term as a practical and conceptual approach: working with the *chaîne opératoire* implies a rigorous methodological framework for reconstructing processes of manufacture and use, and also, as importantly, a theoretically informed commitment to understanding the nature and role of technical activities in past human societies.

A brief and selective historical overview will confirm the broad appeal and potential of the *chaîne opératoire*. Back in the first decades of the nineteenth century (long before the term itself was coined), the French antiquarian François Jouannet found in the Dordogne region a range of stone axes, some perfectly polished and others flaked (chipped). For him, the flaked axes were 'rough-outs' or unfinished examples of the polished ones, and their study could 'reveal the secret of their fabrication'. Challenging this interpretation, the naturalist Casimir Picard cogently argued on statistical and morphological grounds that flaked axes were not rejects but rather finished implements, desired as such and adapted to their function (cf. Cheynier 1936). We now know that the artefacts in contention were quite distinct, respectively Neolithic axes and Acheulean handaxes. Nevertheless, the arguments whereby certain forms could represent interruptions in the shaping process (and thus have technological significance), while other forms, despite their rude or 'imperfect' appearance, could actually be intended as such (and thus have also chrono-stratigraphic and cultural implications) clearly constitute important milestones in the dynamic interpretation of artefact variability.

Similar issues cropped up in 1890s North America, when the high antiquity of man (*see* p. 7) in the New World was being proclaimed on the basis of comparisons between local finds and European Palaeolithic implements (specifically Acheulean handaxes). Opposing this claim, the Smithsonian anthropologist William Henry Holmes conducted ethnographic and stratigraphic investigations at quarry sites to argue that these supposed 'Palaeoliths' were not desired end-products but rather rejected preforms, abandoned by the native artisan because of flaws in the material or imperfect knapping. Holmes then arranged and illustrated lithic specimens in 'a series of progressive steps of manufacture' from nodule to arrowhead, demonstrating that the rude and the finished forms actually constituted 'a unity in art and in time' (cf. Meltzer and Dunnell 1992; Schlanger 1999). Despite its arcane aspects, this insightful 'natural history of implements' effectively anticipates much of the processual 'reduction sequence' approach to lithic analysis developed in the 1970s and later (e.g. Bradley 1975; Dibble 1995).

While Holmes' work was rooted in Victorian evolutionism, the cultural technology developed in France from the 1930s onwards had essentially sociological and anthropological orientations. In a series of influential essays on techniques and their study (notably on 'techniques of the body'), the sociologist Marcel Mauss conceived of techniques as 'traditional efficient acts', a socially practised and transmitted 'habitus' (*see* p. 133), a way of being and doing. Approaching technical activities in practice, as they unfolded, could show how they are at each moment materially determined and also socially mediated and effective (cf. Mauss 2004). Some of these insights were taken up and expanded by Mauss' student, the technologist, ethnologist and prehistorian André Leroi-Gourhan. In *L'Homme et la matière* (1943–6), Leroi-Gourhan developed an ethnographic classification of elementary means of action on matter, as well as a distinction between generic or universal technical 'tendencies' and specific 'degrees of fact', which occur in particular ethnic groups. He then drew on biological models and metaphors to reach the very dynamics of techniques: besides addressing the functions they served, he sought to grasp how techniques themselves functioned, how they were structured, how their different components and phases were integrated and brought to play in the course of action.

By the 1950s Leroi-Gourhan had coined the term of *chaîne opératoire* to describe this process, and in his 1964 masterpiece *Le Geste et la parole* he defined it in the following terms; 'techniques involve both gestures and tools, organised in a chain by a veritable syntax that simultaneously grants to the operational series their fixity and their flexibility' (1964: 164/1993: 114; cf. Schlanger 2004). Building on these crucial terminological and conceptual inputs, the *chaîne opératoire* approach has mainly developed along two interconnected directions, anthropological and archaeological.

With the *chaîne opératoire*, anthropologists of techniques have been exploring the links between techniques and societies, in both modern and traditional settings. They have notably enlisted materialist (*see* p. 163) and Marxist (*see* p. 165) perspectives, as well as Maussian ideas, structuralism and semiotics. Particularly influential has been the work of Pierre Lemonnier, who characterised techniques as socialised action on matter, involving implements, procedures, and knowledge. Lemonnier further distinguished among the components of *chaînes opératoires* between 'strategic tasks' – fixed operations which cannot be tampered with or cancelled without undermining the whole project – and 'technical variants' – flexible choices which are arbitrary in material terms but nevertheless socially and culturally relevant. These choices may include seemingly superficial features (e.g. decoration or 'stylistic variations'), but also more fundamental aspects regarding technical efficacy and reliability. In the slash-and-burn agriculture practised in Papua New Guinea, for example, some groups first burn the felled vegetation in their forest plot, then put a fence around it, then plant it with seeds; others first burn, then plant, then fence; others still begin by fencing, then burn, then plant. Burning before planting is imperative in this gardening *chaîne opératoire*, a strategic task which cannot be deferred and which has an impact on the scheduling and unfolding of subsequent operations. However, the timing of the fencing operation is arbitrary, a technical choice related to the differentiation strategies of the groups, or to their distinct social representations of enclosure, domestication and ownership (Lemonnier 1986, 1992). The productions of matter and of meaning are coincidental, as Lemonnier puts it, and both are enmeshed in social relations. The *chaîne opératoire* approach can thus contribute to contemporary material culture studies, notably by balancing a focus on purely ideational and symbolic considerations with the recognition of the more mundane material aspects of everyday undertakings. Moreover, as *chaînes opératoires* are essentially 'non-linear' (*see* p. 182) and dovetailing, their study can help overcome the divide between production and consumption, and appreciate the intersecting life-histories of objects-in-motion as simultaneously social, technical and symbolic accomplishments.

Although it now encompasses a broad range of archaeological materials and problem-areas (ceramics, metallurgy, textiles, archaeo-botany and -zoology, craft specialisation, ethnoarchaeology (*see* p. 95), the *chaîne opératoire* approach was first developed around the study of stone artefacts; not only do they survive in abundance across the entire human record, their physical properties make them particularly well suited for process-oriented reconstructions. Experimental (*see* p. 110) flintknapping provides contemporary archaeologists with a much better grasp of the material, gestures and dexterity implicated in tool production and usage. Equally informative is the method of artefact refitting, when the various flakes and chips detached in the course of knapping can be physically reconstructed together in their sequence of detachment. In combination with advances in termin-ology and graphic representations (e.g. schemes which indicate directionality and sequence), these inputs have done much to consolidate studies of prehistoric technology across various research traditions (French, Anglo-Saxon, Soviet, Japanese, cf. Bleed 2001). It is now increasingly evident that processes of manufacture must be incorporated in artefact analysis and interpretation, and that conven-tional typologies, for example, will have their chronological or cultural utility considerably undermined if no account is taken of the ways by which forms are reached and modified. By situating technical activities in their temporal and spatial settings (extraction, production, transport, use), *chaîne opératoire* studies can contribute to the reconstruction of the dynamics of past landscapes, both natural and social. At another level, the possibility of finely grasping series of material operations carried out in the remote past opens the way for an investigation of the knowledge, know-how and skills deployed by the prehistoric artisans.

Rather than viewing flintknapping as governed by an immutable plan or a predetermined 'mental template' (a standardised image of the desired end product), or as some adventitious blow-by-blow rock bashing, this goal-oriented activity can be considered as a structured and generative interplay between mental and material possibilities, involving planning and decision-making as well as more tacit or routine reactions (Keller and Keller 1996; Schlanger 1996). This in turn relates to issues of representations, transmission and skills as addressed by cultural anthropologists concerned with cognition in practice, and also to questions of neuro-biological and socio-cultural adaptation in the course of human evolution, as addressed by cognitive archaeology (*see* p. 41) and evolutionary psychology.

In sum, much more than a method for reconstructing past techniques, the *chaîne opératoire* approach can lead from the static remains recovered in the present to the dynamic processes of the past, and thus open up a range of inspiring archaeological and anthropological questions. With the *chaîne opératoire*, it is possible to appreciate that alongside tools, raw materials, energy and various physical or environmental possibilities, technical systems are also composed of such crucial elements as the knowledge, skills, values and symbolic representations brought to bear and generated in the course of action, as well as the social frameworks (including gender, age or ethnic differentiations) implicated in the production and reproduction of everyday life.

Suggested reading

Bleed, P. 2001. Trees or Chains, Links or Branches: Conceptual Alternatives for Consideration of Stone Tool Production and Other Sequential Activities. *Journal of Archaeological Method and Theory* 8: 101–27.
A thorough assessment of recent approaches to the analysis of stone tool manufacture, comparing the strengths of French, North American and Japanese research traditions in this field.

Dobres, M. and Hoffman, C. 1994. Social Agency and the Dynamics of Prehistoric Technology. *Journal of Archaeological Method and Theory* 1: 211–58.

A useful and thought-provoking overview of approaches to the study of technology in archaeology, integrating recent developments in sociological and anthropological theory.

Keller C. and Keller, J. D. 1996. *Cognition and Tool Use: The Blacksmith at Work.* Cambridge: Cambridge University Press.
A concerted anthropological, psychological and experimental study of a technical activity with considerable archaeological visibility (blacksmithing), leading to important conceptual and theoretical insights.

Lemonnier, P. 1992. *Elements for an Anthropology of Technology.* University of Michigan Museum of Anthropology, Anthropological Paper No. 88. Michigan: University of Michigan Museum of Anthropology.
Highly readable and stimulating introduction to the anthropology of technology by one of its leading practitioners, drawing notably on his research in rural France and Papua New Guinea, and hi-tech equipment.

Leroi-Gourhan, A. [1943–6] 1964. *Le Geste et la parole, vol. 1: Technique et langage; vol. 2: La Mémoire et les rythmes.* Paris: Albin Michel. (Translated in 1993 as *Gesture and Speech* by A. Bostock Berger. Cambridge, Mass.: MIT Press.)
Leroi-Gourhan's masterpiece, combining stimulating insights into the study and interpretation of technology with a broader (and sometimes dated) vision of human evolution in its biological and cultural dimensions.

Mauss, M. 2004. *Marcel Mauss. Techniques, Technology and Civilisation* (edited and introduced by N. Schlanger). Oxford: Berghahn Press.
A selection of important texts on the techniques of the body, the comparative study of techniques, the relations between techniques and civilisation, etc. Written between the 1920s and 1940s by the famous French sociologist.

Pelegrin, J. 1993. A Framework for Analysing Prehistoric Stone Tools Manufacture and a Tentative Application to Some Early Lithic Industries, pp. 302–14 in (A. Berthelet and J. Chavaillon, eds) *The Use of Tools by Human and Non-Human Primates.* Oxford: Clarendon Press.
A leading expert in experimental flintknapping and the analysis of prehistoric technology outlines a methodological framework for the *chaîne opératoire* study of stone tool production across human evolution.

Pfaffenberger, B. 1988. Fetishised Objects and Humanised Nature: Toward an Anthropology of Technology. *Man* 23: 236–52.
Drawing on some Marxist insights into the notions of labour and value, as well as on ethnographic fieldwork in India, this is an important acknowledgement by social anthropologists of the centrality of technical phenomena in social life.

Further reading

Bradley, B. 1975. Lithic Reduction Sequences: A Glossary and Discussion, pp. 5–14 in (E. Swanson, ed.) *Stone Tool Use and Manufacture.* The Hague: Mouton Press.
Cheynier, A. 1936. *Jouannet, Grand-père de la préhistoire.* Brive: Chastrusse, Praudel.
Dibble, H. 1995. Middle Paleolithic Scraper Reduction: Background, Clarification, and Review of the Evidence to Date. *Journal of Archaeological Method and Theory* 2: 299–368.
Lemonnier, P. 1986. The Study of Material Culture Today: Toward an

Anthropology of Technical Systems. *Journal of Anthropological Archaeology* 5: 147–86.

Meltzer, D. J. and Dunnell, R. C. 1992. *The Archaeology of William Henry Holmes*. Washington, DC: Smithsonian Institution Press.

Schlanger, N. 1996. Understanding Levallois: Lithic Technology and Cognitive Archaeology. *Cambridge Archaeological Journal* 6 (2): 231–54.

—— 1999. De la rédemption à la sauvegarde: contenu et contexte de la technologie du Bureau of American Ethnology, pp. 483–512 in (J.-L. Jamard, A. Montigny and F.-R. Picon, eds) *Dans le sillage des techniques. Hommage à Robert Cresswell*. Paris: L'Harmattan.

—— 2004. 'Suivre les gestes, éclat par éclat': la chaîne opératoire de Leroi-Gourhan, in (F. Audouze and N. Schlanger, eds) *Autour de l'homme: contexte et actualité de Leroi-Gourhan*. Paris: Editions APDCA.

NATHAN SCHLANGER

CHARACTERISATION AND EXCHANGE THEORY

Characterisation in archaeology refers to the identification of chemical or physical properties in a material which permit it to be assigned to a specific natural source of the material. For instance, the archaeologist in Australia may find a polished stone axe, and wish to determine the specific quarry from which its constituent material came. A suitable characterisation study, for instance the petrological examination of a thin section of material taken from the axe, may allow the recognition of petrological or mineralogical features which pinpoint that natural source. A good example is offered by the so-called 'bluestones' at Stonehenge. These are smaller than the great sarsen stones which form the trilithons of that structure, and are believed to have formed part of an earlier stone monument at the site. As early as 1720, petrological examination showed that they must come from a different source to the sarsens, but it was not until 1923 that the use of the petrological microscope showed them to derive from the Prescelly Mountains of South Wales, over 100 miles away as the crow flies. The distance would be much more by sea and river, since they may have been transported by raft.

The identification of the specific source of the material used for an artefact found on an archaeological site is an obvious indication of the transport either of raw materials or of finished objects. This will often imply trade and hence exchange, and obviously offers indications of early travel and perhaps the development of exchange systems. Distribution maps can show the extent and intensity in the distribution of goods and materials. And the quantitative study of such finds can give useful economic insights. It is often more difficult to decide whether the artefacts in question travelled as a result of exchange, and if so what the other components of the exchange transaction may have been. These remain difficult questions, addressed by a number of analytical techniques.

The early study of trade and exchange in archaeology was based mainly upon the recognition of specific features inherent in the constituent material of artefacts which allowed their assignment to a particular area or place of manufacture. In favourable cases the distribution of such finds could be informative about patterns in the movement of goods, and hence in studying early trade and exchange. An Olmec mask or an Egyptian sculpture could be recognised by its style and workmanship. In favourable cases there might be an inscription, and with coins there could even be a mintmark indicating the place of production. Often, however, the identification of supposedly imported artefacts on archaeological sites was based upon supposed similarities which were less conclusive, or upon resemblances suggesting that the object in question might be an imitation rather than a direct import. The results could be made more conclusive if an exotic material could be identified positively. But only in a few unusual cases, such as that of lapis lazuli, the beautiful dark blue stone from Afghanistan so cherished by the ancient Egyptians, could a specific source be suggested simply on the grounds of the appearance of the material. Nonetheless, useful studies were undertaken in the early years of the twentieth century in which maps were prepared of artefacts of a particular material, such as amber, which could be dated by their context (or their form) and which could indeed be assigned to a source area. The amber finds made in contexts of the Aegean Bronze Age were recognised as coming from the southern coasts of the Baltic Sea, where amber occurs naturally. But without further study, there was always the risk that the amber might derive from some other, perhaps unrecognised source of the material, and that the trade routes proposed might be wrong. The amber question was not put on a thoroughly scientific footing until the application of infra-red spectroscopy in the 1970s.

A great range of techniques is now available for characterisation studies. The earliest to be successfully applied was indeed the petrological study of thin sections, which proved successful for the study of the trade of British Neolithic stone axes, and could also be applied effectively to pottery. In the 1950s the application of trace element analysis to supposedly imported beads of 'faience' (a blue glaze material) from Bronze Age Britain led the way to more definitive later studies. Then trace element analysis (first by optical emission spectroscopy and then by neutron activation analysis) was successfully applied to obsidian. Obsidian is a volcanic glass which fractures conchoidally in the same manner as flint, and was widely used in prehistoric times, especially in the Neolithic period of Europe and the Near East, and in the Formative in Mesoamerica, as well as in the Pacific. Because it is found only in volcanoes of acid (silica-rich) composition, and since it devitrifies (loses its glassy properties) after a few million years, it is found only at a very limited number of sources in nature. It is therefore a very suitable material for characterisation study. Obsidians very often exhibit two characteristics which are important for a successful characterisation study. They are hetero-geneous between sources and homogeneous within sources. That is to say that the products of two different sources are different in their trace element compositions, and so can be distinguished on analysis. And at the same time different samples taken from a single source will show only a small range of variation. They are relatively homogeneous, so that repeated analyses on different samples will consistently show the same characteristics which allow that source to be reliably identified.

Problems may arise if artefacts of the material in question that are found on an archaeological site turn out, on analysis, to have features which cannot be matched with those of any known source. That has happened in the case of obsidian from Anatolia (the modern Turkey), but the missing source was later located and its obsidian analysed successfully. Much more commonly there is the problem that the products of two or more different sources resemble each other so closely (in terms of the analytical procedure being followed) that they cannot be securely distinguished. That has commonly been the experience when potsherds made in different places are subjected to trace element analysis. When numerous samples are available, statistical techniques such as discriminant analysis can be used to try to effect a separation. But if the samples do not in fact differ much on analysis, no amount of statistical sophistication is going to remedy the situation. For some materials it has to be accepted that a completely satisfactory characterisation study may not be possible. That has hitherto proved to be the case for good-quality marble used for sculptures in the classical world. White marble has few impurities, and it has not proved easy to make a successful distinction between different quarries by means of characterisation study.

It is particularly tempting to seek to investigate the trade in metals – gold, silver, bronze or copper – in such a way, since it is known that they were so widely traded. But there are several problems here. In the first place there can be very many possible sources, for instance in the case of copper. Second, it may be difficult to find features of the composition which differ systematically between sources, as has proved to be the case with gold. And then there is the very real problem of 'mixing'. Artefacts of copper or bronze can be melted down and the raw material re-used, often after mixing with material from another source. Fortunately, although trace-element analysis has proved rather disappointing for the characterisation of metals, lead isotope analysis can offer the hope of characterisation, not only for lead but for silver or copper when small quantities of lead are present, which is often the case. Similar issues can pertain to other materials. There is a wide range of analytical methods available from physics (including radioactive methods) and chemistry. In some cases the question may be one of biology – of species identification where exotic species are concerned.

The quantitative study of distribution patterns can also be informative. Trend-surface analysis has been used to study the distribution maps for finds of stone axes, and various mathematical models have been applied to the study of fall-off curves recording the decline in quantity of finds as distance from the source increases. It has been suggested that an exponential decline corresponds to a 'down-the-line' pattern of exchange, where successive villages keep a proportion of the material that they receive from their neighbour nearer the source, and pass on the remainder in the process of exchange to their neighbour down the line. Directional trade, where concentrations of an imported material are found at a particular location, may indicate preferential access or perhaps some pattern of centralised distribution, associated with the functioning of central places, and perhaps of a power hierarchy.

In practice there are difficulties in the application of spatial models for trade and exchange. Among these is the problem of 'equifinality' – the reality that more than one mode of exchange might in fact generate what is in effect the same distribution of artefactual remains. Nor can these patterns of artefact distributions, however painstakingly analysed, cope with the full reality of different patterns of consumption and of deposition, or the personal idiosyncrasies of individual exchanges. As so often in archaeology, the patterns can be difficult to interpret. Yet a sound characterisation study can give hard data about early communication, and has, for instance, given incontrovertible evidence for Upper Palaeolithic seafaring.

The consideration of exchange mechanisms has played a significant role in the development of economic anthropology, and advocates of the 'substantivist' approach of Karl Polanyi have followed him in seeking to identify reciprocity, redistribution and market exchange from the archaeological record.

The development of exchange systems has played an important role in the development of complex societies (*see* p. 101), and the World System approach, with the accompanying notions of 'centre' and 'periphery', has been applied by some scholars to archaeological cases.

Suggested reading

Earle, T. K. and Ericson, J. E. 1977. *Exchange Systems in Prehistory.* New York: Academic Press.
Important collection of papers discussing case studies of characterisation and models of exchange.

Renfrew, C. 1975. Trade as Action at a Distance, pp. 1–59 in (J. Sabloff and C. C. Lamberg-Karlovsky, eds) *Ancient Civilizations and Trade.* Albuquerque: University of New Mexico Press.
Early paper outlining some of the general issues in exchange theory.

Renfrew, C. and Bahn, P. 2004. *Archaeology, Theory, Methods and Practice,* 4th edn, London: Thames and Hudson, Chapter 9.
Up-to-date review of the field.

Scarre, C. and Healy, F. (eds) 1983. *Trade and Exchange in Prehistoric Europe.* Oxford: Oxbow Monograph 33.
Useful collection of case studies.

Further reading

Cauvin, M.-C. (ed.) 1998. *L'Obsidienne au Proche et Moyen Orient.* Oxford: British Archaeological Reports International Series 738.
Earle, T. 2002. *Bronze Age Economics, the Beginnings of Political Economies.* Boulder, Col.: Westview Press.
Polanyi, K. 1957. The Economy as Instituted Process, pp. 243–4 in (K. Polanyi, M. Arensberg and H. Pearson, eds) *Trade and Market in the Early Empires. Economies in History and Theory.* Glencoe, Ill.: Free Press.
Rowlands, M., Larsen, M. and Kristiansen, K. (eds) 1987. *Centre and Periphery in the Ancient World.* Cambridge: Cambridge University Press.
Wallerstein, I. 1974. *The Modern World System.* New York: Academic Press.

COLIN RENFREW

CHILDE'S REVOLUTIONS

Vere Gordon Childe (1892–1957) became one of the foremost prehistorians in Europe in the first half of the twentieth century. Two years before becoming the first Professor of Archaeology at Edinburgh University in 1927, he made his initial scholarly reputation by publishing his first major archaeological work, *The Dawn of European Civilization*, the overall theme of which was 'the foundation of European Civilization as a peculiar and individual manifestation of the human spirit' (Childe 1925: xiii).

The book's method was eclectic; one later commentator harshly judged it 'highly intuitive' (McNairn 1980: 5), while, to another, Childe's work in the 1920s 'contains almost nothing but combinations and permutations of existing ideas from within the canon of archaeological thought at that period' (Trigger 1994: 29–30).

But the third edition of the book, published in 1939, was not only completely rewritten; it possessed a very different method. The emergence of both the Neolithic and urban cultures in the Near East, and the Neolithic in Europe, were firmly characterised by Childe as manifestations of explicit economically based revolutions:

> Stock-breeding and the cultivation of plants were revolu-
> tionary steps in man's emancipation from dependence on the
> external environment. They put man in control of his own
> food-supply so far that population could – and did – expand
> beyond the narrow limits imposed by the naturally available
> supply of wild fruits and game.

> (Childe 1939: 14)

Although earlier scholars (for example, J. L. Myres in *The Dawn of History*, 1911) had written of the transition from hunting and gathering to farming and pastoralism in the Near East, Childe was the first scholar to marshal the wealth of research to discuss the significance of these changes in such precise, predominantly socio-economic, terms.

His new approach was due in part to the fact that in the early 1930s he moved towards a Marxist (*see* p. 165) interpretation of archaeology, especially of those regions of the Old World surveyed in *The Dawn* (see Gathercole 1994: 38–9). This approach, though latent in his *New Light on the Most Ancient East* (1934) – itself a major revision of an earlier work on the same theme – became explicit in Childe's first popular book, *Man Makes Himself* (1936); though, somewhat perversely, he called his approach 'realist' rather than 'Marxist' (Childe 1936: 7), a term borrowed from *What Marx Really Meant*, a book by his old Oxford friend, G. D. H. Cole, published in 1934 (see Childe 1935: 10).

Childe saw the Neolithic revolution as a qualitative process, transforming Palaeolithic hunting and gathering:

> The first revolution that transformed human economy gave man control over his own food supply. Man began to plant, cultivate, and improve by selection edible grasses, roots, and trees. And he succeeded in taming and firmly attaching to his person certain species of animal in return for the fodder he was able to offer, the protection he could afford, and the forethought he could exercise. The two steps are closely related.
>
> (Childe 1936: 74–5)

Regarding the urban revolution, Childe placed more emphasis on complexity:

> And so by 3000 BC the archaeologist's picture of Egypt, Mesopotamia, and the Indus valley no longer focuses attention on communities of simple farmers, but on States embracing various professions and classes. The foreground is occupied by priests, princes, scribes, and officials, and an army of specialized craftsmen, professional soldiers, and miscellaneous labourers, all withdrawn from the primary task of food-production.
>
> (Childe 1936: 159)

Childe's analogy for these revolutions (employed consistently in his writings on the topic thereafter) was the English Industrial Revolution (Childe 1936: 14–16), all three of them manifesting 'an upward kink in the population curve' (Childe 1936: 16).

To Childe these formulations were also important because they both imposed a rational order on history (see Childe 1945), and also, in the fraught political environment of the 1930s, unambiguously demonstrated his opposition to racist interpretations of Old World prehistory (see Childe 1936: 7, where the German fascist apologist, Dr Frick, is named).

These themes were given further prominence in his second popular book, *What Happened in History*, specially commissioned by Penguin Books (Childe 1942: especially 43–61 [Neolithic revolution], 79–100 [urban revolution in Mesopotamia]).

In a posthumously published note, Childe made clear how important the writing of this book, mostly completed before the German attack on the USSR in June 1941, had been

> to convince myself that a Dark Age was not a bottomless cleft in which all traditions of culture were finally engulfed. (I was convinced at the time that European Civilization – Capitalist and Stalinist alike – was irrevocably heading for a Dark Age.)

(Childe 1958: 73)

But *What Happened in History* had further significance, namely in relation to Childe's Marxism. Those Old World civilisations created by the urban revolution ended in collapse. In Marxist terms, they were examples of the Asiatic Mode of Production, where a given economic system could not sustain the social institutions it had established. However, this outcome did not contribute long term (as it should, in the view of Soviet archaeologists, who denied, as Marxist–Leninists, the existence of the AMP) to the ultimate collapse of class society (Childe 1947: 73; see also Sawer 1977: 61–2; Trigger 1984: 8; for British Marxist criticisms of this view, see sources in Gathercole 1994: 41).

Childe often wrote on the Neolithic and urban revolutions in subsequent publications, though increasingly with less emphasis on general statements, giving more attention to the cultural and social implications of the growing quantity of empirical data (see, for example, Childe 1956, 1962 [Neolithic revolution]; Childe 1950, 1952 [urban revolution]). His final synthesis of this thirty-year-old hunt for the origins and development of Old World civilisations, especially within Europe, appeared posthumously as another book commissioned by Penguin, *The Prehistory of European Society* (1958a).

Inevitably Childe's concepts have received much, often critical, comment. Though his use of Marxism (widely misinterpreted as mechanistic Marxism–Leninism) has had both supporters and critics, in the long term the recent views of T. E. Levy regarding Childe's arguments have received considerable endorsement: 'Even today, many decades after Childe introduced the term and after hundreds of new sites have been discovered and excavated, the profound shift from foragers to food producers does indeed warrant the descriptive term of "revolution" ' (Levy 1996: 491 – note the use of 'descriptive'). Regarding the urban revolution, Levy prefers the phrase 'secondary products revolution', first used by Andrew Sherratt in 1981 (Sherratt

1996: 632–4; for the similarity of his views to those of Levy, see Sherratt 1989: 178–80). Much of Childe's work is now primarily of historical interest, but alongside his writings on the sociology of knowledge (see especially Childe 1949), initially often ignored by his archaeological colleagues, those on 'revolutions' have retained much of their topicality.

(Note: see also McNairn 1980: 26–9, 91–103; Trigger 1980: especially 104–14; Green 1981a: 94–9; 1981b; Flannery 1994: 103–10, especially re Childe 1950; Renfrew 1994: 123ff; Rowlands 1971; Tringham 1983: especially 86–7.)

Suggested reading

Publications by V. Gordon Childe
Childe was a prolific writer, who was also meticulous in bringing up to date his most widely used texts. Of those cited above and listed below, readers should also consult the sixth edition of *The Dawn of European Civilization* (London: Routledge and Kegan Paul, 1957) and the fourth edition of *New Light on the Most Ancient East* (London: Routledge and Kegan Paul, 1954). Later reprints of *Man Makes Himself* and *What Happened in History*, however, involved no major changes to their original texts.

Childe, V, G. 1925. *The Dawn of European Civilization*. London: Kegan Paul.
—— 1934. *New Light on the Most Ancient East*. London: Kegan Paul.
—— 1935. Changing Methods and Aims in Prehistory. *Proceedings of the Prehistoric Society* 1: 1–15.
—— 1936. *Man Makes Himself*. London: Watts.
—— 1939. *The Dawn of European Civilization*, 3rd edn. London: Kegan Paul.
—— 1942. *What Happened in History*. Harmondsworth: Penguin Books.
—— 1945. Rational Order in History. *The Rationalist Annual*: 1–26.
—— 1947. *History*. London: Cobbett Press.
—— 1949. *Social Worlds of Knowledge*. L. T. Hobhouse Memorial Lecture 19. London: Oxford University Press.
—— 1950. The Urban Revolution. *The Town Planning Review* XXI (1): 3–17.
—— 1952. The Birth of Civilization. *Past and Present* 2: 1–10.
—— 1953. Old World Prehistory: Neolithic, pp. 193–210 in (A. L. Kroeber, ed.) *Anthropology Today: An Encyclopedic Inventory*. Chicago: Chicago University Press.
—— 1956. The New Stone Age, pp. 95–111 in (H. L. Shapiro, ed.) *Man, Culture, and Society*. New York: Oxford University Press.
—— 1958a. *The Prehistory of European Society*. Harmondsworth: Penguin Books.
—— 1958b. Retrospect. *Antiquity* XXXII: 69–74.
—— 1962. Old World Prehistory: Neolithic, pp. 152–68 in (S. Tax, ed.) *Anthropology Today*. Chicago: Chicago University Press.

In addition to these works, the following are relevant to changes in Childe's approach to archaeology after 1945, which also often provided a broader context than previously to his views on the Neolithic and urban revolutions:

Scotland before the Scots (London: Methuen, 1946) – a Marxist analysis, influenced by then-current trends in Soviet prehistory.
Piecing Together the Past (London: Routledge and Kegan Paul, 1956) – his only detailed study of archaeological interpretation.
Society and Knowledge (London: George Allen and Unwin, 1956) – a philosophical examination of the sociology of knowledge.

Publications by other writers
These include books and articles on Childe, his writings and his significance for archaeology in his time and later (including works cited in the above essay, of which the biographical studies by Green, McNairn and Trigger are especially recommended).

Flannery, K. V. 1994. Childe the Evolutionist: A Perspective from Nuclear America, pp. 101–19 in (D. R. Harris, ed.) *The Archaeology of V. Gordon Childe: Contemporary Perspectives*. London: UCL Press.
Gathercole, P. 1994. Childe in History. *Bulletin, London Institute of Archaeology* 31: 25–52.
—— 2000. Childe among the Penguins. *Australian Archaeology* 50: 7–11.
Gathercole, P., Irving, T. H. and Melleuish, G. (eds) 1995. *Childe and Australia: Archaeology, Politics and Ideas*. St Lucia, Queensland: University of Queensland Press.
Green, S. 1981a. *Prehistorian: A Biography of V. Gordon Childe*. Bradford-on-Avon: Moonraker Press.
—— 1981b. Introduction, pp. 7–23 in (V. Gordon Childe) *Man Makes Himself*. Bradford-on-Avon: Moonraker Press and Pitman Press (reprint of 1956 edn).
Levy, T. E. 1996. The Neolithic and Chalcolithic (Pre-Bronze-Age) Periods in the Near East, pp. 491–4 in (B. M. Fagan, ed.) *The Oxford Companion to Archaeology*. New York: Oxford University Press.
McNairn, B. 1980. *The Method and Theory of V. Gordon Childe*. Edinburgh: Edinburgh University Press.
Renfrew, C. 1994. Concluding Remarks: Childe and the Study of Culture Process, pp. 121–33 in (D. R. Harris, ed.) *The Archaeology of V. Gordon Childe: Contemporary Perspectives*. London: UCL Press.
Rowlands, M. 1971. The Archaeological Interpretation of Prehistoric Metal-working. *World Archaeology* 3: 210–24.
Sawer, M. 1977. *Marxism and the Question of the Asiatic Mode of Production*. The Hague: Martinus Nijhoff.
Sherratt, A., 1989. V. Gordon Childe: Archaeology and Intellectual History. *Past and Present* 125: 151–85.
—— 1996. Secondary Productions Revolution, pp. 632–4 in (B. M. Fagan, ed.) *The Oxford Companion to Archaeology*. New York: Oxford University Press.
Trigger, B. G. 1980. *Gordon Childe: Revolutions in Archaeology*. London: Thames and Hudson.
—— 1984. Childe and Soviet Archaeology. *Australian Archaeology* 18: 1–16.
—— 1994. Childe's Relevance to the 1990s, pp. 9–34 in (D. R. Harris, ed.) *The Archaeology of V. Gordon Childe: Contemporary Perspectives*. London: UCL Press.
—— 1999. Vere Gordon Childe, 1892–1957, pp. 385–99 in (T. Murray, ed.)

Encyclopedia of Archaeology: The Great Archaeologists, vol. 1. Santa Barbara: ABC Clio.

Tringham, R. 1983. V. Gordon Childe 25 Years After: His Relevance for the Archaeology of the Eighties. *Journal of Field Archaeology* 10: 85–100.

PETER GATHERCOLE

COGNITIVE ARCHAEOLOGY

Cognitive archaeology is the study of past ways of thought as inferred from the surviving material remains. Although in the broad sense this initiative might be regarded as including any attempt to reconstruct the 'meaning' to their makers and users of the objects and the symbols from the past which the archaeologist recovers – and the term 'cognitive archaeology' has sometimes been used in this way – it has, over the past decade, come to be employed in a more restricted sense. To many archaeologists today, including those working within the general framework of the processual archaeology which emerged from the 'New Archaeology' of the 1960s and 1970s (*see* p. 212), the evident requirement is to develop a secure methodology by which we can hope to learn *how* the minds of the ancient communities in question worked, and the manner in which that working shaped their actions.

That is deliberately a more modest aim than the quest for the entire 'meaning' which significant symbolic objects or depictions may have originally possessed for those who used them or who understood them. To recover such 'meaning' remains the avowed goal of some researchers working in the recent 'hermeneutic' or interpretive tradition which arose with the 'post-processual' archaeology of the 1980s and 1990s (*see* p. 207). For those working in that tradition, which can be traced back to the earlier work of R. G. Collingwood and of the Italian philosopher Benedetto Croce, it is not enough to make some statements about how the ancient society in question developed and used symbolic concepts with which they could describe and engage with the world. Some interpretive archaeologists have sought instead to 'enter the mind' of the early individuals involved through some effort of active empathy. This total experience of 'being' that other long-dead person, or at least undergoing an experience to be compared with theirs, is what characterises the subjective, idealist and interpretationist approach of the hermeneutic archaeologist. The cognitive archaeologist of today is sceptical of the validity of such

41

empathetic experience, and sceptical too of the privileged status which must invariably be claimed by the idealist who is advancing an interpretation on the basis of this intuitive, 'I-was-there' experience. As in the conduct of all scientific inquiry, it is not the source of the insight which validates the claim, but the explicit nature of the reasoning which sustains it, and the means by which the available data can be brought into relationship with it, for instance by the 'testing' or 'falsification' procedures common in processual archaeology following the hypothetico–deductive approach, such as that outlined by Karl Popper. Validation rests not upon authority, but on testability and on the explicitness of the argumentation, even if testing is not always in practice an easy undertaking.

The field of cognitive archaeology falls naturally into two sub-fields. The first deals with the evolution of the cognitive capacities of our pre-sapient (i.e. before *Homo sapiens sapiens*) ancestors. This is the long story of the developing skills and abilities of such ancestral species as *Australopithecus*, *Homo habilis* and *Homo erectus*, as well as of our relatives *Homo sapiens neanderthalensis*. It is the story therefore of the emergence of human capacities, including the use of language and the development of self-awareness, up to what is sometimes called the 'human revolution' which involves the appearance of our own species, *Homo sapiens sapiens*. The second field of cognitive archaeology involves the subsequent emergence within our species of the varying cognitive capacities and devices associated with the different trajectories of cultural development which diverse human societies have since then followed. Notable among these has been the development of writing, apparently quite independently in different parts of the world.

For the time range up to some 80,000 to 40,000 years ago, prior to which our species was still in process of formation, we are obviously unable to assume that we are discussing beings much like ourselves in our innate capacities. Any interpretive or empathetic approach is very difficult. We have therefore to follow such indications as the evidence, documented by the material remains, may provide. The planning and time-structuring implied in the procurement of raw materials over considerable distances is one promising field of study. The repetitive procedures and skills involved, and the *chaîne opératoire* of tool production is another (*see* p. 25), as is the implication of organised behaviour which may be suggested by the distribution of materials found on living floors. A crucial and still controversial question is just when developed speech first emerged. Many archaeologists share the view of the psychologist Merlin Donald that fully developed speech capacity is essentially a feature of our own species, *Homo sapiens sapiens*, and that earlier hominids, such as *Homo erectus*, operated mainly by 'mimesis', that is to say by learning through demonstration and imitation, rather than primarily by verbal description. But the indications of long-distance sea travel by pre-sapiens hominids, implied, for instance by the finds of Middle Pleistocene artefacts on the island of Flores in Indonesia, raise questions about the communication required by the organisation of the open-sea voyages involved.

With the emergence of our own species, and the subsequent migrations which populated most of the world by 40,000 years ago (with the exception of the Americas and Polynesia), it seems safe to assume that fully developed speech and self-awareness were a feature of all human communities. Indeed, DNA studies suggest that genetically a child born today is very little different in its genetic make-up from one born 40,000 years ago. The hardware is the same. It is the software, the cultural component learnt since birth, which differs. Yet if it is true that the innate potentialities of our species were the same then as they are today, it seems a paradox, sometimes termed the 'sapient paradox' (*see* p. 162), that it took a further 30,000 years before sedentary life first developed, with the first villages and soon the first towns, then cities, and the rapid development in social organisation which the archaeological record documents in Western Asia and then in Europe, in China, in Mesoamerica, in South America and elsewhere.

Cognitive archaeology is only now beginning to grapple with such developments, and with the increasing human use of symbols for measuring the world and for planning. These are dependent upon the formation of new kinds of social relations, which again rely upon the use of symbols to structure and to regulate interpersonal behaviour. At an early stage, also, it is clear that many societies came to think in terms of a supernatural dimension, with the use of symbols to communicate with the other world and to mediate between humans and the world beyond: the birth of religion. A striking and very early feature in the cognitive archaeology of our species is the development of representation, with the production and use of depictions and of other iconic embodiments of reality, notably painting and sculpture. Why the sophisticated cave paintings of south France and north Spain should appear as early as 25,000 years ago and in so localised an area is a difficult question. So too is that of their function, variously interpreted as sympathetic magic for hunting, the work of drug-using shamans, or part of the teaching by which young members of the community were taught the wisdom of the ancestors during some subterranean rites of passage.

Increasingly it is realised that different communities rely upon shared understandings which take on an almost factual reality, concepts which the philosopher John Searle terms 'institutional facts'. In the modern world the notion of 'money' is one of these, and indeed so are most social 'facts', including marriage, property and inheritance, as well as such practical issues as units of weight or of time. The cognitive archaeologist is beginning to realise that it is through the construction and use of such concepts that early societies learnt to cope in new ways with the material world and with each other (see p. 159).

Suggested reading

Donald, M. 1991. *Origins of the Human Mind. Three Stages in the Evolution of Culture and Cognition.* Cambridge, Mass.: Harvard University Press.
Pioneering approach to seeing human evolution in terms of cognitive stages.

Mithen, S. 1996. *The Prehistory of the Mind.* London: Thames and Hudson.
Very readable discussion of some of the problems, although the solution may not be entirely persuasive.

Noble, W. and Davidson, I. 1996. *Human Evolution, Language and Mind, a Psychological and Archaeological Inquiry.* Cambridge: Cambridge University Press.
A standard treatment written too early to take account of some recent developments.

Renfrew, C. and Bahn, P. 2004. What Did They Think? Cognitive Archaeology, Art and Religion, Chapter 10 in (C. Renfrew and P. Bahn) *Archaeology: Theories, Methods and Practice,* 4th edn. London: Thames and Hudson.
A concise introduction to cognitive archaeology.

Renfrew, C. and Scarre, C. (eds) 1998. *Cognition and Material Culture: The Archaeology of Symbolic Storage.* Cambridge: McDonald Institute for Archaeological Research.
A collection of papers dealing with related themes.

Renfrew, C. and Zubrow, E. B. W. (eds) 1994. *The Ancient Mind, Elements of Cognitive Archaeology.* Cambridge: Cambridge University Press.
An early collection of papers introducing some of the problems.

Further reading

Collingwood, R. G. 1946. *The Idea of History.* Oxford: Clarendon Press.
Hodder, I. 1986. *Reading the Past.* Cambridge: Cambridge University Press.
Mellars, P. A. and Gibson, K. (eds) 1996. *Modelling the Early Human Mind.* Cambridge: McDonald Institute for Archaeological Research.
Pearson, J. L. 2002. *Shamanism and the Ancient Mind, a Cognitive Approach to Archaeology.* Walnut Creek, Calif.: AltaMira Press.
Renfrew, C. 1982. *Towards an Archaeology of Mind (Inaugural Lecture).* Cambridge: Cambridge University Press.

Renfrew, C., Peebles, C., Hodder, I., Bender, B., Flannery, K. V. and Marcus, J. 1993. Viewpoint: What is Cognitive Archaeology? *Cambridge Archaeological Journal* 3: 247–70.

Searle, J. R. 1995. *The Construction of Social Reality*. Harmondsworth: Allen Lane.

COLIN RENFREW

ARCHAEOLOGY OF CULT AND RELIGION

The archaeology of cult and religion, although an obvious area of archaeological interest, is substantially neglected. This is, in part, due to the fact that it is not a simple field of investigation, for it comprises the residue associated almost wholly with people's beliefs, both individual and collective, and thus it is in reality remarkably complex.

One of the primary reasons for its neglect is definition. 'Cult' might be fairly easy to define in that it is focused around religious ceremonies though also has connotations of something marginal, 'freakish' and occasional, but 'religion' is far less straightforward to define. What religion is and what it is composed of has been the subject of much debate by anthropologists, sociologists and historians of religions, and their definitions range from simple ones such as that provided by the anthropologist Edward Tylor (1958: 8) that religion is composed of 'the belief in spiritual beings', through to much more complex ones, the latter attempting to define religion as a complex of different elements – beliefs, practices, rituals, experiences, social factors and the like.

At this point it could be asked: what, then, is religion? In answer to this it has to be stated that in many respects it is indefinable, being concerned with thoughts, beliefs, actions and material, and how these are weighted will vary; but in general terms, the simpler the definition the better. The important point to make is that, regardless of all the complexities of definition which have been attempted, in the end we have to recognise as archaeologists that religion also includes the intangible, the irrational and the indefinable. Religion is complex, as is its associated archaeology, and put simply, the material implications of the archaeology of religion are profound and can encompass all dimensions of material culture.

Partly because of this definitional uncertainty archaeologists have tended to avoid the term 'religion' except, predominantly, where historically known or living religions are being considered: world religions (Christianity, Judaism, Islam, Hinduism, Buddhism, etc.) or so-called traditional or primal religions (African religions, Australian Aboriginal religions, etc.). Outside of these contexts archaeologists have tended to use the term 'ritual' to describe material which might often be better described as religious. 'Ritual' is again a problematical term and one also subject to debate as to its definition. Ritual can be both sacred and secular in intent, but this distinction is often blurred and the term is used to describe anything which is not fully understood. Thus ritual becomes a synonym for the 'odd', the unexplained or the otherwise unexplainable, when in fact it can only really be understood on a case-by-case basis, and forms merely an element of religion rather than being a descriptor for religion itself as it is often employed in archaeology.

Turning to a consideration of the impact of the study of religion and cult in archaeological thought and method, it is possible to trace an interest in this subject back to at least the seventeenth century, when the English antiquary John Aubrey interpreted the stone circles of Avebury and Stonehenge in Wiltshire as Druids' temples. He in turn influenced the eighteenth-century English antiquary, William Stukeley, who amplified such interpretations to the extent that druidical ceremonies at sites such as Avebury were thought to 'closely resemble the services in his own parish church at Stamford' (Piggott 1985: 104).

With the development of archaeology proper, we can again see archaeologists taking an interest in 'religious' aspects of their data. For example, Christian Jürgensen Thomsen and Jens Worsaae, two Danish archaeologists who were instrumental in establishing the very discipline of archaeology in the mid-nineteenth century – the former establishing the Three Age System of stone, bronze and iron, for instance (*see* p. 264) – were interested not only in technology and subsistence but also in past beliefs. Yet explicit theorising by archaeologists with regard to religion did not occur until the mid-twentieth century, when the English archaeologist Christopher Hawkes developed his 'ladder of inference'. This was a ladder of interpretation which placed technical processes on the bottom rung, i.e. as easy to interpret from archaeological evidence, followed by 'subsistence economics', social and political institutions, and finally 'religious institutions and spiritual life' (1954: 161–2). The latter held the most elevated position as Hawkes thought this the most difficult area of past life to interpret via archaeology.

More recently, processual or 'New' archaeology (*see* p. 212), especially the work of the American archaeologist Lewis Binford, has also recognised that religion is a factor to be considered by archaeologists. Binford (1962: 218–19) has referred to 'ideological sub-systems' and also what he calls 'ideotechnic artefacts'. Yet ultimately within this processualist framework, religion was discarded as 'epiphenomenal', meaning that it was a superfluous or additional domain of research outside the main concerns of archaeology such as technology and subsistence. Hence the study of religion by archaeologists was classed as an endeavour which fell inside the domain of 'palaeopsychology'. Within the later development of cognitive processualism, however, concerned as it is with past minds as much as with technology or economy, the archaeological study of cult and religion has a definite place. The British archaeologist Colin Renfrew has provided the impetus for this, and though moving away from his earlier 'framework of inference' (1985: 11), has argued that the archaeology of cult and religion can be considered, for example, through archaeological indicators of ritual which have been grouped within four main categories, those concerned with:

- the focusing of attention;
- the boundary zone between this world and the next;
- the presence of the deity;
- participation and offering.

This stands in contrast to other key areas of contemporary archaeological thought. Post-processual, contextual or interpretative archaeology, for instance (*see* p. 207), has largely neglected religion in favour of 'ritual' or 'symbolic' dimensions of material culture. The British archaeologist Ian Hodder provides a case in point, for in considering the 'domestication of Europe' (1990) he emphasises these latter aspects of the data, even though some of the evidence described might more plausibly be described as religious. A similar absence of religion is found in the writings of other post-processual archaeologists, such as those of Michael Shanks and Christopher Tilley, who subsume religion within ideology, though consider ritual as a category of evidence which archaeologists can explore.

The use of the term 'religion' has perhaps been conceptually tainted within post-processual contexts by the sort of generalising approaches to 'prehistoric religion' which used to exist, whereby Middle Palaeolithic 'Cave Bear Cults' or Neolithic religions complete with panoplies of priests and priestesses were created through the transference of modern labels on to inappropriate contexts, or the enthusiastic over-interpretation of limited evidence. Yet, equally, factors such as the perspective of the archaeologists writing about the archaeology of cult and religion must also be isolated as a potentially relevant factor. So that if religion is perhaps not of importance to the individuals themselves, this will inevitably be reflected within their archaeological interpretations as well.

Recently, a more holistic approach to the archaeology of religion has begun to be advocated in which it can be considered as the superstructure into which all other aspects of life can potentially be placed – above and beyond the usually considered domains of sacred sites and burials. This is not in the sense of some form of idealistic religious totality as might have been generated by the Romanian American historian of religions Mircea Eliade, but rather a recognition that academic notions of religion might be failing to do justice to the complexity involved; in fact, what is required in considering the archaeology of cult and religion is a rethink of the method and theory involved in this key area of archaeology.

Suggested reading

Bell, C. 1997. *Ritual Perspectives and Dimensions*. Oxford: Oxford University Press.
An excellent study which introduces the many dimensions to ritual.

Hawkes, C. 1954. Archaeological Theory and Method: Some Suggestions from the Old World. *American Anthropology* 56: 153–68.
The original paper by Christopher Hawkes in which his ideas about the 'ladder of inference' are propounded.

Insoll, T. (ed.). 2001. *Archaeology and World Religion*. London: Routledge.
A collection of papers which looks at the archaeological theory and method involved in the study of world religions such as Hinduism, Christianity, Judaism, Islam and Buddhism.

Insoll, T. (2004). *Archaeology, Ritual, Religion*. London: Routledge.
This volume examines the relationship between archaeology and religion, charts the history of relevant scholarship in detail, and dismantles existing definitions of religion and ritual. A new approach to the archaeological study of religion is suggested.

Renfrew, C. 1994. The Archaeology of Religion, pp. 47–54 in (C. Renfrew and E. Zubrow, eds) *The Ancient Mind*. Cambridge: Cambridge University Press.
A broader summary and treatment of Colin Renfrew's approach to the archaeological study of religion.

Renfrew, C. 1985. *The Archaeology of Cult*. London: Thames and Hudson.
A classic text (especially Chapter 1) which presents a seminal cognitive processual approach to the study of a sanctuary in Greece.

Further reading

Binford, L. 1962. Archaeology as Anthropology. *American Antiquity* 28: 217–25.

Eliade, M. 1969. *The Quest. History and Meaning in Religion.* Chicago: University of Chicago Press.

Hodder, I. 1990. *The Domestication of Europe.* Oxford: Blackwell.

James, E. O. 1957. *Prehistoric Religion.* London: Thames and Hudson.

Piggott, S. 1985. *William Stukeley. An Eighteenth-Century Antiquary.* London: Thames and Hudson.

Shanks, M. and Tilley, C. 1992. *Re-constructing Archaeology. Theory and Practice.* London: Routledge.

Tylor, E. B. 1958. *Religion in Primitive Culture.* New York: Harper and Row.

TIMOTHY INSOLL

CULTURAL EVOLUTION

The term 'cultural evolution' (sometimes used interchangeably with 'social' or 'sociocultural' evolution), as commonly used by archaeologists and anthropologists, has traditionally referred to the history of what are conceived as the key long-term trends in human history: from foraging to farming; from farming to the origins of civilisation and the state; from agrarian civilisations to industrial and now post-industrial society; accompanied by such developments as increased population, greater social complexity and inequality, and more complex technologies. More recently the term has been used to refer to the idea that the processes producing cultural stability and change are analogous in important respects to those of biological evolution: in this view, just as biological evolution is characterised by changing frequencies of genes in populations through time as a result of such processes as natural selection, so cultural evolution refers to the changing distributions of cultural attributes in populations, likewise affected by processes such as natural selection but also by others that have no analogue in genetic evolution.

This essay will be devoted to the more traditional definition. The archaeological approach to studying culture from the newer perspective just described has become known as Darwinian archaeology (*see* p. 58) and its ideas and implications will be presented under that heading.

Directional schemes for the evolution of society have a long history in human thought, although they vary in their view of whether the movement is good or bad: the Greek and Roman idea of the decline from a golden age can be compared with the Christian idea of a movement towards salvation. More secular schemes originated during the eighteenth-century revolution in philosophy known as the

Enlightenment, but the ones which have been most influential are those that developed in the nineteenth century, especially those of Marx (*see* p. 165) and Engels, heavily influenced by L. H. Morgan's sequence from savagery to barbarism to civilisation. In the nineteenth-century industrial societies where the secular schemes were increasingly elaborated, such developments as complex technologies and increased production were seen as improving humanity's lot, and therefore as progressive. In a similar vein, the process of domination of traditional societies by industrial, imperialist ones was seen as a natural and inevitable process of social Darwinist competition, in which weaker societies succumbed to stronger ones.

While the idea of directional evolution was a central part of the intellectual background out of which archaeology emerged in the later nineteenth century, it was less prominent in the first half of the twentieth, when culture history became the main preoccupation of archaeologists. The outstanding exception to this emphasis was Gordon Childe (*see* p. 35), a Marxist by persuasion. Childe's approach was not an inflexibly unilinear and deterministic one, as the titles of such books as *Man Makes Himself* clearly demonstrate. However, he did regard the origins of agriculture (the Neolithic revolution) and the emergence of urban societies (the urban revolution) as major steps in the progress of human societies, because they represented improved adaptations of humans to their environments, witnessed by the greatly increased populations which could now be sustained. Nevertheless, progress was not automatic. Childe argued that the civilisations of the ancient Near East, which had initially been progressive, eventually became stagnant and fossilised as a result of the effects of despotic leadership and social control. Further progress took place elsewhere, he suggested, when the Bronze Age Near East handed on the baton of technological development to the societies of prehistoric Europe. Because these did not have despotic forms of leadership they were able to take the innovations which had developed in the Near East, such as metallurgy, and turn them in new directions. The result, in Childe's scheme, was a kind of direct line of evolution from independent European Bronze Age metal producers to Greek democracy and on eventually to the Industrial Revolution!

In North America the two individuals who brought cultural evolution back to centre-stage were the anthropologists Julian Steward, who was concerned with explaining the adaptive trajectories of particular societies, and Leslie White, who revived a much more generalising view of evolution on a global scale. White saw cultural evolution as an extremely general process, in which societies progressed as a result of harnessing increasing amounts of energy from the environment thanks to the process of technological innovation. A problem with White's idea of cultural evolution as increased energy throughput was how to relate it to the analysis of individual societies so that they could be placed within the scheme. The answer was provided by Elman Service, who proposed that a measure of how much energy a society was able to harness could be obtained by examining how energy was invested in social structure. He suggested that structure could be characterised in terms of four successively more complex social types: bands, tribes, chiefdoms and states. Broadly speaking, bands corresponded to the majority of hunter-gatherer societies, with very few links between local groups. Tribes were seen as usually practising some sort of agriculture and as having certain social institutions that linked individual communities together, such as fairly formal kinship structures. Chiefdoms had a central agency responsible for such activities as redistribution, in which goods are collected from members of the community and then handed out again in some way, often through the organisation of feasts. Finally, there was the state, which involved the presence of a much more centralised decision-making apparatus, dependent on provisioning by the population at large.

Societies were regarded as moving through these stages by responding to adaptive challenges. Thus, redistribution was conceived as a means of organising a territory with a variety of economic potentials, so that communities could benefit from all the resources in the territory as a whole, as opposed to just their particular part of it. It was also suggested that societies with more complex organisation would tend to be more successful if competition between different groups occurred.

Service's scheme and others like it were attractive to archaeologists because they seemed to encapsulate the key patterns in human history, and to offer an appropriate scale of resolution for archaeology, as a discipline that has evidence for long-term patterns in the past, but evidence that is usually coarse-grained in temporal resolution and in detail often open to a variety of interpretations. Thus Colin Renfrew (1974), for example, looked at the archaeological record of Late Neolithic Wessex from the perspective of Service's scheme in an attempt to throw light on the organisation of the societies that produced such monuments as Avebury and Stonehenge. He argued that between the Early Neolithic, with its long burial mounds and causewayed earthwork enclosures, and the Late Neolithic, with its enormous 'henge' monuments, such as Avebury, Wessex society must have evolved from the tribe to the chiefdom stage.

A great deal of useful work has been done within this framework, mainly devoted to tracing patterns of changing complexity in past societies on the basis of the archaeological record and then attempting to explain the changes observed. Nevertheless, the criticisms that the approach has attracted are many. The 'complexity' scale has been seen as one in which 'complex' societies were more highly valued than simple ones, with dubious Eurocentric moral overtones. Moreover, many of the archaeological sequences in different parts of the world failed to show much evidence of increasing complexity. Either these periods and areas had to be left on the sidelines of history, or, more usually, the archaeologists working on them, not wanting to be left out of things, had to become ever more ingenious at showing that some slight increase in social complexity could actually be observed. In any event, it came to seem unrealistic to squash all social variation on to a single dimension of 'complexity', and worse still to divide that dimension into a series of discrete stages; the attempt to do so, it was argued, arose from a gross exaggeration of the extent to which societies can be divided into types characterised by particular sets of features. Moreover, the sequence of stages was not inevitable; for example, societies did not necessarily have to pass through a chiefdom stage before becoming states.

These attacks on conventional directional schemes of cultural evolution have left social archaeology without a clear agenda in terms of the issues it should address. The question is whether they entail a complete rejection of the idea of long-term trends in the history of human societies. Bruce Trigger (1998) has recently argued that the issues the cultural evolutionary approaches were supposed to address remain as important as ever: in the course of human history, novel social and economic forms have come into existence that have had the capacity to dominate increasingly large areas of the world, more often than not to the detriment of the people living in the societies subject to this domination. It is essential, Trigger argues, to recognise that these developments have occurred and to understand how they came about. It is the cultural evolution approach to understanding them that is problematical, especially its focus on the emergence of hierarchies and the development of social control as societies became larger and more differentiated. Other important dimensions of change that impinge on governing institutions, such as the development of property and commercial institutions, have been largely ignored. The same is true of domestic institutions, despite the fact that many aspects of social change are located at the domestic level. Furthermore, many authors have pointed out that attempts at domination always invoke a corresponding resistance: we need to look at what social processes are going on at the bottom as well as at the top.

Studies attempting to remedy these deficiencies in cultural evolutionary understandings of the broad patterns which hindsight enables us to detect in human history have begun to appear. One of the most promising approaches uses a form of 'bottom-up' approach known as 'agent-based modelling'; in contrast to the elite social control models of traditional cultural evolutionary approaches, the actions and interactions of entities attempting to achieve local goals lead to unintended consequences at larger temporal and spatial scales, including new forms of social institutions (see e.g. Kohler and Gumerman 2000). Thus, cultural evolution does not have a preordained direction.

Suggested reading

Earle, T. 1997. *How Chiefs Come to Power*. Stanford: Stanford University Press.
A comparative analysis of the emergence of chiefdoms in prehistoric Denmark, Peru and Hawaii, looking at the different sources of power mobilised by emerging chiefs in the different areas and their effects.

Feinman, G. M. and Marcus, J. (eds) 1998. *Archaic States*. Santa Fe: SAR Press.
An extremely useful survey of the characteristic features of early states in different parts of the world.

Richerson, P. J. and Boyd, R. 2001. Institutional Evolution in the Holocene: The Rise of Complex Societies, pp. 197–234 in (W. G. Runciman, ed.) *The Origin of Social Institutions*. Oxford: Oxford University Press.
An interesting attempt to revise the long standing cultural evolution approaches described above in the light of recent work on the evolution of human and animal social behaviour from a Darwinian perspective.

Trigger, B. G. 1998. *Sociocultural Evolution*. Oxford: Blackwell.
This is a comprehensive critical survey of the history of ideas about cultural evolution within anthropology.

Further reading

Diehl, M. W. (ed.) 2000. *Hierarchies in Action. Cui Bono?* Carbondale, Ill.: Center for Archaeological Investigations, University of Southern Illinois.
Haas, J. (ed.) 2001. *From Leaders to Rulers*. New York: Kluwer/Plenum.
Kohler, T. A. and Gumerman, G. J. (eds) 2000. *Dynamics in Human and Primate Societies: Agent-Based Modelling of Social and Spatial Processes*. New York and Oxford: Oxford University Press (Santa Fe Institute Studies in the Sciences of Complexity).
Peebles, C. and Kus, S. 1977. Some Archaeological Correlates of Ranked Societies. *American Antiquity* 42: 421–48.

Renfrew, C. 1973. Monuments, Mobilisation and Social Organisation in Neolithic Wessex, pp. 539–58 in (C. Renfrew, ed.) *The Explanation of Culture Change*. Duckworth: London. (Reprinted in C. Renfrew (1984) *Approaches to Social Archaeology*. Edinburgh: Edinburgh University Press, pp. 225–57.)

—— 1974. Beyond a Subsistence Economy: The Evolution of Social Organisation in Prehistoric Europe, pp. 69–96 in (C. B. Moore, ed.) *Reconstructing Complex Societies: An Archaeological Colloquium* (Supplement to the Bulletin of the American Schools of Oriental Research No. 20).

Sanderson, S. K. 2001. *The Evolution of Human Sociality: A Darwinian Conflict Perspective*. Lanham: Rowman and Littlefield.

Shennan, S. J. 1999. The Development of Rank Societies, pp. 870–907 in (G. Barker, ed.) *Companion Encyclopaedia of Archaeology* vol. 2. London: Routledge.

Trigger, B. G. 1998. *Sociocultural Evolution*. Oxford: Blackwell.

STEPHEN SHENNAN

'DARK AGES' IN ARCHAEOLOGY/SYSTEMS COLLAPSE

The vanished civilisation, typically a desert city or vine-draped ruins, is an enduring image. These nineteenth-century motifs are recycled often in popular literature and films. Such images are poignant: here are societies that suddenly disappeared rather than experiencing gradual transformation.

Archaeologists use the term 'collapse' to describe societies that rapidly simplified. Cities and monuments quickly disappear, and population greatly diminishes. Famous cases include the collapse of the western Roman Empire in the fifth century AD and the Classic Maya in the ninth century AD. The periods that follow show such simplification that they are sometimes called Dark Ages.

Every society is characterised by a degree of complexity, which describes how extensively a society includes different roles, specialists, technologies and information, and what institutions regulate life. In hunter-gatherer societies, for example, there are few specialised roles other than those arising from age and sex. There are scarcely full-time leaders, and decisions are made by consensus. Industrial societies, conversely, may have as many as 1,000,000 social roles, integrated by many institutions, including government.

Perhaps any society can rapidly simplify under pressure, not just civilisations. There are perhaps two dozen collapses among literate societies, but there may have been many more among societies that must be studied archaeologically.

Many theories attempt to explain collapse. One of the most

common is resource shortages arising from environmental change or mismanagement. Adams describes how intensive irrigation caused salinisation of fields in ancient Mesopotamia, and the collapses of the Third Dynasty of Ur (c. 2100–2000 BC) and the Abbasid Caliphate (tenth century AD). Weiss links the collapse of Tell Leilan, Syria, to climate change c. 2200 BC. Butzer argues that low Nile floods caused the collapse of Old Kingdom Egypt after 2181 BC. Scholars have explored whether deforestation affected the Maya collapse.

Others suggest that catastrophes cause collapse. The volcanic eruption of Thera is said to have doomed Crete's Minoan civilisation (c. 1380 BC), while hurricanes, earthquakes and epidemics are suggested in the Maya collapse.

A popular explanation is that collapses are caused by intruders, colloquially labelled barbarians. The demise of the western Roman Empire is the enduring example. Dorian Greeks have been implicated in the collapse of Mycenaean Greece (eleventh century BC). Intruder theories appear in the literature of nearly every collapse, including the western Chou Dynasty (ended 771 BC), the Maya, Teotihuacán (c. 700 AD), the Hittites (thirteenth century BC) and the Minoans.

Several theories concentrate on internal social factors. A common idea is that societies collapse under challenges to which they cannot adapt. Some scholars suggest that Mesopotamian collapses occurred when states' administrative capacities were exceeded. Willey and Shimkin argued that the Maya bureaucracy could not organise to cope with challenges. It is commonly suggested that the Roman Empire collapsed from inability to respond to internal challenges and external enemies. Some argue that the Maya, and Chacoan society of the US Southwest (collapsed twelfth century AD), had developed complexity that was unsustainable in, respectively, a tropical rainforest and a desert plateau.

A common interpretation is that conflict causes collapse. This idea is found from Plato, Aristotle and Polybius, through the fourteenth-century historian Ibn Khaldun, and continuing from eighteenth-century writers such as Vico and Volney through today. A persistent variation is that peasant rebellions cause collapse. Every ancient state depended on farmers, who were often exploited. Thus nearly every collapse exhibits a peasant revolt theory. Prominent examples include the Maya, Mesopotamia, Peru and China.

Some argue that mystical factors cause collapse. The most common is a biological analogy: societies pass through birth, growth, old age and death. Organic analogies were championed by Greek historians, in the nineteenth century by Danilevsky, and in the twentieth by

Spengler. A second theme is decadence: changing morals cause collapse. Hegel, Petrie and Toynbee asserted that societies succeed when people confront adversity, and disintegrate when individuals pursue self-interest.

The final class is economic explanations, which examine the costs and benefits of complexity. Lattimore once characterised the Chinese dynastic cycle as increasing returns on organisation early in a dynasty, and falling returns during later rulers.

Complexity develops through problem-solving. As problems arise, societies respond by increasing complexity of organisation (e.g., bureaucracies), expanding the military, regimenting behaviour and processing more information. Complexity costs, which in ancient societies meant that people worked harder. As societies exhaust easy solutions, the cost of problem-solving grows, often just to maintain the status quo. Tainter argues that complexity can reach diminishing returns, where problem-solving costs rise but benefits fail to rise proportionately. A society experiencing diminishing returns to complexity in problem-solving extracts more resources to survive and function. Eventually the process generates economic weakness and discontent. A crisis that the society might previously have survived becomes insurmountable. Ultimately it becomes disadvantageous to be a complex society, as the costs of complexity rise too high in relation to benefits.

These explanations are not uniformly useful. Resource shortages, catastrophes and intruders focus narrowly on external factors. Societies always have ways to ameliorate challenges, and rarely succumb to them. Theorists of resource shortages point to the Irish potato famine to illustrate the potential devastation. Yet the potato blight did not cause Irish society to collapse. The eruption of Thera, said to have caused the Minoan collapse, has been compared to the nineteenth-century South Pacific eruption of Krakatoa. But Krakatoa caused no political collapses. As for intruders, if complex societies are worth invading, why destroy the things that repay conquest?

External challenges alone cannot explain collapse. Internal factors are also involved. Yet here, too, there are problems. Conflict is the price of social life, and by itself cannot explain collapse. Rulers often exploit peasants, but this also cannot explain collapse. Why would rulers destroy their vital resource? Where rulers have undermined peasant productivity it is imperative to understand why. Arguing that societies collapse because they cannot meet challenges clarifies nothing. The problem becomes understanding why they cannot adjust. Mystical explanations cannot connect collapse to an empirically observable cause.

Economic explanations link internal and external stresses. The development of complexity is an internal process. If complexity and collapse are both outcomes of problem-solving, the problems to be solved may be either external challenges (resources, catastrophes, intruders) or internal dysfunctions like conflict. Diminishing returns to complexity cause economic weakness, which can clarify why societies cannot respond to challenges.

Post-collapse societies are poorly known. Renfrew and Tainter have synthesised these periods. Before collapse there is often foreboding. Political systems and societies simplify with collapse. There may be a period of post-collapse disorder. Literacy, numeracy and production of art decline. Squatters subdivide decaying buildings. Territories fragment, and succeeding polities rule smaller areas. Trade and knowledge of distant places decline. Widespread styles and common languages differentiate into regional styles and new languages. People may remember the earlier time as a heroic or golden age. Population typically levels or declines before collapse, then may drop precipitously. As societies simplify and the costs of complexity diminish, taxes drop and peasants may be better off. Centuries elapse before societies appear that are comparable in complexity to those before.

In early medieval Europe and post-Mycenaean Greece, Dark Ages are known substantially from burials. Post-Hittite Anatolia reveals almost no archaeological record. This reflects the relationship of complexity to archaeology. Simpler societies produce less material culture, and leave a less substantial archaeological record. Graves may be their most evident remains. Other post-collapse remains can be difficult to detect. In western Europe, decaying Roman buildings were sometimes rebuilt in timber. Earlier archaeologists excavated through such subtle deposits searching for classical remains below. This problem is recognised today, and careful excavations and surveys are revealing much about Dark Age life.

Collapses and their aftermaths are revealing, for they punctuate the common trend towards greater complexity. They show much about why complexity develops and diminishes, and deserve continued study.

Suggested reading

Culbert, T. P. (ed.). 1973. *The Classic Maya Collapse*. Albuquerque: University of New Mexico Press.

A fundamental resource, this volume presents the state of collapse research in the early 1970s.

Renfrew, C. 1979. Systems Collapse as Social Transformation: Catastrophe and Anastrophe in Early State Societies, pp. 481–506 in (C. Renfrew and K. L. Cooke, eds) *Transformations: Mathematical Approaches to Culture Change*. New York: Academic Press.
This chapter observes that collapse can result suddenly from subtle processes changing slowly, and presents a synthesis of post-collapse societies.

Tainter, J. A. 1988. *The Collapse of Complex Societies*. Cambridge: Cambridge University Press.
This book synthesises and criticises earlier theories of collapse, and develops a new theory based on the economics of complexity.

Tainter, J. A. 1999. Post-Collapse Societies, pp. 988–1039 in (G. Barker, ed.) *Companion Encyclopedia of Archaeology*. London: Routledge.
This chapter synthesises the nature of post-collapse societies.

Yoffee, N. and Cowgill, G. L. (eds) 1988. *The Collapse of Ancient States and Civilizations*. Tucson: University of Arizona Press.
This is a compendium of approaches to collapse by a diverse group of leading scholars.

Further reading

Adams, R. McC. 1981. *Heartland of Cities*. Chicago: Aldine.
Bell, B. 1971. The Dark Ages in Ancient History: 1. The First Dark Age in Egypt. *American Journal of Archaeology* 75: 1–26.
Betancourt, P. P. 1976. The End of the Greek Bronze Age. *Antiquity* 50: 40–7.
Diehl, R. A. and Berlo, J. A. (eds) 1989. *Mesoamerica after the Fall of Teotihuacan, AD 700–900*. Washington, DC: Dumbarton Oaks.
Gill, R. B. 2000. *The Great Maya Droughts: Water, Life, and Death*. Albuquerque: University of New Mexico Press.
Lowe, J. W. G. 1985. *The Dynamics of Apocalypse: A Systems Simulation of the Classic Maya Collapse*. Albuquerque: University of New Mexico Press.
Sabloff, J. A. and Andrews, E. W., V (eds) 1986. *Late Lowland Maya Civilization: Classic to Postclassic*. Albuquerque: University of New Mexico Press.
Turchin, P. 2003. *Historical Dynamics: Why States Rise and Fall*. Princeton: Princeton University Press.
Webster, D. 2002. *The Fall of the Ancient Maya*. London: Thames and Hudson.

JOSEPH A. TAINTER

DARWINIAN ARCHAEOLOGY

Darwinian archaeology is an approach that takes as its starting point the idea that the processes producing cultural stability and change are similar, even identical in important respects, to those of biological evolution: in this view, just as biological evolution is characterised by changing frequencies of genes in populations through time as a result of such processes as natural selection, so cultural evolution refers to the changing distributions of cultural attributes in populations, likewise affected by processes such as natural selection but also by others that have no analogue in genetic evolution. In fact, to understand changing patterns of human behaviour and organisation we need to take account of both the biological and cultural dimensions.

To see how this works we need to start by defining what makes evolutionary processes distinctive. In the most general terms they involve mechanisms for inheritance, mutation, selection and drift. In the case of biological evolution inheritance is provided by the genes, which are passed on through the generations at reproduction; mutation involves random copying errors occurring in the genes; selection occurs when gene frequencies change as a result of the effect of the genes on the survival and reproductive success of individuals and their close kin; and drift represents change in gene frequencies arising from processes completely unrelated to the properties of the genes themselves, such as chance events.

In the case of human culture the inheritance mechanism is social learning: people learn ways to think and act from others. It is the process of social learning that leads over time to the creation of cultural traditions. Richard Dawkins (1976) coined the term 'meme' to represent this idea – memes were postulated as the cultural equivalent of genes – but there is no need to accept this particular version of the idea to acknowledge the central importance of inheritance in human culture. What is very clear, however, is that the routes through which culture is inherited are much more diverse than those for genes. The cultural equivalents of mutations are, of course, innovations. Innovations may indeed be unintended copying errors, like genetic mutations, but they can also be intentional changes, perhaps arising from trial-and-error experimentation. However, just because someone has intentionally come up with something new, even if they think that it is better than previous alternatives, there is no guarantee that it will be widely adopted. This depends principally on processes of selection.

Because of the existence of culture, selection is more complex among humans than among most other animals. First, there is standard natural selection. This acts on people, like other animals, via the genetically inherited dispositions that affect their responses to variations in the environment relevant to their survival and reproductive success. Second, there is natural selection acting on people via their cultural traditions. In other words, particular inherited cultural attributes lead to some people having greater survival rates and reproductive success than others. However, in addition to these two processes cultural selection can also occur. Thus, people can decide to switch from what they originally learned, perhaps from their mother or father, to copying someone else, for example because that person is more prestigious or seems to be doing better in some way, or simply in order to conform to what the majority are doing.

Finally, there is the cultural equivalent of genetic drift. In other words, the frequencies of particular cultural attributes can change for essentially chance reasons not involving any preference for a particular attribute. Who you copy may simply be a random choice dependent on who you meet.

Darwinian archaeology attempts to account for the patterns observed in the archaeological record in terms of these processes. The work which has been carried out under this heading is extremely varied and can be roughly divided into two categories: studies that emphasise the role of natural selection in affecting human behaviour and do not attach much importance to culture, and those that emphasise the importance of understanding changing cultural traditions. These two approaches are often seen as opposed to one another.

The key assumption for natural selection approaches is the idea of *optimisation*: that individuals will relate to their environments in ways that maximise their reproductive success. This is not a tautological claim about the world but a framework for generating hypotheses. Foraging provides the context in which we can formulate optimisation models most straightforwardly. This is done most simply by assuming that the foraging strategy which will be most successful in fitness terms will be the one that is most efficient in providing the maximum amount of energy for the minimum amount of effort on the part of the individual doing the work.

What is known as the *diet breadth model* predicts that the resources that will be exploited are not those that are most widely available, but those which provide the best return for a given amount of effort. The effort or cost is divided into two components: the time taken to pursue the prey item and the handling costs which arise when it has been obtained, such as the butchery of game or the processes required to make acorns suitable for eating. Resources can be ranked in terms of the returns they produce once they have been encountered, and we can find out which combination of resources will produce the maximum returns, taking into account the time it takes to locate them. Even if certain resources are plentiful in the environment they will not be included if the handling costs are large and the return rates in terms of calories per unit time are low.

What would lead to change in the optimal diet? One possibility would be a technological innovation that drastically reduced the capture/handling costs of one of the low-ranked resources initially not in the diet and thus made it worth exploiting. Another possibility would arise when the highest-rated resources become rarer as a result of exploitation, so that search times increase. In fact, where optimal foraging assumptions hold, as environments are increasingly exploited, return rates go down, the diet breadth increases as people have to look to other resources, and they have to do more work to maintain the same levels of production as before, unless the opportunity of migration to less heavily exploited areas is available.

One example of the application of this approach is a study of the use of sea and land resources at the site of Shag River Mouth in New Zealand (Nagaoka 2002). This involved looking not just at the different species represented in the bone assemblage, but also at the different bones of the different species, to assess the extent to which people were interested in obtaining every last scrap of meat from the prey they caught or just used the better parts. In the light of their large body-size, seals were argued to be the highest-ranked marine resource and moas, a large flightless bird, the highest-ranked on land. As these high-ranked resources declined, Nagaoka found that the exploitation of seals and moas developed in different ways. Seals were used more intensively, with more different body parts being found at the site. Moas were used more selectively, as evidenced by the body parts represented. The difference was explained in terms of transport costs. Seal transport costs were low, because they were either exploited locally or could be easily moved by canoe. The declining numbers of moas locally led to hunters seeking them further afield, where encounter rates remained high, but transport was an issue. Hunters would use the low-value parts of the moas at their hunting camps and only bring back the parts with the most meat.

The cultural versions of Darwinian archaeology, on the other hand, aim to understand the history of cultural traditions as represented in the archaeological record. In this respect it can be regarded as an updated version of culture history. The first step in the process is to demonstrate that you are really dealing with a tradition – a set of practices linked historically through time by inheritance based on social learning. The most important way of establishing this is by means of the long-established technique of 'seriation', a method by which archaeological assemblages are ordered in such a way that those most similar to one another are closest together in time (O'Brien and Lyman 2000, 2002). The evolutionary approach to cultural traditions transcends the old culture historical approaches with their implicit ethnic foundations by showing that cultural packages come in different sizes. A consequence of this is that the different cultural practices and artefact forms that are found within a population at a given time may have different descent histories. Some may be transmitted together and others not, and they may be affected by very different selective pressures.

Nevertheless, there are cases where large sets of cultural attributes are linked together in time and space – core traditions – and there are grounds for thinking that these may often, if not always, be associated with particular populations, perhaps especially in those cases involving relatively recent history where links with languages can be established. It seems likely that the main processes associated with the origin and spread of these large packages relate to the increasing differentiation of expanding populations as communities become increasingly separated from one another in space and time.

Once such cultural evolutionary lineages, for example pottery traditions, have been identified, the aim is to account for their emergence, their changes and their ultimate demise. One way to establish the processes involved is to start from the hypothesis that the only factor operating is the cultural analogue of genetic drift: the changes are random, depending only on who interacts with whom, and how frequently. Recent analytical work on this subject suggests that such neutral models can be surprisingly successful in accounting for the patterns observed, although equally it is possible in some circumstances to identify departures from neutrality where processes of social selection lead to different outcomes (e.g. Shennan and Wilkinson 2001).

Although the natural selection and cultural selection versions of Darwinian archaeology are often seen as in conflict with one another, by and large they are complementary and the aim in any particular study should be to establish the processes producing the pattern, rather than assuming, in a doctrinaire way, that they fall into one category or another. Furthermore, the costs and benefits of exploitation strategies for human populations depend ultimately on the technologies locally available. These have specific cultural histories and do not automatically come into existence to solve adaptive problems.

Suggested reading

Boone, J. 2000. Status Signalling, Social Power and Lineage Survival, pp. 84–110 in (M. W. Diehl, ed.) *Hierarchies in Action. Cui Bono?* Carbondale: Center for Archaeological Investigations, University of Southern Illinois.

An anthropologically oriented study showing the way in which a Darwinian approach focused on survival and reproductive success can be used to understand social organisation as well as subsistence.

O'Brien, M. and Lyman, R. L. 2002. Evolutionary Archeology: Current Status and Future Prospects. *Evolutionary Anthropology* 11: 26–36.

A brief and clear outline of the main principles behind the evolutionary approach to the archaeology of cultural traditions and the key methods it involves.

Richerson, P. J., Boyd, R. and Bettinger, R. L. 2001. Was Agriculture Impossible during the Pleistocene but Mandatory during the Holocene? *American Antiquity* 66: 387–412.

A Darwinian analysis of a classic archaeological problem: why did it take so long for farming to appear in human history and why was it so successful? It shows that the classic population pressure arguments are unsatisfactory.

Shennan, S. J. 2002. *Genes, Memes and Human History: Darwinian Archaeology and Cultural Evolution.* London: Thames and Hudson.

An overview of the whole field of evolutionary approaches to anthropology and archaeology, from those emphasising the centrality of survival and reproductive success to the analysis of cultural traditions, using a broad range of examples.

Further reading

Dawkins, R. 1976. *The Selfish Gene.* Oxford: Oxford University Press.

Kelly, R. L. 1995. *The Foraging Spectrum.* Washington: Smithsonian Institution Press.

Nagaoka, L. 2002. Explaining Subsistence Change in Southern New Zealand Using Foraging Theory Models. *World Archaeology* 34: 84–102.

Neiman, F. D. 1995. Stylistic Variation in Evolutionary Perspective: Inferences from Decorative Diversity and Inter-Assemblage Distance in Illinois Woodland Ceramic Assemblages. *American Antiquity* 60: 7–36.

O'Brien, M. J. and Lyman, R. L. 2000. *Applying Evolutionary Archaeology.* New York: Plenum.

Shennan, S. J. and Wilkinson, J. R. 2001. Ceramic Style Change and Neutral Evolution: A Case Study from Neolithic Europe. *American Antiquity* 66. 577–93.

Smith, E. A. and Winterhalder, B. (eds) 1992. *Evolutionary Ecology and Human Behaviour.* New York: Aldine de Gruyter.

World Archaeology 34 (1 June 2002). Issue theme: Archaeology and Evolutionary Ecology.

STEPHEN SHENNAN

IDEAS IN RELATIVE AND ABSOLUTE DATING

Today, the numerous and highly technical dating methods available to archaeologists tell us in a very precise way two pieces of information that are critical to archaeology: how old monuments or artefacts are, and how long in duration major periods or processes in human history have been. Sophisticated techniques for measuring minuscule amounts of radioactive matter, in combination with computing and statistical modelling, often produce relatively precise chronological schemes.

For much of the history of professional archaeology, however, this luxury was not available. Instead, archaeologists had to rely upon the observations of repetitive natural phenomena in the Earth, or protohistoric 'chronologies' recording Near Eastern dynasties, and try to link these to archaeological materials across the world. The results were often very wide of the mark. Before even this, antiquarians had only very basic concepts of relative chronology: in Britain and elsewhere, in much of Europe, for example, things were either Roman or pre-Roman. Since the early nineteenth century, the development of dating techniques has gone through three revolutionary periods in which dating was central to changing radically the way archaeologists thought about the past. We are still in the last of these.

Antiquarianism

In the eighteenth century the English antiquarian William Stukeley observed that the great mound of Silbury Hill must be pre-Roman in date, as a Roman road detoured around it. Stukeley was employing relative dating, a means of establishing how monuments or artefacts are of different ages relative to each other. The foundation of relative dating is the principle of stratigraphy on specific sites (*see* p. 243). There are limitations to making simple stratigraphic observations, which led Glyn Daniel (1967: 57), the historian of archaeology, to note that antiquarians like Stukeley could not have created the professional discipline of archaeology as they had no developed relative scheme such as the Three Age System (*see* p. 264). The rationale of this is to extend site-specific stratigraphic principles to make observations at the larger scale. For example, if on all known archaeological sites Iron Age levels always overlie Bronze Age, which in turn always overlie Neolithic, then this may be taken as a general developmental scheme: Neolithic to Bronze Age to Iron Age.

Attempts to glean real dates from relative schemes were made by the seventeenth century, and were taken very seriously. The Reverend James Ussher (1581–1656) used Genesis to infer that the Earth was created in 4004 BC, and that Noah and his family boarded the Ark in 2349 BC. This relied upon the assumption that, as the Word of God, the biblical accounts were true and complete. Ussher therefore did not baulk, for example, when he read that Jared was 162 years old when he 'begot Enoch' (Genesis 5:18) after which 'he lived another 800 years' (5:19). For his work – a chronology of the Earth, no less – Ussher achieved national fame and after his death was buried in Westminster Abbey with full honours (Cohn 1996).

Ussher's scheme dominated concepts of human antiquity until the turn of the nineteenth century. Human existence was thought to have been relatively brief. It was not until the realisation that natural phenomena contained information about their relative ages that the appreciation of the geological and human past took a more academic turn. This can be observed from the turn of the nineteenth century, throughout much of which archaeologists were concerned with establishing regional chronological schemes that gradually coalesced into a general picture, at least for the later prehistoric to early historic periods. Sir Charles Lyell's recognition that some geological deposits must represent tens of millennia of time (*see* p. 276) began the process of recognition that the world – and probably human society – was much older than had been thought.

Archaeological infancy: more sophisticated relative dating

The establishment of deep time, and the realisation that certain animal groups have had fixed periods of existence on Earth, led to the understanding that chronological information may be conveyed by the presence, absence and form of their bones. This is the principle of biostratigraphy. Since the French scholar Georges Cuvier demonstrated in the late eighteenth century that some animals (such as mammoths) had become extinct, and inferred that new forms had come into existence, natural scientists began thinking about how the composition of animal communities differed over time. By the late nineteenth century, formal 'epochs' such as the 'Reindeer age' had been identified by Gabriel de Mortillet. Biostratigraphy remains today at the centre of palaeoanthropology. The development of voles has, for example, been crucial to the dating of the English Lower Palaeolithic site of Boxgrove. De Mortillet and others, such as Edouard Lartet and Henry Christy, also created broad periods using technological and typological characteristics of stone tool assemblages and other artefact categories excavated from caves and rockshelters. By 1865, in his book *Prehistoric Times*, Sir John Lubbock, a friend of Darwin, was able to define two such periods formally as the Palaeolithic and Neolithic.

At the same time, for the period of early states, Egyptian king lists such as that in the tomb of Seti I at Abydos provided the basis for chronological reconstructions for the entire Near East, despite the fact that unfavourable kings such as many of the Eighteenth Dynasty could be omitted; that the rules of others might be expanded out of reality to demonstrate stability; and that some dynasties were listed as successive when in fact they are now known to have been contemporary. Nevertheless, this chronological foundation stone was extended elsewhere to regions for which no such 'protohistorical' information was available, and to Gordon Childe (1934) (*see* p. 35) became 'an indispensable prelude to the true appreciation of European prehistory'.

The degree to which the lack of precise and absolute dates hampered archaeological understanding throughout the nineteenth century cannot be overemphasised. The long debate as to whether major cultural innovations occurred in the east and diffused from there – '*ex oriente lux*' – or independently in the west could not be resolved, and Childe, an enormously influential thinker, often ignored chronology and famously joked that it was like a bellows, which could be expanded or contracted depending on how best it fitted his theories (McNairn 1980).

With the exception of pollen zones identified in lake and peat sequences (*see* p. 85), the first half of the twentieth century saw virtually no improvement over the simple relative chronologies already in existence. Although Rutherford managed to detect radioactive decay in 1905, the concept that this would be of any use for dating Earth history would not be realised for decades. The first real advances in dating came only from the 1930s, when tree ring dating provided absolute dates for sites in the American southwest, and the technique soon spread to Europe. But it was only in the 1950s that the general chronological framework with which archaeologists work today was gradually pieced together.

Archaeological adulthood: absolute dating techniques

The development of absolute dating techniques in the decades following the Second World War resulted in a complete rewriting of European prehistory (Renfrew 1973). In addition to this great surprise, which among other things led to the abandonment of much of Childe's diffusionism, archaeology was provided 'for the first time with a universally applicable chronology and one that allowed the duration as well as the relative order of archaeological manifestations to be determined' (Trigger 1989: 17). As noted by Sir Mortimer Wheeler (1958) it truly 'opened a new era' of archaeological understanding.

The American scientist Willard Libby's recognition that some objects may contain information about their actual age was brilliant. As absolute dating techniques rely on the decay of radioactive matter from one state to another, and measuring the process of this delay, it is no surprise that his discovery came shortly after the Second World War, during the Cold War in which research into radioactivity was intense. Libby soon realised that the decay he had observed occurring in Carbon 14 could be used as a dating technique as long as the original amounts of it in samples and its rate of decay could be ascertained. Initial tests in 1948 were encouraging and the first results were published in 1949 (Libby et al. 1949).

Surprises came almost immediately. The origins of agriculture and the development of copper and bronze metallurgy were shown to have occurred much earlier than had been previously thought. Not everyone agreed with the new results, however. Stuart Piggott (1959) dismissed the first radiocarbon dates for the British Neolithic as 'archaeologically inacceptable' as they did not agree with his setting of Neolithic beginnings around 2000 BC, falling much earlier. By the 1960s, tree ring dating rivalled radiocarbon as a provider of absolute dates, since it was now improved with the assistance of statistics and computing. With the tree ring correction ('calibration') of radiocarbon dates a number of later prehistoric European cultures were shown to be earlier than the Mediterranean ones that supposedly inspired them. Other surprises came from developments in relative dating schemes: at the Natural History Museum in London, Kenneth Oakley in the 1950s used fluorine levels in bones as indicators of their relative ages, to suggest that the Piltdown 'fossils' were actually recent in age, which was finally confirmed in the 1980s when small samples drilled from the bones were dated to the medieval and modern periods by radiocarbon.

By the 1970s increasing use of radioactive decay in dating was further revolutionising archaeology. The dating of volcanic sediments in East Africa by potassium-argon decay caused controversy in the 1970s, when initial results suggested that a crucial marker deposit dated to around 2.4 million years BP. As fossils of early *Homo* underlay this, the results suggested a surprisingly early date for the emergence of our own genus (*see* p. 72), which was entirely at odds with biostratigraphic estimations of the same. The resulting controversy was finally resolved when it was realised that mistakes had been made in the calculation of the original date, and the estimation was revised to around 1.8 million BP, in accordance with the biostratigraphic estimation.

Archaeological frontiers: what we can and cannot do with dating

Measurement methods used for nuclear research were applied to archaeological dating from 1977 onwards, and by the mid-1980s a handful of laboratories were producing dates by counting very small samples of carbon by means of particle accelerators and sophisticated detection apparatus. This radiocarbon dating by Accelerator Mass Spectrometry (AMS) revolutionised archaeology in that for the first time it permitted direct dating of small and valuable items including bone tools, wooden artefacts, papyri and human fossils. The measurement of other high-energy cosmic rays absorbed by rocks and which accumulate over time is also facilitated by AMS techniques (cosmogenic isotope dating). Carbon 14 atoms with an abundance of one in a million million can be counted in microscopically small samples such as charcoal scraped from cave art, human hair or individual cereal grains.

Nowadays, it is very easy to think that the vast battery of scientific dating methods available to archaeologists forms an unproblematic and clear picture of the chronology of the past. While this may apply for some techniques, and at least for the last 6,000 years or so, reality is very different. Most of the methods relying upon radioactive decay require an understanding of the behaviour of the relevant radioactive isotope, which, in the case of uranium (U-Series; Electron Spin Resonance) is poorly understood. Assumptions often need to be made to cover this lack of knowledge, and in some techniques so many of these assumptions need to be made that one wonders whether they will ever be at all reliable (e.g. ESR). This uncertainty is usually expressed in the error of a date, which is very wide in all direct dating techniques other than radiocarbon. For the latter, while relatively few assumptions need to be made, the variation in natural production of 14C in the upper atmosphere alters the ticking of the 'radiocarbon clock' and affects its accuracy. Cross checking of 14C dates on certain items by other techniques, such as wood dated by dendrochronology, has allowed the estimation of these errors. Correction ('calibration') curves now allow us to convert 14C dates to real calendric ages at least back to around 14,000 years ago, but at some points in the past atmospheric production has been so high that large amounts of calendrical time are 'swallowed up' in a single radiocarbon date.

We are reaching the frontiers of dating methods in archaeology. Frontiers are about pushing boundaries such as dating at the molecular level and understanding complex decay chains in radioactive matter. Perhaps it will soon be possible to date directly ancient DNA recovered from fossil bones. But frontiers are also about limits – in this case about what dating can and cannot do. In the last half-century archaeologists have been provided with techniques that scholars only one century ago could not have dreamed of. But there are, and will always be, gaps in what we can hope to achieve in dating. The farther back in deep time we look, the fuzzier our chronology is. It is unlikely to improve. As we scrutinise even the most familiar techniques available to us, we realise that they are never as straightforward as they seem; and as the questions we ask of the human past become more sophisticated, nature will always have the last laugh.

Suggested reading

Aitken, M. J. 1990. *Science-Based Dating in Archaeology*. London: Longman.
Still the most comprehensive manual on absolute dating techniques. Coverage is mainly technical and concerned with applications, but some history of the techniques is included.

Bahn, P. G. (ed.) 1996. *The Cambridge Illustrated History of Archaeology*. Cambridge: Cambridge University Press.
Contains excellent coverage of how dating techniques were developed, their intellectual context, and their effect on the discipline of archaeology.

Pettitt, P. B. 2002. Antiquity and Early Humanity. *Antiquity* 76: 1080–5.
Brief paper reviewing the development of our understanding of the chronology of human evolution, seen from the perspective of the journal *Antiquity*.

Renfrew, C. 1973. *Before Civilization: The Radiocarbon Revolution and Prehistoric Europe*. London: Pelican.
Highly readable and informed account of the radiocarbon 'revolutions' and how they changed perceptions of European prehistory.

Renfrew, C. and Bahn, P. 2004. *Archaeology: Theories, Methods and Practice*, 4th edn. London and New York: Thames and Hudson.
Standard reference for archaeology. Chapter 4 ('When? Dating, Methods and Chronology') is a useful and up-to-date introduction to how archaeologists reconstruct chronologies.

Further reading

Aitken, M. J., Stringer, C. B. and Mellars, P. A. 1993. *The Origin of Modern Humans and the Impact of Chronometric Dating*. Princeton: Princeton University Press.

Childe, V. G. 1934. *New Light on the Most Ancient East: The Oriental Prelude to European Prehistory.* London: Kegan Paul.

Cohn, N. 1996. *Noah's Flood: The Genesis Story in Western Thought.* Yale: Yale University Press.

Daniel, G. 1967. *The Origins and Growth of Archaeology.* London: Penguin.

Gillespie, R. 1986. *Radiocarbon User's Handbook.* Oxford: Oxford University Committee for Archaeology Monograph 3.

Hedges, R. E. M. 1997. Radiocarbon Dating – 50 Years On. *Education in Chemistry* November: 157–64.

Libby, W., Anderson, E. C. and Arnold, J. R. 1949. Age Determination by Radio-carbon Content: Worldwide Assay of Natural Radiocarbons. *Science* 109: 227–8.

Lubbock, J. 1865. *Pre-historic Times as Illustrated by Ancient Remains, and the Manners and Customs of Modern Savages.* London: Williams and Norgate.

McNairn, B. 1980. *The Method and Theory of V. Gordon Childe.* Edinburgh: Edinburgh University Press.

Piggott, S. 1959. The Radiocarbon Date from Durrington Walls. *Antiquity* 33: 289.

Schnapp, A. 1993. *The Discovery of the Past.* London: British Museum Press.

Trigger, B. G. 1989. *A History of Archaeological Thought.* Cambridge: Cambridge University Press.

Waterbolk, H. T. 1971. Working with Radiocarbon Dates. *Proceedings of the Prehistoric Society* 37: 15–33.

Wheeler, M. 1958. Crawford and Antiquity. *Antiquity* 32: 4.

PAUL B. PETTITT

THE DESCENT OF MAN

The modern field of human evolution has its roots in the theory of natural selection that was developed independently in the nineteenth century by Charles Darwin and naturalist Alfred Russell Wallace. The theory of natural selection is based on the simple principle that organisms produce more offspring than can survive. Those less suited to their environment perish while those more suited survive to pass on their genes to succeeding generations. Natural selection is the underlying principle of the modern field of evolutionary biology that is based on the concept of inclusive fitness. This means that the biological and social adaptations of organisms, including humans, are those that have maximised the genetic contribution to succeeding generations of ancestors characterised by those traits.

The only mention of human evolution in Charles Darwin's influential book *On the Origin of Species*, published in 1859,[1] was in the conclusion, where Darwin said: 'Light will be thrown on the origin of man and his history.' In 1864 Darwin's defender, Thomas Henry Huxley, published *Evidence as to Man's Place in Nature*,[2] outlining the anatomical similarities and inferred evolutionary connections between humans and apes. Shortly afterwards, in 1871, Darwin published *The Descent of Man: and Selection in Relation to Sex*,[3] where he posited sexual selection in addition to natural selection as an important mechanism for (human) evolution. Another influential thinker of the time was the German anatomist Ernst Haeckel, who proposed a hypothetical human evolutionary sequence: *Pithecanthropus allalus* (speechless ape man), *Homo stupidus* and *Homo sapiens*. It is no longer acceptable to create fantasy taxa (species and genera), and the naming of new taxa is governed by strict rules of the International Code of Zoological Nomenclature. Each species must have a type specimen and each genus a type species that is demonstrated to be significantly different from the types of any other species and genera.

At the time of the publication of *The Origin of Species* a few human (hominid) fossils had already been discovered, but they had not yet been recognised as such. The first named hominid taxon was *Anthropus neanderthalensis* (1864) (later changed to *Homo neanderthalensis*). The type specimen was the famous Neanderthal skeleton discovered in the Neander Valley in Germany in 1856. Since that time many Neanderthal fossils have been discovered across Europe, and Neanderthals are now known to have lived between approximately 250,000 and 28,000 years ago. Early interpretations of Neanderthals pictured them as the missing link, with stooped posture and some ape-like features. We now know that they were very similar to modern humans but they had large and projecting faces and very robust bodies. Although some palaeoanthropologists place them in the same species as modern humans, *Homo sapiens*, genetic studies demonstrate that they are distinct from us and most probably diverged from our line over a half a million years ago.

Nothing was known of human fossils outside of Europe until the 1870s, when a young Dutch doctor, Eugene Dubois, went to the Far East with the specific purpose of finding the fossil evidence for Haeckel's fantasy evolutionary sequence. The surprising thing is that he succeeded. Dubois found a skullcap and femur (thigh bone) at the site of Trinil on the Solo River in Java in 1891–2, and named the fossils *Pithecanthropus erectus* (erect ape man). These original fossils are now included in the taxon *Homo erectus* and probably date to about 500,000 years ago. *Homo erectus* in its broadest modern interpretation originated in Africa about 1.8 million years ago and is believed by many palaeoanthropologists to have been the first human species to move out of African and into Europe and Asia. The species persisted until approximately 500,000 years ago, and possibly into much more recent times in the Far East (the Ngandong fossils from Java may date to approximately 50,000 years ago).

Based on Dubois' work, some theorists argued that humans first evolved in the Far East. This idea began to change with the discovery of the first human fossil in Africa in 1924. This was the Taung child, the type specimen of *Australopithecus africanus* (southern ape from Africa). Although this fossil of a three-year-old child was highly controversial in its day, later fossils discovered at other rich southern African sites, such as Sterkfontein, Swartkrans, Makapansgat, Kromdraai and, more recently, Drimolen, established that at least two major types of hominid lived in Africa. In addition to *A. africanus* there was a second species with much larger jaws and teeth that was named *A. robustus*. Both of these were earlier in date and much more primitive in form than either *Homo erectus* or Neanderthal.

Until 1959 australopithecines were only known from southern Africa. In that year Louis and Mary Leakey discovered their first significant hominid fossil at the site of Olduvai Gorge in Tanzania. This was *Zinjanthropus boisei* (now known as *Australopithecus boisei*) and represents an eastern African version of the southern African large-toothed *A. robustus*. In the early 1960s the Leakeys also discovered other fossils that they argued were more modern than the australopithecines, being characterised by a relatively larger brain size, a foot adapted to two-footed walking (bipedalism) and a hand capable of tool-making. This material was assigned to *Homo habilis* (handy man) and is still considered by many palaeoanthropologists to be the earliest member of the genus *Homo*. The Olduvai *H. habilis* fossils date to about 1.7 million years ago, while other more recently discovered early *Homo* specimens from Ethiopia date as early as 2.3 million years ago.

In the 1960s some anthropologists thought that the robust australopithecines (*A. boisei* and *A. robustus*) and the gracile forms (*H. habilis* and *A. africanus*) were simply males and females of the same species living in eastern and southern Africa. However, as new dating techniques were developed and applied, palaeoanthropologists recognised that *A. africanus* was older than the other taxa. The dominant opinion now was that the earlier *A. africanus* was the common ancestor of the later species, *H. habilis* on the one hand and *A. robustus* and *A. boisei* on the other. *H. habilis* and the robust australopithecines represented two different adaptations of an African environment that was becoming more arid and seasonal. *H. habilis* was adapting with its brain and tool use, while the robust australopithecines were adapting with their massive teeth and jaws to food resources of lower quality requiring much stronger mastication.

From this time to the present day at least ten more species of hominids have been recognised in Africa that predate, or are contemporaneous with, *Homo erectus*. The picture of human evolution has become correspondingly complicated and difficult to decipher. A few of these discoveries have particularly changed our thinking. The first was the discovery of the fossil material from the Hadar region of Ethiopia that has been assigned to the species *Australopithecus afarensis*. This species dates to between about 3.6 and 2.9 million years ago and its most famous representative is the Lucy skeleton (AL 288–1) which was discovered in 1974. This is the most complete australopithecine skeleton currently described, and has shown us that this species, although bipedal, had relatively short legs and features of the upper body suggesting that they may still have been efficient climbers.

The second important discovery was another almost complete skeleton known as the Nariokotome youth, discovered in 1984 on the western shore of Lake Turkana in Kenya. This skeleton is an early African *Homo erectus* that is also classified by some palaeoanthropologists as *Homo ergaster*. It is very different from Lucy, with long legs and human-like body proportions. The Nariokotome youth, along with other fossils assigned to the same species, demonstrates beyond a shadow of a doubt that *Homo erectus*-like hominids were contemporaneous with the robust australopithecines in eastern Africa but were adapting to their environment in a very different way.

Three additional discoveries have radically extended our knowledge of the antiquity of the human line. *Ardipithecus ramidus* from Ethiopia was first named in 1994 and dates to between about 4.4 and 5.8 million years ago; *Orrorin tugenensis* from Kenya was named in 2001 and dates to about 6 million years ago; while *Shalanthropus tchadensis* from Chad was named in 2002 and dates to 7 million years ago. These new taxa are almost as old as the molecularly determined age for the division of the line leading to humans and our closest relatives, the African apes. They are all quite different from each other and show us that even at this early period there was much diversity among human ancestors. There is considerable debate at the present time in relation to the phylogeny (evolutionary pattern of relatedness) of these fossils.

More recent periods of human evolution have been dominated by the debate between the Multiregional (*see* p. 176) and Out-of-Africa theories for the evolution of modern humans. This has been particularly true since 1986 and the publication of the first mitochondrial DNA studies suggesting that modern humans may have had their origin in Africa. Current opinion suggests that there may have been multiple dispersals of modern humans out of African during the past 200,000 years or so. The discovery of modern humans in 2002 at the site of Herto in Ethiopia provides convincing proof that modern humans were living in Africa 160,000 years ago, at a time that Neanderthals were in Europe and *Homo erectus* may still have survived in Java.

Notes

1   Darwin, Charles. 1859. *On the Origin of Species by Means of Natural Selection, or, The Preservation of Favoured Races in the Struggle for Life.* London: J. Murray.
2   Huxley, Thomas Henry. 1864. *Evidence as to Man's Place in Nature.* London: Williams and Norgate.
3   Darwin, Charles. 1871. *The Descent of Man: and Selection in Relation to Sex.* London: J. Murray.

Suggested reading

Bowler, P. J. 1996. *Charles Darwin: The Man and His Influence.* Cambridge: Cambridge University Press.
A good introduction to Darwin and his influence.

Delson, E, Tattersall, I., Vancouvering, J. and Brooks, A. S. (eds) 2000. *Encyclopedia of Human Evolution and Prehistory.* 2nd edn. New York: Garland Publishers.
A useful reference book for human evolution.

Klein, R. G. 1999. *The Human Career: Human Biological and Cultural Origins.* Chicago and London: University of Chicago Press.
A clear and detailed textbook of human biological and cultural evolution.

Lewin, R. 1997. *Bones of Contention: Controversies in the Search for Human Origins,* 2nd edn. Chicago, Ill.: University of Chicago Press.
An engaging discussion of the controversies surrounding the discovery and interpretation of human fossils.

Tattersall, I. 1998. *Becoming Human: Evolution and Human Uniqueness.* Oxford: Oxford University Press.
A very accessible and engaging discussion of human evolution.

Further reading

Boyd, R. and Silk, J. B. 2003. *How Humans Evolved,* 3rd edn. New York/London: W. W. Norton.
Jobling, M. A, Hurles, M. E. and Tyler-Smith, C. 2003. *Human Evolutionary Genetics.* Oxford: BIOS Scientific.
Lewin, R. 1997. *Bones of Contention: Controversies in the Search for Human Origins,* 2nd edn. Chicago: University of Chicago Press.
Reader, J. 1990. *Missing Links: The Hunt for Earliest Man,* 2nd edn. London: Penguin.

Stringer, C. and McKie, R. 1997. *African Exodus: The Origins of Modern Humanity.* London: Pimlico.

LESLIE C. AIELLO

THEORISING DIFFUSION AND POPULATION MOVEMENTS

What is diffusion?

Diffusion is a concept that describes the transfer of material traits from one culture to another. In the process it may introduce changes in the receiving culture. Diffusion was also employed as an explanatory concept for the spread of cultures and civilisations throughout the world from the late nineteenth century until the 1950s. It was linked to a 'culture historical' framework of interpretation that identified archaeological cultures with peoples or ethnic groups, and considered changes to be the result of a process of diffusion from the centres of civilisation.

Often migrations (population movements) were thought to be the motor of change. Gordon Childe (*see* p. 35) is often referred to as a propagator of such a perspective, especially in his major synthesis *The Dawn of European Civilization*, although he also employed an evolutionary perspective. From the 1960s onwards this culture historical research tradition was replaced by a new theoretical framework that gave priority to internal forces of social, economic and cultural change. This new framework of interpretation was called processual (*see* p. 212) and post-processual (*see* p. 207) archaeology, and has been dominant until today. As a result, diffusion and historical changes beyond the local area or the region have been largely ignored during the last generation. It is therefore timely to add diffusion and migration/population movements to the theoretical and interpretative repertoire of modern archaeology. A mature archaeology should, after all, be able to deal with all types of historical change.

First it should be recognised that diffusion covers a whole range of social, economic and cultural transfers that may have different impacts. One needs therefore to identify what is being diffused. Andrew Sherratt has in several studies traced the diffusion of new technological innovations and economic practices, such as ard ploughing and the use of wheel, wagon and draft animals, which spread from the Near East to Eurasia during the later fourth millennium BC. This package of interrelated technologies he termed 'the secondary products revolution' due to their economic impact over wide areas covering many cultures. Colin Renfrew coined the concept 'peer polity interaction' (*see* p. 196) to account for the diffusion of a package of knowledge and corresponding material culture leading to the formation of a homogeneous regional polity. It may be constituted by a new political or religious institution of warrior chiefs or a new palace organisation.

The two processes of interregional and regional cultural transmission described by Andrew Sherratt and Colin Renfrew often interact. A new economic practice or a new social institution may spread over large areas, but in that process its material culture may change as it is adapted to different local and regional traditions. What matters is if the package of material culture remains intact, even if the objects may change form. This suggests that the knowledge linked to its proper use (a new economic practice or a new social institution) is also transmitted. However, if the original package of objects are separated or selectively adopted it suggests a similar transformation of its original meaning and function.

Tracing and analysing diffusion

The first step in tracing diffusion is to identify and map the distribution and diffusion of single objects, monuments or structures that are new in the region under study. The next step is to analyse whether a package of objects, ritual practices, etc., are being diffused, as this might indicate the transfer of more complex knowledge, linked to their use. Third, one needs to study the local contexts of the package to get a better understanding of its meaning and impact. Finally, one should try to understand how the transfer has taken place, through travels of small groups of people (traders, warriors, craftspeople), or through conquest or population movements of larger groups.

It should be recognised by now that diffusion covers complex social and historical processes where the different elements in the process need to be conceptualised and then analysed. It should also be recognised that diffusion as a concept in itself has no theoretical or interpretative power. It needs to be related to other concepts that define its meaning and direction. The process of diffusion can be analysed and interpreted in three stages: one that describes the process archaeologically from its point of origin to its local acculturation in a new context (diffusion, acculturation and contextualisation); one that interprets this archaeological process, its content and meaning (message, materialisation and meaning); and finally one where its social or economic effects are explained, eventually leading to the formation of a new political or religious institution (transmission, transformation and institutionalisation).

In addition it is necessary to analyse how the process took place and was organised. Knowledge, objects and ideas do not move by themselves. They are always carried by people. Any study of diffusion and interaction is therefore confronted with the question: who travelled, for what reasons, and how many were they – in short, how was the interaction between different cultures and communities organised?

The role of travels and population movements

Finally, one needs to ask why diffusion and population movements are taking place. Travels and interaction are universal features of all societies. No community can reproduce itself without being linked to others in various forms of networks and obligations. Population movements, travels and the diffusion of new knowledge often occurred more frequently when new economic and social strategies were developed that made it possible for populations to expand into new environments, sometimes at the expense of local communities already living there. This characterised the expansion of agriculture in its various stages. Later the spread of metallurgical knowledge and the use of copper and bronze increased the movements of goods and people further. From the Bronze Age onwards the distances encompassed by networks of exchange expanded dramatically, and so did the frequency of interaction, due to the fact that every community needed to be part of long-distance networks to obtain and maintain their metal supplies. This introduced new regional processes of convergence and cultural homogenisation. In such ranked societies changes are often introduced from outside through travels. Power and prestige are linked to exoteric knowledge and heroic fame gained from travels to distant places, often at a higher level of social complexity and cosmological superiority, as demonstrated in several pioneering works by Mary Helms. In this way local chiefs and specialists can return as 'heroic foreigners' and introduce change. Such movements of individuals and groups of people are now also increasingly demonstrated by scientific methods, using strontium isotope analysis on bones to measure whether a person has moved or stayed in the same place throughout his or her life.

What role did population movements play in prehistory? Probably a bigger role than we are normally inclined to believe. Travels were frequent, just as settlement expansion and colonisation have always taken place when new opportunities emerged and/or conditions at home became too burdensome. This was often linked to knowledge gained from travels within already established networks of exchange and alliances, as demonstrated by David Anthony. Most of the time, however, prehistoric communities were highly stable and stayed within the same environment generation after generation. Some people would travel and keep links to the larger world, but they were mostly a restricted group. In periods of major social and economic change, however, new opportunities would arise that could lead to major settlement displacements and population movements on a larger scale, often combined with the incorporation of the new social and cultural institutions by sedentary communities.

Therefore, to trace population movements or migrations is a complex and difficult process in archaeology, as their impact is often combined with diffusion and acculturation that transformed surrounding local cultures. The third millennium BC in Eurasia represents such a period of social and economic expansion of new institutions and practices over large territories, that integrated all of these processes, and is therefore still badly understood.

Migrations, whether by conquest, settlement, expansion or colonisation, can often be identified in the archaeological record when more complex societies colonise areas occupied by less complex societies, as was the case with neolithisation or the colonisation of the west Mediterranean by the Greeks in the eighth and seventh centuries BC. So-called barbarian conquest migrations, such as those by Celtic and Viking settlers and warriors, are sometimes more difficult to trace, as they quickly assimilated much of the indigenous culture. One can therefore rarely expect identical cultural traits to appear in the area of origin and the area of colonisation.

In conclusion: diffusion and population movements, like any general culture historical concepts, need to be theorised at a more finely grained level of analysis, where several concepts are linked together in an interpretative structure that adds meaning and direction to the problem. Theoretical concepts are guiding tools for interpretation and should therefore as far as possible correspond to the historical structures being analysed. This is not achieved at once but through a process of empirical and interpretative approximations that characterise all research.

Suggested reading

Anthony, D. 1997. Prehistoric Migrations as Social Process, in (J. Chapman and H. Hamerow, eds) *Migrations and Invasions in Archaeological Explanation*. Oxford: BAR International Series 664.
An important analysis of migration.

Helms, M. 1986. *Ulysses Sail*. Princeton: Princeton University Press.
——— 1993. *Craft and the Kingly Ideal*. Austin: University of Texas Press.
These works by Helms are specially recommended.

Kristiansen, K. 1998. *Europe before History*. Cambridge: Cambridge University Press.
Another analysis of migration.

Kristiansen, K. and Larsson, T. (in press) *The Rise of Bronze Age Society*. Cambridge: Cambridge University Press.
A new framework for understanding the historical relations between the Near East, the Mediterranean and Eurasia during the Bronze Age is presented, together with a theoretical framework for diffusion and interaction.

Renfrew, C. and Cherry, J. (eds) 1986. *Peer Polity Interaction*. Cambridge: Cambridge University Press.
Shows Renfrew's approach to regional interaction and diffusion.

Sherratt, A. 1997. *Economy and Society in Prehistoric Europe*. Edinburgh: Edinburgh University Press.
A collection of Sherratt's works on processes of diffusion in the Neolithic and Bronze Age.

KRISTIAN KRISTIANSEN

ECOLOGICAL ARCHAEOLOGY

Although the term has been around since shortly after Darwin's seminal publication *On the Origin of Species* (the term *Oecologie* was first coined by Ernst von Haeckel in 1866), ecological ideas really gathered momentum from the beginning of the twentieth century, as something of a reaction against evolutionary arguments that had unfolded in the nineteenth century. Within such arguments, series of natural and cultural groupings had been organised along a linear sequence from lower to higher, from simple to complex, from primitive to advanced. The fate of individual units contained within such sequences was fairly clear; their movement was passive and one-dimensional, on an axis between regress and progress. Twentieth-century ecologists began to treat these units as active, engaging with their environment, with influence flowing in both directions. While nineteenth-century evolutionary approaches emphasised long, gradual evolutionary trajectories, twentieth-century approaches sharpened their focus upon particular times and places, where particular organisms were interacting with their environment, the study which was now defined as ecology.

By the 1920s a series of key concepts within ecology had crystallised, each of which would stimulate and inform different branches of archaeology. These relate to: the dynamics of change and the concept of succession; the dissipation of energy and concept of food web; and the cycling of materials. From the 1930s, these were brought together, for example in Arthur Tansley's *ecosystem*, and integrated with other studies of humanity and time, in the forms of *human ecology, cultural ecology* and *evolutionary ecology*. These different concepts and their bearing upon archaeological thinking will be considered in turn.

The dynamics of change

From the late nineteenth century, observations within European peat bogs had led botanists to speculate about a sequence within Nature that mirrored progress within Culture. Just as human communities were seen as moving from simple, undifferentiated communities to complex, hierarchical societies, so natural communities could be seen to follow the parallel trajectory of succession. Moving upwards through the profile of a peat bog, the traces of undifferentiated herbaceous communities gave way to ever more stratified and differentiated woodland. Just as human communities followed the path of *progress* towards *complexity,* so natural communities followed the path of *succession* to *climax*. Such a path could be seen extending not just across time but also across space, stretching out between optimal and sub-optimal growing conditions. Those geographical sequences, from pioneer to climax communities, were particularly important, both in giving successional ideas their fine detail, and in relating them to human action. In 1916 Lennart Von Post laid the foundations of pollen analysis by marrying stratified sequences of pollen-bearing sediments with the successional sequence observed in space across the southern Russian steppe. Observations of an equivalent sequence in North America, extending from the deserts and prairies to the eastern woodlands lakes, informed the successional arguments of the pioneer ecologists Henry Chandler Coles and Frederick Clements at around the same time.

In observing the disappearing prairies, Clements connected human action with two distinct pathways of ecological change. The indigenous American was seen as contained and passive within a natural successional process, whereas the European American was viewed as deflecting the successional sequence, moving sideways to an alternative cultural path, or even reversing it. This contrast between two modes of human ecological action has been challenged on a number of fronts. On the one hand, it is now believed that indigenous Americans were not quite as passive, and may have played a key role in the expansion of prairie. On the other hand, the ways in which human communities engage with Nature in an exploitative and sometimes quite intensive manner do not always entail deflection from their successional sequence. Nonetheless, the idea of two types of society, variously termed *cold* and *hot*, *traditional* and *modern*, with implicitly different ecologies, still retains widespread currency

The concept of two distinct pathways in human ecology, and the 'flip' from the passive to the active path, underpinned the thinking of Vere Gordon Childe on the Neolithic revolution (*see* p. 35), and indeed the entire ensuing debate on the origins of agriculture. Von Post's use of successional data to make sense of pollen sequence has continued to inform pollen analysis, a technique that forged its closest fusion with archaeology in the collaboration between archaeologist Grahame Clark and palynologists Harry and Mary Godwin. Their work anticipated the concept of *ecosystem*, that Arthur Tansley coined a few years later, to emphasise the interconnections rather than the boundaries between plant and animal, life and death, organism and environment. While ideas of succession and progress greatly informed studies of the origins and development of agriculture, Mesolithic and then Palaeolithic studies shifted the emphasis to ecological adaptation.

The dissipation of energy

Ecologists quickly came to prioritise the movement of energy as a central principle by which entities were interconnected, and from which their form derived. The major form of energy transfer took place during food consumption, and the notion of an *ecological pyramid* conveyed the substantial dissipation of energy at each feeding step, such that the 'sustainable biomass' (i.e. the total mass of organisms occupying each step) reduced dramatically as one moved up the *food chain* or through the *food web*, giving it its pyramidal structure. The feeding relationship between predator and prey lent itself to dynamic modelling, and during the 1920s mathematicians Alfred Lotka and Vito Volterra independently came up with powerful mathematical articulations of that dynamic based on a relatively simple equation known as the logistic equation, which expresses in formulaic terms the relationship between population growth, reproductive rate and 'carrying capacity' (the size of population that environment is able to support). While archaeology has drawn upon the mathematical elements of this relationship far less than some other disciplines, the conceptual elements have underpinned a number of ecological arguments within archaeology, for example in relation to site-catchment analysis (*see* p. 230), optimal foraging theory, and studies of reproductive strategy in natural selection, contrasting *r-strategies* (that maximise offspring number) and *K-strategies* (that optimise the success of a restricted number of offspring).

The cycling of materials

While energy is a non-renewable resource, quickly becoming dissipated along relatively short food chains, there are many renewable resources, such as water and nutrients, which are cycled around ecosystems, and the stability of those cycles influences both the form of natural communities and their sensitivity to human action. The form of a climax community is very much dependent on the status of each of those cycles. The richest and most complex woodlands cycle nutrients and water in a highly effective manner, banking much of their stock of material in organic tissue. The most conspicuous examples of environmental impact by humans have involved the disruption of one or more of those cycles. Without such a disruption, many natural communities display considerable resilience to being eaten, burnt and chopped down, quickly recovering and regaining their biomass. Most enduring disruption of these cycles arises from destabilising the soils beneath the living communities. The principles behind geochemical cycling have thus informed much geo-archaeology, in particular in relation to understanding ancient soils, and how they respond to human disturbance of those cycles.

Integrated systems and human ecologies

During the 1930s, these different building blocks of ecology were brought together within overarching concepts, such as Arthur Tansley's *ecosystem*, which drew the three core dynamics above within the cybernetic system model (*see* p. 261). The ecosystem concept has remained powerful and productive in research, and attempts have subsequently been made to give it a human articulation through a fusion with concepts from sister disciplines. So the Chicago School of

Human Ecology attempted a fusion with urban geography in the work of Ernest Burgess and Robert Park. While they were concerned with explaining the Western City in ecological terms, Julian Steward's *cultural ecology* attempted to explain the cultures of indigenous peoples in ecological terms, as best exemplified in Roy Rappaport's work with the Tsembaga Maring in New Guinea. The most enduring fusion has interwoven the ecological concepts, particularly of food web theory, with the evolutionary concepts of selection and adaption, in the process emphasising niche, competition and reproductive strategy. *Evolutionary ecology*, which draws inferences from the adaptive features of the human skeleton and the biogeography of their remains and artefacts, still provides a most fruitful route for research into early humans and their extinct relatives.

Each of these human ecologies has fed productively into archaeological thinking. The manner in which evolutionary ecology has cast light on human origins has been elucidated by Glynn Isaac and Robert Foley. The geographical theme of human archaeology, while starting from a modern urban focus, has had a major impact on the debate about the origins of agriculture, through Carl Ortwin Sauer and David Harris, and also the palaeo-economy of Eric Higgs (*see* p. 230). The anthropological theme of cultural ecology inspired the 'New Archaeology' (*see* p. 212), explored by Lewis Binford and others. In each of these human ecologies within archaeology, systems thinking is quite prominent, and a starting assumption is the tendency towards equilibrium. Another archaeologist who has been prominent in ecosystemic thinking is Kent Flannery, but his arguments place less emphasis upon equilibrium, and develop themes that are intrinsically linked to disequilibrium.

Beyond equilibrium

The first generation of ecosystem models treated equilibrium as the 'natural' state, and the burden of explanation fell upon accounting for change, rather than stasis, which needed no explanation. Disequilibrium came about as a result of an external force, either a climatic perturbation or an intense human intervention. In 1973, Robert May demonstrated that the logistic equation (see above) could move a predator–prey relationship into a fluctuating, or even chaotic, state, without the requirement for external intervention. In formal terms, equilibrium was deposed from 'natural' status, and instead became a special case. Disequilibrium ecology is itself quite new, but has made a significant contribution to archaeological ideas. Its attraction within archaeology is that humans are fundamentally disequilibrium species, gaining their selective advantage from our cognitive powers of prediction within a highly unpredictable environment. Our awareness of, and means of tracking, very rapid environment change in the past, is currently growing apace, and disequilibrium models will no doubt become increasingly widespread in the future.

Suggested reading

For general texts introducing the approach, see Butzer and Simmons; for Palaeolithic and evolutionary perspectives, see Binford and Foley, and for a focus on the last 10,000 years, see Harris.

Binford, L. R. 1981. *Bones: Ancient Men and Modern Myths*. New York: Academic Press.

Butzer, K. 1981. *Archaeology as Human Ecology: Method and Theory for a Contextual Approach*. Cambridge: Cambridge University Press.

Foley, R. A. 1987. *Another Unique Species: Patterns in Human Evolutionary Ecology*. Harlow: Longman.

Harris, D. R. (ed.) 1996. *The Origins and Spread of Agriculture and Pastoralism in Eurasia*. London: UCL Press.

Harris, D. R. and Thomas, K. D. 1991. *Modelling Ecological Change*. London: Institute of Archaeology.

Simmons, I. G. 1997. *Humanity and Environment: A Cultural Ecology*. Harlow: Addison Wesley Longman.

Further reading

For primary case studies of landmark projects in ecological archaeology, see Clark and Flannery; and for in-depth studies of some of the scientific principles and approaches, see Griffiths and May and Seger.

Clark, J. G. D. 1972. *Star Carr: A Case Study in Bio-archaeology*. Reading, Mass.: Addison Wesley.

Flannery, K. (ed.) 1976. *The Early Mesoamerican Village*. New York: Academic Press.

Griffiths, H. (ed.) 1998. *Stable Isotopes: Integration of Biological, Ecological and Geochemical Processes*. Oxford: Bios Scientific Publishers.

May, R. M. and Seger, J. 1986. Ideas in Ecology. *American Scientist* 74: 256–67.

Odum, E. P. 1971. *Fundamentals of Ecology*, 3rd edn. Philadelphia: Saunders.

Pollard, A. M. and Wilson, L. 2001. Global Biological Cycles and Isotope Systematics – How the World Works, in (A. M. Pollard and D. R. Brothwell, eds) *Handbook of Archaeological Sciences*. New York: John Wiley.

Steward, J. 1955. *A Theory of Culture Change*. Illinois: University of Illinois Press.

MARTIN JONES

ENVIRONMENTAL ARCHAEOLOGY

In the years that immediately followed the publication of Charles
Darwin's *Origin of Species* (*see* p. 70), a series of interconnected debates
and discoveries laid the foundation for environmental archaeology.
First, the implicit deep time scales reduced the potency of historical
explanations and of the human past, and opened the way for biological
explanations of human diversity. Second, nineteenth-century industrial and technological progress was stimulating an emergent debate on
Man's Role in Changing the Face of the Earth, the title of a seminal
volume by George Perkins Marsh (1864) Third, the dry summers of
the mid 1860s lowered the water levels within the Swiss lakes, in the
process exposing the extent to which direct biological evidence from
prehistory could be preserved. Finally, Herbert Spencer had endowed
the hitherto aesthetic concept of *environment* with a new concrete and
scientific meaning.

Environmental archaeology is the study of the relationship between
humans and their natural environment through time. As a sub-
discipline of archaeology, it has grown dramatically since the late
1960s, largely through the stimulus of the 'New Archaeology' (*see*
p. 212) drawing upon systems theory (*see* p. 259) and ecological
archaeology (*see* p. 79). However, its roots go back to those years that
followed Darwin's seminal publication. Many of the principal lines of
enquiry within the sub-discipline were already underway by the end of
the nineteenth century, including the studies of vertebrate remains,
insects, molluscs, plant macrofossils, peat stratigraphy and glacial
geomorphology. In 1916, these were finally complemented by one of
the most pivotal methodologies within environmental archaeology,
pollen analysis. Today, environmental archaeology encompasses the
study of a wide range of materials that have in common that they are
not predominantly shaped by human action. They are not *artefacts* but
ecofacts. Their form reflects human engagement with nature, rather
than culture, with climate, weather, biology and landform. The
boundary is far less clear than was once thought, as all archaeological
materials bear witness to their natural origin and cultural modification.
Recently archaeologists have found it interesting to look upon pottery
as harvested mud, and meals as artefacts, blurring and subverting these
boundaries. Nonetheless, as environmental evidence in broad terms
presents different challenges to artefactual evidence, environmental
archaeology has a range of its own concepts, which not surprisingly
have close parallels with concepts relating to artefact study.

Sequence, process and context

While stratigraphy was borrowed and adapted by archaeology from geology (*see* p. 243), there is more continuity in this concept from geology to environmental archaeology, which some would regard in any case as a facet of quaternary geology. Archaeological stratigraphy *per se* has tended to emphasise sequence: a series of layers and cuts that form a ranked sequence of containers, each bearing its own artefact assemblage. In geology and environmental archaeology, stratigraphy is as much about *process* as sequence. It matters greatly not just in what order sediments were laid down, but how they got there in the first place. There are two reasons for this. First, artefacts tend to be, in sedimentological terms, rather large particles, only moved by such high-energy processes as glaciers and human action. Ecofacts are far more varied in their mobility, and understanding an environmental sequence may depend far more critically upon knowing how the sediment was actually formed. Second, while an isolated artefact may be rich in information about the human past, through its aesthetic form, its technological makeup, its cultural affiliations and date, an isolated ecofact may have essentially lost all its information by losing its context. Third, while the conceptual separation between artefact and 'matrix' (the medium from which it is excavated) is clear, that between ecofact and matrix is not. There is a continuum both in material and in evidential terms; the matrix itself comprises intrinsic environmental data. While the study of artefacts has placed an increasing emphasis on context, process and context have always been the starting point of environmental archaeology; it is impossible to reach any understanding of the contents without first understanding the context.

Proxies and indicators

Ecofacts are frequently studied because of an interest in something other than the ecofact itself. Beetles may be a fascinating and alluring group of animals in their own right, but environmental archaeologists tend to study them in order to draw conclusions about climate or urban living conditions, not about insects. They serve as a proxy for something else. The proxies we study may be one step, or several, away from the target of interest. A fragment of the exoskeleton of the elm bark beetle is one step away from an elm tree, two steps away from a deciduous woodland, and three steps away from a mild interglacial climate, and it may serve as a proxy for all or any of these. Each step involves certain premises and assumptions, not least that natural communities and ecosystems are currently organised much as they have been in the distant past. This is the principle of *uniformitarianism* (*see* p. 274). It is a principle that is safer in systems that are close to equilibrium, and becomes increasingly unsafe as they depart from equilibrium.

There are various kinds of proxies. The most frequently encountered are proxies for climate (especially temperature), for vegetation cover and for human action/disturbance. The best proxies are those that have a narrow ecological range or niche, and a rapid turnover and response time. However, those with a slower response time can also be of value in revealing the nature of environmental change. For example, Early Holocene mismatches between temperature-sensitive insects and temperature-sensitive trees can be related to the rapidity of post-glacial warming.

Individuals and communities

Environmental archaeology works from both sedimentological and biological data. In the case of biological data, there are two routes to interpretation. One follows individual species and draws upon the fine points of their ecology to draw environmental inferences; the other assembles species into communities, and it is those communities that act as proxies. The selection of route comes down in part to intellectual tradition, and in part to the nature of the material. Plant macrofossils have tended to explore following the individual approach in Britain and America but the community approach in Germany and Central Europe, for example. Vertebrates are more commonly studied following the individual approach, while several invertebrate groups are typically analysed in community terms. Each approach is constrained by the uniformitarian assumption in different ways. In the individual approach, too much interpretation can come to rest on the fluctuations of a single species. In the community approach, the assumption that species groupings remain intact is highly problematic. Indeed, direct comparison of modern and prehistoric pollen rains would suggest that 50 per cent of the plant communities encountered in Europe after the glacial maximum disappeared during the period of rapid warming that introduced the Holocene. However, these *non-analogue communities* are of great interest in their own right, and include some of the major human ecosystems of the Palaeolithic.

Death assemblages and taphonomic sequences

Especially in the case of community approaches, it is important to distinguish between the living community and the death assemblage, which may differ in striking ways. For example, species with short life-cycles will comprise a much higher proportion of the latter than the former. In addition to such life-cycle features, the depositional process itself can radically modify the proportions in a death assemblage. To understand and interpret an assemblage of biological fragments within the mouth of a cave, for example, we will need to factor in: features of the original life-cycle of the organisms yielding those fragments; the behaviour of birds and bats that preyed on and transported them; and the karstic geomorphology of the cave itself. This is part of the larger field of *taphonomy* (*see* p. 122) that examines the transformations that occur in the transition from the biosphere (our planet's 'skin' of living organisms) to the lithosphere (the Earth's mineral crust). As well as exploring natural transformations, taphonomic studies also emphasise the cultural transformations which provide one form of insight into the factor that most directly concerns archaeologists, human action.

Human action and response

Environmental archaeology has been concerned with reconstructing past human environments in order to understand their influence on shaping life. It has also been concerned with detecting the impact of humans on the environment and its shape. Many of these involve the detection of some kind of deflection of a quaternary sequence, a departure from the natural *succession to climax* (*see* p. 80). In pollen sequences, this may entail the reduction of tree pollen, indicating the shrinkage of climax woodland, giving way to an open agrarian landscape. At a more subtle level, disturbance may not drastically reduce tree cover but, nevertheless, human action may be perceived in the fluctuations of specific components, such as elm, which decline over much of Europe during the Early Neolithic. The problem with automatically connecting fluctuations in tree cover with human action is that other factors such as climate and disease can have similar effects. A securer approach follows proxies of disturbance of the soil matrix, which at certain levels can only be attributed to either human or glacial action. Markers of such disturbance include plants whose cycle strategies are particularly resilient in the face of intense soil disruption. These are referred to as weeds. There are similarly a range of invertebrates, such as molluscs and insects, that are particularly resilient in the face of repeated devastation of their immediate environment, and which also serve as proxies of disturbance.

Suggested reading

Each of the following texts effectively introduces the entire field, but from different perspectives: Burglund and Roberts from quaternary science, Evans and O'Connor and Dincauze from archaeology, while Bell and Walker draw on both perspectives.

Bell, M. and Walker, M. 1992. *Late Quaternary Environmental Change: Physical and Human Perspectives*. London: Longman.
Burglund, B. E. (ed.) 1986. *Handbook of Holocene Palaeoecology and Palaeohydrology*. Chichester: John Wiley.
Dincauze, D. F. 2000. *Environmental Archaeology: Principles and Practice*. Cambridge: Cambridge University Press.
Evans, J. G. and O'Connor, T. 1999. *Environmental Archaeology: Principles and Methods*. Stroud: Sutton.
Goudie, A. 1993. *The Human Impact on the Natural Environment*, 3rd edn. Oxford: Blackwell.
Roberts, N. 1989. *The Holocene: An Environmental History*. Oxford: Blackwell.

Further reading

Of the following texts, Marsh is purely of historical interest, Bintliff *et al.* explore some theoretical issues, while Pearsall and French take archaeobotany and geoarchaeology to greater depths.

Bintliff, J. L., Davidson, D. A. and Grant, E. G. (eds) 1988. *Conceptual Issues in Environmental Archaeology*. Edinburgh: Edinburgh University Press.
French, C. A. I. 2002. *Geoarchaeology in Action: Studies in Soil Micromorphology and Landscape Evolution*. London: Routledge.
Marsh, G. P. 1965 (1864). *Man and Nature or, Physical Geography as Modified by Human Action*. Cambridge, Mass.: Belknap.
Moore, P. D., Webb, J. A. and Collinson. M. E. 1991. *Pollen Analysis*, 2nd edn. Oxford: Blackwell.
Pearsall, D. M. 1989. *Palaeoethnobotany*. San Diego: Academic.

MARTIN JONES

EPISTEMOLOGY

Not interested in a word that looks like 'epistemology'? Consider this routine description: an archaeological site is excavated and objects of various materials recovered. By observing the colours, shapes and other properties of the objects, and their associations with one another and with features like house structures, archaeologists reconstruct the way of life of the people who lived at the site. A post-processualist (*see* p. 207) even writes a paper on the symbolic meaning of the community's settlement structure. Sounds like standard, contemporary archaeology, doesn't it? Epistemology is about the nature and integrity of such knowledge claims. It is of fundamental importance to everyone interested in the human past, for if archaeologists cannot demonstrate in a convincing way that their statements about the past are true or at least well supported, then why should their stories be privileged over more entertaining stories about moonbeams and Stonehenge? This entry provides an introduction to epistemology and to the current epistemological crisis in archaeology.

What is epistemology?

Epistemology (from the Greek *episteme*, 'knowledge', and *-logy*, 'discoursing') is that branch of philosophy concerned with the nature, sources and validity of human knowledge, and, by extension, with issues like the nature of reality. Among the questions it attempts to answer are: What is knowledge? How is it produced? How is it justified? Although rooted in the work of Plato and other early philosophers, epistemology only took centre-stage in philosophy with the rise of modern science in the seventeenth century, due in large part to the increasing use of notions like perception, observation, evidence and method. This review focuses on the 'empiricist' (*contra* 'rationalist') school's answer to how knowledge is acquired, which is principally through the use of the senses aided where possible by scientific instruments, for this answer is shared by most contemporary archaeologists. (Rationalism is the view that reason – rather than sense experience – is the chief source and test of knowledge.)

Appearance and reality

If asked, most archaeologists would agree that the world consists of material objects like artefacts, the stuffs of which they are composed, their properties and relationships, and the processes, such as decomposition and erosion, which they undergo. They would likely agree, too, that these objects exist independently of how they as archaeologists think of or experience them, and that the objects are directly accessible to them through their sense organs. By implication, the information they record about the objects is largely objective.

This widely held, commonsense view of reality ('direct realism') has been a focus of attack since the rise of modern science. Doubters are quick to point out that our senses can and do deceive us. Simple examples are the straight stick that looks bent in water and the parallel lines of railroad tracks that seem to converge in the distance. More seriously, colour sceptics have convincingly argued that colours have no objective reality in the external world; they are an effect of the stimulation of our visual organs and the manner in which that stimulation is processed through the optic nerve and brain. Moreover, when compared to the process of seeing in bats, dogs and other animal species, some of which see in colour and three dimensions while others do not, it is clear that humans see in a decidedly species-specific way.

Arguments by Locke, Berkeley and others also maintain that other qualities we seem to perceive in objects – like taste, smell, sound and texture – are not 'in the objects themselves' but vary according to how they are perceived, and the species of the perceiver. When the culturally conditioned way humans see is added, it is apparent that there is at least some difference between what we see and whatever it is that is 'out there'.

These arguments draw attention to a fundamental challenge for archaeologists: if reconstructions of the past are grounded in sense experience, and if there is (inevitable) discordance between what is seen and what is 'out there', then how can they be sure they are reconstructing the past-in-itself?

Theories of knowledge and justification

Given these doubts about our ability to directly access reality, then what is knowledge? Again, it cannot simply be sense awareness of the world around us, for to know that something is an artefact, say, one must not only have the artefact in one's field of vision, but must judge that it is an artefact. The possession of knowledge of this sort ('knowing that') involves not just sense awareness, but the power of judgement within a cultural context. Does this mean that knowledge is necessarily simply judgement within a cultural context? The most common response among philosophers has been that knowledge is not just true belief, but justified true belief. Of course, this definition merely shifts the debate from theories of knowledge to theories of justification.

Attempts to identify what justifies a belief include foundationalism (in which a given belief is justified by appeal to other 'foundational' beliefs that are thought to require no justification), coherence (in which a belief is justified if it is consistent with other already accepted beliefs) and reliabilism (in which a belief is justified if it is supported by a reliable process, such as perception under scientifically controlled conditions). The plausibility of these attempts is weakened, however, by their reliance on assumptions about our access to reality, assumptions that themselves need justification. This and other difficulties open the door to a variety of sceptical positions.

Scepticism

The roots of arguments of scepticism in early modern times are in Descartes' *Meditations*, in which he attempts to disentangle knowledge from nonsense, and methods of inquiry that yield genuine knowledge from those that promote ignorance. Using his 'method of doubt', he tries to determine what cannot be doubted. His sceptical considerations about perception, error, delusion and dreams raise troubling challenges for knowledge gained through sense awareness.

Responses to sceptical arguments include attempts to reframe the task of epistemology and to bridge the gap (if a gap is acknowledged at all) between knowledge claims and the grounds put forward for them. An example of the first response is the claim that Descartes' quest for certainty is misguided, for certainty is a psychological state independent of the truth or falsity of a belief. Attempts to bridge the gap include Kantian transcendentalism, Berkeley's idealism, sceptical epistemology, phenomenalism and, increasingly, reworked versions of realism (the belief that the objects of sense perception exist independently of the mind). John Searle, in his *The Construction of Social Reality*, for instance, attempts to show how social and institutional facts like money, marriage and governments 'fit into a world consisting entirely of physical particles in fields of forces' (1995: xi). (Searle's response is a particularly instructive one for archaeologists, for, whether adequate or not, it is an exemplar of one epistemic route that can be travelled if one's subject matter is culture.)

The postmodern turn

Since the 1980s, there has been an increasing tendency within the disciplines, including archaeology, to accept the strong sceptical thesis that nothing is – or, even more strongly, can be – known. More sceptical postmodernists argue that there is no real world, that 'reality' (if that concept is useful at all) is merely a linguistic convention; according to 'epistemological impossibilism', our focus is limited to the play of words and meanings around us. More 'affirmative' postmodernists retain the possibility of saying something about the world, though they accept the notion that events and objects have no meaning apart from the meanings attributed to them by culture-permeated perceivers. Given this theory of 'reality', their modes of interpretation tend to be idealist, subjective and hermeneutic (that is, geared to comprehending individual and cultural understandings rather than an understanding of the world as it is in some objective, empirical sense). Postmodernists as a group reject (or find trivial) 'standard' epistemological concerns with belief, justification and truth; they favour instead epistemological standpoints that involve power, inequality, narrative and other non-traditional perspectives. In archaeology, this range of sceptical stances is most clearly visible within the post-processual research programme.

Is there a crisis in archaeology?

Increasingly, more archaeologists are adopting the view that since statements about the past are always uncertain, they cannot know anything (for sure) about the past. The result is a growing pragmatism according to which the purpose of archaeology is to tell stories about the past that will help people cope with contemporary issues, such as inequality and alternative 'native' views of the past. Other archaeologists believe that this sceptical view repeats Descartes' mistake of mingling the psychological state of feeling certain with knowledge. It is based, too, they argue, on the trivial (because circular) claim that we cannot know anything because ... well ... we cannot know anything.

Is there an epistemological crisis in archaeology? My own view is that scepticism is a challenge, not a settled claim that renders meaningless the epistemic endeavours of archaeologists. An agenda for the future is required in which the framework of perception and thought in archaeology is made more explicit, and its implications developed and criticised. Current studies by cognitive psychologists, philosophers like Searle and others already provide critical insight into the nature of 'brute' reality and our ability as a species to apprehend it. It seems likely that these studies, while supporting the notion that there is something worth observing 'out there', will nonetheless transform how archaeologists understand their stories about the past.

Suggested reading

Alcoff, L. M. (ed.) 1998. *Epistemology: The Big Questions*. Malden, Mass.: Blackwell.

A wide-ranging anthology that covers key contemporary issues in epistemology. Sections on knowledge, justification, truth, scepticism, the structure of knowledge, and the politics of knowledge are each preceded by a brief, accessible introduction.

Bernecker, S. and Dretske, F. (eds) 2000. *Knowledge: Readings in Contemporary Epistemology.* New York: Oxford University Press.
A collection of some of the most important and influential writings in epistemology. Difficult, but typical of this branch of philosophy.

Johnson, M. 1999. *Archaeological Theory: An Introduction.* Malden, Mass.: Blackwell.
An example of the use of the word 'epistemology' in post-processual archaeology.

Landesman, C. 2002. *An Introduction to Epistemology.* Malden, Mass.: Blackwell.
An introduction to the fundamental problems and issues of epistemology for beginning students.

Landesman, C. 2002. *Skepticism: The Central Issues.* Malden, Mass.: Blackwell.
Since epistemological arguments must necessarily engage sceptical arguments, students with an interest in epistemology should be thoroughly familiar with these arguments. Landesman provides a comprehensive, accessible review.

Rosenau, P. M. 1992. *Post-Modernism and the Social Sciences.* Princeton: Princeton University Press.
Chapter 7 provides a lucid review of the assumptions and consequences of postmodern epistemological positions.

Searle, J. R. 1995. *The Construction of Social Reality.* New York: Free Press.
Contra postmodernists, Searle argues that social realities are firmly rooted in a world made up entirely of physical particles in fields of forces. An illuminating read for archaeologists, whose medium is necessarily material culture.

Further reading

Audi, R. 2003. *Epistemology: A Contemporary Introduction to the Theory of Knowledge,* 2nd edn. New York: Routledge.
Bonjour, L. 2002. *Epistemology: Classical Problems and Contemporary Responses.* Lanham: Rowman and Littlefield.
Crumley, J. S., II. 1999. *An Introduction to Epistemology.* Mountain View, Calif.: Mayfield.
Dancy, J. and Sosa, E. (eds) 1994. *A Companion to Epistemology.* Malden, Mass.: Blackwell.
Greco, J. and Sosa, E. (eds) 1998. *The Blackwell Guide to Epistemology.* Malden, Mass.: Blackwell.
Moser, P. K. (ed.). 2002. *The Oxford Handbook of Epistemology.* New York: Oxford University Press.
Sosa, E., Kim, J. and McGrath, M. (eds) 2000. *Epistemology: An Anthology.* Malden, Mass.: Blackwell.

GUY GIBBON

ETHNOARCHAEOLOGY

Ethnoarchaeology is the study of present-day lifestyles to enable understanding of the processes that generate archaeological evidence, or are responsible for its preservation or destruction. Ethnoarchaeology usually involves fieldwork, which might be complemented by archival research or the analysis of museum collections, to look at such subjects as the making of artefacts (pots, stone and metal being the favourites), food-getting (hunter-gatherer studies are more common than those of farmers), space architecture and settlement patterns, and general formation processes of archaeological evidence (Donnan and Clelow 1974; Gould 1978, 1980; Moore 1986).

Ethnoarchaeology differs from ethnography in that the latter aims to document and understand a culture in its own terms, while the former documents the material aspects of people's lives in order to understand archaeological evidence, either from the same region or from a totally different part of the world.

The strengths of ethnoarchaeology are that it involves 'actualistic studies' of the practices of everyday life through which observations are made, measurements taken and recordings carried out of activities generally beyond the direct cultural experience of the investigator. An understanding of pottery-making, or of the layout of a cattle-herding compound, provides the basis for comparisons with archaeological evidence of interest. Problems arise from the nature of the comparisons made, and how far these might be considered legitimate across cultures and over time. Problems of comparison are heightened by differences of time scale (*see* p. 265): even the longest ethnoarchaeological project is only carried out over decades, which falls within one standard deviation of a relatively precise radiocarbon date (*see* p. 68). There are also ethical issues raised by studying one culture to throw light on others.

In order to give readers some sense of how ethnoarchaeology proceeds I shall look at a number of different projects before returning to more general questions of the benefits and limits of ethnoarchaeology.

The main materials that survive in archaeological sites include pottery, metalwork and stone. It is therefore unsurprising that many studies have been carried out on the making and discard of these materials (*see* p. 121). Many particular studies have been carried out, which have also been used as the basis for generalisations about the nature of production and particularly issues of specialisation and divisions of labour (see, for instance, Rice 1987 for an influential example). Part way between the specific and the general is Gosselain's study of potters in southern Cameroon (Gosselain 1992, 1998). He looked at eighty-two potters in twenty-one ethnic groups, spread across two different language families in southern Cameroon. Gosselain was interested in the complex links between identity, technology and symbolism, using the French concept of *chaîne opératoire* (*see* p. 25), which details the sequence of steps needed to make an object. The idea of *chaîne opératoire* has a lineage going back ultimately to Mauss's concern with the techniques of the body and the body's relationships with objects, cohering as a concept in the work of Leroi-Gourhan. The *chaîne opératoire* works most intuitively with a reductive technology, such as stoneknapping, where the steps taken can be charted directly from the changing form of an object and its debitage. However, additive and transformative techniques, like basketry, pottery-making or metalworking, proceed by set steps which will be more or less evident in the form of the finished object and the by-products of working. The *chaîne opératoire* is seen as a series of steps which are initially learned, and are therefore culturally based, but which become habitual and invisible as skills build up. Differences in pots, for instance, are due partly to variability in the nature of raw materials, but also to the skilled and habitual actions of potters based in the local cultural repertoire of bodily actions generally, and potting traditions more particularly.

Gosselain's studies are complex in that he considers both the unconscious nature of production and the exercise of cultural choice. For instance, one group, the Bafia, prefer clays available for immediate use and which only need pounding to make them workable, whereas other groups are willing to put more effort into clay preparation. He found little individual choice or influence from the nature of the raw material in terms of the forms of the pots being made by different groups. Form was dictated to a great extent by cultural traditions. There was considerably more variation in the nature of finishing and firing, and here faster-moving fashion and personal preferences played a part. The *chaîne opératoire* proved very useful in disaggregating elements of the production process and showing the sorts of influence on each, although the overall complexity of the choices made at varying steps may prove daunting for the archaeologist.

A most wide-ranging attempt to understand the production of material culture is that carried out by Paul Sillitoe with the Wola of the Southern Highlands of Papua New Guinea. Sillitoe's study is not framed as a piece of ethnoarchaeology, but rather as salvage ethnography on the part of an anthropologist working on exchange relations who realised that the stone tools still in use in 1973 and 1982 would soon be superseded by steel. Nevertheless, the book that resulted, *Made in Niugini* (Sillitoe 1988), is of fundamental importance for archaeologists interested in how material things operate as a totality in a period when many were made with non-metal technologies. The Wola lived in small family groups, with a marked separation of men and women in terms of where people lived and worked. Relations of kinship were 'cognatic', i.e. people could claim land and other rights through either their mother's or father's line. Small groups came together in larger temporary coalitions for exchange and ceremony, with exchange being the main way in which group relations were worked through. Exchanges involved wealth items such as pigs, pearl and cowrie shells, salt, feather headdresses, stone axes and oil. Many of people's productive efforts were ultimately geared towards ceremonial exchange, even though their immediate object was subsistence or obtaining basic raw materials. Sillitoe investigated the 169 major objects that the Wola made themselves through a household inventory of what objects people had, how long they had been in their houses, who they obtained them from, etc. He also set up a workshop and commissioned people to make all the major types of objects, meticulously recording their making, noting how long they took to make, what techniques were used, the sources of raw materials and who had the skills to make various things. Individuals usually made things on their own; the only cooperation was in obtaining raw materials, which usually happened when people went to their gardens or into the rainforest to hunt.

The Wola ideology was that women make things and men transact them, but this was not really true. A more accurate view was that men made strong things (axes, shields and bows, for instance) and women made softer, complex things (such as bags, aprons, string, etc.). Women said that this division of labour existed because men's thoughts split, whereas theirs formed a whole. Men made about 75 per cent of the total assemblage and usually made things for their own use or for them to exchange. Women made things for men as well as for themselves, and although they made fewer artefacts, what they did make was much more time-consuming, so that the overall time they spent on production was considerably more than men. Some informal differences in skill were noted, but little, if no, prestige derived from production – all kudos came from successful exchanges. The value of objects partly derived from the difficulty of obtaining raw materials and the degree of labour involved. But the only items with consistently high values were those used as ceremonial exchange objects, which did not always need more labour or rare raw materials than more mundane items. Sillitoe did not look in depth at the history of production and its changes, but did note that custom determined who made which items, the techniques and the raw materials used, and there was little innovation in any of these areas. Sillitoe's work on agricultural production and exchange can be combined with his study of technology to give a rich overview of the various elements of Wola society and its material dimension, of considerable interest to archaeologists (see his synthetic work – Sillitoe 1998 – for an overview and guide to the literature). Lemonnier (1986) has also worked in the New Guinea Highlands making use of the concept of *chaîne opératoire*.

A particularly ambitious attempt to understand a broad range of material culture is the Mandara Archaeological Project, which has focused on a range of artefacts and settlement types in order to elucidate how these are used to create and change forms of identity and belonging. The Mandara Mountains of northern Cameroon and north-eastern Nigeria are presently home to large, dense populations, which have grown up partly through local developments and partly due to people fleeing the political manoeuvrings and fighting surrounding the emergence of various states (such as the Fulbe and Wandala) on the plains, as well as longer-term flight from slavers. Since the 1980s a team led by Nicholas David has been documenting present ways of life in an historical context. The variety in material culture in the present can be seen as variations on long-term histories and common themes. For instance, some specific vessel types, such as red-ware tripod vessels and black-ware food bowls, can be traced back to the middle of the first millennium BC. Links between identity and material culture are complex, partly because the division and classification of people into groups derive from colonial and administrative convenience, not lived experience; but also because a single person has a variety of links to groups of varying types, ranging from individual households to patrilineal descent groups, kin connections traced through women, various political groupings of a chiefly nature and finally language groups (although multi-lingualism further complicates this last category). David and his team conclude that identity is a process, not a state (David and Kramer 2001: 209).

Unsurprisingly in such a complex situation, some elements of material culture are used to create regional differences and others are found more widely spread, conforming to no obvious boundaries of identity. For instance, among the Mafa speakers around Mokolo, settlements take the form of a spiral with a linked series of rooms, whose order depends on who uses them (the male household head's room is first, then that of the first wife, which is followed by a room containing granaries and shrines and ending in the first wife's kitchen – at the centre of all this is a stall for stock). In some areas (the Mafa and their neighbours) linguistic groups are well distinguished by their pots, but this is less true in the northeastern sub-region. Patterns of movement on marriage of female potters are partially responsible, as are differential influences of markets. Iron-making furnaces and iron objects, like hoes, seem to conform more directly to differences of language and identity. The Mafa region of the southeast shows good correlations between costume, compound layout, forge types and pots on the one hand, and language on the other. However, this synchronic variation might not show up clearly archaeologically due to the speed at which communities coalesce and then go out of existence. Variations in material culture and identity are maintained for a small number of generations before reformulating. Populations rise and fall due to famine, war and in-migration, although overall the levels of population have risen in the mountains considerably over the last few centuries.

The Mandara Archaeological Project has been exemplary in its consideration of history and the manner in which changes will have been manifested in material culture, and also how much of this change might have showed up archaeologically. History matters, but it does complicate things, which in itself is a useful lesson for archaeologists. Style and identity are both best seen as relational categories, deriving from complex linkages between people and things, which themselves have fluid and complicated outcomes.

What these brief examples show are some of the benefits of ethnoarchaeology (although I have not touched upon important areas like settlement patterns, or the nature of discard). There has been an enormous accumulation of information on the material world and its links to aspects like style and identity, as well as to the manner in which any of these things will be manifest in archaeological evidence. Information has been collected, and made sense of, from within a number of different theoretical positions, including processualism (*see* p. 212), where the need to generalise is strong (Binford's global hunter-gatherer model, for instance, is partly based on ethnoarchaeo-logical evidence – Binford 2001). Post-processualists (*see* p. 207) have strong feelings on generalisation, but this time have an aversion to it, stressing instead the creative role of material culture in making social relations, the fluidity of these relations and their local specificity. The

French tradition stressing techniques of the body and *chaînes opératoires* cuts across both the Anglophone approaches, with some attempt to generalise on the basis of similar responses to materials and the mechanics of the body, but also looking at how local meanings may derive from artefacts.

Ethnoarchaeology has had a big impact on the discipline as a whole, the high point of which was the disputes between Binford and Hodder which gave rise to post-processualism, and in these disputes their respective ethnoarchaeological work, among the Nunamiut (Binford 1978) and in Baringo (Hodder 1982), loomed large. Since then ethnoarchaeology has had less impact, and this might in part be due to the general influence of post-processualism and the fear of generalising from particular culturally and socially grounded case studies.

There are ethical issues, I feel, around the conduct of ethnoarchaeological research. These concern how far one should use the study of a particular area and group of people to throw light on general problems of archaeology, rather than their present and past. These concerns are part and parcel of broader ethical issues to do with returning the results of research to people whom it concerns most directly, which are relevant to any form of archaeological or anthropological work. Balancing this are the numbers of people from non-western backgrounds now carrying out ethnoarchaeology in areas from which they come (Agorsah 1988; Kusimba 1996).

Overall, ethnoarchaeology is an exciting and dynamic area of archaeology, of some importance to both the past and the present of the discipline in both theoretical and empirical terms. More use could be made of ethnoarchaeological results to develop some general theory concerning material culture, settlement and identity, as well as discard and deposition. It shares with the discipline as a whole a need to include local people in field research and to make results accessible to them.

Suggested reading

Binford, L. 1978. *Nunamiut Ethnoarchaeology.* New York: Academic Press.
David, N. and Kramer, C. 2001. *Ethnoarchaeology in Action.* Cambridge: Cambridge University Press.
The best current overview of the subject.

Donnan, C. and Clelow, C. (eds) 1974. *Ethnoarchaeology.* Institute of Archaeology Monograph 4. Los Angeles: University of California.
Hodder, I. 1982. *Symbols in Action: Ethnoarchaeological Studies of Material Culture.* Cambridge: Cambridge University Press.

Further reading

Agorsah, K. 1988. Evaluating Spatial Behavior Patterns of Prehistoric Societies. *Journal of Anthropological Archaeology* 7: 231–47.

Binford, L. 2001. *Constructing Frames of Reference: An Analytical Method for Archaeological Theory Building using Hunter-Gatherer and Environmental Datasets.* Berkeley: University of California Press.

Gosselain, O. P. 1992. Technology and Style: Potters and Pottery among the Bafia of Cameroon. *Man* 27: 559–86.

—— 1998. Social and Technical Identity in a Clay Crystal Ball, pp. 78–106 in (M. T. Stark, ed.) *The Archaeology of Social Boundaries*. Washington, DC and London: Smithsonian Institution Press.

Gould, R. (ed.) 1978. *Explorations in Ethnoarchaeology.* Albuquerque: University of New Mexico Press.

—— 1980. *Living Archaeology.* Cambridge: Cambridge University Press.

Kusimba, C. 1996. Social Context of Iron Forging on the Kenya Coast. *Africa* 66: 386–410.

Lemonnier, P. 1986. The Study of Material Culture Today: Toward an Anthropology of Technical Systems. *Journal of Anthropological Archaeology* 5: 147–86.

Moore, H. 1986. *Space, Text and Gender: An Anthropological Study of the Marakwet of Kenya.* Cambridge: Cambridge University Press.

Rice, P. 1987. *Pottery Analysis: A Sourcebook.* Chicago: Chicago University Press.

Sillitoe, P. 1988. *Made in Niugini. Technology in the Highlands of Papua New Guinea.* London: British Museum Publications.

—— 1998. *An Introduction to the Anthropology of Melanesia: Culture and Tradition.* Cambridge: Cambridge University Press.

CHRIS GOSDEN

THE EVOLUTION OF SOCIAL COMPLEXITY AND THE STATE

For thousands of years, philosophers have been asking questions about the nature of government and politics. How did societies come to have governments? What is the ideal form of government? Did people want a government because it could provide benefits to everyone? Or was government imposed against the will of the people? The work of contemporary archaeologists on the origins and evolution of government is an outgrowth of these kinds of questions. Rather than engaging in philosophical arguments, however, archaeologists actually study the places and time periods where these social changes took place.

The study of the origin and evolution of governments is one part of a larger research question archaeologists refer to as the evolution of social complexity and the state. The phrase 'social complexity' refers to the variety of life experiences and activities within or between groups making up a society. Today most humans live in societies that are socially complex. Most people practise a highly specialised occupation, including the political leaders and administrative staffs of nation-states that govern millions or even billions in a single polity. Differences in degrees of economic privilege ('social differentiation') are also marked. People live in diverse kinds of communities from small villages to cities with populations in the millions.

But social complexity is a comparatively recent development. While our species first evolved some 400,000 years ago, the shift towards social complexity began only some 10,000 years ago. At that time, the Earth's total population was only about 10 million (compared with 6.3 billion today). Ten thousand years ago, most people lived in small impermanent settlements, families were largely economically self-sufficient, and they tended to be socially equivalent in wealth. And societies were 'politically egalitarian', implying that most adults could participate in societal governance. Archaeologists want to know: when, where and how did complex societies develop over the comparatively short time-span of 10,000 years, and why?

From archaeological investigation and from ethnographic analogies (*see* p. 143) we can identify a developmental sequence of governments from simplest and earliest to the more complex forms of later periods. In the earliest and most simple governments, each community or local territory had a leader, but was independent of leaders of other communities. If a number of community leaders recognised the authority of a single paramount chief above them, we call the polity a 'chiefdom'. In what we call a 'state' numerous local leaders in a large territory recognised the authority of several levels of leaders above them, culminating in the paramount, a king or some other form of paramount authority such as a governing council. Most early states had kings, but the early Greek polis (c. 500 BC) and the republican form of the Vedic Period states in the Ganges area of India (also c. 500 BC), among others, illustrate the latter type.

A key problem for archaeologists of the twentieth century has been: how do states first form? Where and when did this development first happen? Archaeological research has shown that state formation was a rare occurrence. The very earliest states developed independently in only six places. In north China, there were definitely states by 1700 BC, but state origins were probably earlier, sometime after 3000 BC. In the Indus Valley, in what is now Pakistan and northwestern India, an early phase of state development dates to 2600–1900 BC, followed by a second and largely separate South Asian phase beginning around 500 BC, in the Ganges River area, from which later Hindu states can be traced. The earliest states developed in Mesopotamia (now Iraq and Iran) at roughly 3500 BC, while in the Nile Valley, in Egypt, the state was in place by 3100 BC. Native Americans developed their first states in Mesoamerica (now Mexico) by 500 BC and in what is now Peru by 200 BC. Later, the state form of government spread outward from the six areas into sub-Saharan Africa, the Mediterranean, Europe, Central Asia and Southeast Asia.

As they formed, early states had an enormous influence on people's lives; in fact, one prominent anthropologist, Elman Service, refers to state development as the 'great transformation' in human societies. As governments became more complex, so did other aspects of society. State growth is associated with overall population growth, although we are not sure whether growth caused political evolution or was a result of it. Population growth is often evident in cities, with only a few exceptions (e.g. most periods of ancient Egypt). People migrated to the emerging urban centres to serve as administrative staffs, soldiers, artisans and labourers. Production and commerce were intensified because states require surplus production, and because state authorities can enforce the peace of the market place. New kinds of occupations appeared in tandem with state formation. For example, archaeologists argue that specialised nomadic pastoralism in the Mesopotamian region was a response to an increased demand for animal products required by growing urban populations and by farm families who were becoming more specialised in irrigated grain production. In this and similar ways, there was intense interaction between early complex societies and their surrounding populations, some of whom even developed their own states.

The ideas, technologies and forms of social organisation that developed in early states are passed on in some form to later states. Some later states – one could mention hundreds of examples – whose growth reflects some combination of interaction and continuity from the very earliest states include the Bronze Age polities of Crete and later Mediterranean states, Srivijaya and Melaka in Southeast Asia, and the Aztecs of central Mexico. To varying degrees, the social transformations initiated in the six earliest states echo through all later political systems right down to the modern world and its system of nation-states.

As archaeologists have learned more about the evolution of social complexity and the state, so this research problem has influenced the way contemporary archaeologists go about doing their fieldwork.

Social complexity implies growing differences across sectors of a population. While a hundred years ago archaeologists often excavated the tombs and palaces of a ruling elite, now archaeologists interested in the evolution of social complexity want to know more about the causes and consequences of variation and change across all social sectors of a society. One way to do this is by studying whole cities ('urban archaeology') rather than focusing on elite zones. This presents methodological problems for archaeologists because some of the early centres were large, with populations in the tens of thousands or even hundreds of thousands. Research methods have also changed in recognition of the fact that the stages, so to speak, on which early complex societies and states developed were very large ones. Early cities and palace centres developed in relation to their agricultural hinterlands of hundreds or even thousands of towns and villages. Warfare, trade and diplomacy among groups of nearly equivalent polities can be a social force bringing about political change in the direction of state formation ('peer polity interaction' – *see* p. 196), necessitating a large geographical scale for archaeological research. To answer these research questions, since the middle of the twentieth century archaeologists have developed methods for systematically recording and studying the distributions of large numbers of archaeological sites over whole regions, a method called settlement pattern archaeology.

But to fully understand an early state requires a geographical perspective that goes beyond even city hinterlands and peer polities. Nomadic pastoralists and producers of other kinds of raw materials crucial to the economy of a growing state may be found at great distances from the main cities or other concentrations of population. For example, during the fourth millennium BC (Uruk Period), when the earliest Mesopotamian states developed, raw materials such as copper were being imported into the main cities from as far away as Turkey and the Saudi Arabian peninsula. Here, as elsewhere where early states developed, social change in the direction of greater complexity occurred within the framework of a very large region where diverse cultural groups were linked by trade, migration and other forms of social interaction.

Studying past social change at the scale of whole cities, hinterlands and even larger interaction zones strains the resources available to archaeologists and forces them to develop new research methods. By approaching the study of complex societies in this way, however, we learn more about how diverse social sectors and cultural groups contributed to the evolution of social complexity and the state.

Suggested reading

Adams, R. McC. 1981. *Heartland of Cities: Surveys of Ancient Settlement and Land Use on the Central Floodplain of the Euphrates.* Chicago: University of Chicago Press.
This is one of the first applications of settlement pattern archaeology in the study of early state formation.

Blanton, R. E., Kowalewski, S. A., Feinman, G. M. and Finsten, L. M. 1993. *Ancient Mesoamerica: A Comparison of Change in Three Regions.* Cambridge: Cambridge University Press.
Compares archaeological sequences of state formation in various regions of pre-Hispanic Mesoamerica, and highlights the growing significance of settlement pattern research in Mesoamerican archaeology.

Chang, K. C. 1983. *Art, Myth, and Ritual: The Path to Political Authority in Ancient China.* Cambridge: Harvard University Press.
A somewhat dated, but still useful, summary of the cultural basis for state formation in China, written by one of the foremost authorities on the archaeology of this region.

Hoffman, M. 1991. *Egypt before the Pharaohs: The Prehistoric Foundations of Egyptian Civilization,* 2nd edn. New York: Knopf.
Summarises the background to state formation in Egypt in a readable format.

Millon, R. 1973. *Urbanization at Teotihuacán, Mexico, Volume One, The Teotihuacán Map, Part One: Text.* Austin: University of Texas Press.
This is the first major publication of urban archaeology. In it, Millon reports on the completion of a map of Teotihuacán, in the Valley of Mexico, one of the earliest cities of the Native Americans that was also one of the world's largest cities of the time.

Postgate, J. N. 1992. *Early Mesopotamia: Society and Economy at the Dawn of History.* London: Routledge.
A useful summary of the early state in Mesopotamia that synthesises archaeological and early written sources.

Possehl, G. L. 2002. *The Indus Civilization: A Contemporary Perspective.* Walnut Creek, Calif.: AltaMira Press.
An up-to-date synthesis of archaeological research on state formation in the Indus Valley region.

Service, E. R. 1975. *Origins of the State and Civilization: The Process of Cultural Evolution.* New York: W. W. Norton.
Service was one of the most influential anthropologists interested in the evolution of social complexity and the state, and his comparative method combined ethnographic information on contemporary chiefdoms and early states with the results of archaeological research from areas of primary state formation.

Further reading

Algaze, G. 1993. *The Uruk World System: The Dynamics of Expansion of Early Mesopotamian Civilization.* Chicago: University of Chicago Press.
Charvat, P. 2002. *Mesopotamia before History.* London: Routledge.
Cribb, R. 1991. *Nomads in Archaeology.* Cambridge: Cambridge University Press.

Earle, T. 2002. *Bronze Age Economics: The Beginnings of Political Economies*. Boulder, Col.: Westview Press.

Feinman, G. and Marcus, J. (eds) 1998. *Archaic States*. Santa Fe: School of American Research Press.

Nichols, D. L. and Charlton, T. H. (eds) 1997. *The Archaeology of City-States: Cross-Cultural Approaches*. Washington: Smithsonian Institution Press.

Price, T. D. and Feinman, G. M. (eds) 1995. *Foundations of Social Inequality*. New York: Plenum Press.

RICHARD BLANTON

KEY IDEAS IN EXCAVATION

Excavators may dig one big hole or many small holes, and these strategies have varied – and still vary – according to the way that archaeologists imagine the past and visualise what lies under the ground. Cultural historians like to see sites as fossilised historical events, and investigate them with targeted trenches. For example, Mortimer Wheeler dug a trench through the earth rampart at the British Iron Age hill fort of Maiden Castle and interpreted the sequence of layers he saw in the vertical section at the edge of the trench as showing how it was built, repaired and rebuilt through time. Wheeler liked sections, and in order to have as many as possible he dug in boxes – a set of square areas separated by baulks 3 feet wide. The *deposit* (the ground) inside each box was excavated stratigraphically, that is layer by layer, using a builder's trowel, and the finds kept with each layer. When complete, the box had four vertical sections each carrying a version of the sequence of events – making up the story of the site (the place chosen for investigation).

Processual or 'New' archaeologists (*see* p. 212), such as Lewis Binford and Kent Flannery, see sites as parts of buried systems and, like social scientists, seek to understand the dead society by 'sampling' its behaviour. In field archaeology this translates into numerous small square or rectangular areas which are the samples to be surveyed or excavated. There are many ways of laying out the samples – at regular intervals, or randomly where the position of each trench (*transect*) or test pit (*quadrat*) is chosen by random numbers, each of which is excavated to the bottom, either in arbitrary layers (spits) or in natural layers (strata). The assumption is that, as in a social group, a set of questions put to an individual can provide answers applicable to all, and the more randomly they are put, the less likely is the answer to be biased.

At some levels this is certainly true. For example, the pollen falling into a bog can be determined from a single measure; the seeds of plants eaten on a site can be extracted by screening (sieving) the contents of a single pit. These are thought to be 'representative samples'. But excavated test pits distributed across a piece of ground seldom produce representative samples, because in most matters, like houses, meals or burials, each one was different, so one cannot stand for all. At Qsar es-Seghir, American excavator Charles Redman began by exploring the early Islamic ruined town with a number of quadrats distributed randomly; but as the pattern of the streets and buildings stared to appear, he opened up large areas so he could map their form and activities more clearly.

In countries where people built in timber, the buildings tend to rot away and only survive as sockets where the posts stood. The *schnitt* (slice) method popular on the European continent helps to show them up by cleaning square areas with hoes and shovels, so producing a *horizontal section* in which the posts appear as rows of dark blobs in the natural sand. The site is recorded as set of horizontal and vertical sections which together provide a controlled, checkable model of the original deposit. If the deposit lies deep, however, it may conceal structures which the schnitt method cuts through. In Scandinavia, archaeologists in the 1930s began following layer surfaces and dispensing with vertical sections to see elusive buildings better. This *open area excavation* was championed in Britain in the 1960s by Martin Biddle at Winchester and Philip Barker at Wroxeter and Hen Domen, who applied it to deep stratified sites. The deposit was taken apart on the largest possible scale layer by layer, the shape and position of each layer being recorded individually.

This idea of *total excavation* was well received by the British 'Rescue' movement (an early form of Cultural Resource Management). In 1972 the *context* was invented by Max Foster and taken into use in York and subsequently in London, where big contract archaeology companies were at work. The context is defined as the prime stratigraphic unit, and can be a layer, or an interface like the surface of a floor or the edge of a pit, the foundation stones of a building or the sides of the trench into which they were cut. Winchester archaeologist Edward Harris has showed how the sequence of contexts could be represented on a diagram (his *matrix*) with the earliest at the bottom and the latest at the top. Urban archaeologists such as London excavator Steve Roskams find it logical to record the whole of a deposit context by context, each given its own description on a form and its own drawing on a separate piece of plastic film. Interpretation on site is not encouraged, but reserved until after the sequence has been put together and the finds have been analysed. This practice was known as *single context recording*. It works well in towns and is convenient for the 'rescue' sector because many contexts can be recorded and lifted in different parts of a site at the same time. The method also achieves a consistency which is essential for analysis.

The total and systematic dissection of a deposit still leaves open the question of how much of it to dig and what it means. Post-processual archaeologists (*see* p. 207), like Ian Hodder and Gavin Lucas, want to re-introduce interpretation on site, and record thoughts in progress using video cameras as well as the old site journal long favoured by researchers. Excavators should be conscious of why they do what they do (*reflexivity*) and should share the business of interpretation with those around them (*multi-vocality*). York archaeologist Martin Carver turned these principles into practice with his 'Field Research Procedure', which champions the key ideas of evaluation and design, and embeds interpretation in the excavation records.

Evaluation happens before excavation starts, and draws up an account of what we want to know (the research agenda), the character of the deposits (the terrain), the techniques, and the local social circumstances which may exercise restraint on what we can do; in other words, it works out what we can know out of what we want to know. The first site evaluation was probably that of the early nineteenth-century flute-playing diplomat Claudius Rich at Babylon. Instead of weighing in with a trench and pulling out antiquities, he undertook a careful surface survey, made a map showing the location of the ruins and suggested what they might have originally belonged to. At the abandoned Mexican city of Teotihuacán, George Cowgill mapped the surface and used the type and quantities of pottery to divided the ruined area into zones which could answer different questions about this seventh-century Maya society. At the English barrow site of Sutton Hoo the evaluation lasted three years and used topographical, geophysical survey and the re-excavation of old trenches to create a *deposit model* showing what was left of this Early Bronze Age settlement and the Anglo-Saxon cemetery of burial mounds which had been placed on top of it. This model mapped the edges of a cemetery 4 hectares in extent and formed the basis for a *project design* which included an excavation of a quarter of it.

The *design* of an excavation relies on the evaluation and is multi-vocal in the sense that it solicits opinions from groups of 'stake-holders'. Once consensus is achieved, the design takes the form of a contract with the rest of society (who are not on site and cannot see what is going on). Value-led excavation therefore sees itself as reconciling ethical and academic concerns by holding to a widely advertised project design. In most countries, project designs can be debated and agreed through the planning system, and this applies to all projects whether they are mainly research or mainly cultural research management. Nowadays, field projects also use both excavation and survey (*see* p. 249) in integrated programmes.

On-site 'reflexivity' may be achieved by 'recording the recording' as well as the interpretations made 'at the trowel's edge' (in Ian Hodder's words). Carver's *recovery levels* monitor the different intensities of digging required by a design – so Level A might use a mechanical excavator, Level B a shovel, Level C and D trowels and Level E a spatula. Level F is taking it home with you in a block. For example, the coarser recovery levels might be applied to open up the site and the finer to excavate a grave. To record interpretations made on site, while creating a consistent record, context recording is backed up with additional higher-order concepts – the *feature* (seen as a set of contexts as defined by the excavator) and the *structure* (seen as a set of features), each of which has its own form and numbering system. These *multi-level records* are used to compose the interpreted sequence or 'site model'.

Excavation records are not only multi-level but multi-media, consisting of written notebooks, sheets, drawings, photographs, videos, digital files and boxes of samples, animal bones, seeds, plants and artefacts. How can all this be made known? A key idea here is Barry Cunliffe's 'Levels of Publication', which matches the information won from the ground to those who need it. Level 1 is the site itself, now a target for long-term conservation, since it still stores as yet unrealised information. Level 2 describes the records made on site or *Field Records*, the first-hand accounts of what the excavators saw. Level 3 consists of the excavators' first analyses and synthesis, the stratigraphic sequence, the plans of buildings, the maps of artefact distributions. These *Field Reports* offer the first full account of the project. Level 4, the *Research Report*, puts those findings into their research context. In general, Levels 2 and 3 are stored in an archive for future researchers to study. Level 4 is the selected research results of interest to the academic community now. Further selection may be applied to offer to the public (Level 5) and the media (Level 6). The trick is to raise interest from a new audience at each stage, without ever losing the primacy of the encounter on the ground, the thoughts of the person holding the trowel.

Suggested reading

Barker, P. 1993. *Techniques of Archaeological Excavation*. London: Batsford.
The case for total excavation.

Carver, M. 1998. *Sutton Hoo. Burial Ground of Kings?* London: British Museum Press.
The value-led system in action.

Carver, M. and Rothschild, N. 2004. *Field Archaeology. Principles, Techniques and Design*. London and New York: Thames and Hudson.
A comprehensive manual of the integrated approach to excavation and survey.

Flannery, K. (ed.) 1976. *The Early Mesoamerican Village*. New York: Academic Press.
The best, and most entertaining, discussion about how sampling works.

Hodder, I. 1999. *The Archaeological Process*. London: Blackwell.
The case for interpretation on site, as practised at Çatal Hüyük.

Lucas, G. 2001. *Critical Approaches to Fieldwork. Contemporary and Historical Archaeological Practice*. London and New York: Routledge.
A thoughtful discursive history of field work (especially Chapter 2).

Roskams, S. 2000. *Excavation*. Cambridge: Cambridge University Press.
The case for single context recording.

Wheeler, R. E. M. 1954. *Archaeology from the Earth*. Oxford: Oxford University Press.
The case for the use of sections and the box system.

MARTIN CARVER

EXPERIMENTAL ARCHAEOLOGY

Experimental archaeology is the investigation of archaeological issues using experiments. It has been part of archaeology from the very beginning of the discipline. As artefacts were identified and sorted into chronological sequences, so assumptions were made about their manufacture and use. Occasionally, someone would try out an object to see how it worked or how it could be made. These very early experiments were mostly ad hoc, but the value of practical experiments was nonetheless recognised by archaeologists of the nineteenth and early twentieth centuries.

Some of the most systematic experiments in prehistoric agriculture were conducted in Denmark in the first half of the twentieth century, but the concept became more formally recognised as an archaeological tool in the second half of the century with the initiation of long-term projects in the 1960s such as the experimental earthworks created at

Overton Down, Wiltshire, which were envisaged as a 128-year experiment in how vegetation, soils and artefacts changed as part of earthwork structures and weathering processes. The formal recognition of experimental archaeology culminated in two key books written by the Cambridge academic John Coles and another American-based edited volume, all published in the 1970s. Other major projects at Butser (Hampshire) and Lejre (Denmark) integrated agriculture and technology with buildings and crafts. These were very influential and served as centres for both research and the presentation of archaeology to the public. The research vs presentation dichotomy lies at the heart of current discussion over what constitutes experimental archaeology.

At its widest the term encompasses all experiments used to elucidate an archaeological issue, encapsulated by Coles' *Archaeology by Experiment*. It is generally agreed that experimental archaeology includes all artefact technology and function experiments, the creation of above-ground structures based on ground level or below archaeological features, the investigation of destruction and decay processes of objects and structures (*see* p. 121) and the full range of agricultural practices and resource management experiments. However, there are more contentious uses of the term. Experimental archaeology has become synonymous with large demonstration centres, many of which contain buildings believed to mimic those of the past. Not all such centres undertake archaeological research and thus engage in the practice of experimental archaeology, but the best of them combine a public accessibility with some form of research, and many use the results of previous experiments. These centres present tableaux of a possible past with some features based on good evidence but other aspects conjectural, a distinction that is not always clear to visitors. The buildings and structures are often referred to as 'reconstructions' but, since the past cannot be recreated and there is always some element which is unknown, recent discussion has suggested using 'construct' instead. The public, walking around visitor centres, are not doing experimental archaeology any more than is a visitor to a museum, but the centres are more likely to offer demonstrations or participation in some activities allowing the public to learn about the past by means of experience. Since active participation is a powerful educational tool, such centres offer good opportunities for promoting archaeology to individuals, educational groups and organisations. Archaeologists have been concerned to distinguish this experiential learning from experimental archaeology. Some would also exclude experiments on the effectiveness of archaeological methods, but such research is indeed part of 'archaeology by experiment'.

Since experiments are a major feature of science, they are also a method of investigation widely used in all the scientific branches of archaeology. Thus experimental archaeology forms part of research into subjects such as environmental archaeology (see p. 85) and taphonomy (see p. 122). In these spheres especially, but ideally also in other areas, the experiments tend to follow the tenets of the scientific philosopher Karl Popper. Theories or hypotheses are tested by means of experiments, with the results carefully observed and measured. The results are used to disprove an idea or suggest modifications to a theory; results can never give complete proof, but they can show a possibility. The investigation is fully written up so that others can replicate the experiments if they wish. In this way the concept of experimental archaeology is a tool which demonstrates incorrect assumptions and inaccuracies, and refines theories and methodologies.

A good experiment will have a clearly stated idea of what archaeological issue it will investigate and how. The factors or variables affecting the experiment will be carefully considered. Some may be held constant, others will vary, and so records of observed changes and measurements will be needed. What is to be recorded and when is an integral part of the experiment design, and experiments generally take more time to plan than to execute. In some cases an experiment will need to be repeated so that statistically meaningful results are obtained. All of these issues will be tempered by the archaeological question and practical limits.

Full-scale, open-air experiments might be the most realistic but it may be difficult to monitor, control or repeat conditions in the field, whereas scaled-down or laboratory experiments might offer more control or better recording facilities, or be safer. In practice, all experiments are a compromise and the experiment design relates to the archaeological purpose.

Open-air experiments for smelting may be hard to control but the interaction of variables may be crucial: e.g. the Sri Lankan experiments with hillside iron-smelting furnaces demonstrated that the trade winds of the area and the position on the hillside allowed the strong wind to act as natural bellows, resulting in successful smelting. Agricultural experiments are carried out in the field. It is not possible to control wind, rain and temperature, but it is possible to record these and look at cause and effect over many years' worth of experiments.

Large-scale projects such as Overton Down Earthwork, or construct-ing a full-scale ancient Greek ship, cannot in practice be endlessly repeated to obtain a larger sample size, but the time scale and environmental conditions of the earthwork would be difficult to recreate in the laboratory, and the ship's performance and three-tier rowing system could not otherwise be appreciated.

Issues of time are especially complex (*see* p. 268). First, it is always difficult to complete a project which will outlast the initial funding period and even the researchers. Second, many experiments record the time taken to do something, but if the task is performed by a less skilled modern counterpart this can be meaningless, and even then our concept of time may have little relevance to the archaeological society. It may be pertinent to the archaeological issue to use a skilled flintknapper to replicate stone tool production, but working out the average time to produce blades in seconds correct to two decimal places is spurious numerical accuracy. Ideally, similar materials and methods to those available in the past should be used if to do otherwise will affect the results. However, experiments investigating the pitch of archaeological bone flutes used high-resolution synthetic casts, because this did not affect the musical capabilities but did reduce the time taken to make the objects, allowing more replicas to be made, and also avoided the slight variations in shape that would occur in real bones. Ideally, a series of experiments might be designed holding all variables except one constant, but this can be impractical. Sets of experiments which integrate experimental buildings, above and below ground storage, tools, technologies, ecology and plant and animal husbandry for a period or culture have been informative because of the way these aspects are interrelated in the past society.

The achievements of experimental archaeology are numerous. The Butser and Lejre projects have been especially influential. Peter Reynolds' Butser project experiments showed that Romano-British 'grain-driers' did not dry grain, and that Iron Age storage pits could be used to store grain but, since they did so successfully over many years, could not be used to give population estimates. It also tested possible above-ground structures based on ground-level features from real archaeological sites. The thatched roundhouse at Butser was once novel, but there are now many more roundhouses to be seen at various kinds of centre. Jake Keen's Ancient Technology Centre (southern England), with a variety of buildings and crafts available, is an educational tool based in a school, and funded as part of local education. In contrast, some centres are run privately by individuals or funded by local authorities. Tourism and educational parties usually provide the bulk of visitors, and so location and relationship to school curricula can prove influential. The funding base for these kinds of centre can be crucial to their role and development. Butser was originally envisaged as a twenty-year project but, without owning the land and lacking secure long-term funding, it has had to adapt to changing situations and has moved sites. In contrast, Lejre with state funding and a large area of land has, over time, been able to develop areas focusing on different time-periods, as well as an area for technology and crafts and a section devoted to practical visitor participation.

Experiments can aid interpretation by giving comparative data, e.g. of usewear on stone tools or pots, or provide quantitative data, e.g. on the amount of meat and other resources from different animals. They can evaluate different archaeological techniques or the most efficient way to recover data, e.g. phytolith extraction techniques, and show how natural processes affect the formation of archaeological sites. Experimental archaeology is usually thought of as dealing with the tangible, but it can contribute to more esoteric and enigmatic issues. There are experiments investigating the methods of designing prehistoric stone circles, or the tool-using capabilities of bonobo chimpanzees as an alternative source of ideas on the origins of tool-using, and the musical tuning frameworks for bone flutes. 'Archaeology by experiment' is widespread and wide-ranging, though it is the presentational aspects which tend to be the most well known. Thus many more people are doing archaeology by experiment than would think of themselves as experimental archaeologists.

Suggested reading

The two books by John Coles are classic texts and very accessible:

Coles, J. M. 1973. *Archaeology by Experiment*. London: Hutchinson.
Introduces the key elements of the subject and presents succinct overviews of food production and craft.

Coles, J. M. 1979. *Experimental Archaeology*. London: Academic Press.
Gives the historical background and more detailed overviews of different topics such as subsistence, settlement and crafts.

Harding, A. F. (ed.) 1999. *Experiment and Design*. Oxford: Oxbow.
The section on experimental archaeology features Reynolds' thought-provoking general paper reassessing the methodological issues and divisions originally identified by Coles' 1973 introduction, and is especially concerned to identify the

problem of using the term 'reconstructions'; see also Lawson's research on the musical frameworks of bone flutes as well as papers on Danish ship-building work and Polish tar production experiments.

Ingersoll, D., Yellen, J. and MacDonald, W. (eds) 1977. *Experimental Archeology.* New York, Guildford: Columbia University Press.
A useful introduction and a collection of papers on a range of aspects.

Mathieu, J. R. (ed.) 2002. *Experimental Archaeology: Replicating Past Objects, Behaviours and Processes.* British Archaeological Reports International Series 1035. Oxford: Archaeopress.
A good collection of papers on a range of issues.

Stone, P. G. and Planel, P. G. (eds) 1999. *The Constructed Past: Experimental Archaeology, Education and the Public.* London: Routledge.
Excellent overviews of the heritage aspects of experimental archaeology including reflective but succinct papers on some of the most famous research initiatives, e.g. Butser and Lejre.

The two Overton Down publications together show the original aims and the continuing research data produced by a long-term study of taphonomic processes with Bell's assessment of the strengths and weaknesses of the project to date:
Bell, M., Fowler, P. J. and Hillson, S. 1996. *The Experimental Earthwork 1962–90.* York: Council for British Archaeology.
Jewell, P. A. (ed.) 1963. *The Experimental Earthwork on Overton Down.* London: British Association for the Advancement of Science.

Further reading

Amick, D. S. and Mauldin, R. P. (eds) 1989. *Experiments in Lithic Technology.* Oxford: British Archaeological Reports International Series S28.
Anderson, P. C. (ed.) 1999. *The Prehistory of Agriculture: New Experimental and Ethnographic Approaches.* Monograph 40. Los Angeles: Institute of Archaeology, University of California.
Barnatt, J. and Herring, P. 1986. Stone Circles and Megalithic Geometry: An Experiment to Test Alternative Design Practices. *Journal of Archaeological Science* 13: 431–50.
Coates, J. F. 1989. The Trireme Sails Again. *Scientific American* 260 (4): 68–75.
Juleff, G. 1998. *Iron and Steel in Sri Lanka.* Mainz am Rhein: Verlag Philipp von Zabern.
Outram, A. and Rowley-Conwy, P. 1998. Meat and Marrow Utility Indices for Horse (*Equus*). *Journal of Archaeological Science* 25: 839–49.
Reynolds, P. J. 1974. Experimental Iron-Age Storage Pits, an Interim Report. *Proceedings of the Prehistoric Society* 40: 118–31.
Schick, K. D., Toth, N. and Sevcik, R. 1999. Continuing Investigations into the Stone Tool-Making and Tool-Using Capabilities of a Bonobo (*Pan paniscus*). *Journal of Archaeological Science* 26: 821–33.
Zhao, Z. and Pearsall, D. M. 1998. Experiments for Improving Phytolith Extraction from Soils. *Journal of Archaeological Science* 25: 587–98.

LINDA HURCOMBE

FEMINIST ARCHAEOLOGY

What is feminist archaeology?

Feminist archaeology refers to an approach that uses feminist critique as the basis for archaeological work. Feminist archaeology developed from the women's movement in the 1970s–1980s together with gender archaeology (*see* p. 127). The two approaches, sharing many of their aims and having similar roots, were originally merely different nuances and emphases within a women-dominated call for attention towards gender as an essential element of any society – past ones as well as our own. Recently, different emphases and increasing distinctions in their epistemological (*see* p. 89) foundation and corresponding practice have, however, emerged, and it is now often more useful to see the two as closely related but different approaches within archaeology.

The two approaches share a concern with the recognition of women's contributions and importance both in the archaeological record and in the professional and public spheres of the discipline. Feminist archaeology has, however, increasingly sought its inspiration in feminism and in its epistemological claims. This has meant that practice, the practising of being feminist archaeologists, rather than the project of investigating and interpreting the past has come to the fore. This does not mean that investigation and interpretations have become irrelevant; but it does mean that the process of generating knowledge, and how gender plays into this and is actively utilised and incorporated into that process, is seen as just as significant as any knowledge claim that may result from it. This development is clearly captured in statements to the effect that the notion of feminist archaeology, with its implication of partaking in and contributing to disciplinary structure, should be replaced with an emphasis upon *being* feminist archaeologists, which stresses the practices of individuals.

For feminist archaeology, sex and gender are not just basic structures of society, they are integrated aspects of our subjectivities and therefore explicit influences upon all dimensions of how we, as individuals, organise and experience life, including what it means to be a woman. In addition, the earlier concern with inequality has been taken in new directions and interpreted with various strategies in mind. This leads to a positive emphasis upon women being distinct and different from men. Rather than striving to overcome this difference by insisting upon equality, recent feminist arguments stress

116

difference as an enabling quality that should be celebrated rather than denied. Difference, rather than a social problem, should be recognised as a constructive force behind how we act in and upon the world. This emphasis means that subjectivity becomes a major aspect of archaeological practice.

The strong emphasis upon feminist archaeology being not just an intellectual approach but a way of being has resulted in some distinct differences between gender and feminist archaeology. The former may be seen as closely associated with archaeology in its aims and goals but concerned with ensuring greater inclusiveness and reflexivity, while feminist archaeology does not see itself as a sub-discipline, but rather as a reaction and a distinct solution to the question of what constitutes (scientific) knowledge.

Feminist archaeology seems to be more clearly present as a distinct approach in North American academic circles than in other parts of the world, and many of the seminal arguments that have fuelled the debate have been formulated there. In Europe the medievalist Roberta Gilchrist from England and some Scandinavian scholars, such as Erica Engelstad, may be seen as exponents of a similar approach. There has, however, been distinctly less experimentation with multivocality among European scholars, and the underlying aim of reasserting the female role and participation in past societies continues to underwrite much of their research.

Simultaneous with the development of feminist archaeology has been an academically more marginal and often cross-disciplinary focus upon women's spirituality, such as the Goddess movement, which often uses archaeological data in its arguments. Their tendency to produce absolute interpretations of conditions in the past has, however, meant that feminist scholars in general have been critical towards these approaches, and there is not a simple equation between the two approaches to women.

The philosophical basis of feminist archaeology is in part similar to gender archaeology, but also in part affected by a more explicit embrace of the feminist epistemological debates that have taken place over the last two decades. One consequence is that although the two approaches share an emphasis upon sex and gender as basic structures of society, and both agree to sex having social dimensions, they give different significance and meaning to these constructions and respond in different ways to the concerns to which they give rise.

The philosopher Alison Wylie has played a central role in guiding feminist archaeology in its concern with epistemology. In particular, she has been concerned with establishing what a feminist archaeology may mean, and on what basis it will make knowledge claims. The central philosophical concern is how to reconcile the fact that feminist archaeology argues that some interpretations are better than others, with the fact that, at the same time, it embraces notions of multivocality and subjectivity. In response to this challenge, feminist archaeology tends to refer to practice as the basis for evaluating knowledge claims or interpretations. This position is complicated, and some have argued that there is not a sound philosophical foundation for this, while others see the solution in a rejection of the acceptance of authority. The debate is still ongoing, and different perceptions of both the problem and possible responses can be seen among feminist archaeologists.

A related aspect of the epistemological debate is the extent and acknowledgement of political influence on questions, research agenda, and also results. The theoretical basis of feminist archaeology makes it easy to accept that data are affected by theory and intentions. It does make less clear, however, how one may discriminate between different intentions. Using practice as the final point of discrimination leaves feminist archaeology open to the attack that political correctness becomes decisive for the results of the research process. For some this is an acceptable and welcome insight, while for others it is still a problem to be resolved. Feminist archaeology does, however, in general accept that knowledge bears the mark of its maker, that objectivism is always qualified by intentions and that the truth is only ever true from a certain standpoint or perspective.

It is these tensions in the epistemological basis that have been used to criticise the project of a feminist archaeology. It is argued, for example, that the disjunction between the notion of truth and politics undermines any claim to knowledge. Such critiques argue that feminists project themselves on to the past and that they do not explain the past but rather use it to give credence to contemporary feminist claims. In this regard the epistemological basis of feminism is, however, not distinctly different from that of various post-processual approaches (see p. 207).

There is also a somewhat muted tension between gender archaeology and feminist archaeology, but rather than their differences being based on radically separate epistemological positions they seem due to different relationships to the world, the discipline and the aims of the interpretative project.

Feminist archaeology has undergone substantial transformation over the last decade largely due to influences from the social sciences and the arts. This means it has increasingly moved from theoretical discussions to focusing upon developing and challenging archaeological practice. This has resulted in a strong focus upon *the doing* of archaeology, such as developing new approaches to fieldwork, teaching methods, the construction of data, and the relationship to the larger community. Within this development, three areas of special attention can be discerned. One is the gendered aspects of fieldwork. Here Joan Gero's work can be singled out, as she was one of the first to argue that gender affects even basic aspects of fieldwork. She exemplifies this through different behaviour patterns (different ways of seeing and being) between men and women working on excavations. Such studies aim to bring attention to the gendered dimension of the power relations which emerge in the field (and thus the discipline). This means that questions about how the past is controlled become central concerns. The second area of development has been concerned with multivocality. This interest has arisen from the post-processual claim that there is neither a single past nor should there exist a single authoritative account of what the past should be. The interest of feminist archaeology in enhancing the individual and subjective element of practice has furthered this interest. Exploring the concept of voices and to some extent also that of the gaze has meant that various narrative forms and especially the potentials of the internet and virtual realities have become a distinct interest of feminist archaeologists. This celebration of multivocality can be found early on in Ruth Tringham and her work on Çatal Hüyük. More recently, similar experimentation is found among a wider group of feminist archaeologists including in the work of Rosemary Joyce. Their works are particularly exemplary of this approach due to their use of various media such as hypertexts and virtual sites. They are also distinct in their use of stories as a means of bringing out the alternative and different voices.

The third related emphasis has been experimentation, especially with regard to the communication of archaeology and the involvement of wider groups. Here the strategy of telling stories, rather than claiming the truth or aiming at an unambiguous account of the 'past', has come into favour. This was most influentially started by Janet Spector's volume *What This Awl Means* (1993), in which she interwove ethnographic accounts of a girl's relationship to her awl with the archaeological description of the similar object; as a device for bringing different narrators into the account of life in a Dakota village, she literally used a past voice as a means of unlocking the stories in the object. This volume may be seen as a seminal starting point for the experimentation with alternative texts – mapping, so to speak, different possible travels through archaeological data.

Due to these developments the most explicit and significant feminist documents may now be found on the web in the form of hypertext and virtual sites. These 'sites' in various ways encourage visitors to engage with the past for themselves. It is here that the underlying aim of producing contingent and humanly compelling forms of social knowledge is currently seen most clearly.

Suggested reading

Conkey, M. W. and Gero, J. W. 1991. Tensions, Pluralities, and Engendering Archaeology: An Introduction to Women in Prehistory, pp. 3–30 in (J. W. Gero and M. W. Conkey, eds) *Engendering Archaeology: Women and Prehistory*. Oxford: Blackwell.
This is one of the 'classic' texts for gender and feminist archaeology, since it is seen as providing the arguments for focusing upon gender as a specific concern of archaeology.

Conkey, M. W. and Tringham, R. E. 1995. Archaeology and the Goddess: Exploring the Contours of Feminist Archaeology, pp. 199–247 in (A. Steward and D. Stanton, eds) *Feminisms in the Academy: Rethinking the Disciplines*. Ann Arbor: University of Michigan Press.
This article is of substantial importance for the clarification of the differences between feminist archaeology and the Goddess movement.

Engelstad, E. 1991. Images of Power and Contradiction: Feminist Theory and Post Processual Archaeology. *Antiquity* 65 (248): 502–14.
The article is important in clarifying some of the divergent aims of post-processual approaches and feminist ones. It is also an interesting documentation of the early interest in explicit use of feminist philosophy.

Gero, J. 1996. Archaeological Practice and Gendered Encounters, pp. 251–80 in (R. P. Wright, ed.) *Gender and Archaeology*. Philadelphia: University of Pennsylvania Press.
One of the first investigations of how gender affects the working practice of archaeology.

Gero, J. M. and Conkey, M. W. (eds) 1990. *Engendering Archaeology: Women in Prehistory*. Oxford: Blackwell.
This is a classic volume for gender and feminist archaeology, containing important case studies from different periods and areas.

Gilchrist, R. 1999. *Gender and Archaeology. Contesting the Past*. London: Routledge.
A good discussion of the main components of feminist archaeology, with interesting case studies from the medieval period.

Spector, J. 1993. *What This Awl Means. Feminist Archaeology at a Wahpeton Dakota Village*. St Paul: Minnesota Historical Society Press.
The first distinct experimentation with the use of narrative in an archaeological interpretation.

Tringham, R. 1991 Households with Faces: The Challenge of Gender in Prehistoric Architectural Remains, pp. 93–131 in (J. Gero and M. Conkey, eds) *Engendering Archaeology: Women and Prehistory.* Oxford: Blackwell.
This text is a classic insofar as it challenges earlier approaches that ignore people in the past and acknowledges the author's subjectivity as a significant source of insight.

Further reading

Hager, L. D. (ed) 1997. *Women in Human Evolution.* Routledge: London.
Meskell, L. 1996. The Somatization of Archaeology: Institutions, Discourses, Corporeality. *Norwegian Archaeological Review* 29 (1): 1–16.
Moore, H. L. 1994. *A Passion for Difference.* Cambridge: Polity Press.
Nelson, S. N. 1997. *Gender in Archaeology. Analyzing Power and Prestige.* Walnut Creek, Calif.: AltaMira Press.
Sørensen, M. L. S. 1999. *Gender Archaeology.* Cambridge: Polity Press.
Wright, R. P. (ed.) 1996. *Gender and Archaeology.* Philadelphia: University of Pennsylvania Press.
Wylie, A. 1992. The Interplay of Evidential Constraints and Political Interests: Recent Archaeological Research on Gender. *American Antiquity* 52: 15–35.
—— 1997. Good Science, Bad Science, or Science as Usual? Feminist Critiques of Science, pp. 29–55 in (L. D. Hager, ed.) *Women in Human Evolution.* Routledge: London.
—— 2002. *Thinking from Things: Essays in the Philosophy of Archaeology.* Berkeley: University of California Press.

MARIE LOUISE STIG SØRENSEN

ARCHAEOLOGICAL FORMATION PROCESSES

Archaeologists learn about the human societies of the past by studying debris that has survived into the present. However, these material remains have not come down to us unchanged. In fact, virtually all of the 'objects' that archaeologists study – artefacts, plant and animal remains, and architectural spaces – have been altered in significant ways by *archaeological formation processes* (also known as *'site' formation processes*). This term refers to all of the behavioural, mechanical and chemical processes that have modified an object, from the time it was first made or used by people until its remains are recovered and studied. Formation processes can modify or obliterate important evidence of past human activities. Some processes alter objects physically, fragmenting or eroding them. Others can move objects away from their places of use in past activities; objects that were habitually used together can become dissociated, and spurious associations of unrelated objects may be created. Through selective destruction, formation processes can increase or decrease the quantities of some object types. Archaeologists ascertain how formation processes have modified the portion of the archaeological record they wish to study, because these effects have implications for the kinds of questions they can ask, their choice of analytical tools, and the quality of their conclusions.

In the past thirty years, much specialised research has been devoted to studying formation processes and the traces they leave in the archaeological record. Today, some subfields of archaeology deal almost exclusively with such issues. Zooarchaeologists who specialise in *taphonomy*, for instance, study the processes which modify animal remains (bones, teeth and residues of other tissues) as they pass through human cultural systems and enter the archaeological record. 'Taphonomy' means literally the 'laws of burial' (from the Greek *taphos*, 'burial', and *nomos*, 'law'), and refers specifically to the field of study that is concerned with the physical and chemical processes (induced by human, animal or natural agents) that modify an organism after its death and through which its remains are incorporated into geological deposits. The study of discard and abandonment behaviours has also become an important area of specialisation because such formation processes can provide important windows into social organisation, residential mobility patterns, and ritual and religion. Continuing research into archaeological formation processes is enabling archaeologists to draw ever more accurate and sophisticated conclusions about past societies from their material remains.

Some of the earliest examples of research into archaeological formation processes date to the early nineteenth century, when claims were made that geological deposits of great age, in Europe and elsewhere, contained evidence of human activity (*see* p. 7). Sometimes resorting to experiments, scholars debated what constituted unequi-vocal evidence of human modification on stones and animal bones. Apart from this kind of work, which continued into the twentieth century, whenever disputed claims of human occupation arose (such as pre-Clovis in the New World), archaeologists were little concerned with formation processes.

This neglect ended in the late 1960s with the advent of *processual archaeology* (*see* p. 212), as archaeologists began to recognise the need for a systematic investigation of formation processes and their impact on the archaeological record. The processual movement, with its interests in the organisation and evolution of past societies, stimulated new research into archaeological formation processes along several fronts. Archaeologists like L. R. Binford and his colleagues conducted research among living peoples (*ethnoarchaeology, see* p. 95) to determine how variation in residential mobility and other aspects of social organisation conditioned when, where and how people abandoned artefacts and activity spaces, thus producing characteristic patterns in the archaeological record. By the early 1970s, archaeologists were beginning to develop an appreciation for the sheer complexity of processes, cultural and natural or environmental, that could play a role in the formation of archaeological deposits and potentially confound inferences about the past. M. B. Schiffer, along with J. J. Reid, and their colleagues and students at the University of Arizona, spearheaded an effort to document these processes and to establish methods for assessing their impacts on archaeological remains. Theory and methods developed and synthesised by these scholars in the 1970s and 1980s, under the umbrella of the *behavioural archaeology* programme, provide a framework (outlined below) that has guided and stimulated more than three decades of research into archaeological formation processes.

The theoretical framework developed by behavioural archaeologists emphasises the historical nature of the archaeological record. Archaeological remains at every scale – artefact, site and region – are cumulative records of past events (for the sake of brevity, the examples below are restricted to the scale of individual artefacts). That is, traces of events (and processes) accumulate over time; sometimes the traces of earlier events are obscured or obliterated by the traces of later events. In order to make accurate statements about a particular past event, one isolates the most relevant traces by analytically 'peeling back' the traces of later events that have accumulated Accordingly, much research into formation processes is organised in terms of *object histories.*[1]

An object history is simply the chronological sequence of events (and processes) that involved a particular object of interest (e.g. a ceramic bowl, a bison carcass, a Hopi pueblo) from the time that object was first created until its remains were unearthed and studied by the archaeologist. For any general class of objects (e.g. portable artefacts, animal skeletons, extended-family domiciles), sequences of events tend to recur in a predictable fashion. All such objects tend to go through the same general sequence of processes (procurement, manufacture, use, deposition, decay) and some may pass through one or more secondary cycles (reclamation, reuse, recycling). When studying a group of artefacts to answer a specific question about the past, the investigator determines where exactly within this flow-model the main focus of the question lies. Does the question concern how a certain type of ceramic vessel was made (*manufacture*), or does it concern what foods were cooked in those vessels and where cooking activities took place (*use*)? Once this is decided, the researcher can determine from the model which kinds of events might have acted upon, and added traces to, the vessels *after* the events of interest.

Happily, there is already a fairly extensive literature on the specific material traces left by different kinds of past behaviour and formation processes. Many of these data have been acquired through direct observation of the actual processes at work – during ethnoarchaeological fieldwork or in controlled laboratory experiments on replicated artefacts (*experimental archaeology, see* p. 110). Recognising these processes is the first step in assessing their impact on an artefact assemblage. For instance, scholars interested in studying ancient cooking activities can find experimental and ethnoarchaeological data on the chemical residues and physical traces (patterns of carbonisation and abrasion) left on ceramic vessels when different foods are cooked in them and when different cooking techniques are used. They might be able to infer what an ancient pot was used to cook, and how, by comparing residues and abrasion marks found on it with known patterns that have been established through direct observation. Ethnoarchaeologists have also compiled an extensive database on the reuse of broken or worn-out ceramic cooking vessels. When an old cooking vessel is reused for something else (e.g. as a storage vessel), this non-cooking activity can modify or obliterate traces of the original use. Archaeologists have found that reuse can add or remove chemical residues, create new abrasion patterns, or move vessels far from their original use location. These are all formation processes that the researcher considers before offering statements about past cooking activities (the original *use*).

The use and reuse activities discussed so far fall under the heading of *cultural formation processes* – human activities that leave material traces on archaeological remains. There is also a host of *non-cultural* or *environmental formation processes* that the archaeologist must contend with: forces of nature (animals, chemical or physical processes) that act upon objects, especially after they have been discarded, abandoned or otherwise removed from the realm of human activities and left to decay. Archaeologists have turned to research from fields such as chemistry, ethology and geology to identify traces of such processes in the archaeological record and to assess their potential impact on material remains.

In recent years, archaeologists have taken research into cultural formation processes in new directions, making it possible to study aspects of past human behaviour that were previously less accessible. Sometimes cultural formation processes themselves take centre-stage. Among the most salient of these new directions is the movement to understand how ritual activities can be identified in the archaeological record. For example, W. H. Walker and his colleagues have studied *ritual discard* (a kind of cultural formation process) in ethnoarchaeological settings, examining how modern-day ritual practitioners 'throw away' objects used in ritual activities. Often, ritual paraphernalia must be burned, buried or deposited in some safe, out-of-the-way location. These studies have shown that ritual discard can leave robust traces on artefacts and on deposits, which often remain discernible despite the layering effects of subsequent formation processes. Such findings have provided a sound basis for identifying deposits of 'ritual trash' in prehistoric contexts, allowing archaeologists to explore religion and ritual through the material debris preserved in the archaeological record.

The careful consideration of archaeological formation processes is a necessary component of any investigation that yields well-supported statements about the past based on archaeological remains. Today, archaeologists devote considerable time and effort to developing methods for identifying and understanding these processes. As scholars seek to make ever-more sophisticated statements about the past, research into archaeological formation processes is likely to increase in importance.

Notes

1   This general concept, or one very similar to it, appears under various names (e.g. 'taphonomic history') in different sectors of the archaeological literature; it is synonymous with what behavioural archaeologists have referred to as an 'object [or artefact] life history'.

Suggested reading

Hayden, B. and Cannon, A. 1983. Where the Garbage Goes: Refuse Disposal in the Maya Highlands. *Journal of Anthropological Archaeology* 2: 117–63.
Hayden and Cannon explore where and how broken artefacts are discarded in three contemporary Maya villages. The results suggest that archaeologists need to be cautious in interpreting the spatial distribution of artefacts at prehistoric sites.

LaMotta, V. M. and Schiffer, M. B. 1999. Formation Processes of House Floor Assemblages, pp. 19–29 in (P. Allison, ed.) *The Archaeology of Household Activities*. London: Routledge.

This article provides a generalised object history for domestic dwellings, and synthesises data on formation processes that potentially contribute to the contents of artefact assemblages found in abandoned houses. It focuses especially on ritual abandonment processes.

Lyman, R. L. 1994. *Vertebrate Taphonomy.* Cambridge: Cambridge University Press.
Lyman's work synthesises a large body of method and theory from vertebrate taphonomy as it is applied in zooarchaeology. This volume covers many of the formation processes, environmental and cultural, that act on assemblages of animal remains, and discusses techniques for identifying those processes at work.

Miksicek, C. H. 1987. Formation Processes of the Archaeobotanical Record, in (M. B. Schiffer, ed.) *Advances in Archaeological Method and Theory,* 10: 211–47. San Diego: Academic Press.
This paper on plant taphonomy synthesises information on natural and environmental processes that affect preservation of food plants, wood and charcoal, fibre, pollen, phytoliths (plant crystals) and coprolites (fossil faeces) in archaeological deposits. The impacts of different sampling and recovery techniques are also considered.

Schiffer, M. B. 1996. *Formation Processes of the Archaeological Record.* Salt Lake City: University of Utah Press.
This volume is the single most comprehensive treatment of archaeological formation processes available, documenting and describing a wide range of cultural and natural environmental formation processes and their potential impacts on archaeological remains. Theory, methods and case studies are presented in detail.

Skibo, J. M. 1992. *Pottery Function: A Use-Alteration Perspective.* New York: Plenum Press.
This seminal work on the formation processes of ceramic assemblages discusses the organic residues and patterns of abrasion left on ceramic cooking vessels as a result of use activities. Skibo's experimental and ethnoarchaeological research provides techniques for determining what kinds of food prehistoric ceramic vessels were used to cook, and what cooking methods were employed.

Walker, W. H. 1995. Ceremonial Trash?, pp. 67–79 in (J. M. Skibo, W. H. Walker, and A. E. Nielsen, eds) *Expanding Archaeology.* Salt Lake City: University of Utah Press.
Walker's ethnoarchaeological study of ritual behaviour details the object histories of artefacts used in modern-day religious rituals, with particular attention to how and where these objects are discarded. This work provides suggestions for identifying ritual formation processes at work that contributed to the archaeological record.

Wood, W. R. and Johnson, D. L. 1978. A Survey of Disturbance Processes in Archaeological Site Formation, in (M. B. Schiffer, ed.) *Advances in Archaeological Method and Theory,* 1: 315–81. New York: Academic Press; reprinted in (M. B. Schiffer, ed., 1982) *Advances in Archaeological Method and Theory, Selections for Students from Volumes 1 through 4,* New York: Academic Press.
This article is a detailed catalogue of natural soil-disturbance processes that can cause artefacts to be moved around in the ground after deposition, and of other

distortion processes that can lead to spurious inferences about the past. The authors draw data from a number of outside fields, especially geology.

Further reading

Binford, L. R. 1978. Dimensional Analysis of Behavior and Site Structure: Learning from an Eskimo Hunting Stand. *American Antiquity* 43: 330–61; reprinted in (L. R. Binford, 1983) *Working at Archaeology*. New York: Academic Press.

—— 1980. Willow Smoke and Dogs' Tails: Hunter-Gatherer Settlement Systems and Archaeological Site Formation. *American Antiquity* 45: 4–20; reprinted in (L. R. Binford, 1983) *Working at Archaeology*. New York: Academic Press.

Brain, C. K. 1981. *The Hunters or the Hunted? An Introduction to African Cave Taphonomy*. Chicago: University of Chicago Press.

Cameron, C. M. and Tomka, S. A. (eds) 1993. *Abandonment of Settlements and Regions: Ethnoarchaeological and Archaeological Approaches*. Cambridge: Cambridge University Press.

Inomata, T. and Webb, R. W. (eds) 2003. *The Archaeology of Settlement Abandonment in Middle America*. Salt Lake City: University of Utah Press.

Schiffer, M. B. 1983. Toward the Identification of Formation Processes. *American Antiquity* 48: 675–706; reprinted in (M. B. Schiffer, 1995) *Behavioral Archaeology: First Principles*. Salt Lake City: University of Utah Press.

—— 1985. Is there a 'Pompeii' Premise in Archaeology? *Journal of Anthropological Research* 41: 18–41; reprinted in (M. B. Schiffer, 1995) *Behavioral Archaeology: First Principles*. Salt Lake City: University of Utah Press.

Schiffer, M. B., Downing, T. E. and McCarthy, M. 1981. Waste Not, Want Not: An Ethnoarchaeological Study of Reuse in Tucson, Arizona, pp. 68–86 in (R. A. Gould and M. B. Schiffer, eds) *Modern Material Culture: The Archaeology of Us*. New York: Academic Press; reprinted in (M. B. Schiffer, 1995) *Behavioral Archaeology: First Principles*. Salt Lake City: University of Utah Press.

Stiner, M. C. 1994. *Honor among Thieves: A Zooarchaeological Study of Neanderthal Ecology*. Princeton: Princeton University Press.

Walker, W. H. 1998. Where are the Witches of Prehistory? *Journal of Archaeological Method and Theory* 5: 245–308.

VINCENT M. LAMOTTA AND MICHAEL B. SCHIFFER

GENDER ARCHAEOLOGY

The archaeology of gender is the study of the roles, activities, ideologies and identities of men and women, and the differences between them. This topic is important to counteract several previous tendencies. These include perceiving everything in archaeology through the eyes of men (this is called androcentrism), understanding women only in biological roles such as mother and sexual partner, and describing the differences between men and women as polar opposites.

It should be clear that the idea of gender differences is not the same as oppositions. While it is perceived in some cultures, for example, that men are stronger than women, there are probably none where all men are stronger than all women (but there are cultures in which women are believed to be stronger than men). Thus, the archaeology of gender was created to balance archaeological interest in men and women by directing as much attention to women's activities as to men's, to demonstrate that women are not the same in all cultures and that therefore their activities are of interest for comparative studies, and to help make archaeology into a discipline that concerns people, rather than merely artefacts.

The need for an anthropology of gender became clear with the development of the world-wide Women's Movement, but the idea of an archaeology of gender was slower to take hold. The concept was fuelled by increasing numbers of women archaeologists, who saw that their own access to training, jobs and promotions was not equal to that of their male peers. In the process of trying to understand the situation and searching for ways to obtain equity in these issues, some women began to question the way that women of the past were ignored or trivialised in archaeological reports, or lumped all together into an undifferentiated mass.

Although the topic of gender in archaeology was not taken seriously at first by archaeologists as a whole, some related fields tackled gendered topics. Women who studied fossils of early humans contested the 'Man the Hunter' model of the creation of humanity by proposing 'Woman the Gatherer'. Adrienne Zihlman and Nancy Tanner, both at the University of California at Santa Cruz, developed this line of research as early as the 1970s. However, they did not focus on archaeology as much as on human fossils. The first book on women in the ancient Mediterranean world was by a classicist and art historian, Sarah Pomeroy (*Goddess, Whores, Wives, and Slaves*, 1975). Her data included myths, documents, painted images and statues, but not archaeological sites as such. Historic archaeologists, with a variety of written material such as diaries, wills and deeds, along with artefacts and features, had the tools to discuss gender issues as soon as the topic was on the table. The American historical archaeologist Suzanne Spencer-Wood organised the first session on gender at a historic archaeology meeting in 1986. Women in prehistoric archaeology, with neither images nor texts to work with, did not immediately follow suit.

Stirrings of interest in gender in prehistoric archaeology began to be perceptible as early as the 1970s in Europe, the Americas and

Australia. The earliest meeting organised to focus attention on women as subjects of archaeology took place in Norway in 1979, and was later published in 1987 under the title 'Were They All Men?' Focusing on the question of the organisation of archaeological practice, Joan Gero and Alison Wylie published papers in 1983 in a departmental publication that was not widely advertised, but influential nevertheless. In May 1991 women in Germany founded an association and a newsletter, *Netzwerk der Archaeologishe Arbeitende Frauen* (which is still active).

The first published article by prehistoric archaeologists was co-authored by Margaret Conkey, at the University of California at Berkeley, and Janet Spector, at the University of Minnesota. Between them they represented both New World and Old World Archaeology, which added strength to their argument. This article explains why the archaeology of gender is an important topic, and provides examples of how attention to gender without androcentrism would have improved the published conclusions about several well-known sites.

Meetings and conferences proliferated. Joan Gero and Margaret Conkey organised an invitational conference, which resulted in *Engendering Archaeology: Women in Prehistory*. At about the same time Margaret Ehrenberg, a European archaeologist, published *Women in Prehistory*, using all the then available evidence, but with most of her data coming from European archaeology. The largest group of archaeologists interested in gender came together at the Chacmool Conference of 1989, in Calgary, Canada. The announcement of the gender theme produced an outpouring of papers from women in the English-speaking world. It was published in 1991 as *The Archaeology of Gender*. Cheryl Claassen, an archaeologist specialising in the American southeast, organised the first Boone Conference in 1992, and others in subsequent years. This conference continues as the biennial *Gender in Archaeology Conference*, meeting at various universities around the USA. It is often attended by archaeologists from other countries. The same is true of the Australian *Women in Archaeology* conferences. The Theoretical Archaeology Group in the UK heard papers on gender in archaeology in the 1980s.

The number of papers on gender in archaeology was multiplying rapidly. Archaeology students at the University of Michigan demanded a class on the topic, which they used to review all the gender publications they could find. These insightful student reviews were published in 1993 as *A Gendered Past: A Critical Bibliography of Gender in Archaeology*. Still, publications on gender were almost entirely found in proceedings of gender conferences. They were avidly read by students (mostly women) and those who saw the potential of the topic, but they did not reach most of the readers of established journals. The journal KAN (*Kvinner in Archaeologi*, Women in Archaeology) was published in Norway as the first journal devoted to the archaeology of gender. It is now published in English to reach a wider audience. The British journal *Antiquity* was more responsive than American journals to gender-related papers from the 1990s onward.

Edited regional books on archaeology and gender began to appear in the 1990s, including Africa, Italy, Mesoamerica and various parts of North America. Topical books on gender also appeared, for example with a focus on power or technology. Monographs began appearing in the 1990s. *Gender in Archaeology, Analyzing Power and Prestige* (Nelson 1997) makes the point that the treatment of women in archaeology and learning about women in the past are intertwined in practice if not in theory. Roberta Gilchrist published *Gender and Archaeology, Contesting the Past* in 1999, using her work on women in medieval cloisters as an extended example. Marie Louise Sørensen, in *Gender Archaeology* (1999) took the perspective of material culture as a way into discussing gender and archaeology. Since then the number of books on gender in archaeology has at least doubled, with series on the topic supported by two academic presses.

At first it was not clear whether the topic should be adding women to archaeological understandings of the past, or whether the relationship between women and men should become the main focus of attention: that is, whether women or gender should be the main topic. Both strategies have been followed, but for strategic as well as theoretical reasons the focus became gender in the past. Roberta Gilchrist noted that three strands could be teased apart: a feminist thread which exposed inequities for women archaeologists, a thread which followed women archaeologists of the past, and one that worked to include women in the archaeology of past societies. All three threads are still of interest, but it is the last that is the most directly relevant to the archaeology of gender.

The relationship between gender and sex was drawn from other social sciences. Gender was the word chosen to express social constructions of men and women, and sex used for biological differences. Therefore gender was considered to reflect sex: two sexes, two genders. But it has become commonplace to note that other genders have been recognised by many societies. Attempts to discover other genders by means of archaeology have been increasing, especially in America, where 'Two Spirits' are known ethnographically. Other new avenues to gender in archaeology include the archaeology of childhood, the archaeology of sexuality, and a focus on bodies. Not all work on these topics is about gender, but much of it is related. Childhood can be studied as the time when people learn about the gender roles they are expected to follow and the activities and attitudes that define their gender. Sexuality, too, leaves material remains for the archaeologist. Human bodies are sexed, so sexuality often plays into an understanding of gender, especially the fact that restrictions on sexuality are often different for women and men.

Some archaeologists have emphasised gender as an element of personal identity. They consider how people become gendered, how gender affects their possibilities and life choices within a particular culture, and the changes that may occur in perceived gender as a person ages. Do some cultures only emphasise gender during the years of young adulthood? Do old women have more freedom to express themselves than young women in some cultures? Even within one group of people, there may be differences in the way that gender is expressed, depending on race, or work, or social status. The study of gender has thus become increasingly complex.

Two examples provide a brief view of the value of focusing on gender. Julia Hendon's work on the Late Classic Maya studies households. Rather than treating the domestic group as homogeneous, she shows that with different genders, ages and statuses, the people within the household may have different goals. In analysing relationships between households and the state, Hendon demonstrates that political action can be informal as well as formal, and that both men and women have active roles in mediating between household and state. Janet Levy considers metals and symbols in Bronze Age Denmark, noting differences by gender in both the types of metal artefacts used and the places that the artefacts were deposited. Gender differences, she finds, are an important aspect of social complexity in this case.

Gender in archaeology has had a mixed impact on archaeological methods and theories, although its influence is growing. It fits well with the methods and aims of post-processual archaeology (see p. 207), and generally has been welcomed in Europe. Processual archaeology (see p. 212) has been less interested in gender, possibly because gender and other social variables simply do not fit into its agenda, which has tended to treat whole cultures as adaptive, rather than considering the constituent parts as factions with possibly competing or incompatible goals. Even with some adamant processualists, however, gender has made inroads. Michelle Hegmon, an archaeologist who works in the American southwest, lists gender among other topics that she calls 'processual-plus'. On the whole, gender in archaeology is a topic that changes all perspectives on archaeology.

Suggested reading

Bacus, E. A., Barker, A., Bonevish, J. D., Dunavan, S. L., Fitzhugh, J. B., Gold, D. L., Goldman-Finn, N. S., Griffin, W. and Mudar, K. 1993. *A Gendered Past: A Critical Bibliography of Gender in Archaeology.* Ann Arbor: University of Michigan Museum of Anthropology.
For a quick exposure to all the early gender literature, this book is invaluable. It reveals both the unevenness in quality of these early attempts, and the broad variety of topics that were tackled.

Conkey, M. W. and Spector, J. 1984. Archaeology and the Study of Gender. *Advances in Archaeological Method and Theory* 7: 1–38.
This is the classic beginning of a serious interest in gender in archaeology. It outlines the problems that are to be addressed, and suggests ways of achieving the goals.

Gero, J. and Conkey, M. W. (eds) 1991. *Engendering Archaeology: Women and Prehistory.* Oxford: Blackwell.
The papers in this book define gender as a useful tool for examining the past. Most of them have become classics.

Gilchrist, R. 1999. *Gender and Archaeology: Contesting the Past.* London: Routledge.
A British perspective on gender in archaeology, with an extended example using her own work on medieval women.

Joyce, R. 2000. *Gender and Power in Prehispanic Mesoamerica.* Austin: University of Texas Press.
A richly textured book that considers gender identity through various life stages.

Nelson, S. M. 1997. *Gender in Archaeology: Analyzing Power and Prestige.* Walnut Creek, Calif.: AltaMira Press.
Includes the history of gender archaeology, anthropological topics, and how they have been approached with archaeological data.

Sørensen, M. L. S. 1999. *Gender Archaeology.* Cambridge: Polity Press.
Focusing on material culture, this book demonstrates how objects become gendered.

Wylie, A. 1991. Gender Theory and the Archaeological Record: Why is there No Archaeology of Gender? pp. 31–54 in (J. M. Gero and M. W. Conkey, eds) *Engendering Archaeology: Women and Prehistory.* Oxford: Blackwell.
This paper set the philosophical and theoretical standard for gender in archaeology.

Further reading

Arnold, B. and Wicker, N. (eds) 2001. *Gender and the Archaeology of Death.* Walnut Creek, Calif.: AltaMira Press.
Gilchrist, R. 1991. Women's Archaeology? Political Feminism, Gender Theory, and Historical Revision. *Antiquity* 65: 495–501.

Hegmon, M. 2003. Setting Theoretical Egos Aside: Issues and Theory in North American Archaeology. *American Antiquity* 68 (2): 214–43.

Hendon, J. 1996. Archaeological Approaches to the Organization of Domestic Labor: Household Practices and Domestic Relations. *Annual Review of Anthropology* 25: 45–62.

Kent, S. 1998. *Gender in African Prehistory.* Walnut Creek, Calif.: AltaMira Press.

Levy, J. E. 1999. Metals, Symbols and Society in Bronze Age Denmark, in (J. E. Robb, ed.) *Material Symbols: Culture and Economy in Prehistory.* Carbondale: Center for Archaeological Investigations.

Nelson, S. M. and Rosen-Ayalon, M. (eds) 2002. *In Pursuit of Gender: Worldwide Archaeological Approaches.* Walnut Creek, Calif;: AltaMira Press.

Whitehouse, R. (ed.) 1996. *Gender and Italian Archaeology: Challenging the Stereotypes.* Vol. 7, Accordia Specialist Studies on Italy. London: Accordia Research Institute, University of London.

SARAH MILLEDGE NELSON

HABITUS

The concept of *habitus* originates in the work of Pierre Bourdieu (1930–2002), one of the pre-eminent French social theorists working in the late twentieth century. We need not suppose that the concept of habitus is particularly easy to understand, but nonetheless it would be wrong to avoid the challenge of such an understanding by offering, in its place, a definition. Definitions give the image of a finished product, something clear-cut that we can take away and use in our own work, a 'concept' for archaeology. But this would miss the point of Bourdieu's work and of an idea whose real strength is to draw our attention to issues that require our closer attention and more detailed work. If habitus is a concept for archaeology, then it is such not because archaeology will be improved as a result of its application, but because the issues that it raises must be addressed before archaeology can contribute more fully to the historical understanding of the study of humanity.

What are these issues? Bourdieu introduced the idea of habitus in an attempt to identify a quality of, or a resource that facilitates, human action. The implication is that there are certain qualities that are specific to human action and, as such, presumably distinguish it from animal behaviour. We would therefore not expect to apply the concept of habitus to the rest of nature. We may have little initial difficulty in accepting this possibility – after all, human consciousness, the deployment of complex systems of communication, and the cultural, ethnic and racial diversity of humanity all involve distinctions in action of various kinds, and this considerable diversity of humanity would seem to mark out the distinctiveness of the human species within the animal kingdom. However, these observations alone do not give much indication as to how we might grasp the mechanisms that generate the particularity of human diversity. Perhaps it is the structure of the human brain, or the human ability to speak, or a combination of these and other factors. Whatever we might propose at this stage, it is generally accepted that the conditions from which human diversity arises are a product both of history and of our biology. For example numerous studies have attempted to demonstrate the ways the evolution of the brain has given rise to a biological facility whose structure can generate cultural concepts. In other words, since Darwin, humanity has been taken to be the product of nature and of evolution. However, we must also accept that the distinguishing characteristics of humanity are now sustained historically through mechanisms that appear to be distinct from nature, namely social institutions and cultural conventions.

There is therefore a problem in maintaining that the two sides of the dualism of nature:culture comprise independent entities. The historical conditions that gave rise to culture must have operated through the processes that gave rise to nature. This recalls other similarly problematic dualisms such as that between social structure and human agency. In this case social institutions (structure) are maintained by the actions of individuals (agency), although the routines displayed by individuals appear to be structured by social conventions and rules (see p. 240). The problem is often avoided by assuming that one side of the dualism can be reduced to the other: in other words, that culture can be reduced to nature and that agency can be reduced to social structures. Such a reductionism is difficult to maintain: human agency works as a set of cultural practices (see p. 3) and it is these that bring social structures into being. And if culture is a product of nature then it is unlikely to be a uniquely human attribute.

We may now begin to approach the concept of habitus. Bourdieu brings the concept to bear upon the problems raised by the dualisms of nature:culture and social structure:human agency. The effectiveness of introducing the concept is that it lays the groundwork for rendering this kind of dualistic thinking and the circularities to which it leads irrelevant. It does this by reminding us that humanity is physically embodied, that agency works through the body, and that, although embodiment is fundamental as a product of nature and a bearer of culture, it cannot be easily accommodated by these dualisms.

Various attempts have been made to transcend approaches that establish nature:culture, and social structure:human agency as dualisms operating between binary opposites. One such has been Giddens' theory of structuration that recasts the relationship between human agency and social institutions into a single duality that drives the historical process (structuration). Bourdieu's concept of habitus approaches the problem of dualistic thinking from a slightly different perspective. Despite Bourdieu's notoriously convoluted language, habitus is far less abstract than the concepts employed by Giddens because it concerns itself empirically with the ways the embodied actions of people cope with daily practicalities. On the face of it, Bourdieu's observation that human presence and human actions are embodied seems to state the stunningly obvious, but we should note that the body has only recently become a focus for sociological and anthropological study and, with certain notable exceptions, hardly features at all as an archaeological concern, unless of course it occurs as the object in funerary archaeology.

If we are to develop the issue of embodiment in a way that is helpful, we are going to have to do more than propose that the body has qualities that are natural/biological and qualities that are cultural/social. This will achieve nothing because it leaves the opposing natural:cultural categories intact and this in turn leads to the irresolvable question of whether nature or culture are, under certain conditions, determinate of the body's actions. Such questions often locate the natural qualities in the biological functioning of the body, and the social qualities in various cultural characteristics that are learnt or are 'inscribed' upon the body. This neat distinction between internal biology and external society leaves us with a seemingly irresolvable dilemma regarding the division between brain (biological) and mind (cultural), also often expressed as a mind:body dichotomy. But notice again how the position of the body is always left suspended between inner drives and external constraints.

The challenge of avoiding the dichotomy, therefore, impacts directly upon our assumptions first that human action can be characterised as an issue of internal motivation or external stimulation, and second that the body can be conceived as a vessel or container. Bourdieu directs our attention towards qualities in human action that include the disposition to act in certain ways without the obedience to rules, and where the dispositions that organise practices do not involve conscious intentions. This all sounds remarkably unhelpful until we notice that what he aims to avoid, among other things, is to explain the regularity of human practices in terms of external and abstract determinates (rules) and inner conscious motivations directed to intended outcomes. This is not to deny that regulations make demands of humans and that people consciously formulate plans to achieve certain things, but they do all these in the context of a habitus that is lived as an embodied existence. We might now assume that reference to unconscious embodied practice as a feature of this habitus marks a return to a biological determinacy, a kind of primitive, non-cultural motivation that is carried by the biological body. This is not the case, as the examples Bourdieu uses make clear. The body makes its appearance as expressive of values in the ways it moves and engages with others; such values express the proud and the haughty, the subservient and passive, the elegant and spiritual, the outcast and abused. Participants share these values which express power operating between people, and the power a person has to make themselves seen and heard. These are the actions of becoming whom one is in the way one moves through, and responds to, the world and to others around us. They are the inflections by which the body is not only known but by which it comes to know of itself. It is the building of a security of knowing how to occupy the world of things and people, knowing implicitly what is possible. This security is emotional, a question of well-being, as well as a question of rights and of pride. And it is in his failure to fully develop the emotional aspects of solidarity and belonging that Bourdieu fails to fully exploit the strength of his own argument.

Archaeologists can only study the past by means of surviving material, and it is perhaps understandable that the primary archaeological concern has been to explain the creation of the archaeological record by reference to past human actions. It would, however, be futile to claim that habitus leaves an unambiguous imprint upon the archaeological record. Habitus marks out a way of being; it is not expressed in the mechanical relationship between an action and its material consequence, nor is it the symbolic representation of an idea. Habitus is how people enter the world, where staking a claim upon their place in the world is also staking a claim upon their identity. The securities that this involves are fundamental to the point of being 'natural', as in 'it is natural for her to act in that way'. The naturalisation of core values links people to the material world around them: it is as fundamental as knowing when to stand aside or where to sit, or how to admire a work of art, or how to inflect the body towards an altar. These subtleties make sense in the contexts of everyday life. For archaeology, the contexts in which such lives are lived are the material contexts that we investigate. The questions that we might now ask would concern how such primary values, ranging between honour and debasement, trust and uncertainty, and the security of knowing how to live, were grounded upon the material references that occur in the conditions that we investigate.

Suggested reading

Bourdieu, P. 1990. *The Logic of Practice*. Cambridge: Polity Press.
Certainly not an easy text but essential to gain a grasp of Bourdieu's way of working around the issues of human practice.

Calhoun, C., LiPuma, E. and Postone, M. 1993. *Bourdieu: Critical Perspectives*. Cambridge: Polity Press.
A collection of well-written essays that help to unpack and to evaluate Bourdieu's writings.

Hamilakis, Y., Pluciennik, M. and Tarlow, S. (eds) 2002. *Thinking Through the Body: Archaeologies of Corporeality*. New York: Kluwer Academic.
A collection of archaeological studies that deal critically with the issues of embodiment and provide a guide to current archaeological thinking.

Jenkins, R. 2002. *Pierre Bourdieu*, revised edn. London: Routledge.
A reader-friendly and critical account of Bourdieu's work.

Jones, S. 1997. *The Archaeology of Ethnicity: Constructing Identities in the Past and Present*. London: Routledge.
An archaeological treatment of identity that draws upon the concept of habitus and Bourdieu's work more generally.

Shilling, C. 1993. *The Body and Social Theory*. London: Sage Publications.
A clear and concise account of the development of sociological approaches to human embodiment.

JOHN C. BARRETT

HISTORICAL ARCHAEOLOGY AND TEXT

Historical archaeology is defined here as the archaeology of all societies with written records, including non-literate peoples recorded by their literate neighbours. Some authors define the subject more narrowly, as the archaeology of the past 500 years, especially in relation to western European colonial expansion and its impact. The broader definition includes subjects usually described and studied separately within a specific area/period subject division, such as Egyptology, ancient China, biblical or classical archaeology. General themes are the role of literacy, the nature of the written and material record, and the relationship between them, all of which have varied considerably across time and space and within and between different societies.

Writing was first invented in Mesopotamia about 5,000 years ago, and appears in Egypt not long afterwards. It seems to have developed independently in China, where the earliest texts known are those inscribed on oracle bones from about 1200 BC, and also in pre-Columbian America. It is difficult to be precise about dates of origin, since clearly recognisable scripts must have emerged from less easily identifiable earlier symbols. We cannot be sure the earliest surviving texts are the earliest written nor that what we have is a representative sample of the uses to which writing was put in ancient societies. The texts which have been preserved on durable media such as stone, metal or baked clay include a high proportion of official documents. Writing was created by and for the elite, who used it for administration, legal transactions, religion and propaganda. In later periods informal and personal texts were often written on perishable materials such as wood, papyrus or paper, which may also have existed in earlier periods.

Historical archaeology has come to be a separate subject only since the recognition in the mid-nineteenth century of the antiquity of man (*see* p. 7). Before then it had been assumed by Europeans that human existence began with the Creation, as described in the Bible, at a date calculated by Archbishop Ussher of Armagh (1581–1656) as 4004 BC. All archaeological evidence could therefore come only from the period of recorded history, and all archaeology by definition was historical archaeology. Early investigations of the past were driven by interest in recorded people or events. As early as the sixth century BC a Babylonian king uncovered and restored a temple built by his predecessors, and classical historians and ethnographers described monuments and objects with reference to recorded historical or mythological figures. In medieval Europe, saints' relics were sought to promote cults, and rulers deployed Roman material culture to present themselves in an imperial guise. As early as the eleventh century in China critical comparisons were made between written records and artefacts, but in Europe antiquarians began to record and describe ancient monuments in a more systematic way only in the sixteenth and seventeenth centuries. They attributed them to recorded peoples, hence the association of Stonehenge by William Stukeley (1687–1765) with the Druids.

The study of classical art and monuments was part of the education of European aristocracy from the Renaissance, while interest in ancient Egypt was encouraged by Napoleon's expedition there, especially the discovery of the Rosetta Stone in 1799, which allowed decipherment of hieroglyphic texts. Major achievements in classical and biblical archaeology in the nineteenth century included the excavations of Layard at Nineveh and Schliemann at Troy. Finds from these sites came to European museums to impress the public with the reality of the ancient world at the same time that the recognition of the existence of humans long before the invention of writing established a new subject, prehistory.

Prehistory includes the whole time-span of human existence, and addresses fundamental questions about human evolution and the emergence of human society. It is within prehistory that archaeologists play the key role, developing ways of interpreting the material record without reference to written texts. Historical archaeology, by contrast, co-exists with documentary history, to which it often seems subordinate. Even an outline of historical events, let alone the complex detailed body of written sources available for more recent centuries, can appear to make archaeological theory unnecessary, and reduce material evidence to a source of illustrations, rather than providing, as it should, an independent basis for interpretation. Attempts to use archaeology as a substitute for political narrative are often misleading because archaeological evidence is seldom susceptible to interpretation in terms of specific events. Such attempts raise false expectations among historians, who are then disappointed that archaeological evidence has not given the answers to the questions they are asking.

Historical archaeology has also suffered in recent years because in all parts of the world it has been put to political use: the peoples and dynasties of the earliest written sources are equated with material culture of apparently contemporary date, and the distribution and chronology of that material are then used as a proxy for the historical people, and often as justification for current political claims. This has led to a relationship with nationalism, conservative tradition and authoritarian governments to which most modern archaeologists are unsympathetic. Attempts to deconstruct these relationships pose the most difficult – and most rewarding – challenge for historical archaeologists today.

The lines between history, archaeology and prehistory should not, however, be drawn too sharply. The distinction between writing and other forms of communication is not always clear. Precise messages can be conveyed by symbols, by narrative pictures or by any form of visual representation. Numerical and calendrical notations may have been recorded as early as the Palaeolithic, and could be embodied in the form of some monuments. In a society with limited literacy, the meaning of any text would depend on form and context as much as content. Records of the deeds and ancestry of ruling dynasties were inscribed on large monuments visible to all. The Bible was ornamented with gold leaf and intricate patterns to show the value of the Word of God. The boundary between literacy and orality can be fluid: a Maya text, an Anglo–Saxon genealogy or the biblical pictures on the walls of a medieval church were the inspiration for the stories and sermons of the priests or poets, who interpreted them to the wider audience who could not read for themselves. All documents, even those on computer screens, are themselves a part of material culture and evidence of the technology and organisational systems of the societies which create them – and so a part of the subject matter of archaeology.

Archaeology can throw light on aspects of society which documents did not record, either because they were taken for granted or because they did not seem important to those in control of society. To understand a text which describes a city, an army or even a house we need to know what was in the mind of the writer when he used those terms. Material culture can allow access to the non–elite majority of society, and the everyday life even of the elite. It complements the written record even in areas where documents seem to dominate. Military historians have long understood that replaying a battle involves putting it back into its original terrain, and the same is true of all events and processes: context is essential.

Archaeologists share the tendency to give priority to the written word, because it is a permanent version of speech, one of the characteristics we believe define us as human. Yet we all constantly receive and translate non–verbal messages, from facial expressions and clothes to shapes of buildings or cars and TV advertisements. Both written and material records survive and are transmitted in fragments which are subject to interpretation, and writing can only be meaningfully read within the context of its original purpose. Speech and writing are crucial parts of human existence, but so is our material environment and our use of it, now and in the past. The two are inextricably connected and the evidence of both, where they exist, should be studied together. That is the role of historical archaeology.

Suggested reading

Andren, A. 1998. *Between Artefacts and Texts. Historical Archaeology in Global Perspective.* New York and London: Plenum.
An account of the development of historical archaeology in several parts of the world. Comprehensive introduction, extensive bibliography.

Johnson, M. 1999. Archaeology and History, Chapter 10, pp. 149–61 in (M. Johnson) *Archaeological Theory.* Oxford: Blackwell.
Concise discussion of key issues in chapter of good textbook.

Moreland, J. 2001. *Archaeology and Text.* London: Duckworth.
Readable and stimulating discussion, focusing especially on medieval Britain and Europe

Schnapp, A. 1996. *The Discovery of the Past.* London: British Museum Press.
Account of the prehistory of archaeology, from Babylon to the nineteenth century. Lavishly illustrated with striking pictures from manuscripts and early printed books.

Further reading

Beaudry, M. (ed.) 1988. *Documentary Archaeology in the New World.* New Directions in Archaeology. Cambridge: Cambridge University Press.
Hooker, J. T. (ed.) 1990. *Reading the Past: Ancient Writing from Cuneiform to the Alphabet.* London: British Museum Press.
Marcus, J. 1995. Writing, Literacy and Performance in the New and Old Worlds. *Cambridge Archaeological Journal* 5: 325–31.
International Journal of Historical Archaeology. New York and London: Plenum.

CATHERINE HILLS

HOLISTIC/CONTEXTUAL ARCHAEOLOGY

Holistic archaeology, as its name suggests, involves a broad and inclusive approach to archaeological research. Articulated in a series of publications by American archaeologists Joyce Marcus and Kent Flannery since the 1970s, holistic archaeology involves the comprehensive investigation of all aspects of human societies, from ecological relationships and economy, to social organisation and politics, to art and ideology. The theory and methods of holistic archaeology are particularly suited to the work of anthropological archaeologists and especially those interested in complex societies (such as the Olmec, Maya, Aztec, Moche or Inca) for which the archaeological record is rich and complex. As a wide-ranging investigation of different phenomena and their interrelationships, holistic archaeology also encompasses diverse methods and sources, including ethnography, ethnohistory and contextual archaeology.

During the 1960s, as processual archaeology emerged (*see* p. 212), archaeologists developed ecological models and emphasised the reconstruction of past environments using scientific techniques. In line with cultural evolutionary theory (*see* p. 49), these archaeologists saw societies as adaptive systems; innovations in technology that facilitated the production of a surplus were given primary emphasis in explanations for societal change. Changes in other spheres of life, from social institutions to religion and ideology, were of interest to these scholars, although for many they were epiphenomenal – i.e. of secondary importance. This bias, coupled with the difficulties inherent in studying symbols and their meanings in the archaeological record, meant that the study of religion or art was often relegated to the sidelines or left entirely to researchers in other disciplines such as art history.

In developing an alternative model of cultural evolution, Flannery (1972) contested the notion that religion, ritual or art was epiphenomenal. Instead, he argued that, as societies grew larger and more complex, the processing of information (and communication) was as critical for the functioning of society as the production of food and other resources. Flannery believed that human societies depended critically upon ritual activities and socio-political institutions that managed and regulated social relations and monitored human use of the natural environment. In developing this argument, Flannery was influenced by his colleague, anthropologist Roy Rappaport (1971), who had highlighted the central role of ritual in small-scale societies. Rappaport showed that economic, social and political interaction was governed by ritual, arguing further that the content as well as the occurrence of ritual carried information. Rituals tied to the agricultural cycle signalled the times for planting or harvesting; ritual feasts, in turn, allowed the redistribution of surplus while facilitating political goals such as alliance-building or mediation of disputes. Feasts could also foster solidarity within a group to facilitate cooperative activities.

Flannery used these insights to develop a 'multivariate' model for the origins of the state. He argued that since ritual, religion and ideology were essential for regulation and co-ordination, they should be given equal weight with ecological variables in models of cultural evolution. As societies grew larger and more complex, decision-making processes became more hierarchical, organised under a central authority. Rejecting models that sought to identify a single 'prime-mover' (such as the managerial requirements of irrigation networks or population growth), Flannery insisted that states emerged through complex interactions of multiple variables, from technology and the economy to social institutions and the symbolic.

Building upon these theoretical foundations, holistic archaeology helped to bridge an intellectual divide that has often separated anthropological archaeologists (with interests in subsistence and ecology) from humanist scholars (whose emphasis is on art, symbolic systems or religion). This divide has been particularly evident in the Americas, where complex societies have received sustained attention from processual archaeologists at the same time that their art and iconography has fascinated art historians. Working to overcome this split in the Valley of Oaxaca (Mexico), Marcus and Flannery (1996) have conducted a comprehensive, long-term study of Zapotec civilisation using a holistic approach.

A holistic approach involves archaeological study conducted with careful reference to information from the related disciplines of ethnohistory and ethnography wherever possible. As with other New World societies, scholarship on the Zapotecs includes ethnohistory, the study of sources from the Spanish colonial period. These documents, written or commissioned by Spanish missionaries and administrators during the sixteenth and seventeenth centuries, record detailed information about indigenous societies and aspects of their ritual practices, beliefs and ideology. Although the Spaniards' main objective was the eradication of these traditions, the details in the accounts are invaluable to archaeologists. There is also, in Oaxaca, an opportunity to learn from Zapotec writing, which appears on numerous monuments erected by elites to legitimate their claims to power (Marcus 1992).

Ethnography, the study of contemporary peoples, is another source used widely in conjunction with a holistic approach in the Americas. Analogies drawn from contemporary societies are most effective in regions where there is strong evidence for cultural continuity, as for example when contemporary peoples share an ethnic identity or language with past inhabitants of the region. Because the Valley of Oaxaca has such a record, ethnographic data allow use of the direct historical approach, which involves working back in time from the present to the past, with great care taken to establish (rather than assume) cultural continuity. Data from ethnohistory are also used as part of the direct historical approach. In using analogies, researchers must be prepared to find discrepancies – evidence of change in some institutions and continuity in others. Since religion and ritual are often conservative or resistant to change, however, they may be especially suited to analysis using the direct historical approach.

While holistic archaeology encourages the use of ethnohistoric and ethnographic evidence, it also offers a clear methodology – called contextual archaeology – for the study of archaeological remains. This approach was presented in one chapter of Flannery's (1976) edited volume, *The Early Mesoamerican Village*. In this book, processual archaeologists explored new techniques of statistical and spatial analysis using data from Formative Period (1500 BC to AD 100) villages in Mesoamerica. The book itself – encompassing analyses from household to community to region and covering topics ranging from agriculture to ritual – exemplified a holistic approach. Flannery's discussion of contextual archaeology, in turn, formulated a rigorous and systematic approach to interpretation of excavated materials.

In a contextual analysis, a researcher asks about an artefact's context (e.g. its location within the site and its associations with other artefacts), with the goal of inferring the nature of the human behaviour or activity that led to the artefact being deposited there. Contextual archaeology is concerned, therefore, not only with single artefacts, but also with the associations among artefacts. Researchers are also interested in whether some artefacts are typically found together or in association with features (such as near a hearth or in a cache), and in their overall frequencies across a site or a region. To cite Flannery's example, if a figurine is found in all households, it may have been used in daily household rituals. Conversely, if a different figurine is found in only a single location, such as a temple, it probably had a role in more formal, community-wide rituals. Further clues to the nature and scale of public activities may be revealed by the designs of buildings (open to the public or restricted in access) and their location within the community.

Contextual archaeology also offers insights into social organisation and status differences. If objects are rare or valuable, concentrated in only a few households, then they may have been owned by elites who used them as symbols of status or social position. The general principle is that the context in which an artefact is found can help to answer questions about its function and the information that it communicated to members of a society. If one is interested in ritual, for example, the contextual approach leads one to ask: 'What information was this ritual feature or artefact designed to transmit?' (Flannery 1976: 333). Rituals must be regularly performed, and these performances leave traces in the archaeological record. Artefacts used in rituals, left behind in ritual settings, placed as offerings or discarded in trash heaps, may indicate where rituals took place, who participated and how often they were repeated.

Although elements of holistic archaeology have been criticised, many of its tenets are now taken for granted and its methods have been widely adopted throughout the world. Post-processual/interpretive archaeologists (*see* p. 207) object to a view of societies as adaptive systems, arguing that analysis at the system level leads archaeologists to ignore the individual. Others argue that studying the function of a ritual object or symbol means ignoring the meaning it had for the people who made or used it. Yet the holistic approach has had lasting effects on the practice of archaeology. Because it provides an integrated framework of theoretical principles and a robust set of methods, holistic archaeology has had – and continues to have – an enduring impact on archaeological research.

Suggested reading

Flannery, K. 1972. The Cultural Evolution of Civilizations. *Annual Review of Ecology and Systematics* 3: 399–426.
This article contains the argument for a 'multivariate' model for the origins of the state.

Flannery, K. (ed.) 1976. *The Early Mesoamerican Village*. New York: Academic Press.
A wide-ranging discussion of approaches and methods appropriate to holistic archaeology. Flannery's chapter, entitled 'Contextual Analysis of Ritual Paraphernalia from Formative Oaxaca' (pp. 333–45) presents the methodology of contextual archaeology in detail.

Flannery, K. V. and Marcus, J. 1983. *The Cloud People: Divergent Evolution of the Zapotec and Mixtec Civilizations*. New York: Academic Press.
An edited volume, more challenging for the general reader than *Zapotec Civilization* (see below), but contains detailed discussion of the data set in an explicitly comparative framework.

Marcus, J. 1992. *Mesoamerican Writing Systems*. Princeton: Princeton University Press.
A detailed analysis of writing systems in Mesoamerica, with chapters on Zapotec writing and the uses to which it was put by elites.

Marcus, J. and Flannery, K. V. 1994. Ancient Zapotec Ritual and Religion: An Application of the Direct Historical Approach, pp. 55–74 in (C. Renfrew and E. Zubrow, eds) *The Ancient Mind: Elements of Cognitive Archaeology*. Cambridge: Cambridge University Press.
This chapter presents a readable account of efforts to reconstruct Zapotec religion and its development through time, employing data from three sources: ethnography, ethnohistory and contextual archaeology.

Marcus, J. and Flannery, K. V. 1996. *Zapotec Civilization*. London: Thames and Hudson.
An up-to-date and richly illustrated account of the Zapotecs, showing the potential of the holistic approach in archaeology.

Rappaport, R. 1971. The Sacred in Human Evolution. *Annual Review of Ecology and Systematics* 2: 23–44.
Rappaport's initial statement of the role of ritual in human societies.

Further reading

Conrad, G. and Demarest, A. 1984. *Religion and Empire*. Cambridge: Cambridge University Press.

Flannery, K. V. and Marcus, J. 1976. Formative Oaxaca and the Zapotec Cosmos. *American Scientist* 64 (4): 374–83.

Jones, G. and Kautz, R. 1981. *The Transition to Statehood in the New World*. Cambridge: Cambridge University Press.

Rappaport, R. 1999. *Ritual and Religion in the Making of Humanity*. Cambridge: Cambridge University Press.

Trigger, B. 1998. *Sociocultural Evolution*. Oxford: Blackwell.

Willey, G. and Sabloff, J. 1993. *A History of American Archaeology*, 3rd edn. London: Thames and Hudson.

ELIZABETH DEMARRAIS

INDIGENOUS ARCHAEOLOGIES

Indigenous archaeology is a rather fuzzy category seen to consist of archaeology carried out by First Nations or First Peoples: that is, the displaced original inhabitants of North America, Australia, New Zealand or South America. However, some of the most interesting forms of archaeology are carried out by archaeologists (often of European descent) but in close collaboration with indigenous peoples and with people who have no formal archaeological training. The notion of indigenous archaeology, which I will critique as much as explain, overlaps with the more general issue of public participation in archaeology.

> In my language my name is Bine-si-ikwe, Thunderbird Woman. I am an Anishinabe, Leech Lake Reservation enrolee, and a member of the Minnesota Chippewa Tribe. I was taught that the Anishinabe people are the Keepers of the Earth, and that as an Anishinabe person, it is our responsibility to protect the water and land, and all things related. I also believe that I have a responsibility to preserve my cultural ways.

> (Kluth and Munnell 1997: 117)

The above quote is from a woman whose European name is Kathy Munnell, made in an article where she discusses the role of Native Americans in American archaeology and the uses that her people can make of archaeological data. Kathy concludes by saying that her grand-daughter is keen to become an archaeologist, and she can think of no one better to carry out archaeology in Anishinabe lands, as only a native person can accord the right levels of respect to local cultural materials but only a trained archaeologist has the full range of skills to find, excavate and interpret archaeological materials.

An important part of archaeology's origin myth is that the nineteenth-century origins of professional archaeology came about through battles between science and religion in which a scientific and non-biblical view of the past triumphed. It came as a shock to many archaeologists to be criticised in the later twentieth century by those of religious views, albeit non-Christian ones, such as Kathy Munnell whose attachment to her cultural ways was in large part spiritual. Initially at least, these discussions were seen as confrontational, harking back to debates between the nineteenth-century evolutionists and the church establishment. Such discussions took place at a time of change within archaeology and of important new forms of legislation giving First Peoples more legal control over their own sites and cultural property.

The most influential law was one passed in the US – the Native American Graves and Protection and Repatriation Act (Public Law 101–601, known generally as NAGPRA) in 1990. As the title of the Act indicates, the crucial points at issue are what, to Whites, might seem an overly specific issue, the right to dispose of human bones and bodies. Since NAGPRA, the legal basis for a repatriation claim of skeletal remains or certain classes of artefacts is cultural affiliation. This is defined in the act as 'a relationship of shared group identity that can be reasonably traced historically or prehistorically between a present-day Indian tribe or Native Hawaiian organisation, and an identifiable earlier group'. There are problems here of what constitutes groups in the present and the nature of their claims. Three groups are currently recognised as having claims: lineal descendants; tribal members, other individuals or groups who claim some degree of Native American heritage. Lineal descendants have a straightforward claim in law, showing the importance of genetic inheritance in these issues. NAGPRA allows that admissible evidence for cultural affiliation can be geographic, genealogical, biological, archaeological, anthropological, linguistic, folkloric and historic information. The effect of NAGPRA has been that all institutions receiving funds from the Federal government have had to inventory all Native American items in their holdings and make these inventories available to tribal groups (they are listed on a national NAGPRA database –

147

http://www.cast.uark.edu/other/nps/nagpra/nagpra.html) who can then request that culturally sensitive materials be returned to them, for keeping in tribal museums or other keeping places. The early arguments over NAGPRA were repeated in many parts of the world and were sharpest around the issue of the return of human remains. Physical anthropologists and archaeologists tended to claim that ancient human remains were of interest to all humanity as containing the story of human evolution both globally and regionally, although most very readily conceded that recent remains of known cultural affiliation (and especially of named individuals) were a special case and should be returned. Native American groups felt that all human remains, irrespective of age, should be returned to Native groups in the areas from which they came, because they are ancestral to the groups living there today.

The most controversial case surrounds the so-called 'Kennewick Man' or 'the Ancient One' found in July 1996 below the surface of Lake Wallula, a pooled part of the Columbia River behind McNary Dam in Kennewick, Washington. This skeleton has been dated to around 9500 cal BP. It is thus undoubtedly pre-Columbian and non-Caucasian, but whether the skeleton can be linked biologically or culturally to present-day tribes is still at issue. The bones were turned over to tribal control by the Army Corps of Engineers after brief study by physical anthropologists, unauthorised by local tribal groups, who claim oral histories which stretch back 10,000 years. The physical anthropologists say their brief investigations of the unusually complete skeleton show considerable affinities with Polynesian or Asian groups, outside the main range of variation of present Native American groups, casting doubt on claims of affiliation with local groups in the present. The legal battles continue at present and seem likely eventually to be decided by the US Supreme Court, so that any real decision on the skeleton is currently years away. In Britain, a government Working Group is looking into the legal and ethical issues surrounding the roughly 60,000 sets of human remains held in museums and universities in Britain, less than 10 per cent of which probably come from First Peoples (the bulk derive from archaeological excavations in Britain and are relatively uncontentious). Physical anthropologists point out that many new techniques of DNA and isotopic analysis have recently been developed which can provide much new information on past genealogies and diets. First Peoples counter by saying that most bones were taken without consultation or local permission and that the majority have never been subject to study. If the debates surrounding human remains have continued to be confrontational and heated, then elsewhere there are signs of accommodation and dialogue.

The notion has grown up of 'covenantal archaeology' which takes place through a worked set of agreements between archaeologists and local people as to aims, methods, forms of analysis and the eventual disposition of artefacts deriving from excavations (Zimmerman 1997). This has led archaeologists away from a generalised liberal view of knowledge, which sees information about the past as being of potential interest to people everywhere, to more locally based views, deriving from culturally specific notions of history and what is appropriate subject matter for debate. The influence of post-processual archaeology (*see* p. 207), with its stress on multivocality and different views of the past, has made many archaeologists more receptive to views from outside academia in many parts of the world.

Indigenous archaeology suffers from problems of definition, as does any mention of the term indigenous. Does indigenous mean local to an area or is it a shorthand for non-western or post-colonial? It would seem absurd to include Chinese or Japanese archaeologies in such a category, although they are definitely non-western. Would Zimbabwean archaeology carried out by western-trained Zimbabweans count or not? Much archaeology in places like Zimbabwe has been constructed to overthrow colonial stereotypes of the past, such as Cecil Rhodes' assertion that Great Zimbabwe was too sophisticated to have been constructed by Africans (Pikirayi 2001).

A most interesting aspect of indigenous archaeology is the participation of local communities in places like Britain. The site of Seahenge on Holme-next-the-Sea on the north Norfolk coast raised considerable controversy when a circle of wooden posts around an up-turned tree bole dating to 2050 BC were raised and removed for conservation. The archaeological arguments for removing the structure concerned conservation: the erosion of the beach would eventually cause the drying out and destruction of a unique monument. Furthermore, lifting the timbers allowed scientific analysis of the wood-working techniques (which showed some three dozen different copper alloy axes and adzes were used to cut the timbers). A final consideration was fragile local habitats for wading birds which were disturbed by the large numbers of visitors to the site (some 19,000 people came to see the excavations in May 1999). On the other hand, local people and not so local neo-Pagans and Druids objected to the excavations and especially to the removal of the timbers. Various groups occupied the site during excavation, trying to prevent the work from happening, and this received much coverage through the popular archaeological television programme *Time Team*. Local opinion was not necessarily against the work (and indeed many were in favour), although significant numbers of local people felt that there had been insufficient discussion of the issues surrounding the site prior to excavation. The neo-Pagans objected to the desecration of an ancient site. The timbers are presently under conservation and analysis at Flag Fen in Peterborough, but negotiations are underway between a range of official bodies including local councils and English Heritage, plus local people and the neo-Pagan community. Quite what the agreed outcome will be and where the timbers will eventually be placed is presently unclear (Miles 2001).

Indigenous archaeology covers many different contacts between archaeologists and local people with an interest in archaeology. Such connections are not always harmonious and easy, but should be seen to represent a set of possibilities, rather than problems, for archaeologists and all those interested in the past. These possibilities cover two main areas. First, connections between archaeologists and displaced First Peoples have caused much debate on the political importance of cultural heritage and claims to the past. In many parts of the world, claims to land and attempts at cultural regeneration depend upon the ability to demonstrate a continuing attachment to place and long-term cultural integrity. Archaeology clearly has a potential role to play here, causing archaeologists to consider deeply their attitudes to such political claims. As well as becoming more deeply aware of the political context of their work, archaeologists have also been called on to consider basic theoretical questions concerning the nature of historical continuity and change and the sources for writing histories. How seriously are archaeologists to take claims that oral histories provide some access to the last 10,000 years, and how can such oral histories complement archaeological evidence? What can form evidence of cultural continuity in the face of change evident everywhere, and how are we to weigh up various aspects of biological heritage, spiritual links to land and artefactual continuity or change? Do accounts of the past need to be verifiable to be valid? None of these questions is easy to answer. Archaeologists have been inclined to scepticism about many forms of claim to know the past; scepticism can be healthy but should not become too limiting either to our breadth of thought or to the range of people drawn to collaborate with archaeologists. As a discipline that is funded by the public, archaeology needs to take seriously its public links and connections.

Further reading

Biolsi, T. and Zimmerman, L. J. (eds) 1997. *Indians and Anthropologists. Vine Deloria Jr. and the Critique of Anthropology.* Tucson: University of Arizona Press.

Deloria, V. 1970. *Custer Died for your Sins: An Indian Manifesto.* New York: Avon.

Kluth, R. and Munnell, K. 1997. The Integration of Tradition and Scientific Knowledge on the Leech Lake Reservation, pp. 112–19 in (N. Swidler, K. E. Dongoske, R. Anyon and A. S. Downer, eds) *Native Americans and Archaeologists: Stepping Stones to Common Ground.* Walnut Creek, Calif.: AltaMira Press.

Miles, D. 2001. Ramsar Designation and the Case of Seahenge, pp. 157–64 in (B. Coles and A. Oliver, eds) *The Heritage Management of Wetlands.* Exeter: Short Run Press.

Pikirayi, I. 2001. *The Zimbabwe Culture: Origins and Decline of Southern Zambezi and States.* Walnut Creek, Calif.: AltaMira Press.

Swidler, N. , Dongoske, K. E., Anyon, R. and Downer, A. (eds) 1997. *Native Americans and Archaeologists: Stepping Stones to Common Grounds.* Walnut Creek, Calif.: AltaMira Press.

Trigger, B. G. 1985. *Natives and Newcomers. Canada's 'Heroic Age' Reconsidered.* Kingston: McGill-Queen's University Press.

Zimmerman, L. 1997. Remythologising the Relationship between Indians and Archaeologists, pp. 44–56 in (N. Swidler, K. E. Dongoske, R. Anyon and A. S. Downer, eds) *Native Americans and Archaeologists: Stepping Stones to Common Ground.* Walnut Creek, Calif.: AltaMira Press.

CHRIS GOSDEN

INNOVATION AND INVENTION – INDEPENDENT EVENT OR HISTORICAL PROCESS?

What is an invention and how does it relate to innovation? An invention introduces a completely new concept in the field of technology that makes a new construction or system possible, such as wheel and wagon, allowing the introduction of new social and economic practices. It is thus an event. Innovation, on the contrary, is part of an ongoing process that gradually adds new elements to an existing pattern of use, refining routines and efficiency. It may include everything from improved pottery technology to the reformulation of myth and rituals. The pairing of invention and innovation defines a difference between fundamental new ideas versus improvements of a known pattern. But invention presupposes the ongoing process of innovation. All societies are truly innovating in terms of creating and recreating a distinctive material culture of their own defined by social and symbolic meaning. It may be considered a universal feature of modern humans. All societies, however, are not truly inventive, as we shall see. Therefore innovation can also be employed to characterise the social and spatial process of accepting inventions, including their practical implementation and use (*see* p. 75).

Let us exemplify the difference between invention and innovation. The domestication of grains, cattle and sheep was the result of a long historical process of step-by-step innovations within a well-known framework of economic practice and experiment. By contrast, the combination of wheel and wagon is considered an invention, a historical event. And so is the invention of writing. It demanded experiments and hard intellectual work, it was part of a historical development towards writing characterised by many innovations along the way. But the formulation of cuneiform or the alphabet was carried out by a single individual or a specialist team at a specific moment in time, where suddenly everything fell into place within a new system of order and logic. Consequently, original and important inventions are few and far between, just as they demand the existence of specialists who can spend most of their time on the task.

From this it also follows that the number of inventions increases with the development of complex societies and states which have not only new needs but also the potential to fulfil them. From the early states inventions were normally adopted by neighbouring cultures in a process of diffusion (*see* p. 75).

However, the process could also be reversed. Sometimes a combination of organisational knowledge from urban centres with specialised knowledge from their periphery might lead to new inventions and practices. As an example let us consider the war chariot. It was based upon a new two-wheeled concept that employed a lightweight construction with spoked wheels and a small platform for the charioteer and the archer. Knowledge of steambowed wood was needed, in combination with the use of select types of wood, some of them only found in the temperate zone. This had to be combined with a new superior control of horses, that was developed in the steppe, as also, most probably, was the invention of the composite bow. All of these elements were then adopted to a new use of the chariot as a shooting platform in warfare based on speed and manoeuvrability, that completely changed the nature of warfare in the palace and state societies of the Bronze Age.

The anatomy of invention and innovation

A number of preconditions are necessary for an invention to take place. The most important are:

- the development of new needs, e.g. to record and calculate tribute and taxes more efficiently, or to move goods faster than sledges or pack animals could do. The responses were the invention of writing and wheeled vehicles;
- availability of most of the components of the invention. Often they are functionally separated, their potential not being fully recognised or utilised until combined in a new way. Symbolic representation of objects had been known and employed before the invention of a system of writing, and the frame of the wagon had previously been employed as a sledge;
- a mastermind, who is already a specialist in the field. The invention is made by adding a new formula for the combination and use of pre-existing elements and/or by inventing and integrating components that make the new construction possible. The pottery and wagon wheel exemplify connected areas of new inventions by changing the context of use. Later the wheel would be adopted as a religious symbol representing the sun, a change of use from a practical to a symbolic context.

Inventions are thus the result of a historical process of multiple innovations, often in many separate fields. In the process, new evolving social and economic needs finally trigger a solution through an invention that makes better use of the existing structures and allows them to expand further. Thus, wagons demanded both a pre-existing tradition of draft animals and the existence of roads or trackways. Since the fourth millennium BC wheel and wagon have undergone a series of innovations that gradually improved their construction, and through new inventions have taken us to cars and trains. However, the historical process of inventions and innovations is often discontinuous. Periods of openness to innovations alternate with periods and societies that preserve tradition and refuse certain types of innovations. We therefore need to consider the social context and cultural meaning of innovations to understand these historical dynamics, not least the resistance to change.

Resistance to inventions and innovations

While creativity is in human nature, this does not automatically imply that inventions and innovations are always readily accepted. If that had been the case, social evolution would have progressed much faster. All material and technological practices are inscribed with social and

symbolic meaning, embodied in routines that tend to preserve existing
ways of doing things. Pierre Lemonnier formulated this paradox very
succinctly: 'But as soon as one looks closely at a particular period or
human group, it appears that, time and time again, people exhibit
technical behaviours that do not correspond with any logic of material
efficiency or progress' (1993:).

More often than not, innovations are resisted if they cannot be
integrated within an existing social and cosmological framework. That
has been the case with several fundamental technological innovations.
The expansion of a Neolithic economy stopped for one millennium
just south of the Baltic, where it was resisted by an advanced Late
Mesolithic society, the Ertebølle Culture. They incorporated several
elements from the farmers into their material culture, such as the shape
of axes and primitive pottery, and thus knew about farming. But they
apparently had no incentive to change their way of life as long as it
provided a stable social and economic platform. Likewise, the diffusion
of iron technology occurred in steps, and it also stopped for several
hundred years south of Scandinavia, where a millennium-old social
organisation based upon the employment of bronze in the building
and maintenance of social prestige and chiefly networks would resist
iron technology. The reasons seem perfectly clear: iron could be
obtained and produced locally and thus undermined the whole chiefly
structure of Bronze Age society, including the symbolic and
cosmological value inscribed into its use as prestige goods.

It can further be observed that there existed in all societies cultural
mechanisms by which external innovations were internalised. Thus,
while an innovation might be applied (e.g. a new tool), its shape
would often be changed into the local cultural idiom of doing things,
e.g. by adding local decoration to it. In this way the innovation would
seem to be autonomous, and could therefore be accepted more easily.
Such strategies were part of the complex ways in which societies in
prehistory coped with the adoption of innovations and inventions.
This leads to a discussion of the role of diffusion versus independent
evolution in the spread of inventions and innovations.

Independent evolution and inventions

The same inventions and innovations are sometimes known to have
been made independently in societies widely separated in time and
space. Basic tools such as pottery or axes were invented in both
America and Europe, as were domestication and farming. Once
invented they spread in a process of diffusion. Major inventions and

innovations are thus linked to the social evolution of independent historical trajectories, each of them with their own history of inventions and technological traditions that goes back to the origin and spread of agriculture. Independent historical and evolutionary trajectories often comprise most of a continent, such as Eurasia, Southeast Asia, South America or Africa, and may comprise a wide variety of social complexity. Societies within each of these evolutionary trajectories were historically interconnected and shared elementary technological and social/cosmological properties, sometimes called 'great traditions'.

It is therefore difficult to demonstrate that important inventions, such as wheel and wagon, were invented more than once within the same historical trajectory. And in some continents, such as America, wheel and wagon were never invented. From this we may conclude that it is a universal feature of human societies at all levels of social complexity to interact with each other, and in that process inventions and innovations are transmitted, transformed and recontextualised within local and regional cultural traditions.

Suggested reading

Literature on inventions and innovations in prehistory is surprisingly scarce. Some basic readings include:

Lemonnier, P. (ed.) 1993. *Technological Choices. Transformation in Material Cultures since the Neolithic.* London: Routledge.
See especially Lemonnier's introduction, and Pierre Pétrequin's 'North Wind, South Wind. Neolithic Technical Choices in the Jura Mountains, 3700–2400 BC'.

Odner, K. 2000. *Tradition and Transmission. Bantu, Indo-European and Circumpolar Great Traditions.* Bergen Studies in Social Anthropology. Bergen: Norse Publications.
Concerns the persistence of 'great traditions'.

Piggott, S. 1983. *The Earliest Wheeled Transport. From the Atlantic Coast to the Caspian Sea.* London: Thames and Hudson.
The best source for information about wheel and wagon.

Renfrew, C. 1984. *Approaches to Social Archaeology.* Edinburgh: Edinburgh University Press
See especially the paper entitled 'The Anatomy of Invention', which looks at innovation as a process of adoption.

Van der Leeuw, S. E. and Torrence, R. (eds) 1989. *What's New? A Closer Look at the Process of Innovation.* London: Unwin Hyman.
In this book, see especially M. L. Stig Sørensen's 'Ignoring Innovation – Denying Change: The Role of Iron and the Impact of External Influences on the Transformation of Scandinavian Societies 800–500 BC'.

KRISTIAN KRISTIANSEN

THINKING ABOUT LANDSCAPE

The first principle of thinking about landscape is very simple. People in the past did not simply live, discard items, and build on sites, but they also interacted with the landscape beyond. Landscape archaeology, then, is about what lies beyond the site.

In modern archaeology, the practical impetus for thinking about landscape was observation of more and more features on the land. Many of the large-scale projects of the 1960s and 1970s, whether 'rescue' (salvage) surveys in advance of large-scale destruction such as highway constriction or quarrying, or research projects, threw up a huge number and density of archaeological sites. Moreover, these sites were not just dots on a map. Many more linear and large-scale features – field boundaries, remains of irrigation and agricultural systems, dykes, etc. – were shown to be of great antiquity. As a result, so much archaeology was found that many 'sites' overlapped with each other, and/or were linked by these linear features.

It began to make less sense to think of sites as a limited number of dots on a map, and much more sense to think of an entire *landscape*. The English archaeologist O. G. S. Crawford drew an analogy with a palimpsest, that is:

> a document that has been written on and erased over and over again; and it is the business of the field archaeologist to decipher it. The features concerned are of course the roads and field boundaries, the woods, the farms and other habitations, and all the other products of human labour; these are the letters and words inscribed on the land. But it is not easy to read them because, whereas the vellum document was seldom wiped clean more than once or twice, the land has been subjected to continual change throughout the ages.

> (Crawford 1953: 51)

Many archaeologists, particularly those working in landscapes that have been densely and successively settled over the millennia such as those of Europe, view their task as one of 'reading the landscape' in this way, working backwards by unpeeling successive layers of traces of settlement in a process akin to that of excavation as analytical procedure (*see* p. 106). To do this, a variety of off-site techniques can be used, including fieldwalking, air photography and the use of documents such as tax records and field surveys. Even standard maps such as OS maps and IGN maps record basic information such as the shape and layout of field boundaries and settlement forms that can be used. There are close links between this form of archaeology and traditional historical geography.

In more theoretical terms, the study of landscape is as old as the study of archaeology itself. The Renaissance saw the development of archaeological interest in the past, and also saw the rise of an analytical view of landscape in which features of antiquity were noted, described and classified by leisured antiquarians. Such a view of landscape was seen, for example, in the development of new techniques of surveying, and the production of maps. Scholars of the sixteenth to the eighteenth centuries combined elements of what we would see as archaeology, history and cartography in their writings on topography.

These views of landscape were transformed by two developments: the rise of the Romantic movement in the later eighteenth century, which stressed the aesthetic appreciation of landscapes and the landscape as spectacle, and nineteenth-century geology, which demonstrated how the landscape we see today is the end result of often very slow processes of change (*see* p. 274), processes which, moreover, are comparable in different places and times (for example, processes of deposition and erosion). The aesthetic/emotive view of landscape and its geological understanding remain driving forces of landscape archaeology today.

Archaeologists have thought about landscape in a variety of ways:

1   Landscape as a set of economic resources, or site catchment/ territorial analysis (*see* p. 230). Many archaeologists stress that 'site catchment analysis' examines the location of sites in terms of what resources are available within a given distance or travel time from the site. Viewing sites such as gatherer-hunter camps of early agricultural settlements in economic terms immediately leads one to examine the landscape beyond – for example, the soil type and terrain, the presence of migratory routes of animals, and so on. Large-scale modifications of the landscape for economic reasons have been extensively studied. Gatherer-hunter communities will often set fire to or otherwise modify the landscape in order to encourage the growth of certain flora and fauna; agricultural communities will engage in irrigation, terracing of hillsides, clearance of fields and so on.

2   Landscape as a reflection of society, and its relation to theories of the formation of complex societies and states (*see* p. 101). Sites

have been categorised into 'settlement hierarchies' on the basis of size, presence of monumental architecture or the complexity of the overall settlement system. Large-scale transformations of landscape, for example through the use of irrigation, are linked to social transformations such as the rise of chiefdoms or early states.

3   Landscape as expressive of a system of cultural meaning. In line with the increasing stress on cognitive (see p. 41) and post-processual (see p. 207) perspectives, many archaeologists have come to interpret the landscape as an expression of people's way of thinking and acting upon the world. The two senses of the term 'land-scape' are important here: not just the land, but how it is viewed or mentally constructed. Richard Bradley, for example, has looked at the use and reuse of monuments in the past. Many areas have been interpreted as large-scale 'ritual landscapes': Stonehenge, for instance, is surrounded by groups of barrows, linear earthworks and other features; other large-scale ceremonial landscapes include Aztec and Maya ritual complexes, and the Nazca lines. Many of the approaches to these landscapes, and their intersection with everyday patterns of life, are characteristic of phenomenological archaeology (see p. 201).

Still other archaeologists, harking back to the Crawford tradition, simply write about landscape in a way that is not obviously linked to any theoretical perspective. There is a very strong tradition, particularly in historical archaeology (see p. 137), of an emotional attachment to landscape and the understanding of particular places and localities as an end in itself. It is this tradition, of seeking to understand nothing more nor less than the puzzles in one's own back yard, that can easily be criticised, but which remains the central and inspiring motivation of many local archaeologists.

Suggested reading

Ashmore, W. and Knapp, A. B. (eds) 1999. *Archaeologies of Landscape*. Oxford: Blackwell.
A good selection of case studies illustrating theoretical approaches.

Bender, B. 1998. *Stonehenge: Making Space*. Oxford: Berg.
The archaeology and politics of the Stonehenge landscape.

Bradley, R. 1998. *The Significance of Monuments: On the Shaping of Human Experience in Neolithic and Bronze Age Europe*. London: Routledge.
One of the best of the recent crop of books on prehistoric landscape.

Crumley, C. L. (ed.) 1994. *Historical Ecology: Cultural Knowledge and Changing Landscapes*. Santa Fe: SAR Press.
A good selection of recent ecological approaches.

Hoskins, W. G. 1978. *The Making of the English Landscape*. London: Hodder and Stoughton (1st edn 1955; this edition with useful marginal comments by C. C. Taylor).
Read for its passionate tone and approach, which has been hugely influential.

Johnson, M. H. Forthcoming. *Ideas of Landscape*.
An introduction to the subject.

Further reading

Aveni, A. F. 1986. The Nazca Lines: Patterns in the Desert. *Archaeology* 39: 32–9.
Bender, B. (ed.) 1993. *Landscape: Politics and Perspectives*. Oxford: Berg.
Crawford, O. G. S. 1953. *Archaeology in the Field*. London: Phoenix House.
Head, L. 1993. Unearthing Prehistoric Cultural Landscapes: A View from Australia. *Transactions of the Institute of British Geographers* 18: 481–99.
Piggott, S. 1976. *Ruins in a Landscape: Essays in Antiquarianism*. Edinburgh: Edinburgh University Press.
Tilley, C. 1994. *A Phenomenology of Landscape: Places, Paths and Monuments*. Oxford: Berg.
Yamon, R. and Metheny, K. B. (eds) 1996. *Landscape Archaeology: Reading and Interpreting the American Historical Landscape*. Knoxville: University of Tennessee Press.

MATTHEW JOHNSON

MATERIAL ENGAGEMENT AND MATERIALISATION

The 'material engagement' approach towards the study of past societies implies an emphasis upon informed and intelligent action, and the recognition in them of the simultaneous application of cognitive as well as physical aspects of the human involvement with the world. It is an approach which endeavours to transcend the duality implied in the long-standing contrasts drawn between mind and matter, soul and body, or cognition and the material world. It recognises that the contrast between idealist and materialist approaches (in the traditional sense) can work against a fuller understanding of the nature of the human engagement with the world, which is not only knowledgeable but which involves also the use of symbolic values with a social dimension that is specific to the society in question in its time and the place. It emphasises therefore the embodiment of the human condition – we do not exist without our bodies and all their

159

limitations and capacities – and that the reality of that embodiment changes with knowledge and experience and with the range of material culture which we in our society have come to develop and use. The current emphasis upon materialisation similarly emphasises the active role of material culture in the development of social structures and of religious concepts. The approach thus aspires to escape the anti-idealist stance often associated with traditional materialism and with earlier versions of Marxist archaeology (*see* p. 165), and at the same time to avoid what often seems the anti-materialist position of some versions of post-processual or interpretive archaeology (*see* p. 207).

Material engagement theory considers the processes by which human individuals and communities engage with the material world through actions which have simultaneously a material reality and a cognitive or intelligent component (*see* p. 41). This component is not genetically determined or transmitted, as are some of the activities of such species as various social insects, which construct their nests in quite elaborate ways, something that at first sight could be taken as the result of intelligent planning. They are based instead upon culturally determined patterns of learned behaviour which are themselves the product of human experience and innovation over long trajectories of time and which may be regarded as the result of human agency (*see* p. 3).

The engagement process is seen as critical in shaping the paths of development and change within societies, and as a fundamental feature of the human condition. And while all evolutionary change, including that in other species, can be seen as one of engagement between the individual or community and the environment, it is the cognitive component which is particularly human and which introduces choice and decision (or 'agency') into what would otherwise be a process of natural selection.

The consideration of materialisation similarly takes account of the way human societies use aspects of the material world to give expression to symbolic concepts, as in the development and elaboration of religious beliefs through the use of iconic representations and the construction of temples or sanctuaries. Here the ideational or cognitive component could not work effectively or find adequate expression in social behaviour without the use, for instance, of divine images or the construction of sanctuaries in which the behaviour of those participating in the ritual is conditioned and facilitated by the materiality of the constructed environment. In general the physical arrangement of temples or sanctuaries functions in this way, as in the much discussed example of Chavín de Huantar in north-central Peru in the first millennium BC. There, monumental platforms enclose a sunken plaza, giving access to a central passageway leading to a small chamber containing the Lanzón or Great Image. Hidden passageways may have been used for ritual cleansing and to use running water to produce roaring sounds used to heighten the impact of the ceremonies. There is in addition evidence for the use of drugs to heighten perception, and of a rich accompanying iconography. The consideration of materialisation analyses the way in which different aspects of materiality are used to structure the religious experiences and the social relationships involved in ritual practices.

The religious dimension offers just one example of the wider range of social relationships which are mediated by the intelligent use of *things*, for instance in the recognition (or definition) of valuable materials. These may be used to structure social relations, as in gift exchange or in the production of emblems of rank or status, or indeed in the production of money. Many of the material aspects involved in such processes of materialisation or of engagement involve the recognition of 'institutional facts' as defined by the philosopher John Searle (*see* p. 41).

A good example is the development of systems of measure, such as weight. A weight might at first be regarded as 'symbolic'. But on closer examination it does not quite fit the signifier/thing-signified relationship implied in the usual definition of a symbol, namely as the term X in the relationship 'X represents Y in context C'. There X is the 'signifier' and Y the thing signified. This can be made clearer by an example. The term 'kilogram' is indeed the symbol or signifier representing a given mass in the real world. But the actual lump of matter of appropriate size and mass (i.e. a kilogram) which we term 'a kilogram weight' actually *embodies* the thing signified (i.e. the appropriate quantity of actual stuff measured not by volume but by weight). The symbol is insubstantial, but the actual kilogram weight (which is needed in order to define how much stuff you need to have a kilogram of it) has an inseparable material reality. The symbol cannot do its work without the stuff. This exemplifies an important feature of engagement theory: that the symbol (signifier) and the reality (thing signified) are not to be separated into some dual relationship in terms of 'concept' and 'matter'. They often co-exist in what may be termed a 'hypostatic' (i.e. indivisible) relationship where the symbolic and the material are both present.

Material engagement theory sets out to recognise and analyse some of these features which underlie the reality of human societies. It may hope in this way to overcome or transcend what may be termed the 'sapient paradox'. The sapient paradox refers to the strange circumstance that although the human revolution (i.e. the emergence of our species *Homo sapiens sapiens*) took place more than 40,000 years ago, it is only 10,000 years ago that we see the emergence of settled, village life and with it other innovations that led, quite rapidly in some areas, to the development of urbanism, of literacy and of state societies. Why, if those early sapient ancestors were hard-wired with just those innate, genetically determined cognitive capacities which we share today, did it take so long for these major developments to occur? That is the paradox. And the answer seems to be that it was difficult for many other key innovations to develop before the emergence of sedentism, and soon of farming. Some of these innovations, including new social relationships mediated by the notion of property, arose following the development of sedentary life and of farming.

The property relationships (between individuals and objects) of Upper Palaeolithic hunter-gatherers may have been rather limited: individual property may have been restricted to clothing and adornment, and personal kit. With sedentary life and farming came the potential for ownership of the house, of cultivable fields, and of flocks or cattle. And there soon came the first recognition of new kinds of valuables – of precious stones, like jade, or of valuable commodities such as gold, which do not seem to have been regarded as 'valuable' earlier. Material engagement theory sets out to analyse such relationships implied by measure, value, wealth and commodity, and later by money. Nor is the engagement process restricted to the economic sphere, as the earlier reference to materiality and religion indicated.

Suggested reading

Appadurai, A. (ed.) 1986. *The Social Life of Things*. Cambridge: Cambridge University Press.
Series of essays illustrating the active role of material culture.

DeMarrais, E., Castillo, L. J. and Earle, T. 1996. Ideology, Materialization and Power Ideologies. *Current Anthropology* 37: 15–31.
Key paper, introducing the idea of materialisation.

DeMarrais, E., Gosdon, C. and Renfrew, C. (eds), in press, *Rethinking Materiality: the engagement of mind with the material world*. Cambridge: McDonald Institute.
Up to date review of many of the main issues.

Renfrew, C. 2001a. Symbol before Concept: Material Engagement and the Early Development of Society, pp. 122–40 in (I. Hodder, ed.) *Archaeological Theory Today*. Cambridge: Polity Press.
Paper which introduces the concept of material engagement as discussed here.

Renfrew, C. 2001b. Commodification and Institution in Group-Oriented and Individualising Societies, pp. 93–117 in (W. G. Runciman, ed.) *The Origin of Human Social Institutions*. Oxford: Oxford University Press for the British Academy.
Further discussion of material engagement theory.

Further reading

Donald, M. 1991. *Origins of the Modern Mind: Three Stages in the Evolution of Culture and Cognition*. Cambridge, Mass.: Harvard University Press.
Lesure, R. 1999. On the Genesis of Value in Early Hierarchical Societies, pp. 23–55 in (J. E. Robb, ed.) *Material Symbols, Culture and Economy in Prehistory*. Carbondale, Ill.: Southern Illinois University.
Michailidou, A. 1999. Systems of Weight and Social Relations of 'Private' Production in the Late Bronze Age Aegean, pp. 87–113 in (A. Chaniotis, ed.) *From Minoan Farmers to Roman Traders*. Stuttgart: Franz Steiner Verlag.
Mithen, S. 1998. The Supernatural Beings of Prehistory and the External Storage of Religious Ideas, pp. 977–106 in (C. Renfrew and C. Scarre, eds) *Cognition and Material Culture: The Archaeology of Symbolic Storage*. Cambridge: Cambridge University Press.
Renfrew, C. 1996. The Sapient Behaviour Paradox: How to Test for Potential?, pp. 11–14 in (P. A. Mellars and K. Gibson, eds) *Modelling the Early Human Mind*. Cambridge: McDonald Institute for Archaeological Research.
Searle, J. R. 1995. *The Construction of Social Reality*. Harmondsworth: Allen Lane/Penguin Press.

COLIN RENFREW

MATERIALISM, MARXISM AND ARCHAEOLOGY

There is a long historical relationship between various forms of materialism and archaeology. It stands to reason, of course, that archaeology's dependence upon the material should make it conducive to influences of such approaches, but this is not a necessity. Materialism, whether historical or cultural, has had a tendency to view social and cultural forms as a product of material relations. A particular influential form of materialism argues that the nature of society is determined by the material conditions of production, which in turn are defined by the bare necessity of the human need to extract a living from the physical environment. In the neo-evolutionism of anthropological writers such as Leslie White (1959) and Julian Steward (1955) as well as the more stringent cultural materialism developed by Marvin Harris (1979), the material consists of demographic, ecological and technological conditions that are assumed to be free of particular social forms determining the appropriation of such conditions. Instead the social relations are determined by them in a rather direct way.

In the work of Leslie White, cultural evolution is explained in terms of the increased capture of energy surpluses or free energy by suggesting that culture is an adaptive system. By including everything from technology to religion as adaptive in the relationship between society and environment, and by including inbuilt demands for energy input as well as adaptive mechanisms, White claimed that cultural evolution could be explained on the grounds of efficiency in extracting energy from environment. This also enabled him, while maintaining a generally technological evolutionary perspective, to address issues of civilisational collapse as a result of maladaptation or due to crises in environmental adaptation. His work had a significant influence on discussion of South American archaeology, especially evident in the work of his student Betty Meggers. Julian Steward, however, had a more powerful direct influence in the development of what was called the 'New Archaeology' (see p. 212), in the 1950s and 1960s. His 'cultural ecological' approach proposed that the actual structures of technology were the significant variables, rather than their efficiency in the promotion of energy capture. He attempted to show the ways in which hunting and gathering techno-ecology could be used to deduce an appropriate social form called 'band society'. In this form of society, small groups roamed large territories, reproducing themselves by maintaining an equilibrium between their local conditions of environmental appropriation and gaining access to a larger region for which maintaining social relations of alliance would be crucial.

This kind of argument was extended to swidden (slash-and-burn) agriculture and to its intensification, and was presented in a historically crucial article in 1949 (Steward 1955) in which he compared parallel technological and social evolutionary processes in the emergence of irrigation-based civilisations in several parts of the world. The results of this work were massive in both anthropology and archaeology. The categories 'band', 'tribe', 'chiefdom', 'state' became textbook categories for a generation of both anthropologists and archaeologists (see p. 191). The classificatory power of this approach resonated throughout the field. The history of ancient civilisations, the social prehistory of the world, the classification of contemporary 'traditional' societies, all were subjected to the same principle of ordering. The massive volume *Handbook of the South American Indians* is a case in point. Here anthropologists as well as archaeologists made significant contributions to a master plan in which ecology and technology were primary variables for the understanding of the distribution of social forms throughout the continent. It should be noted that the explanatory framework adopted in this approach was primarily of a functionalist nature. The institutions and culture of a society were the product of adaptation. They existed in order to fulfil an ecological, demographic or otherwise economic function.

But the approach started to come under increasing fire in the 1960s. There were, of course, other ways of understanding the archaeological data. But this basically technological determinist approach had great appeal, and seemed to correlate quite well with the data at hand. Certain versions of Marxism were quite compatible with the results of neo-evolutionism, but there were others who criticised the foundations of the model. If hunting-and-gathering was supposed to generate band society, what then to do with the Northwest Coast Indians whose society was quite stratified? How could one interpret the Calusa Indian society of Florida, which was urbanised? What about the monumental architecture of the Mesolithic Lepenski Vir site in the Balkans? The critique was of the explanatory model, its functionalist bias or reductionism. Steward had been influenced by Karl Wittfogel (1957) whose work on irrigation society proposed that, in arid areas devoid of significant rainfall, irrigation was necessary for any concentration of population, and such irrigation had to be *organised*. This implied for Wittfogel the necessity of a managerial state. Thus the early irrigation civilisations were all reduced to the 'hydraulic hypothesis' in which the elaborate bureaucratic state apparatus was generated as a necessary organiser of the irrigation systems that, in their turn, were the support for the higher population densities required by large civilisations. This hypothesis gained support in the early New Archaeology, but it was eventually shown to be a gross oversimplification, and even false. In the case of China, irrigation was the product of the state and not vice versa, and it could as easily be understood as part of a project of increasing political power. The existence of elaborate irrigation systems without state-level organisation, e.g. in the Philippines and other areas, contradicted the material causality implied in this approach.

The contribution of Marxist theory to all of this lies in its rejection of functionalist approaches, even if many Marxists did embrace this kind of reductionism. Rather than searching for adaptive mechanisms, Marxism held the possibility of envisaging long-term social change as a contradictory and dynamic process. Gordon Childe (*see* p. 35) had already argued for this approach in archaeology by rejecting the influence of Soviet-style unilinear evolutionism in order to show that technical change in prehistory had regularly been impeded by social hierarchy, except for the unique case of the European Bronze Age (cf. Patterson 2003). Marxist anthropology developed as a true field in France in the 1960s and 1970s in the work of Terray, Meillassoux, Rey and Godelier. Only the latter was interested in archaeology and wrote about the nature of theocratic power in his work on Marx's 'Asiatic mode of production', which he later applied to the Inca. But the work of Meillassoux, Rey, Godelier and Friedman did provide models of social dynamics and control that were later utilised in archaeology. In contrast to a materialism that emphasised the determination of techno-ecological factors, they emphasised instead that production was always socially organised and, in particular, the ways in which surpluses of labour and materials were extracted and monopolised by some could be used to define differences in social forms.

Using an approach based on the notion of the monopoly of exchange of 'prestige goods' inherent in the work of Rey, Ekholm-Friedman developed a model of the political expansion and collapse of the Kongo kingdom as a result of the loss of control over and decentralisation of long-distance exchange, a model that has been applied to historical as well as prehistorical data (Frankenstein and Rowlands 1978; Friedman 1982; Friedman and Rowlands 1977). It is to be noted, however, that the Marxist anthropology of the 1960s and 1970s began to have an impact in archaeology at the same time as a more orthodox Marxism itself was under internal and external attack. The latter was a product of the decline of the eastern bloc and of modernist and developmentalist thinking in the west. The internal critique questioned the materialist reductionism of the approach and also argued for the primacy of social relations and strategies. But another development was perhaps more important, one that led to the establishment of a global systemic approach to the field. Here again, Marxism was criticised for its excessively local model of materialist determinism, and the notion of social reproduction was used to open the analysis to a larger regional and global framework. Social systems were conceived within the framework of processes of social reproduction that spanned large areas. Notions of centre, periphery and semi-periphery began to be applied to ancient history and prehistory.

It should also be noted that the generalisation of the global framework was contrary to the accepted notion that the world system was a modern European phenomenon dating from the fifteenth century at best. This position has been criticised in recent work (Abu-Lughod 1989; Frank and Gills 1993). These were not, of course, new ideas as such, but the framework of reproduction supplied a systemic way of dealing with such large-scale flows. In Friedman and Rowlands (1977) a framework was proposed in which long-term social transformation was linked to global dynamics. The world system perspective was adopted and debated in the late 1970s and 1980s, and a large number of works were published dealing with centre/periphery relations in the Middle East and Europe. The seminal work of Algaze, *The Uruk World System*, is a landmark from this period. One might say that the assumptions of the world system framework were modified in this period to deal with other kinds of processes in previous regional systems. But the need to deal with social process in larger arenas was clearly recognised and led to a range of applications.

In some cases, questioning what constituted the larger region of social reproduction led to wide-ranging surveys of archaeological interconnections, in which the idea of centre and periphery was more loosely applied in order to designate regions of inequalities and dependency. Kohl's discussion of trading entities in ancient Mesopotamia and Weigand writing on complex societies in the classic period in western Mexico shared a common concern with inequalities through controlling access to trade routes and circulation. How much control actually lay in the core and to what extent peripheries were really linked to cores in a systematic manner became a matter of debate, and Kohl in particular argued that in Mesopotamia, for most of the ancient period, trading links were established between semi-autonomous regions rather than cores and peripheries (Kohl 1987). Stein has pointed to the fact that colonies and diaspora populations were more characteristic of trading empires than the technology-driven integration of markets characteristic of modern world systems. It is perhaps not surprising, therefore, that the concept of semi-periphery has been more eloquently developed by archaeologists influenced by this approach (cf. Chase Dunn and Hall 1997: 37). The emphasis that peripheries are not voiceless agencies and totally dominated by their cores is also the point made by Kohl in showing that many of the more significant technological innovations in Mesopotamia occurred in the so-called peripheries of the Caucasus and beyond. Of course, the image of the passive periphery is based on some of the schematic and political texts of imperialism theory, but historically informed works have tended to acknowledge the actor status of peripheral zones, even as the range of their choices is somewhat limited. In many cases, of course, the strategies of peripheral elites in exchanging slaves and raw materials, but sometimes prestigious items, is related to maintaining local power. The work of

Hedeager (1992) on Scandinavia in the Roman Iron Age argues convincingly for the development of a periphery that exchanged local products for imported prestige goods, an exchange system that seems to have configured local chiefly hierarchy as well. Kristiansen, in his extensive work on the European Bronze Age and its connections with the Mediterranean world and the Near East, argues in similar fashion for widely dispersed elites forming nodes in large regional and inter-regional networks (Kristiansen and Rowlands 1998). There are also a great number of other works that have invoked regional dynamic models, and still others that use less regional but dynamic models based on internally contradictory processes.

One significant development has been the result of the enthusiastic entry of a group of political scientists, sociologists and anthropologists of the world system persuasion into the study of long-term change. Researchers such as Modelski and Thompson, Chase-Dunn and Hall, Frank and Gills, have revived the issues of world history and the modelling of the latter. They have done their best to begin a dialogue with archaeologists, and there are interesting results from this encounter. Frank, who has been the most provocative in recent years, has attempted to show the degree to which the entire area linking Europe with the Middle East, India and China was a true system in which cycles of expansion and contraction are synchronised over the entire region. The issue of the continuity of such global systems has been hotly debated within this group. Sherratt (1997) has developed a mapping system in which he has tried to depict the ways in which different zones within larger regions are related to one another in the process of change. Most important in this development is the opening of transdisciplinary discussions between archaeologists, anthropologists, political scientists and sociologists. A number of works have emerged from this cooperation.

In conclusion, it may be appropriate to ask whether a materialist approach, Marxist or otherwise, remains a viable option in archaeology. Cultural evolution is equally pursued from both Darwinian and cognitivist (*see* p. 58, 41) perspectives . Materialism itself could be said to have diversified into a range of 'Foucauldian' and 'post-Marxist' forms that escape any single definition. At the present time archaeology is strongly motivated by phenomenological (*see* p. 201) and interpretative approaches that emphasise experience as the motivating force for engagement with the past and its apparent relevance for understanding the present. In this idiom, the idea of a region is more likely to evoke the thought of landscape, rather than an entity containing the material conditions of social reproduction. Materialism, in the sense made famous by Marx as the dominance of sensory practice over intellectual abstraction, is quite compatible with a notion of subjectivity in which 'making the self' subsumes identity inscribed symbolically in material forms. But this shift must raise the question of the purpose of archaeology if, effectively, we no longer wish to be concerned with the long term as generating later social forms, or materiality as unintended consequences that allow us to see how emerging structures constrain and inform the range of alternative possibilities for action in given social and historical circumstances.

On the other hand, Marxism as critique appears to retain its influence in the field. The politicisation of archaeology, like that of anthropology in the 1980s and 1990s, has been related to the rise of cultural politics, not least among indigenous peoples who have fought the activities of archaeologists with numerous claims over land rights and sacred remains. This kind of activity also highlights the contestation of a formerly stable power relationship between representatives of western science and indigenous populations. This, of course, is paralleled by similar confrontations between indigenous populations and anthropologists in which the latter have struggled to gain control of the way in which knowledge about them is produced. And it is to be noted that this phenomenon can itself be understood in global systemic terms. The relation between cultural identity and archaeology is a significant phenomenon that is worthy of serious analysis. The politics of archaeology is in fact closely related to issues of Marxist analysis in so far as the latter implies the necessity for a socially contextualised understanding of the field.

Suggested reading

Algaze, G. 1993. *The Uruk World System: The Dynamics of Expansion of Early Mesopotamian Civilization*. Chicago: University of Chicago Press.
Applies world system theory to early Mesopotamia while modifying the framework in doing so.

Chase-Dunn, C. K. and Hall, T. D. 1997. *Rise and Demise: Comparing World Systems*. Boulder, Col.: Westview Press.
First attempt to create a large-scale comparative study of early world systems.

Friedman, J. and Rowlands, M. J. 1977. *The Evolution of Social Systems. Proceedings of a Meeting of the Research Seminar in Archaeology and Related Subjects held at the Institute of Archaeology, London University*. London: Duckworth.
A collection of papers that illustrates the use of various strands of Marxism in archaeological and ethnohistorical analyses.

Kristiansen, K. and Rowlands, M. 1998. *Social Transformations in Archaeology.* London: Routledge.
A collection of papers that applies structural Marxist and world systems theory to prehistory and the archaeology of colonialism.

Patterson, T. C. 2003. *Marx's Ghost. Conversations with Archaeologists.* Oxford: Berg.
Discussion of Marx's influence in archaeological interpretation.

Roseberry, W. 1997. Marx and Anthropology. *Annual Review of Anthropology* 26: 25–46.
Surveys theoretical developments of Marxian political economy in anthropology.

Sherratt, A. 1997. *Economy and Society in Prehistoric Europe: Changing Perspectives.* Princeton, NJ: Princeton University Press.
Large-scale approach to use of world systems theory in Old World prehistory.

Wolf, E. 1982. *Europe and the People without History.* Berkeley: University of California Press.
Comparative study of the application of the Modes of Production approach to development of the modern world system.

Further reading

Abu-Lughod, J. L. 1989. *Before European Hegemony: The World System AD 1250–1350.* New York: Oxford University Press.
Denemark, R. A. 2000. *World System History: The Social Science of Long Term Change.* London: Routledge.
Foster, J. 2000. *Marx's Ecology: Materialism and Nature.* New York: Monthly Review Press.
Frank, A. G. and Gills, B. K. 1993. *The World System: Five Hundred Years or Five Thousand?* London /New York: Routledge.
Frankenstein, S. and Rowlands, M. 1978. The Internal Structure and Regional Context of Early Iron Age Society in South-Western Germany. *Bull Institute of Archaeology* 15: 73–113.
Friedman, J. 1982 Catastrophe and Continuity in Social Evolution, in (C. Renfrew, M. Rowlands and B. Seagraves, eds) *Theory and Explanation in Archaeology.* London: Blackwell.
Harris, M. 1979. *Cultural Materialism: The Struggle for a Science of Culture.* New York: Random House.
Hedeager, L. 1992. *Iron-Age Societies: From Tribe to State in Northern Europe, 500 BC to AD 700. Social Archaeology.* Oxford, UK, and Cambridge, Mass.: Blackwell.
Kohl, P. 1987. The Ancient Economy, Transferable Technologies and the Bronze Age World System, in (M. Rowlands, M. Larsen and K. Kristiansen, eds) *Centre and Periphery in the Ancient World.* Cambridge: Cambridge University Press.
Kohl, P. and Fawcett, C. 1995. *Nationalism, Politics and the Practice of Archaeology.* Cambridge: Cambridge University Press.
Meillassoux, C. 1981. *Maidens, Meal and Money: Capitalism and the Domestic Community.* Cambridge: Cambridge University Press.
Orser, C. E. 1996. *A Historical Archaeology of the Modern World.* New York: Plenum.

Paynter, R. 1999. The Archaeology of Equality and Inequality. *Annual Review of Anthropology* 18: 369–99.

Spriggs, M. (ed.) 1984. *Marxist Perspectives in Archaeology.* Cambridge: Cambridge University Press.

Stein, G. 1999. *Rethinking World-Systems: Diasporas, Colonies and Interaction in Uruk Mesopotamia.* Tucson: University of Arizona Press.

Steward, J. H. 1955. *Theory of Culture Change; The Methodology of Multilinear Evolution.* Urbana: University of Illinois Press.

White, L. A. 1959. *The Evolution of Culture; The Development of Civilization to the Fall of Rome.* New York: McGraw-Hill.

Wittfogel, K. A. 1957. *Oriental Despotism; A Comparative Study of Total Power.* New Haven: Yale University Press.

JONATHAN FRIEDMAN AND MICHAEL ROWLANDS

MENTAL MODULARITY

Archaeologists are concerned with the nature of the human mind. Whenever they propose an interpretation for a collection of artefacts or an explanation for a particular trajectory of cultural change, they make either an implicit or an explicit reference to how the mind perceives the world and influences human behaviour. Such references often remain as hidden assumptions about human nature, especially in archaeological studies prior to the development of processual (*see* p. 212) and then post-processual (*see* p. 207) archaeology. Cognitive archaeology (*see* p. 41), as developed since the 1980s, requires that such references are made explicit and prioritised in archaeological studies. In this regard, because 'mental modularity' is a key concept in the psychological, philosophical and neurological study of the human mind, so too must it be in archaeology.

Mental modularity is the notion that the human mind is constituted by a series of discrete components, each of which functions with a degree of independence and is likely to have its own evolutionary history. Although the idea of mental modularity originated in the nineteenth century, it gained its pre-eminent position in the cognitive sciences from Jerry Fodor's seminal 1983 book, entitled *The Modularity of Mind*. Fodor argued that the input and output systems of the mind, such as vision, hearing and language, are modular. By this he meant they were mandatory in operation (we can't help seeing or hearing), swift in operation, inaccessible to the rest of cognition and liable to specific patterns of breakdown that would leave other systems intact. In contrast, thinking and problem-solving, described by Fodor as central systems, were distinctly unmodular, having access to the diverse range of information acquired by the input systems.

While Fodor's characterisation of input systems has effectively gone unchallenged, several philosophers and psychologists have extended the notion of modularity to central systems. They argue that thinking about, say, other people, numbers, artefacts and animals requires different types of knowledge and different ways of processing relevant information. As a consequence, it is likely that they are undertaken by discrete mental modules, which may or may not map on to specific areas of the brain. This approach has been championed by so-called evolutionary psychologists, notably Steven Pinker (1997), Leda Cosmides and John Tooby (1994), and Barkow *et al.* (1992). They propose that each module evolved to solve a specific adaptive problem faced by our ancestors because those with specialised ways of thinking about, for instance, wild animals, social relations and material objects would be the most likely to survive and reproduce and consequently natural selection would lead to a highly modular mind. This characterisation of the mind has been termed the 'massive modularity' thesis (Samuels 1998; see Carruthers (2003) for a 'moderately massive modularity' thesis).

Other psychologists, most notably Annette Karmiloff-Smith (1992), reject such evolutionary approaches and argue that mental modules arise during the course of development. Consequently human minds might develop mental modules for reading, writing and playing chess, even though these are recent inventions in human history. Equally contentious is the manner in which mental modules interact. The evolutionary psychologists claim that there is effectively no such interaction, while development psychologists stress the significance of learning to build links across mental modules. Dan Sperber (1994) has argued that there is a mental module specifically devoted to integrating the output from other modules, while Carruthers (2002) proposes that the function of 'inner speech' is to convey information between modules.

While there is considerable disagreement about the precise nature of mental modules, there is substantial evidence that the mind is indeed essentially modular in structure. This partly comes from neuropsychological studies of people who have either been born with cognitive deficits or suffered brain damage. In numerous cases one or more modules appear to have become inhibited while other aspects of the mind remain intact. Autistic children, for instance, appear to lack a 'theory of mind' module – they are unable to understand that other people have beliefs and desires that differ from their own – while maintaining normal function in other areas (Baron-Cohen 1995). Peretz and Coltheart (2003) and Butterworth (1999) review studies of people who have 'lost' their musical and mathematical abilities following brain damage, while maintaining all other cognitive functions.

The rate at which very young children acquire knowledge about the world has also been used as evidence for modularity. Language is the classic example. As Noam Chomsky, the distinguished American linguist, originally argued, humans appear to be born with a language acquisition device innately wired into their brains, enabling them to rapidly acquire a vast lexicon and the grammatical rules of the specific language of their culture. Similar arguments have been made that infants are born with an intuitive understanding of psychology (Leslie 1994), physics (Spelke 1991) and biology (Atran 2002).

As mental modularity is such a key concept in the cognitive sciences, it must also be central to archaeological debate about the evolution of the human mind and cultural evolution. When archaeological studies of cognitive evolution lack any reference to mental modularity (e.g. Noble and Davidson 1996) they appear inherently flawed because they cannot engage with current understanding of the modern mind. Indeed, it is essential that archaeologists contribute to the debates about mental modularity, rather than simply adopt the views of psychologists. This is most evident from some of the naive writing from evolutionary psychologists about the human past, in which a lack of attention to archaeological data and theories has led to invalid assumptions about past lives and hence the selective pressures that may have operated on the human mind. For instance, Pinker, Cosmides and Tooby have frequently invoked the 'environmental of evolutionary adaptedness' for the human mind, implying this was the Plio-Pleistocene African savannah. This fails to account for the many cognitive processes humans share with primates (and other species), and for those, such as language, that most likely evolved during the Middle Pleistocene.

My own attempts to understand the evolution of the human mind argued that the notion of mental modularity can resolve paradoxes in the archaeological record that have baffled archaeologists for many years (Mithen 1996). Why, for instance, do Neanderthals appear to be so intelligent in some domains of behaviour, such as hunting and tool-making, and so unintelligent in others, such as their use of material symbols and the innovation of new technology? This might be explained by the presence/absence of specific mental modules, or different patterns of connection between modules from that found in the modern mind. I suspect the latter and that the evolution of language in *H. sapiens* resulted in greater degrees of interaction between mental modules – something I termed 'cognitive fluidity' – than in Neanderthals and other pre-modern humans. This idea has since received substantial support from the studies by Carruthers (2002) on the cognitive function of language.

The notion of mental modularity is also invaluable for studies of the earliest hominids, especially when comparisons are drawn with the extant African apes, our closest living relatives. Although chimpanzees appear to have high degrees of social intelligence, their abilities at tool use appear limited. A diverse range of sticks and stones are used for numerous tasks, and patterns of cultural transmission have been detected (Whiten *et al.* 1999). But the rate at which infants learn about tool use, the marked lack of innovation, and observations of ineffective tool use, suggest that specialised modules for tool-making and -using have not evolved in these species (Mithen 1996) and, by implication, in the common ancestor of Africa apes and humans of 10–6 million years ago. The evolution of such modules in the hominid line might explain the appearance of Oldowan technology among australopithecines, species that in other respects appear very similar to modern-day apes.

Mental modularity should also be a key concept in studies of later prehistory and indeed historic archaeology. If Karmiloff-Smith (1992) is correct and mental modules are partly the consequence of one's developmental environment, then as culture changes through time so will the types of modules within the mind. In this regard there is a clear feedback process between culture and biology that may explain why the rate of culture change appears to continually accelerate. The invention of writing at c. 3000 BC may have led to the development of new types of neural networks in children's brains as they matured. Once present, such modules may have provided the basis for further types of cultural innovation, which would provide the cognitive basis for the next generation. Such 'ratchet' effects would be especially prevalent in societies where craft specialisation is present and skills pass from parent to child.

In summary, mental modularity is a key concept for all periods of archaeological study because all archaeologists ought to make explicit reference to the human mind when proposing their interpretations. It has had most impact on studies of pre-modern humans and the origin of the modern mind. But as developments are gained in our understanding of brain maturation and the interactions between biology and culture, later prehistorians and historic archaeologists will increasingly find a need to embrace the concept of mental modularity.

Suggested reading

Butterworth, B. 1999. *The Mathematical Brain*. London: Macmillan.
Brian Butterworth argues that mathematical abilities have a modular basis within the human mind by drawing on case studies of patients who have lost their abilities at mathematical reasoning but maintained all other cognitive functions, and vice versa. It is highly readable and covers the key arguments regarding the nature of modularity.

Cosmides L. and Tooby, J. 1994. Origins of Domain Specificity: The Evolution of Functional Organization, pp. 85–116 in (L. A. Hirschfeld and S. A. Gelman, eds) *Mapping the Mind*. Cambridge: Cambridge University Press.
Leda Cosmides and John Tooby have been the most ardent proponents of the 'massive modularity thesis'. This is their best contribution as they clearly explain why, from an evolutionary perspective, we should expect the human mind to have a modular structure.

Fodor, J. 1983. *The Modularity of Mind*. Cambridge, Mass.: MIT Press.
Jerry Fodor's slim volume was a seminal work in the study of the human mind. He argues that whereas perceptual processes, such as vision and hearing, are modular, central thought processes are distinctly non-modular in fashion and are effectively beyond human understanding. This is one of the most widely cited works and essential background reading for anyone concerned with current debates about the mind.

Mithen, S. 1996. *The Prehistory of the Mind: A Search for the Origin of Art, Religion and Science*. London: Orion.
My book attempted to integrate data and theories from archaeology and the cognitive sciences to explain the evolution of the human mind and the development of culture. It argued that pre-modern human minds, such as those of *Homo ergaster* and *H. neanderthalensis*, were modular in structure while the key cognitive development of modern humans was 'cognitive fluidity' which allowed an enhanced degree of creative thought.

Further reading

Atran, S. 2002. Modular and Cultural Factors in Biological Understanding, pp 41–72 in (P. Carruthers, S. Stitch and M. Siegal, eds) *The Cognitive Basis of Science*, Cambridge: Cambridge University Press.
Barkow, J. H., Cosmides, L. and Tooby, J. 1992. *The Adapted Mind: Evolutionary Psychology and the Generation of Culture*. Oxford: Oxford University Press.
Baron-Cohen, S. 1995. *Mindblindness*. Cambridge, Mass.: MIT Press.
Carruthers, P. 2002. The Cognitive Function of Language. *Brain and Behavioral Sciences* 25: 657–726.
—— 2003. Moderately Massive Modularity, pp. 69–91 in (A. O'Hear, ed.) *Mind and Persons*. Cambridge: Cambridge University Press.
Karmiloff-Smith, A. 1992. *Beyond Modularity: A Development Perspective on Cognitive Science*. Cambridge, Mass.: MIT Press.

Leslie, A. 1994. ToMM, ToBY, and Agency: Core Architecture and Domain Specificity, pp. 119–48 in (L. A. Hirschfeld and S. A. Gelman, eds) *Mapping the Mind*. Cambridge: Cambridge University Press.

Noble, W. and Davidson, I. 1996. *Human Evolution, Language and Mind*. Cambridge: Cambridge University Press.

Peretz, I. and Coltheart, M. 2003. Modularity of Music Processing. *Nature Neuroscience* 6: 688–91.

Pinker, S. 1997. *How the Mind Works*. London: Penguin.

Samuels, R. 1998. Evolutionary Psychology and the Massive Modularity Hypothesis. *British Journal for the Philosophy of Science* 49: 575–602.

Spelke, E. S. 1991. Physical Knowledge in Infancy: Reflections on Piaget's Theory, pp. 133–69 in (S. Carey and R. Gelman, eds) *Epigenesis of Mind: Studies in Biology and Culture*. Hillsdale, NJ: Erlbaum.

Sperber, D, 1994. The Modularity of Thought and the Epidemiology of Representations, pp. 39–67 in (L. A. Hirschfeld and S. A. Gelman, eds) *Mapping the Mind*. Cambridge: Cambridge University Press.

Whiten, A., Goodall, J., McGrew, W. C., Nishida, T., Reynolds, V., Sugiyama, Y., Tutin, C. E. G., Wrangham, R. W. and Boesch, C. 1999. Cultures in Chimpanzees. *Nature* 399: 682–5.

STEVEN MITHEN

MULTIREGIONAL EVOLUTION

Multiregional evolution is often described as a theory of modern human origins, explaining how modern humans are defined by many features and behaviours that appeared at different places and different times and dispersed across the human range, sometimes together and sometimes independently. However, it is more than an explanation of the origin of humans today: multiregional evolution is meant to account for the pattern of evolution within a diversified species distributed widely across many environments. Whether this accurately describes human evolution is a much-debated hypothesis within palaeoanthropology.

As the human fossil record accumulated through the twentieth century (*see* p. 70) and a sense of its pattern of variation and change developed, it was soon evident that there was a paradox. Even the most peripheral populations today are not genetically or culturally isolated from the rest of humanity, and all the significant changes that took place in the course of human evolution over the past several million years, such as the great increases in brain size, appear throughout the global human range. Yet there are some anatomical distinctions, most common in different regions of the world today, that can be found in those same areas for very long periods of time – these are called 'regional continuities'. Most regionally distinct skeletal features, no matter how common, do disappear sooner or later, but fossil evidence suggests that some can be very long lasting. Widespread evolution of common features implies population mixing, while long-lasting differences between regions imply population isolation. Therein lies the dilemma.

One explanation that had been advanced was that the regional populations were races that were similar to distinct species, competing with each other and evolving at different rates along similar pathways that were dictated by evolutionary constraints such as the control of evolutionary change by the limitations imposed by the growth process. A second explanation was that all living human populations had a single, recent origin, accounting for their shared similarities, while current variation between regions appeared quickly and for the most part reflected different environmental adaptations.

Both of these explanations have significant drawbacks: the first requires the improbability of isolated populations evolving the same way; the second requires that observations of regional continuities extending over time are illusions or misinterpretations. Furthermore, neither explanation can account for the details of genetic variation discovered over the past decade. A valid explanation resolving this paradox must reconcile evidence from the human fossil record and the pattern of variation in nuclear DNA.

Multiregional evolution is an explanation of how evolution occurs *within* a species. Its antithesis is when the evolutionary changes take place during the speciation process as a species splits into two; the new species may differ enough to successfully replace the other descendants of the original species. For humans, the multiregional explanation accounts for the significant changes throughout a single, widespread species that evolves *without* any speciations, and the preservation of some regional variations across its broad range. It relies on known and well-understood forces of evolution such as natural selection and gene flow to account for the pattern of variation and change over time.

According to the multiregional model, natural selection is the explanation of why characteristics and behaviours that promote success in reproduction and survivorship can be expected to spread throughout the human range. The mechanism that allows this dispersal is gene flow, the movements of peoples, or of genes when there are mate exchanges between populations. Genes promoted by natural selection disperse because they bring advantages to individuals that have them, and are more frequent in number with each generation. Even with only a slight advantage, genes could quickly spread through the range of the human species. The best example of such a characteristic is cranial capacity, a feature linking anatomical and behavioural evolution that increased very significantly *after* human populations first disseminated out of Africa and colonised the tropics and subtropical regions of the Old World, some two million years ago.

The existing pattern of human geographic variation is a consequence both of these first colonisations, and of differences in adaptation that evolved between various parts of this range as different environments were encountered. Geographic variation also reflects population size expansions and the many population movements that occurred later, both into and out of Africa, and the genetic network linking populations because of mate exchanges throughout the human range that were promoted by exogamy and regulated by language and culture. The consequence of these population movements and exchanges is that human populations each descend from multiple antecedents; they ultimately divide and have descendants that may become extinct or merge with other populations, creating a network of changing relations in a process called 'ethnogenesis' that is similar to the channels in a river that can separate and recombine numerous times. An ethnogenic pattern cannot be topologically transformed into a branching tree, and therefore no tree analysis – no model that assumes only population branching – can validly describe human evolution.

Today, while human differences are evident, their social context and expressions make them seem more regular and significant than they actually are. Human variation is much greater within populations than it is between them because of the long history of population mixing and mate exchanges, and compared with other animals the total amount of human variation is quite small. It is said that differences between the most disparate human populations amount to less than what one finds between adjacent populations of a single frog species!

Is this pattern of human variation, so evident in the present, validly explained by multiregional evolution? Because multiregional evolution is within a species, it could potentially be invalidated by evidence that Pleistocene human evolution was the consequence of species replacements, as successive species replaced earlier ones without mixture (the most recent would be the event presumably described by the 'Eve theory' (*see* p. 17)). Because the sample sizes for diagnostic fossils are small, the question of whether or not there have been such species replacements is still debated among palaeoanthropologists, but the genetic evidence is more abundant and less ambiguous.

Humans evolved from an australopithecine ancestor in Africa two million or more years ago. The dramatic change in anatomy and behaviour that took place then indicates that the mechanism of this evolution was speciation, when a small peripheral population became isolated and evolved quickly, leaving two closely related but significantly differing species. Indeed, some australopithecine species survived the emergence of humans by up to a half million years. There are expected genetic consequences caused by the initial period of very small population size in the new human species. It is a time when genetic variation is dramatically reduced because of the small population size. Many genes that appear with different varieties in the parental species will retain only one of the variations in the new descendant species because when the population size is very small, many or most varieties of a gene can become accidentally lost. This process can be described as a 'bottleneck' because it is a time when genetic variation is constricted and limited, just as the neck of a bottle constricts and limits the movement of the liquid in the bottle. Later in time, as the population size increased, new varieties of the genes appeared, restoring the genetic variation. The evidence that remains of this is seen in the fact that, with the earlier variation removed, most of these gene varieties have their origin at about the time of the bottleneck, or later.

The pattern of variation in genes on the nuclear chromosomes is compatible with this description. Virtually all of the several hundred nuclear genes studied so far have varieties that are close in age to the time when the human line first appeared, or younger. However, human genetic variation is not a simple reflection of this key speciation, because it has geographic structure. Human population variation became more complex during the colonisations that followed the appearance of the human species. New fossil remains from Dmanisi in Georgia, and dates established for the earliest remains from Sangiran in Indonesia, show that this colonisation was almost as early as when the human line emerged. While the earliest human populations in Africa quickly attained higher numbers and came to encompass considerable variation, the initial dispersals out of Africa were by very small populations that suffered additional genetic bottlenecks resulting in different patterns of restricted variation in each. This created shorter histories of genetic variation for some of the genes in each of these populations and, to this day, genetic variation is greater in Africa than it is anywhere else. These small colonising populations also differed as they adapted to local environments. The various population histories and different adaptations form the basis of human geographic variation.

However, the earlier geographic differences are not always clearly seen today because of the subsequent population movements and mixing, and continued population divisions and extinctions through-out human evolution. What can be seen is that there were earlier appearances and greater numbers of regional continuities at the world's peripheries than at the African centre; there is a greater amount of genetic variation in the more populous Africans than anywhere else, and there were more population movements out of Africa than between any other regions or back into Africa.

Regional features are important because they reflect the con-sequences of intraspecies evolution; these describe how we differ. However, the predominant pattern seen in human evolution is not of local continuity but of worldwide change, created as advantageous variations spread widely through the matrix of interconnected populations, linked by both genic exchanges and the common background of the evolving cultural system whose elements also could disperse. These changes created the uniquely human things we have in common.

Suggested reading

Lasker, G. W. and Crews, C. E. 1996. Behavioral Influences on the Evolution of Human Genetic Diversity. *Molecular Phylogenetics and Evolution* 5 (1): 232–40.
Marriage data from recent Native Australian populations are used to describe the pattern and magnitude of gene flow over wide areas that the authors believe occurred throughout most of human prehistory. The magnitude is significant and the pattern is trellis-like, not one of successive fissioning.

Moore, J. H. 1994. Putting Anthropology Back Together Again: The Ethnogenetic Critique of Cladistic Theory. *American Anthropologist* 96 (4): 925–48.
The description of 'ethnogenesis', the trellis-like pattern of population change in which populations may diverge and later merge again.

Relethford, J. H. 2003. *Reflections of the Past*. Boulder, Col.: Westview.
An insider's account of how population size shapes genetic variation and how this affects the modern human origins controversy. Nobody better explains why the evidence that initially appeared to favour one model generally can be found to fit the other as well.

Templeton, A. R. 1993. The 'Eve' Hypotheses: A Genetic Critique and Reanalysis. *American Anthropologist* 95 (1): 51–72.
Templeton describes the replacement theory and shows that genetic data taken from living populations refutes it. All humanity evolved as a single entity, without any major splits.

Templeton, A. R. 2002 Out of Africa Again and Again. *Nature* 416: 45–51.
A statistical analysis of mitochondrial and nuclear DNA shows that Africa played a dominant role in world-wide human evolution, and genetic interchanges between human populations have been ubiquitous in terms of recurrent gene flow

constrained by geographic distance and major population expansions that resulted in interbreeding, not replacement.

Thorne, A. G. and Wolpoff, M. H. 2003. The Multiregional Evolution of Humans, revised paper, in (M. Fischetti, ed.) *New Look at Human Evolution. Scientific American* 13 (2): 46–53.
The authors describe the multiregional hypothesis and present some of the evidence supporting it. Both fossil and genetic evidence argues that the ancient ancestors of many living groups lived where they are found today.

Wolpoff, M. H. and Caspari, R. 1997. *Race and Human Evolution*. New York: Simon and Schuster.
A readily accessible explanation of multiregional evolution and its historic development. The debate over the Eve replacement theory reflects a long history of controversy over theories about human origins and race that have been fraught with social and political implications.

Wolpoff, M. H., Hawks, J. D., Frayer, D. W. and Hunley, K. 2001. Modern Human Ancestry at the Peripheries: A Test of the Replacement Theory. *Science* 291: 293–7.
The predictions of multiregional evolution and the Eve replacement theory were tested with the Late Pleistocene evolutionary sequence at two human peripheries: Australasia and Europe. In both places the authors could not disprove the hypothesis that the earliest 'modern' humans of the region had equal ancestry in their local antecedents and earlier modern humans from the centre of the human range. This disproves replacement theories.

Further reading

Etler, D. A. 1996. The Fossil Evidence for Human Evolution in Asia. *Annual Review of Anthropology* 25: 275–301.
Frayer, D. W. 1997. Perspectives on Neanderthals as Ancestors, pp. 220–34 in (G. A. Clark and C. M. Willermet, eds) *Conceptual Issues in Modern Human Origins Research*. New York: Aldine de Gruyter; and combined bibliography on pp. 437–92.
Hawks, J. and Wolpoff, M. H. 2003. Sixty Years of Modern Human Origins in the American Anthropological Association. *American Anthropologist* 105 (1): 87–98.
Kennedy, K. A. R. 1994. Evolution of South Asian Pleistocene Hominids: Demic Displacement or Regional Continuity?, pp. 337–44 in (A. Parpola and P. Koskikallio, eds) *South Asian Archaeology*. Helsinki: Suomalainen Tiedeakatemia.
Pope, G. G. 1992. Craniofacial Evidence for the Origin of Modern Humans in China. *Yearbook of Physical Anthropology* 35: 243–98.
Relethford, J. H. 2001. *Genetics and the Search for Modern Human Origins*. New York: Wiley-Liss.
Templeton, A. R. 1998. Human Races: A Genetic and Evolutionary Perspective. *American Anthropologist* 100 (3): 632–50.
Wolpoff, M. H. 1989. Multiregional Evolution: The Fossil Alternative to Eden, pp. 62–108 in (P. Mellars and C. B. Stringer, eds) *The Human Revolution: Behavioural and Biological Perspectives on the Origins of Modern Humans*. Edinburgh: Edinburgh University Press.

MILFORD H. WOLPOFF

NON-LINEAR PROCESSES AND ARCHAEOLOGY

In its early years, archaeology conceived the past as a sequence of more or less stable periods in which the state of individual human societies changed very little, alternating with almost instantaneous, profound changes. Stability was assumed, change needed to be explained. In the archaeological literature, this is often called the 'staircase' model of cultural change.

In the second half of the twentieth century, an evolutionary perspective was dominant, in which incremental change was considered to be permanently ongoing and its absence had to be explained. Such explanations could, for example, argue that the powers dominating society suppressed change. Since about 1980, many areas of research that are of interest to archaeologists witnessed an increasing use of yet another approach, which subsumes both these positions into a single one. According to this perspective, changes do not always occur at the same rate. Periods of gradual change may alternate with very rapid changes, or with time-spans in which there is very little change. Whereas a constant rate of change is graphically represented as a straight line in calculus, such accelerations and decelerations in the rate of change give rise to a curved graph. The processes concerned are therefore called 'non-linear'.

Renfrew and Cooke (1979) introduced these ideas in archaeology. They drew upon the work of mathematician René Thom in order to describe sudden transitions as the result of the interaction of different kinds of slow processes. Thom's work was one of the early contributions to what is currently called the 'Theory of Complex Systems'. This approach postulates that most social systems, if not all of them, are potentially unstable because among the many processes that occur in societies, there are always interactions that may unexpectedly cause sudden structural transformations. It re-conceptualises 'social institutions' and 'social structure' in dynamic terms, as phenomena that may temporarily appear to be the stable foundations of society, but which are in reality as much subject to change as everything else, albeit temporarily at a slower rate.

The initial development of the Theory of Complex Systems is associated with the names of, among many others, theoretical physicist Murray Gell-Mann, chemist Ilya Prigogine (both Nobel laureates), mathematician David Ruelle, biologist Stuart Kauffman and ecologist Sir Robert May. But it was soon found to be useful in certain domains of the social sciences, in particular in economics (by Brian Arthur and

Ken Arrow) and finance. In archaeology, the names of George Gumerman, Tim Kohler, James McGlade and Sander van der Leeuw spring to mind.

What are some of the other hallmarks of this approach? First, its emphasis upon the constant renewal of social institutions. In the process, society adapts itself to internal changes as well as changes in the environment with which it interacts. It is thus a fundamental characteristic of societies and social institutions that they are flexible. That flexibility is essential for their survival. Societies survive by changing, rather than by avoiding or suppressing change.

In research, the focus is therefore on emergence, structural transformation and discontinuity in all things social. The Complex Systems approach assumes that processes observed at the macro-scale (in the society as a whole) are the result of dynamic interactions between various diverse entities at smaller scales, such as individuals, groups, institutions and other constituent parts of the society. Many of these interactions are deemed to be part of self-amplifying processes. Increases in population, for example, require more resources. To make these available, new techniques are developed. Such innovations produce exchangeable products, for which the society receives other goods in return. The desirability of such goods stimulates the population to increase production, and to harness more labour. That in turn prompts people to have more children, further increasing the population and the need for resources.

With this emphasis on change comes a focus on differences rather than similarities. Dynamical (social and other) systems transform themselves by not always reproducing their existing features, by introducing differences between the old and the new, or by amplifying anomalies and unexpected conditions they encounter on their way. Hence, considerable importance is accorded to the fact that not all processes occurring in dynamic systems lead to optimisation. Indeed, because future conditions are always different from present ones, optimal adaptation to the present is inherently sub-optimal in the future. Conversely, sub-optimal system behaviour in the present may be optimal in the future, and a dose of it is therefore essential to the system's survival.

Change can come from within as well as from outside, and it often occurs as a consequence of the interplay between dynamics within and dynamics outside the system. Observations of many kinds of systems, both social and natural, point to the fact that the role of the interaction between a system and its environment is essential. If the environment is highly variable, for example due to climatic variation, the system will in time learn how to cope with a wider range of conditions and dynamics than if the environment were uniform. Populations living in 'difficult' desert conditions, for example, permanently anticipate a range of potentially dire circumstances, and learn how to cope with them. Those living in fertile valleys, on the other hand, do not usually anticipate difficulties, and such circumstances therefore hit them all the more heavily when they occur – possibly leading to famine or even mass extinction.

Conceptually, it is assumed that the trajectory that a system follows through time is the result of a continuous dynamic interaction between that system and the multiple 'attractors' in its environment. At any point in time, a system can come to interact with one or more of the many different processes occurring in its environment. This will transform both the system and its environment, and make the former more dependent on a specific part of the latter. One could thus say that the two are 'attracted' to each other. The changes that this triggers may either drive the system to engage even more with that particular part of the environment, or drive it to engage with another 'attractor', another set of environmental dynamics. Different kinds of relationships between a system and its attractors have been observed. The system may, for example, be driven into a long-term 'stable' state in which it does not change. In that case one speaks of a 'point attractor' on which the system, as it were, 'zooms in'.

Alternatively, it may periodically alternate between two or more different attractors. That implies a stable state of oscillation, also called a 'limit cycle'. If the periodicity of attraction to two or more different attractors differs, the system trajectory is said to be 'quasi-periodic'. This leads to a predictable trajectory that, graphically, takes the shape of a doughnut. But many systems are subject to more complex dynamics, which graphically show no regularity. Predictions about the future of such 'strange attractors' are impossible, even in the short term. Of course this presumes that, at any time, the society disposes of a set of different potential ways to survive, different sets of dynamic interactions with its environment, which can be activated by self-amplifying processes. A social system that has a relatively wide range of such options open to it is said to be 'resilient', as it can adapt to a wide range of changes in its environment without losing coherence. On the other hand, if the system has only a few options at its disposal, it is inflexible and vulnerable. The chances are that it will not survive intact.

Because the adaptive changes are triggered by – often minuscule and invisible – changes in the external or internal dynamics of a complex system, such systems are said to operate 'between chance and necessity': at times they behave predictably, while at other times chance determines the way things will go. Hence, apparently similar situations can lead to different outcomes, but apparently different situations may also lead to highly similar outcomes. As a result, the 'law of cause and effect' does not apply. Although we sometimes know what might happen next, we can never predict the longer-term trajectory that complex systems will ultimately follow, nor 'post-dict' the trajectory followed in order to become the way they currently are.

Applying the Complex Systems perspective to past social systems points to a fundamental flaw in archaeological method, the tendency to simplify that is inherent in our whole chain of reasoning, from the moment we group our artefacts into types. We urgently need to investigate more, rather than fewer, dimensions of variability in our data so as to be able to identify the full range of potential behaviours of the social systems we study. This is inherently difficult, due to the nature and scarcity of our data. But modern technology has provided us in recent years with a powerful tool to understand the full complexity of many processes: the computer model. Building dynamic models of many processes, both simple and complex, allows us to do 'virtual experiments' to study the effect of all kinds of hypothetical dynamics, and thus to decide on the most probable ones among them. Volumes by Gumerman and Gell-Mann (1994), Kohler and Gumerman (2000) and van der Leeuw and McGlade (1997) apply this approach to archaeology.

Suggested reading

Gumerman, G. J. and Gell-Mann, M. (eds) 1994. *Understanding Complexity in the Prehistoric Southwest*. Santa Fe Institute, Studies in the Sciences of Complexity. Reading: Addison-Wesley.

Hemelrijk, C. K. and Kunz, H. P. (eds) 2003. *Artificial Life* 9 (4) Special Issue on Collective Effects of Human Behaviour.

Kohler, T. and Gumerman, G. (eds) 2000. *Dynamics in Human and Primitive Societies: Agent-based Modeling of Social and Spatial Processes*. Santa Fe Institute Studies in the Sciences of Complexity. New York: Oxford University Press.

Tainter, J. A. and Tainter, B. B. (eds) 1995. *Evolving Complexity and Environmental Risk in the Prehistoric Southwest*. Santa Fe Institute, Studies in the Sciences of Complexity. Reading: Addison-Wesley.

van der Leeuw, S. E. and McGlade, J. (eds) 1997. *Archaeology: Time, Process and Structural Transformations*. London: Routledge.

Further reading

Gell-Mann, M. 1994. *The Quark and the Jaguar: Adventures in the Simple and the Complex*. New York: W. H. Freeman.

Kauffman, S. 1993. *The Origins of Order: Self-Organization and Selection in Evolution.* Oxford: Oxford University Press.

—— 1995. *At Home in the Universe: The Search for the Laws of Self-Organization and Complexity.* Oxford: Oxford University Press.

Renfrew, C. and Cooke, K. L. (eds) 1979. *Transformations: Mathematical Approaches to Culture Change.* New York: Academic Press.

Renfrew, A. C., Rowlands, M. J. and Segraves, B. A. (eds) 1982. *Theory and Explanation in Archaeology*, Part III. New York: Academic Press.

van der Leeuw, S. E. (ed.) 1998. *The Archaeomedes Project – Understanding the Natural and Anthropogenic Causes of Land Degradation and Desertification in the Mediterranean.* Luxemburg: Office for Official Publications of the European Union.

SANDER E. VAN DER LEEUW

NOTIONS OF THE PERSON

The emergence of an 'archaeology of personhood' is a relatively recent development, and is concerned with identifying the forms of human identity, selfhood and embodiment that existed in the past. The traditional archaeology of the earlier twentieth century paid rather little attention to these issues, being more preoccupied with the cultural norms that characterised 'peoples' or ethnic groups in their entirety. In some cases of exceptional preservation, descriptions of the lives of particular people might have been attempted, but these were rarely integrated into synthetic accounts of the past. The particularities of human experience in specific times and places were also of little interest to many of the early New Archaeologists. Lewis Binford, for instance, advocated the pursuit of universal laws of culture, rather than the details of 'individual psychology'. In this respect he adhered to the cultural evolutionary perspective of the American anthropologist Leslie White, who argued that the history of ancient Egypt 'would have been the same had Ikhnaton been but a sack of sawdust' (1949: 279). That is, the actions of particular people are of little consequence when viewed at the large scale and in the long term. This view was not universal among processual archaeologists, however. Hill and Gunn (1977) argued that cultural variation at the level of the individual organism was significant in evolutionary processes, and sought to identify groups of artefacts which had been made by specific persons. This was to be achieved by distinguishing the personal 'motor habits' (i.e. repeated, habitual bodily actions) of particular artisans manifested in the form and style of material culture.

More recently, an emphasis on the actions and identities of singular persons in the past has been more marked. In feminist archaeology, it has been argued that perspectives that emphasise the social whole and its relationship with the environment tend to dismiss gender as a mere 'ethnographic variable', resulting in accounts of the past in which people are no more than 'faceless pink blobs'. Yet we are aware that in most societies gender relations are a significant element in the internal dynamics of communities. A particularly important set of arguments was presented by Hodder (1982), who suggested that processual archaeology's 'ecological functionalism' (i.e. an approach in which aspects of human culture are principally explained in terms of their functional role in a community's adaptation to its environment) over-emphasised the long-term survival of social systems. As a result, people's actions appeared to be determined by the system, and amounted to a means of achieving the goals of the social whole, in responding to selective pressures at the group level. Hodder stressed instead the role of purposive action and human creativity, which were related to the particular understandings that people developed of their own circumstances. He proposed to integrate a concern with human intentions and indeterminacy into social analysis through structuration theory, in which the relationship between individual actions and long-term structures is explicitly addressed. Arguably, though, this can give the impression that the human individual and the social whole are separate entities, in some kind of relationship with one another, and this problem is perhaps compounded by Hodder's identification of the individual with the small-scale and the singular event.

Hodder's more recent discussions of people in the past continue to dwell on the question of scale (2000). Here he points out that although archaeology studies immense depths of time, it does so through a record made up of the residues of ephemeral activities conducted at the human scale. As a result, he suggests that events and event-sequences on archaeological sites can be used as a means of addressing 'embodied individuals' (i.e. individual people whom we can understand in corporeal terms). This reflects a growing tendency within post-processual archaeology which seeks to move beyond the study of the individual as an abstract category, the basic atom or unit from which societies are built up, and to identify particular personalities and their singular biographies. For Meskell (1999) this is a means of overcoming the discipline's reluctance to consider the subjective and emotional experiences of past people, which is a consequence of an overemphasis on objective knowledge. Meskell presents human individuality as the combination of agency, intentionality and creativity, and suggests that at its most fundamental level this is a universal. All human beings experience themselves in the same way as 'embodied entities' (i.e. having a corporeal existence), but culturally specific interpretations of what it is to be a person are layered on this foundation, and there are also particular life-experiences that are quite singular, making all people separate and non-repeatable. In a way similar to Hodder, Meskell opposes the individual and subjectivity to the social and objectivity, maintaining dichotomies which some would consider to be particular to modern western thought.

Much recent debate over the archaeology of personhood has come to focus on the question of whether the category of the individual is indeed universal. This much is questioned by the British anthropologist Marilyn Strathern's ethnographic work in Melanesia (1988), which reveals people for whom the western conception of individuality is practically incomprehensible. For Strathern, Melanesians are 'dividuals', who consider themselves to be manifestations of structures of kinship and exchange that pre-exist them. Rather than bounded entities, they understand their bodies to be an amalgam of separate parts, each of which has a particular gender. Conversely, in southern India, Cecelia Busby (1997) has described persons who conceive of their bodies as 'permeable' instead of autonomous, linked by the exchange of bodily substances in sex and eating. The anthropological literature contains continuing debates over whether dividual and individual selves form two ends of a continuum, or whether all forms of selfhood contain dividual and individual aspects, or whether there is a potentially wider range of ways of being human. These are important issues for archaeology, for the diversity of forms of personal identity that may have existed in the past remains an open question.

There is certainly a strong argument that the autonomous, rational individual is a form of personhood that is peculiar to the western world in the period since the Renaissance. This is a person who is a free moral and political agent, whose mind is distinct from their body, and who exists in the first instance separately from society, which they enter into as a kind of contract. For seventeenth- and eighteenth-century philosophers like René Descartes and Immanuel Kant it is consciousness, free will and the ability to use reason that make such a person human. However, there is a counter-argument that suggests that even in the modern west all people are to some degree a product of their community, and never have an existence that is prior or external to society and culture. In this view, the unencumbered autonomous individual with an inner world of thought and reflection is a way of understanding oneself that only developed in the Christian era (Taylor 1989).

Those archaeologists who advocate the identification of 'individuals in the past' would not deny that forms of personhood have varied culturally and through time, but they would distinguish between being an individual, which is common to all human beings, and individualism, which is a specifically modern form of individuality. However, individualism properly refers to a celebration and valorisation of the individual that arose in the period following the French Revolution (Lukes 1973), and which relied on the prior existence of the autonomous western self.

These debates have begun to have an impact on accounts of the past in a number of ways. For instance, the study of prehistoric monuments and landscapes has been characterised in recent years by investigations which dwell on the embodied experience of moving through space and architecture (e.g. Tilley 1994). Hodder (2000) criticises these phenomenological archaeologies for failing to address the individual lived experiences of people in the past, as opposed to the generic experiences of indistinguishable past people. However, if we accept the point that past forms of personhood may have been very diverse, the problem is more complex than this would suggest.

Some archaeologists have nonetheless begun to wrestle with the question of what the past would look like if people had not identified themselves as individuals in the familiar sense. Joanna Bruck (2001), for example, has discussed the way that human bodies in the Middle and Late Bronze Age of southern Britain were treated in a similar fashion to particular classes of artefacts. In being cremated after death, bodies were subjected to processes of burning and crushing that are comparable with contemporary cooking, metal-smelting and potting practices. Bruck suggests that the lives of people and artefacts were understood as cycles of birth, death and regeneration, and that both humans and objects could be broken into fragments and reconstituted. Equally, Chris Fowler (2002) has used the notions of dividual and 'partible' (i.e. divisible into parts) personhood to discuss Neolithic mortuary practices on the Isle of Man. More generally, the circulation of body parts between megalithic tombs and other monuments in earlier Neolithic Britain may indicate a notion of the person as dissolvable into its constituent parts, in contrast to an Early Bronze Age in which the emphasis on bodily integrity in death may be related to a new focus on descent and genealogy (Thomas 2000).

Suggested reading

Bruck, J. 2001. Body Metaphors and Technologies of Transformation in the English Middle and Late Bronze Age, pp. 149–60 in (J. Bruck, ed.) *Bronze Age Landscapes: Tradition and Transformation*. Oxford: Oxbow.

Fowler, C. 2002. Body Parts: Personhood and Materiality in the Earlier Manx Neolithic, pp. 47–69 in (Y. Hamilakis, M. Pluciennik and S. Tarlow, eds) *Thinking Through the Body: Archaeologies of Corporeality*. Dordrecht: Kluwer.
These two references are good examples of the way in which novel conceptions of personhood can inform interesting interpretations of the past.

Fowler, C. 2004. *The Archaeology of Personhood: An Anthropological Approach*. London: Routledge.
This is the first full-length treatment of the issue of personal identity in archaeology, in a form that should be accessible to students. These arguments are usefully placed in the context of the archaeology of ancient Egypt.

Hill, J. N. and Gunn, J. 1977. Introducing the Individual in Prehistory, pp. 1–12 in (J. N. Hill and J. Gunn, eds) *The Individual in Prehistory: Studies of Variability in Style in Prehistoric Technologies*. New York: Academic Press.
One of the earliest serious attempts to discuss the role of individuals in past societies, much concerned with the way that variability at the level of the human organism affects the composition of artefact assemblages.

Hodder, I. R. 1982. Theoretical Archaeology: A Reactionary View, pp. 1–16 in (I. R. Hodder, ed.) *Symbolic and Structural Archaeology*. Cambridge: Cambridge University Press.
A singularly important statement, which presented criticisms of ecological functionalism in archaeology from a position which sought to emphasise individual agency and creativity.

Hodder, I. R. 2000. Agency and Individuals in Long-Term Process, pp. 21–33 in (M.-A. Dobres and J. Robb, eds) *Agency in Archaeology*. London: Routledge.
A more recent development from the arguments in the paper above, which goes beyond the recognition of the human individual as the basic element of society, to the identification of particular personalities in the past, who may embody and illuminate long-term social processes at the small scale.

Meskell, L. 1999. *Archaeologies of Social Life*. Oxford: Blackwell.
The most thoroughly articulated account within archaeology of a perspective which stresses the universality of the category of the individual, and argues that fundamental characteristics of individuality are shared by all human beings.

Thomas, J. S. 2002. Archaeology's Humanism and the Materiality of the Body, pp. 29–46 in (Y. Hamilakis, M. Pluciennik and S. Tarlow, eds) *Thinking Through the Body: Archaeologies of Corporeality*. Dordrecht: Kluwer.
Critical of the 'humanist' view that universal characteristics underlie all human identities, and uses this perspective to suggest that British Neolithic funerary practices relate to something other than bounded autonomous western individuals.

Further reading

Busby, C. 1997. Permeable and Partible Persons: A Comparative Analysis of Gender and Body in South India and Melanesia. *Journal of the Royal Anthropological Institute* 3: 261–78.

Lukes, S. 1973. *Individualism*. Oxford: Blackwell.

Morris, B. 1991. *Western Conceptions of the Individual*. Oxford: Berg.

Strathern, M. 1988. *The Gender of the Gift*. Berkeley: University of California Press.

Taylor, C. 1989. *Sources of the Self: The Making of the Modern Identity*. Cambridge: Cambridge University Press.

Thomas, J. S. 2000 Death, Identity and the Body in Neolithic Britain. *Journal of the Royal Anthropological Institute* 6: 603–17.

—— 2004. *Archaeology and Modernity*. London: Routledge.

Tilley, C.Y. 1994 *A Phenomenology of Landscape: Places, Paths and Monuments*. London: Berg.

Treherne, P. 1995. The Warrior's Beauty: The Masculine Body and Self-Identity in Bronze Age Europe. *Journal of European Archaeology* 3: 105–44.

White, L. 1949. *The Science of Culture: A Study of Man and Civilization*. New York: Grove.

JULIAN THOMAS

ORGANISATION OF SOCIETIES, INCLUDING CHIEFDOMS

Human societies, ancient and modern, vary dramatically in their scale and organisation. Archaeological investigations across the globe reveal an enormous diversity of human settlements, from the temporary campsites of foragers to the villages of early farmers to the vast cities of the ancient world. The archaeological record shows gradual (and occasionally dramatic) change through time in the scale of human societies and also in their complexity. In America after World War II, a close alliance between archaeology and anthropology fostered comparative studies that shared the aims of describing the diversity of human societies as well as explaining how and why they changed. In Britain, practitioners of 'social archaeology' (*see* p. 235) sought likewise to reconstruct social institutions and to understand long-term change.

The influential scheme of American anthropologist Elman Service (1962) was widely adopted – and endures today despite criticism – to classify societies into four evolutionary stages: bands, tribes, chiefdoms and states. 'Bands' are mobile family groups who collect wild plants and hunt animals. Band-level groups occupy a range of camps or cave sites, usually on a seasonal basis. In the Valley of Oaxaca (Mexico), for example, American archaeologist Kent Flannery (1986) excavated the cave site of Guila Naquitz, recovering the remains of plants and animal bones deposited during the Archaic Period (8000–2000 BC) by members of 'micro-bands'. Other sites nearby included quarries for stone and an open-air site on the valley floor where several micro-bands gathered, probably for social and ritual activities, when food was plentiful.

'Tribe' is a broad term referring to larger social units, comprising a number of families who are related through a web of kinship. Members of tribal societies earn a living as either herders, horticulturalists or agriculturalists; accordingly, some tribes are nomadic while others live in semi-permanent or permanent villages. Tribes have informal leadership; some are headed by influential 'Big Men', who sponsor feasts, coordinate defence or supervise cooperative projects on behalf of the village. The political influence of a Big Man depends upon his personal initiative but often extends beyond a single village (Sahlins 1963). Some villages also have evidence for food storage (such as pits), defence (walls or fences) or ritual (plazas or dance grounds). The site of Ain Mallaha in Israel is an example of an early sedentary village (9000–8000 BC) associated with the Natufian culture, where excavations revealed the remains of about fifty huts and grinding tools used to process plant foods. Anthropologist Peter Wilson (1988) identifies village life as a critical threshold, arguing that settling down fostered dramatic changes in social relations and material culture.

'Chiefdoms', as 'polities' intermediate between tribes and states, involve the control of productive resources by a chief, integration of multiple settlements under a central authority, and a hereditary elite. As chiefdoms develop, political authority becomes more strongly institutionalised and social inequalities are elaborated; individuals born into the chiefly lineage are ascribed status from birth. Chiefdoms are particularly visible in the archaeological record, as evidenced by Stonehenge in Wessex, the mounds of the Mississippian chiefdoms, or the massive sculpted stone heads of the Olmec in Mesoamerica. In each of these cultures, leaders oversaw large labour forces to move the stones and build the monuments. Monuments and other features of the landscape symbolise the group's presence in a territory (Renfrew 1973) or mark ownership of critical resources (Earle 1997). Because they integrate larger populations (from a thousand to tens of thousands), chiefdom-level societies depend upon agricultural intensification, reflected in terraces, irrigation and storage facilities. Members of the elite occupy elaborate houses, acquire and display rare or exotic goods, and are often buried with numerous or valuable grave goods.

The fourth stage, the 'state', will be most familiar to readers, who belong to nation-states themselves. States encompass still larger populations, more formal institutions of government, a class-structured society, and the means to enforce laws and administer taxes (the state is discussed at length elsewhere; see p. 101).

As a neo-evolutionist (see p. 49), Service hoped to demonstrate (and to explain) cross-cultural regularities in human social organisation. Emphasising ecological relationships, he postulated that social evolution would occur in settings where leadership was necessary to oversee redistribution (collection and reallocation) of products from diverse ecological zones. In his view, leadership developed in response to needs for co-ordination and management as societies grew more complex.

Not all of his colleagues agreed. Anthropologist Morton Fried (1967) shifted the emphasis from ecology to political relationships, proposing a three-stage scheme encompassing egalitarian, ranked and stratified societies. Fried, influenced by Marx, argued that, as agriculture allowed more permanent and reliable production of surplus, ambitious leaders would redistribute accumulated wealth as part of their efforts to enhance their own prestige and social standing. As Marx had argued earlier, Fried thought that control of strategic resources – such as land or capital would foster increasing social inequality, allowing leaders to exploit their followers in pursuit of status or political power.

In Britain, archaeology was less closely allied with anthropology, but proponents of the developing field of 'social archaeology' pursued similar questions. In crystallising the aims of social archaeology, Colin Renfrew (1984) focused upon reconstructing social institutions and on understanding long-term change. Renfrew and other British collea-gues focused on the archaeological record of Europe to ask, 'How many people belong to the society?' 'Are there different roles or statuses within the society?' 'Is there formalised leadership?' 'How do members of the society make a living?' (Renfrew 1984).

Close study of archaeological remains – especially material culture – within a regional context would reveal the answers. Assessing the size and position of sites within a landscape, for example, could reveal the structure of political units. Likewise, reconstructing trade networks held promise for illuminating aspects of the ancient economy or understanding the role of 'prestige goods' in trajectories of change in Bronze Age Europe. Renfrew's (1974) distinction between 'group-oriented' chiefdoms and 'individualising' chiefdoms has been widely cited by archaeologists interested in the strategies of political elites and their impacts on society. Group-oriented chiefdoms included the polities of southern Britain responsible for the construction of the henge monuments, while individualising chiefdoms were typified by the Mycenaean polities of c. 1500 BC, where political power derived from the control of gold and other valuables.

More recently, in both Britain and America, the study of social organisation has broadened considerably in response to criticism. Service himself acknowledged (1971) that the concept of 'tribe' was too broad to be of much use, and critics argue more generally that typologies are simplistic. Classifying a society as a chiefdom, they argue, obscures precisely the interesting and unique variation that should be the focus of study. Worse, researchers overly concerned with typology may approach the archaeological record armed with preconceptions, finding only evidence that fulfils their expectations. Scholars also cite examples of societies that fail to fit into a single stage or category, as exemplified by complex chiefdoms that develop some political institutions more typical of early states.

Seeking to overcome these shortcomings while retaining an evolutionary perspective, American ethnographer Allen Johnson and his colleague, archaeologist Timothy Earle (2000), suggest that human societies are engaged in continuous change. They see societies arrayed along a continuum of scale and complexity marked by certain critical thresholds – points at which new forms of social integration emerge. They group societies into three global categories: the family-level group, the local group (including the Big Man collectivity), and the regional polity (chiefdoms and states). Emphasising the dynamics common to societies of comparable scale and complexity, Johnson and Earle explain societal change through reference to local variables including population growth, intensification of food production, exchange, warfare and competition for power. Importantly, they make few assumptions about the direction or timing of change, allowing that polities may go through cycles of growth and integration alternating with periods of fragmentation into smaller units. Johnson and Earle strongly question whether increases in social complexity or scale can be associated uncritically with notions of 'progress'.

Others, dissatisfied with evolutionary models, have sought more dramatic alternatives. Proponents of practice or agency (*see* p. 3) approaches, for example, believe that social evolution is inadequate to explain the diversity and variability observed in human societies. They argue, following Giddens (1979, 1984), that individuals are the primary 'agents of change'. Human beings, born into specific historical circumstances and shaped by their social worlds (e.g. by culture, norms, social practices and beliefs), construct and transform social reality through their actions. Models for change, these scholars argue, must therefore take account of what people do in particular circumstances, accepting that the course of change can never easily be predicted. Other scholars question the assumption that increases in social complexity and scale inevitably generate strongly centralised or hierarchically structured polities. Alternatives centre on the proposition that power might, in some cases, have been shared (as for example in a confederacy), rather than concentrated in the hands of only a few. As archaeologists increasingly turn their attention to the study of power relations, there is great promise for further new ideas in the study of social organisation.

Suggested reading

Earle, T. 1997. *How Chiefs Come to Power*. Stanford: Stanford University Press.
A readable account of the emergence of chiefdoms, comparing chiefdoms in Bronze Age Denmark, late pre-Hispanic Peru, and Hawaii.

Fried, M. 1967. *The Evolution of Political Society*. New York: Random House.
This book contains Fried's response to Service's (1962) influential typology. Fried emphasised political relationships, arguing that societies developed from egalitarian to ranked to stratified societies.

Johnson, A. and Earle, T. 2000. *The Evolution of Human Societies*. Stanford: Stanford University Press.
A readable introduction to current evolutionary approaches. The introductory chapter presents a new approach to understanding evolutionary dynamics. Nineteen individual case studies follow, to illustrate the variability of human societies throughout the world.

Renfrew, C. 1984. *Approaches to Social Archaeology*. Cambridge, Mass.: Harvard University Press.
A collection of essays that traces the development of social archaeology in Britain. Topics include megaliths, spatial analysis and trade.

Sahlins, M. 1963. Poor Man, Rich Man, Big Man, Chief: Political Types in Melanesia and Polynesia. *Comparative Studies in Society and History* 5. 285–303.
A classic statement on the different forms of political leadership in Polynesia by an anthropologist who strongly influenced Service and Fried.

Service, E. 1962. *Primitive Social Organization*. New York: Random House.
This book contains the initial formulation of Service's influential typology: bands, tribes, chiefdoms, states.

Further reading

Earle, T. 1991. *Chiefdoms: Power, Economy, and Ideology.* Cambridge: Cambridge University Press.

Ehrenreich, R., Crumley, C. and Levy, J. (eds) 1995. *Heterarchy and the Analysis of Complex Societies.* Archaeological papers of the American Anthropological Association, No. 6. Washington, DC: American Anthropological Association.

Flannery, K. (ed.) 1986. *Guilá Naquitz: Archaic Foraging and Early Agriculture in Oaxaca, Mexico.* Orlando: Academic Press.

Giddens, A. 1979. *Central Problems in Social Theory.* London: Macmillan.

—— 1984. *The Constitution of Society: Outline of the Theory of Structuration.* Cambridge: Polity Press.

McIntosh, S. 1999. *Beyond Chiefdoms: Pathways to Complexity in Africa.* Cambridge: Cambridge University Press.

Renfrew, C. 1973. *Before Civilization; The Radiocarbon Revolution and Prehistoric Europe.* London: Cape.

—— 1974. Beyond a Subsistence Economy: The Evolution of Social Organization in Prehistoric Europe, pp. 69–95 in (C. Moore, ed.) *Reconstructing Complex Societies: An Archaeological Colloquium.* Bulletin of the American Schools of Oriental Research 20. Cambridge, Mass.: American Schools of Oriental Research.

Service, E. 1971. *Cultural Evolutionism.* New York: Holt, Rinehart and Winston.

Trigger, B. 1998. *Sociocultural Evolution.* Oxford: Blackwell.

Wilson, P. 1988. *The Domestication of the Human Species.* New Haven: Yale University Press.

Yoffee, N. and Sherratt, A. 1993. *Archaeological Theory: Who Sets the Agenda?* Cambridge: Cambridge University Press.

ELIZABETH DEMARRAIS

PEER POLITY INTERACTION

Peer Polity Interaction (PPI), a theoretical framework developed in the 1980s, is intended to help account for social and political change, or the overall level of organisation complexity, among the equivalent ('peer'), highest-order, autonomous political units that exist in a specific, delimited region. It places special emphasis on the wide range of interactions that may take place between such units – not only exchanges of goods, but also transactions involving information, ideas, symbols, and even hostile confrontations, including outright warfare. The PPI explanatory model has been widely applied in both Old World and New World contexts, and on scales ranging from the small city-states of classical Greece to the whole of Europe in later prehistory.

Prior to the formulation of the PPI approach, archaeologists had certainly given some attention to interactions taking place within and between early societies, leading in some cases to the emergence of a degree of cultural and symbolic unity throughout an entire region. PPI thus shares some similarities with earlier concepts, such as 'interaction sphere' or 'cluster interaction' models. It was the British prehistorian and theoretical archaeologist Colin Renfrew, however, who extended and refined these ideas as a more formal model.

In his important 1975 article 'Trade as Action at a Distance', Renfrew had noted how often it is the case that small-scale early state polities have tended to arise not in isolation, but in clusters whose members show remarkable similarities in size, institutional structure, styles of material culture, belief systems, and so on: the palace-states of Minoan and Mycenaean Greece, the Etruscan city-states, or the cities of the Mayan lowlands are all good examples. One of the mechanisms underlying these regularities and resemblances, Renfrew suggested, must surely be trade (taken in its widest sense to include interactions of various sorts and at differing scales). Yet attempts to explain the social dynamics behind the emergence of state political economies of this kind seemed unsatisfactorily split between either a traditional preoccupation with diffusion and the significance of 'influences' from outside the region ('exogenous' change), or the opposing tendency to concentrate entirely on social and economic processes within a single polity or territory ('endogenous' change). Some of the most important processes and interactions, however, take place between neighbouring societies. So there seemed to be scope for studying *intermediate-level* flows of energy, information and materials occurring *within* a given region between adjacent, but independent and broadly equivalent sociopolitical units.

These ideas coalesced, in a first sketch of the PPI model, as Renfrew sought to account for data from excavations and survey on the Greek island of Melos, as part of his concluding chapter in *An Island Polity* (1982); they were further refined and considerably extended in his introduction to Renfrew and Cherry's *Peer Polity Interaction and Socio-Political Change* (1986), which contains a number of varied case studies exemplifying the approach. The main feature was an understanding of social structures – political institutions, ritual systems, symbolic 'languages', etc. – as the outcome of interactions over a long period among adjacent polities. Renfrew suggested that polities of comparable scale and organisation (early forms of state, for example) tend to be found in the same region, and that they tend to experience transformational changes at about the same time. New institutional features that might appear, as such societies become more complex, include monumental buildings of closely similar form (e.g. temples), ways of communicating information (e.g. writing, measurement systems), special types of artefacts for displaying high status (e.g. royal insignia), and various ritual practices and customs that help reinforce complex social organisation (e.g. burial practices). Significantly, the archaeological record seems to indicate that such changes tend, at first, not to emanate from a single source of innovation, but to crop up roughly contemporaneously in a number of interacting polities. What might account for such observations as these?

In the PPI framework, the explanatory focus is on the interactions taking place *between* peer polities, particularly those tending to promote the intensification of production. Prolonged warfare, for example, which requires support of an army and uses up resources as a result of destruction and looting, has the effect of both intensifying production and favouring the emergence of hierarchical institutions. But competition of less overtly hostile sorts may also have similar effects. When one group seeks to outdo another and achieve higher inter-polity status (by gift exchange, for example, or the construction of impressive monuments), competitive emulation can involve gestures that are not only expensive, but similar in kind: that is, authority is established by doing the same things as other nearby groups – but bigger and better. However, not all relevant interactions need be competitive. Renfrew also coined the term 'symbolic entrainment' to refer to processes whereby more complex symbolic or non-symbolic innovations (some of the institutions of kingship, for example, or the use of writing as an effective system for bureaucratic recording) come to be adopted by less developed neighbouring societies. He argued that the prior existence, or parallel growth, of a political or belief system in one polity would tend to favour the acceptance and stability of a similar social order in a neighbouring one (this applies equally to the transmission and acceptance of innovations). Finally, increased exchange (both imports and exports) can foster new levels of production and forms of specialisation, as well as institutions to manage the allocation and distribution of goods.

A convincing example of the PPI idea in action concerns the processes that led to the development of the Greek city-state in the earlier first millennium BC. Hundreds of such political units came to be established throughout southern Greece, on the islands and along the coasts of the Aegean, and further afield too, in the Black Sea area and in southern Italy and Sicily. Despite their generally small scale in terms of territory and population, they were self-governing (at least at first); and, although many of them engaged in trading and other cultural contacts with the Near East or Egypt, they do not represent instances of a civilisation 'secondary' to the states that had developed earlier in those areas. Individual city-states, to be sure, exploited different local resources, underwent dissimilar paths of agricultural or industrial intensification, and developed distinctive local political and cultural institutions. But more significant is the social, cultural and religious framework in which these processes occurred, one very widely shared with other city-states (i.e. peer polities) throughout the Greek world, and created via the interactions taking place among them. As Renfrew put it:

> The small states of Greece emerged *together*, pulling each other up by the bootstraps, as it were. What they shared were the common elements of Greek civilization: language, religion, shared history, similar (but not identical) institutions, equivalent agricultural and commercial practices.
>
> (Renfrew and Cherry 1986: 11)

Archaeological evidence in support of this approach is plentiful. The temple, as the focus of religious expression in every city-state, developed at an early stage, yet was invariably constructed according to the same, widely shared architectural conventions (the Doric and Ionic orders), leaving scope only for outdoing one's neighbours by building on a grander scale. Clear instances of inter-polity competitive emulation and conspicuous community display may be found in the treasuries of different city-states, built literally side by side and in closely similar styles, at the sanctuaries of Olympia and Delphi; these sites and others that hosted pan-Hellenic games and festivals provided important contexts where members of different polities interacted and competed with each other. Heavy infantrymen (hoplites) drawn from the citizen bodies did battle with each other, in a highly conventional and even ritualistic manner – almost a game whose rules were seemingly accepted by every Greek state without question. The adoption and public display of law-codes, and the rapid dissemination of the practice of minting silver coinage, reveal the extent to which individual city-states kept an alert eye on the constitutional and economic progress of their peers.

This example concerns small-scale states in Greece, the type of polity whose development the PPI concept was first formulated to explain. It was intended, nonetheless, that the same framework would have applicability to societies in other parts of the world, and of markedly different levels of complexity. Other studies have indeed extended the approach to cases ranging as widely in space and time as prehistoric Europe, the American Midwest and early historic East Asia. PPI obviously presupposes a regional approach, but the regions involved can go well beyond the scale of the small states of Greece, to encompass areas as large as the quarter-million square kilometres of the lowland Maya region, the whole of Britain and Ireland, or even European-wide phenomena such as Beaker burials or the La Tène complexes. When PPI is extended in this way into fully prehistoric settings, some operational difficulties emerge. It is not easy, for example, to provide a spatial definition of the independent polities, or to demonstrate their autonomy and peer status; chronological imprecision makes it tricky to identify clear archaeological evidence of inter-polity contact *before* the changes in organisational complexity for which PPI hopes to provide an explanation; finding archaeological indications of the relevant flows of commodities and information is often far from straightforward, and can sometimes lead to circular explanations. For these reasons, especially, there is general agreement that the approach works best in settings where historical sources afford some measure of control (some relevant recent examples include studies of medieval central India, and political formations in Hellenistic Greece).

PPI was proposed at the outset not as a formal model for 'testing', but as an approach to encourage a shift of perspective. It has stimulated fresh ideas about the processes underlying the emergence of influential symbolic systems that helped to establish power relationships and to promote socio-economic change, and even about the formation of ethnic groups, the spread of languages, and the widespread distribution of certain archaeological phenomena (such as Hopewellian ceremonial behaviour). The term has now become a widely recognised element in the archaeologist's vocabulary.

Suggested reading

Knapp, A. B. 1986. Peer Polity Pressure? *The Quarterly Review of Archaeology*, September–December: 3–5.
A thoughtful review article discussing the PPI concept.

Preucel, R. W. and Hodder, I. 1996. The Production of Value, pp. 99–113 in (R. W. Preucel and I. Hodder, eds) *Contemporary Archaeology in Theory: A Reader*, Oxford: Blackwell.
Useful critical introduction to readings on archaeological approaches to political

control and legitimisation, situating PPI alongside a range of related research directions.

Renfrew, C. 1975. Trade as Action at a Distance: Questions of Integration and Communication, pp. 3–59 in (J. A. Sabloff and C. C. Lamberg-Karlovsky, eds) *Ancient Civilization and Trade*. Albuquerque: University of New Mexico Press.
Seminal paper that urged archaeologists to consider 'trade' as encompassing a wide range of forms of interaction between societies.

Renfrew, C. 1982. Polity and Power: Interaction, Intensification and Exploitation, pp. 264–90 in (C. Renfrew and M. Wagstaff, eds) *An Island Polity: The Archaeology of Exploitation in Melos*. Cambridge: Cambridge University Press.
First sketch of a PPI approach, with particular reference to the nature of Greek city-states and their Bronze Age predecessors.

Renfrew, C. and Cherry, J. F. (eds). 1986. *Peer Polity Interaction and Socio-Political Change*. Cambridge: Cambridge University Press.
Papers from a symposium in which the PPI concept is thoroughly explored and critiqued in very diverse situations in both the Old and New Worlds.

Further reading

Caldwell, J. A. 1964. Interaction Spheres in Prehistory, pp. 133–43 in (J. R. Caldwell and R. L. Hall, eds) *Hopewellian Studies*. Illinois State Museum Papers 12, no. 6. Springfield: Illinois State Museum.
Price, B. J. 1977. Shifts in Production and Organization: A Cluster Interaction Model. *Current Anthropology* 18: 209–34.

JOHN F. CHERRY

PHENOMENOLOGICAL ARCHAEOLOGY

An explicit concern with a 'phenomenological' perspective in archaeological research has only developed during the last decade, although as in many other 'new' positions intellectual precursors can be traced back, or read into, the earlier literature. Put most simply, phenomenology involves the study and description of phenomena. A phenomenon is any entity (thing or event) that appears or presents itself to a subject in the world. So the central concern is with the conceptualisation of subject–object relations. It involves a description of things as they are experienced in the world by a human subject. The presupposition is that the more precise and detailed this description is, the better our understanding will be. Thus the description and redescription of material culture lead to a better understanding of it and fresh insights with regard to its meaning and significance. Describing the world allows us to explain it. Processes of ordinary human perception are of central significance: seeing, hearing, touching, smelling, tasting. Phenomenologists try to ground their descriptions of the social and material world in the manner in which people think and feel about it rather than in an abstract manner. It is a humanist approach which puts people and the manner in which they perceive and relate to the world at the centre of research.

A phenomenological perspective provides a general philosophical background for understanding material forms: an attitude, an orientation, a disposition, a mode of understanding. This does not translate well into a formal theory, nor a fixed set of methodological techniques, as to how one can carry out 'good' research. There are no rule books for a phenomenological analysis and there is no logical end to research since specific material forms can be endlessly described in a multitude of ways in a plethora of different social and material contexts.

The work of the German philosopher Husserl is generally regarded as providing the impetus for a phenomenological approach. His general position was reworked and extended in various ways by Heidegger, Merleau-Ponty and Sartre, who remain today the primary philosophical influences on research (Tilley 1994, 2004; Thomas 1996). The central and most important point of Husserl's work, which forms a starting point for all the various forms of phenomenological positions which have developed subsequently, was his critique of scientific empiricism (*see* p. 92). Husserl argued that there is a fundamental distinction between the manner in which the world is represented in scientific descriptions and the manner in which humans actually experience it. In short, a scientific account is both inhuman and very impoverished. While this might be claimed not to matter so much when we are studying purely physical, biological or chemical processes, which have no human meaning, such a criticism becomes quite devastating when human beings and their artefacts are the focus of study.

In a scientific description primacy is given to variables that can be quantified and measured: size, weight, distance, etc. But what of aspects of things that cannot be abstractly measured such as colour, taste, smell, touch and feeling? All these may be very important aspects of the meaning of an artefact but they inevitably become regarded as of secondary importance from the prejudice of a scientific approach pretending to represent the world in an objective and realistic manner. While the archaeological literature is filled with measurements (e.g. of the size and shape and distances between stones) it has had relatively little to say about other arguably much more important *material* qualities of things. It is quite clear that simply measuring and quantifying aspects of a thing tell us very little about it. As a form of representation of that thing these measurements are a very poor substitute for the rich sensuous qualities that we know to be characteristic of actual human experience and dwelling in the world. It is these, through elaborate and precise description, from the point of view of a human subject, that a phenomenologist attempts to capture and re-present.

The human body itself (Tilley 1994; Thomas 2002) provides a starting point for knowledge of the world, and all modern human beings (*Homo sapiens sapiens*) have the same kinds of bodies and perceive and experience the world in similar human ways at a basic biological level. This is what links past and present, me and you, us and the people who constructed an ancient monument or made a pot. For the phenomenologist his or her body and the experience of this body is the essential research tool: an assertion of our common human experience. To gain fresh knowledge of the archaeological past requires experiencing the surviving traces of that past ourselves. However, in our interpretations, the accounts which we produce of research experiences, we clearly need to go beyond the limiting and 'essentialist' (i.e. simplifying something to a core or basic essence and, in so doing, destroying differences and complexity) notion of a universal human body and try to think through all those other factors mediating human experience that are specific to time and place, such as age and gender and socioeconomic status: access to material and non-material (e.g. knowledge) resources.

The key methodological tool of anthropology has always been participant observation: being there, experiencing the social events and practices which one wants to understand. And so it is with a phenomenological archaeology. We cannot, of course, go back into the past but we can still experience what is left of it today through phenomenologically exploring the practices of excavation, through examining collections of artefacts in museums, and through visiting monuments and places in the landscape. In other words, through precisely the kinds of basic research practices that archaeologists have always carried out but whose potential and significance for understanding the past have not been fully realised because of precisely the kind of scientific prejudice that Husserl criticised. So, in one sense, there is nothing new about a phenomenological approach at all. Looked at in another way everything is new. To attempt to illustrate this I will discuss landscape archaeology and the study of megalithic tombs.

From the birth of the discipline, archaeology has been about the study of landscape. Distribution maps of categories of artefacts, sites and monuments have always been of central importance. Every statistical and analytical technique derived from geographical spatial science has been used to try and understand the locations of sites from 'nearest neighbour analysis' to 'central place theory' to GIS, the new spatial technology currently in vogue. Despite the elementary fact that we can still walk around in the landscape and describe the experience of sites and monuments in it from the sensuous bodily perspective of being there, until the advent of an explicit phenomenological approach understandings were primarily based on measuring and discussing things (literally dots) on paper. Such a two-dimensional abstracted map-based approach can never even approximate an understanding derived from the nuances of being in the field, of experiencing place.

Ten years ago I walked along the traces of the Dorset cursus, a 10 km-long Neolithic linear monument consisting of two parallel banks with internal ditches, and attempted to describe in detail its relationship to the local topography (ridges, hills, valleys, water-courses) and other broadly contemporary Neolithic monuments in its vicinity: how this landscape and these monuments might have been encountered and understood. The cursus had already been exhaustively surveyed and mapped and parts of it excavated. It was well known, but nobody had apparently ever walked along it before while describing its impact on and relationship to the landscape, which led to a more nuanced perspective on its significance. There are now a growing number of similar studies (e.g. Edmonds 2001; Fraser 1998; Scarre 2002).

Similarly, while an enormous amount of ink has been spilled on the problem of European megalithic tombs, until quite recently no archaeologists had attempted to describe what it feels like to move around inside the passages and chambers: the experiences of light and darkness, constricted spaces and open spaces, the sounds, textures, colours, touch and texture, and other material qualities of the stones (e.g. Richards 1993; Bradley 1999; 2000; Fowler and Cummings 2003).

Some critics have claimed that such studies are just a matter of purely personal experience of place. The approach is therefore entirely subjective and, by implication, worthless. I would maintain such a criticism is entirely unfounded: we cannot experience landscapes and artefacts in any way we like. Their very materiality constrains the kinds of observations and understandings we can reach. There is a 'dialectic', or two-way process, at work between thing, or place, and person. Every phenomenological study is not subjective rather than objective because this opposition is itself meaningless. As human beings, we can only study things as we experience them. All such studies are, necessarily, limited and therefore can be criticised. We can never give an account of everything we experience.

The bodily experience of a tomb, or a place in the landscape, or an artefact, can sometimes be powerful and overwhelming. We become aware of the manner in which material culture has an *agency* (*see* p. 3), that it has effects on our minds and our bodies: I can only move in a certain manner down this passage, here I must stoop, there I can stand up. What a phenomenological approach to material culture emphasises is that the manifold sensory qualities of things have effects on persons. Things are active rather than passive and we cannot interpret them in any way we like, precisely because, unlike texts, they have direct sensory effects on us.

Embodied human experiences are absolutely central to a phenomenological approach. What is important here is that human experience is always perspectival and limited. We experience the world as we move around in it, from different angles, different places, different points of view. We never experience it all at once. There is not one landscape but many landscapes, and the manner in which we encounter sites and monuments in the landscape, how we approach and experience them, may radically alter our understanding of their meaning and significance. By contrast, from the peculiar perspective of a ground plan, or a map, we see everything at once, but such maps and plans provide only an abstracted spatial knowledge of places and landscapes: a bird's eye view which is entirely removed from human experience. Because we tend to spend so much time gazing at these maps and plans we tend to interpret the world, in a distorted sense, in their image and end up with a very peculiar perspective on the past. The same is true for the depiction and study of artefacts.

Our experience of the world is, in an important sense, carnal. Human perception involves a fusion of all the senses. We never just see the world, hear sounds, experience smell, touch things independently. Experience involves a structure of sensuous feeling in which different aspects of our sensory engagement overlap, although in any one context it may be sound or sight or vision which may be dominant. A phenomenological archaeology thus tries to take account of the full range of our sensory engagement with the world in order to understand the past (see e.g. Watson and Keating 1999; Jones and MacGregor eds. 2002; Tilley 2004). Our contemporary culture, it has been claimed, is dominated by the visual. In other historical periods, other senses such as sound and smell seem to have been far more important according to some historians. There is much to explore here archaeologically: why should we assume that a view across the sea might be more significant than the smell of the salt or rotting seaweed?

Phenomenological archaeology teaches us about prejudices, it teaches us about ourselves and our relation with that which we study. Its overriding imperative is to demand a 'synaesthetic' (i.e. blending of all the senses through which we experience the world) sensuous engagement with the past.

Suggested reading

Bradley, R. 2000. *An Archaeology of Natural Places*. London: Routledge.
A wide-ranging study which discusses the significance of unaltered features of the landscape in relation to European prehistoric material culture, including votive deposits, stone axe production sites, rock art and monuments.

Edmonds, M. 2001. *Prehistory in the Peak*. Stroud: Tempus Publishing.
An evocative, poetic and well-illustrated study of landscape and monuments in the Peak District of northern England.

Jones, A. and MacGregor, G. 2002. *Colouring the Past: The Significance of Colour in Archaeological Research*. Oxford: Berg.
The first book-length study of the significance of colour for archaeological interpretation.

Richards, C. 1993. Monumental Choreography: Architecture and Spatial Representation in Late Neolithic Orkney, pp. 143–78 in (C. Tilley, ed.) *Interpretative Archaeology*. Oxford: Berg.
An excellent discussion of the sensory dimensions of the internal spaces of megalithic tombs.

Thomas. J. 1996. *Time, Culture and Identity*. London: Routledge.
A philosophical discussion of time in relation to culture and identity based on a reading of Heidegger's work which is used to produce a fresh and stimulating perspective on the significance of monuments and material culture in the British Neolithic.

Tilley, C. 1994. *A Phenomenology of Landscape*. Oxford: Berg.
This book sets out the theoretical basis for a phenomenological approach to the study of landscape, discusses ethnographic work, and presents studies of prehistoric monuments in relation to landscape from southern Britain.

Tilley, C. 2004. *The Materiality of Stone: Explorations in Landscape Phenomenology*. Oxford: Berg.
A detailed discussion of Merleau-Ponty's work is used to understand the manifold sensuous qualities of stone in relation to landscape, with case studies of menhirs in Neolithic Brittany, Maltese Neolithic temples and Bronze Age rock carvings and cairns from southeast Sweden.

Further reading

Bradley, R. 1999. Darkness and Light in the Design of Megalithic Tombs. *Oxford Journal of Archaeology* 8: 251–9.

Fowler, C. and Cummings, V. 2003. Places of Transformation: Building Monuments from Water and Stone in the Neolithic of the Irish Sea. *Journal of the Royal Anthropological Institute* 9 (1): 1–20.

Fraser, S. 1998. The Public Forum and the Space Between: The Materiality of Social Strategy in the Irish Neolithic. *Proceedings of the Prehistoric Society* 64: 203–24.

Scarre, C. (ed.) 2002. *Monuments and Landscape in Atlantic Europe.* London: Routledge.

Thomas, J. 2002. Archaeology's Humanism and the Materiality of the Body, in (Y. Hamilakis, M. Pluciennek and S. Tarlow, eds) *Thinking Through the Body: Archaeologies of Corporeality.* New York: Kluwer Academic.

Tilley, C. 1999. *Metaphor and Material Culture.* Oxford: Blackwell.

Watson, A. and Keating, D. 1999. Architecture and Sound: An Acoustic Analysis of Megalithic Monuments in Western Britain. *Antiquity* 73: 325–36.

CHRISTOPHER TILLEY

POST-PROCESSUAL AND INTERPRETIVE ARCHAEOLOGY

Post-processual archaeology began as a critical response to a set of perceived failings of processual archaeology (*see* p. 212) (Hodder 1982a, 1982b, 1985; Shanks and Tilley 1987a, 1987b; Miller and Tilley 1984; Leone 1982). The critique primarily focused on the processual concern with adaptive technologies, its embrace of a cross-cultural anthropology at the expense of historical context, and its restrictive definition of archaeological science as 'positivist' (positivism, as used in archaeology, is the belief that arguments are built by testing theories against independent and objective data). Initially a wide range of authors, including those influenced by feminism (*see* p. 116), entered into such critiques, and it was difficult to identify common themes of an alternative agenda. The strongest impact of the post-processual critique was at first in Britain and Scandinavia, although important contributions were made from historical archaeology in the United States (Leone *et al.* 1987).

The main struts of the post-processual critique dealt with meaning or symbolism, history, agency (*see* p. 3) and critical approaches. Within processual archaeology of the 1960s and 1970s it was suggested that material culture should be studied in terms of long-term adaptive processes. Even the symbolism of material culture was studied in terms of how it enabled group size to increase, for example (Wobst 1977). The wider anthropological evidence that material culture had meanings that themselves influenced how social actors understood the world seemed to be largely discounted. It was claimed by post-processual archaeologists, following anthropologists such as Bourdieu (1977), Sahlins (1976) and Turner (1969), that material culture was meaningfully constituted. Indeed, it was claimed that symbolism was everywhere, and that even refuse was discarded in terms of meanings and concepts about, for example, cleanliness or purity or dirt.

This emphasis on meaning and symbolism also seemed to undermine the processual emphasis on cross-cultural generalisation. While it might be possible to claim that certain technologies universally allowed certain types of use of the environment, the meanings of symbols were at least partly arbitrary. In other words, the meanings of bow ties or pot shapes came about in particular historical contexts, dependent on specific relations between people in particular circumstances. This emphasis on history had long been argued by Trigger (1978), and post-processual archaeology embraced the need to return to history in parallel with the symbolic and historical turns in anthropology. Indeed, post-processual archaeology immediately had more impact in historical archaeology, both in the United States (see above) and in Britain (Johnson 1996). In prehistoric archaeology the emphasis on context involved a parallel critique of the universal (e.g. Barrett 1987).

An additional critique argued that in much processual archaeology material culture was passive. It was seen simply as a tool to respond to the environment. People too seemed faceless and without agency, responding passively to the exigencies of the world around them. Post-processual archaeologists argued instead that material culture was active – that it was used and manipulated by people to effect social change (Hodder 1982a), and that it could transform the ideologies through which people understood their world (Miller and Tilley 1984). Also, following on from the anthropologist Bourdieu (1977) and the sociologist Giddens (1979), humans were not seen as behavioural dupes, but as able to monitor and transform the world around them – they had agency.

The final strut of the post-processual critique concerned the embrace by processual archaeology in the 1960s and 1970s of a hypothetico-deductive positivism derived from Hempel. The latter approach involved deducing statements from general theories and then testing them against observable data. For post-processual archaeologists the embrace of this epistemology seemed outdated and ironic –

outdated because the epistemology had already undergone considerable critique in the natural sciences, and ironic because archaeology is a discipline that spends most of its time talking about the unobservable – past cultural systems (Wylie 1982). Indeed, anthropology and many other social sciences had already undertaken a thorough critique of positivism. Other critiques of positivism came from feminist archaeology (*see* p. 116) which pointed to the male bias in positivist archaeology (Gero and Conkey 1991), and increasingly from indigenous archaeologists who pointed out that their interests were not always best served by archaeology as a positivist science (Anyon *et al.* 1996).

During the 1980s, post-processual archaeology was simply 'post', in that it was based on a diverse set of critiques of processual archaeology. But within the diversity some unifying features can be identified. One theme was the attempt to 'catch up with' debates in anthropology and the other social sciences and humanities. An overall critique of processual archaeology was that it had rather severed archaeology from developments in adjacent fields, and in each of the four areas of critique identified above some rapprochement between archaeology and related disciplines is defined. Another unifying theme was a focus on social aspects of life at the expense of economic, technological and environmental factors. Finally, a unifying emphasis was perhaps the recognition that diversity of approach was preferable to the unity of science claimed by some processual archaeologists. It was OK to be simply 'post'.

During the 1990s several post-processual archaeologists moved from critique to rebuilding method and theory in archaeology, while at the same time encouraging diversity of approach. The term 'interpretive archaeology' was often used to define this more positive approach (Tilley 1993; Thomas 2000; Hodder 1991). The emphasis on interpretation (rather than the processual emphasis on explanation) is that different people with different social interests will construct the past differently. There is thus an uncertainty and ambiguity in the scientific process that cannot simply be resolved by appeal to objective data, because what people see as objective data also varies (Hodder 1999). Rather, interpretation involves a to-and-fro between data and theory as more and more bits of information are fitted together into a coherent argument – this fitting process is best described as 'hermeneutic' (*ibid.*). It allows some interpretations to be favoured over others and 'best fits' to be identified. But the belief that theories can be tested against objective data is seen as an incorrect description of archaeological (or any other social or natural) science. Interpretive archaeology retains a commitment to social critique of the basis for truth claims, while at the same time embedding truth claims within archaeological data. New forms of writing have become common (e.g. Joyce 2002; Mithen 2003; Edmonds 1999) and reflexive methods developed which explore the implications of interpretive approaches for field and laboratory practice (Andrews *et al.* 2000; Hodder 1999).

Other central components of interpretive archaeology involve an engagement with agency theories (Dobres and Robb 2000) and 'practice theories' (Barrett 1994; Tilley 1994). The major theoretical shift within interpretive archaeology through the 1990s was away from text as a metaphor for material culture and towards practice and 'embodiment' (the breaking down of oppositions between mind and body) . The idea that material culture could be considered as a text was derived from structuralist and symbolic archaeology (Hodder 1986), but such an approach tended to separate material symbols from the practices of daily life. In fact, material culture is not made up of abstract symbols. Its meanings come about through practical engagement with the world (the meaning of an axe is linked to its use to cut down trees), and these non-discursive meanings may influence the conscious discursive meanings. The attempt to break down oppositions between mind and matter, subject and object is most clearly identified with phenomenological approaches in archaeology (*see* p. 201) (Thomas 1996). But new developments in feminist archaeology have also led to an understanding of embodiment (Meskell 1998, 1999; Tringham 1994). The study of landscape (*see* p. 156) has also been an important arena for the application of experiential approaches (Tilley 1994).

By the early twenty-first century, the term 'post-processual archaeology' has come to be used in two different ways. On the one hand, it can be equated with interpretive archaeology. On the other hand, the term can be used to refer to all the varieties of social critical response to processual archaeology including feminist and indigenous archaeology. There has also been much absorbing of post-processual archaeology into mainstream archaeology even in the United States, where processual archaeology was most widely adopted. Thus a recent review of theory in archaeology in the United States argues that the majority of archaeologists select from processual-plus approaches which incorporate the archaeology of symbolism and meaning, agency, gender and critique (Hegmon 2003). In another branch of processual archaeology – cognitive processual archaeology (*see* p. 41) – there has been a parallel acceptance of the main struts of post-processual and interpretive archaeology (Renfrew 1989), although differences remain insofar as cognitive processual archaeologists at times separate cognition from its social context. Today it seems that the old processual/post-processual battlegrounds have largely been abandoned and there is widespread acceptance of a broader range of social theories in archaeology, from which individual researchers select arguments appropriate for particular data-sets and problems.

Suggested reading

Dobres, M.-A. and Robb, J. (eds) 2000. *Agency in Archaeology*. London: Routledge.
A helpful and extensive coverage of the debates about agency in archaeology.

Hodder, I. 1986. *Reading the Past*. Cambridge: Cambridge University Press.
This text summarises the critique of processual archaeology and defines post-processual archaeology.

Leone, M., Potter, P. B. and Shackel, P. 1987. Toward a Critical Archaeology. *Current Anthropology* 28: 251–82.
An important statement defining critical archaeology from the point of view of Marxist North American historical archaeology.

Meskell, L. 1999. *Archaeologies of Social Life: Age, Sex, Class etcetera in Ancient Egypt*. Oxford: Blackwell.
An extensive application of theories about embodiment and social difference.

Shanks, M. and Tilley, C. 1987a. *Reconstructing Archaeology*. Cambridge: Cambridge University Press.
An important founding and radical text within post-processual archaeology.

Thomas, J. 1996. *Time, Culture and Identity*. Cambridge: Cambridge University Press.
A major application of phenomenological approaches to British prehistory.

Further reading

Andrews, G., Barrett, J and Lewis, J. 2000. Interpretation not Record: The Practice of Archaeology. *Antiquity* 74: 525–30.
Anyon, R., Ferguson, T. J., Jackson, L. and Lane, L. 1996. Native American Oral Traditions and Archaeology. *Society for American Archaeology Bulletin* 14: 2, 14–16
Barrett, J. 1987 Contextual Archaeology. *Antiquity* 61: 468–73.
—— 1994. *Fragments from Antiquity*. Oxford: Blackwell.
Bourdieu, P. 1977. *Outline of a Theory of Practice*. Cambridge: Cambridge University Press.
Edmonds, M. 1999. *Ancestral Geographies of the Neolithic. Landscapes, Monuments and Memory*. London: Routledge.
Gero, J. and Conkey, M. (eds) 1991. *Engendering Archaeology*. Oxford: Blackwell.
Giddens, A. 1979. *Central Problems in Social Theory*. London: Macmillan.
Hegmon, M. 2003. Setting Theoretical Egos Aside: Issues and Theory in North American Archaeology. *American Antiquity* 68 (2): 213–43.
Hodder, I. 1982a. *Symbols in Action*. Cambridge: Cambridge University Press.

—— (ed) 1982b. *Symbolic and Structural Archaeology*. Cambridge: Cambridge University Press.

—— 1985. Post-processual Archaeology, pp. 1–26 in (M. Schiffer, ed.) *Advances in Archaeological Method and Theory*, vol. 8. New York: Academic Press.

—— 1991. Interpretative Archaeology and its Role. *American Antiquity* 56: 7–18.

—— 1999. *The Archaeological Process*. Oxford: Blackwell.

Johnson, M. 1996. *An Archaeology of Capitalism*. Oxford: Blackwell.

Joyce, R. 2002. *The Languages of Archaeology: Dialogue, Narrative and Writing*. Oxford: Blackwell.

Leone, M. 1982. Some Opinions about Recovering Mind. *American Antiquity* 47: 742–60.

Meskell, L. 1998. Intimate Archaeologies: The Case of Kha and Merit. *World Archaeology* 29: 363–79.

Miller, D. and Tilley, C. (eds) 1984. *Ideology, Power and Prehistory*. Cambridge: Cambridge University Press.

Mithen, S. 2003. *After the Ice*. London: Weidenfeld and Nicolson.

Renfrew, C. 1989. Comments on 'Archaeology into the 1990s'. *Norwegian Archaeological Review* 22: 33–41.

Sahlins, M. 1976. *Culture and Practical Reason*. Chicago: University of Chicago Press.

Shanks, M. and Tilley, C. 1987b. *Social Theory in Archaeology*. Cambridge: Polity Press.

Thomas, J. 2000. *Interpretive Archaeology. A Reader*. Leicester: Leicester University Press.

Tilley, C. (ed.) 1993. *Interpretative Archaeology*. Oxford: Berg.

—— 1994. *The Phenomenology of Landscape*. Oxford: Berg.

Trigger, B. 1978. *Time and Tradition*. Edinburgh: Edinburgh University Press.

Tringham, R. 1994. Engendered Places in Prehistory. *Gender, Place and Culture* 1: 2, 169–203.

Turner, V. 1969. *The Ritual Process*. London: Routledge and Kegan Paul.

Wobst, M. 1977. Stylistic Behaviour and Information Exchange, pp. 317–42 in (C. E. Cleland, ed.) *For the Director: Research Essays in Honor of James B. Griffin*, University of Michigan Museum of Anthropology, Anthropological Paper 61. Ann Arbor: University of Michigan.

Wylie, A. 1982. Epistemological Issues Raised by a Structuralist Archaeology, pp. 39–46 in (I. Hodder, ed.) *Symbolic and Structural Archaeology*. Cambridge: Cambridge University Press.

IAN HODDER

PROCESSUAL ARCHAEOLOGY

Processual archaeology, also called the 'New Archaeology', has been a highly influential theoretical and methodological approach in the discipline of anthropological archaeology since the early 1960s. The major thrust of this approach has been the contention that the understanding of the causes of culture change (process) in varying environmental and cultural settings should be the principal goal of archaeology. While its greatest impact has been on the practice of archaeology in the United States, its influence has been felt in varying degrees throughout the scholarly world. Processual archaeology has been dynamic in its development, and the approach has significantly changed over the past four decades.

In its original configuration, processual archaeology was formulated as an alternative to the traditional culture historical approach, which was the dominant paradigm, or widely accepted way of thought and action among archaeologists, in the mid-twentieth century. The leading proponent of the new way of thinking in the 1960s was the American archaeologist Lewis R. Binford, whose 1962 article 'Archaeology as Anthropology' and several articles that followed set the initial agenda for the processual approach. While some scholars have viewed processual archaeology as a passing phase in archaeological method and theory, this approach continues to play a key role in archaeological thinking and practice today.

By the 1960s, the traditional culture historical paradigm, with its focus on placing archaeological materials in time and space, had guided archaeologists in their successful development of archaeological sequences around the world. Through careful analyses and classifications of artefacts such as pottery vessels or stone tools, obtained in archaeological excavations in different geographic areas, archaeologists were able to place these objects in chronological order, chart their distributions across the landscape, and group related materials into 'cultures' with clear spatial and temporal boundaries. The emphasis on 'what, where, and when' questions further enabled scholars to create histories of different areas by examining the chronological phases of these cultures and their replacement through time by succeeding cultures.

Some archaeologists, however, were not satisfied with these accomplishments. They felt that understandings of ancient peoples and their activities were being forgotten with all the attention on time–space classifications and that the 'cultures' that archaeologists talked about were skeletal frameworks at best and showed little insight into the functioning of these ancient cultures. The American archaeologist Walter W. Taylor, for example, argued in an influential 1948 book that scholars needed to use their artefact analyses to uncover the functions of the materials they were studying and not just pigeon-hole them in time and space. Others contended that archaeologists should pay more attention to past culture–environment interactions, while some thought that the evolutionary development of cultures deserved more archaeological attention.

Binford focused these challenges in a forceful polemic and argued that archaeologists' basic culture historical approach put unacceptable limits on their archaeological activities. Archaeology, he maintained, could produce much more than an impoverished history of the past. With the proper theories and methods, Binford wrote, it could and should attempt to understand the processes of culture change in the past, just as cultural anthropologists were doing in their studies of modern cultures. Moreover, with the deep time depth of their materials, he believed that archaeologists could see long-term evolutionary trends in cultural development that would not be visible to their cultural anthropological colleagues.

Archaeologists should see explanation as their goal, not description, processual archaeologists argued. Furthermore, archaeological explanations should not be speculations but should be clearly supported by understandings of the archaeological record. In effect, the 'what, where, when' questions of the cultural historical approach were to be supplemented by 'how and why' ones, with the ultimate goal the finding of answers to the latter two queries.

Binford's agenda for the New Archaeology contained a number of key points. First, the processual archaeologists stressed that culture should be viewed as a system with its technological, economic, social, political and ideological aspects all closely intertwined. Second, they noted the importance of cultural ecology, and the necessity to view the interaction of the environment and culture systemically, just as culture itself should be viewed systemically. They particularly stressed the relationship between environment and technology. Third, they argued that archaeologists should study the evolution of these cultural systems through time. Binford, following the American cultural anthropologist Leslie White, argued that scholars should focus their attention on the evolution of the efficient capture of energy by cultures. However, most archaeologists have taken a more general view that the focus should be on searching for regularities through time in the development of cultural complexity. The understanding of these regularities or processes of cultural change was at the heart of processual archaeology. Binford and his colleagues further contended that such understandings of past processes could lead to better appreciation of current ones, and thus make archaeology not just an arcane study of the past but a discipline whose studies would be directly relevant to better understandings of the processes of change in the modern world.

More specifically, processual archaeologists emphasised the importance of developing explicit research strategy designs to further archaeological understanding of cultural processes. Every archaeological study should focus on a particular problem or group of problems.

Acceptance of the 'systems view' of culture also had a variety of implications for archaeological practice. Most importantly, this view of culture as cultural systems, composed of the interactions of different subsystems, emphasised the variability of culture rather than its homogeneity. The implications of the emphasis on cultural variability were immense. Excavation of the biggest mound at an archaeological site or of several test pits at the centre of the site would not necessarily reveal the complete picture of the culture of the people who had lived there, as the data from these excavations might only reveal aspects of one subsystem of the culture and almost certainly would not represent the whole culture. Given this situation in the field, the question of sampling in an archaeological research design became paramount. Since archaeologists rarely could excavate whole sites, it was crucial that they employ sampling strategies that would allow them to draw reliable conclusions about the whole cultural system of the past based on their partial knowledge. Understanding of statistical procedures to be used in sampling strategies became important too. Questions of scale also came to the fore, as it was important for processual archaeologists to understand the size of the cultural system they were studying (e.g. site, region or area).

This new archaeological perspective, with all of its implications for archaeological thought and practice, was coupled with an unbounded optimism that, given a productive outlook and strategy, the past could be knowable to an archaeologist. Processual archaeologists rejected the older view that emphasised the incompleteness of the archaeological record and the relative poverty of archaeological data as compared to historical or anthropological data. The processual archaeologists fervently believed that archaeological research could clearly contribute to scholarly understanding of the nature and causes of cultural change.

The processual approach hit the archaeological scene like an intellectual hurricane in the 1960s; but by the 1970s a series of problems began to emerge, and the initial optimism created by the processual archaeologists started to fade. To some, these problems sounded the death knell of the New Archaeology, but the latter showed great resilience and, as the problems were addressed, it emerged as the strong, viable approach that it is today.

Among these problems was the strong rhetoric employed by Binford and his colleagues in their initial polemic against the traditional, culture historical approach. This early rhetoric raised unrealistic expectations in the field and led to some disillusionment as promised results failed to appear, and no major theories or new understandings emerged in the first decade of the processual approach.

Another problem was that, as part of their rhetorical argument that processual archaeology was more rigorous and scientific than traditional archaeology, some New Archaeologists also asserted that to be scientific archaeologists should use deductive explanatory procedures in their research. Although it garnered a great deal of attention, this contentious issue proved short-lived, as scholars focused their efforts on making their research more rigorous without worrying about detailed explanatory modes.

A third problem was that although processual archaeologists had emphasised the importance of a 'holistic' systems approach to culture (i.e. one that focused on all aspects – the whole – of cultural systems), most attention was paid to the relationships between environment, technology and economics and very little at all to ideology and religion and their interconnections with other aspects of culture.

Perhaps the greatest problem that the processual archaeologists faced, however, in their pursuit of the goal of building new archaeological theories about how and why cultures changed in particular environmental and cultural settings, was how to link the static archaeological record visible today to the dynamic cultural behaviours that created the material record. To give a simple example: if archaeologists find a place with a number of flint flakes, they may infer that someone in the past – by other means, they may know the approximate date – was chipping flint there to make stone axes. But the important thing to stress is that they have not found a stone tool-manufacturing site. They have found a modern location with chipped flakes from which they infer a past activity. The more secure they can make this link, the more useful their inference. Neither traditional nor processual archaeology had procedures in place to make such inferences in a consistent, reliable manner, as archaeologists generally relied on personal experience and widely accepted, but usually implicit, analogies to make the inferences. These analogies frequently were so ingrained that scholars often forgot they were even making them. They might fall into the trap of believing they were actually finding a tool-manufacturing site and not inferring it!

In the past three decades, processual archaeologists have worked diligently to pursue their goal of finding and understanding regularities in cultural change through time and to find solutions to the challenges and problems that their initial efforts raised. For example, their solution to the problem of making rigorous interpretations of the archaeological record was to build what was termed 'middle-range theory'. Such efforts might better be termed 'bridging' or 'linking' theory, as they attempted to bridge the gap between the modern archaeological record and past behaviours. Binford called such attempts 'giving meaning to the archaeological record'. Middle-range theory building was in effect an effort to strengthen the analogies that archaeologists use to interpret the record. These efforts were used in conjunction with the study of archaeological formation processes, which attempted to better understand the cultural and natural processes that led to the creation of the record archaeologists see today.

The most productive way to link behaviours with their material consequences, processualists argued, was through 'ethnoarchaeology'. This method involved archaeologists studying modern peoples to understand how patterned behaviours can produce consistent material 'signatures', given certain environmental and cultural situations. Then if similar signatures were found in the archaeological record, it could reasonably be inferred by analogy that the same behaviour that produced such signatures in the present had done so in the past.

Processual archaeologists have also begun to pay more attention to the key roles that ideology plays in changing cultural systems. One area of work where processual archaeologists have successfully incorporated ideology into their research strategies and interpretations is settlement pattern studies, where ideologically laden landscapes are seen to play powerful roles in determining settlement layouts at different scales from the site to the region.

In sum, processual archaeology, now more than forty years old, continues to be a major approach to the past. Rising beyond its initial polemic, it has shown its adaptability to changing archaeological questions and concerns. Although challenged by other perspectives, including post-processual archaeology (see p. 207), processual archaeology, with its goal of understanding the regularities in cultural evolution and its emphasis on cultural systems and cultural variability, problem orientation, methodological rigour and the use of middle-range theory in archaeological interpretation, retains its decades-old optimism of knowing the past and relating this knowledge to modern social issues. It has had and continues to have a profound impact on the practice of archaeology all over the globe.

Suggested reading

Binford, L. R. 1972. *An Archaeological Perspective*. New York: Seminar Press.
Contains the major writings that helped give rise to processual archaeology in the
1960s.

Binford, L. R., with the editorial collaboration of Cherry, F. J. and Torrence, R.
    1983. *In Pursuit of the Past: Decoding the Archaeological Record*. New York: Thames
    and Hudson. (Reprinted with a new 'Afterword' by Binford in 2002 by the
    University of California Press.)
A popular overview of Binford's view of the aims and methods of processual
archaeology.

Lyman, R. L., O'Brien, M. J. and Dunnell, R. C. 1997. *The Rise and Fall of
    Culture History*. New York: Plenum Press.
A view of the culture historical perspective, which was supplanted in part by
processual archaeology.

Sabloff, P. L. W. 1998. *Conversations with Lew Binford: Drafting the New Archaeology*.
    Norman: University of Oklahoma Press.
An extended interview with Binford in which he discusses the background of the
rise of processual archaeology.

Schiffer, M. B. 1976. *Behavioral Archaeology*. New York: Academic Press.
The pioneering introduction to the study of the processes leading to the formation
of the archaeological record.

Taylor, W. W. 1948. *A Study of Archaeology*. American Anthropological
    Association, Memoir Number 69. Menasha: American Anthropological
    Association (reprinted by the Southern Illinois University Press).
The first full-length challenge to the tenets of the traditional culture historical
approach.

Willey, G. R. and Sabloff, J. A. 1993. *A History of American Archaeology*, 3rd edn.
    New York: W. H. Freeman.
Places the rise of processual archaeology in a historical context.

Wylie, A. 2002. *Thinking from Things: Essays in the Philosophy of Archaeology*.
    Berkeley and Los Angeles: University of California Press.
Includes several clear, if technical, essays on the crucial role of analogy in
archaeological reasoning in general, and middle-range theory in particular.

Further reading

Ashmore, W. and Knapp, A. B. (eds) 1999. *Archaeologies of Landscape: Contemporary
    Perspectives*. Oxford: Blackwell.
Clarke, D. L. 1968. *Analytical Archaeology*. London: Methuen.
Feinman, G. M. and Price, T. D. (eds) 2001. *Archaeology at the Millennium: A
    Sourcebook*. New York: Kluwer Academic/Plenum.
Johnson, A. W. and Earle, T. 2000. *The Evolution of Human Societies: From Foraging
    Group to Agrarian State*, 2nd edn. Stanford: Stanford University Press.
Preucel, R. W. (ed.) 1991. *Processual and Postprocessual Archaeologies: Multiple Ways
    of Knowing the Past*. Center for Archaeological Investigations Occasional Paper
    No. 10. Carbondale, Ill.: Southern Illinois University at Carbondale.

Trigger, B. G. 1989. *A History of Archaeological Thought*. Cambridge: Cambridge University Press.

Wandsnider, L. 1992. *Quandaries and Quests: Visions of Archaeology's Future*. Center for Archaeological Investigations Occasional Paper No. 20. Carbondale, Ill.: Southern Illinois University at Carbondale.

Watson, P. J., LeBlanc, S. A. and Redman, C. R. 1971. *Explanation in Archaeology: An Explicitly Scientific Approach*. New York: Columbia University Press.

JEREMY SABLOFF

PUBLIC ARCHAEOLOGY/MUSEOLOGY/ CONSERVATION/HERITAGE

Public archaeology is where professional archaeologists work with public interests, upholding legislation designed to conserve ancient sites and finds, managing museum collections, presenting the past to the general public, working with developers to reduce the impact of building and construction projects on the remains of the past. Most archaeologists now work in public archaeology rather than in universities, the traditional home of academic archaeological research.

Archaeology has always engaged popular interest. The discipline has its roots in antiquarian collection and study of ancient artefacts like Greek and Roman sculpture and coins. Local archaeology societies, founded from the eighteenth century onwards, were an early focus for amateur excavation and discussion of archaeology. Great archaeological discoveries like those of Schliemann in the Aegean in the late nineteenth century, or those of Carter and Carnarvon in Egypt in the 1920s, attracted enormous coverage in the press. But, in spite of this popular interest, most archaeology aimed to create and publish academic knowledge. Since the 1970s, however, archaeology has become a set of professional fields that extends far beyond academic interests. The term 'Public Archaeology' covers this growth and diversity.

Museums have multiplied considerably in the last thirty years and are now seen as much more than storerooms for the past, with the best pieces displayed in glass cases for the educated public to admire. Great international museums like the Louvre carry enormous cultural prestige. Smaller and specialised museums attract many visitors and are, with the famous international institutions, the cornerstone of the tourist trade. Museums are now more concerned with visitor experience and may take up a role of educating or entertaining the public in all sorts of issues, with animated display techniques used by the likes of Disney in its theme parks. Museum curators are more active in interpreting, rather than simply displaying, their collections for the public. Hence museum displays have come to use a lot more text and visual information to give context and help people understand the items displayed. They may be supplemented by interactive computer presentation or websites. Museums have been joined by interpretation and visitor centres, and indeed theme parks, as places where people encounter archaeology. Museology, or Museum Studies, is the field that covers research into museums as contemporary cultural institutions as well as the professional practice of the curation, interpretation and presentation of collections and archives.

In the nineteenth century some countries in northern Europe passed legislation designed to protect ancient monuments. National and international statutes and agreements designed to protect and conserve the past have multiplied since the 1970s. Organisations like UNESCO take an active role in promoting the conservation of the remains of the past in all parts of the world. Planning and development procedures in many parts of the world now require that account be taken of impact upon archaeological remains. These changes have created a growing need for archaeologists and museum curators to manage the remains of the past for the present and future. The professional field of Cultural Resource Management (as it is called in the United States), or Archaeological Heritage Management (in Europe and elsewhere,) deals with such care of sites, monuments, artefacts and landscapes. Much of this public archaeology takes the form of survey and excavation done to comply with legislation and as part of planning procedures. It is done by private commercial firms operating under contract, as well as public agencies such as the National Parks Service in the United States, or English Heritage in the UK. Hence this kind of archaeology has been called 'Contract Archaeology'.

What this all means is that archaeologists have come to accept an obligation and professional responsibility to share their archaeological knowledge with the public as well as colleagues. And more – to carry out work for public as well as academic interests.

As well as these professional sectors, the term 'Public Archaeology' still covers general public interest in the archaeological past. Treasure hunting, the antiquities trade and private collecting are more popular and lucrative than ever. Books, magazines, movies and TV programmes cover the latest finds and theories, as well as indulging fringe and fantasy interest in the likes of forgotten ancient wisdoms, or the lost civilisation of Atlantis. There is also a whole new genre of computer games, like 'Lara Croft Tomb Raider', that feed on archaeology.

What is driving this growth of public archaeology?

1   The conservation movement. A major factor is the scale of building and construction since the Second World War. It was clear by the 1960s that urban and infrastructural development was a serious threat to archaeological remains. A mile of freeway construction in Europe might well expose a thousand archaeological sites. At first the response was to call for rescue or salvage archaeology as a kind of emergency service. A more effective response has been to incorporate attention to the past early on in planning and building development. A connection with the 'green' agenda of nature conservation was made in the 1970s: Public Archaeology is often connected with what is called a conservation ethic – that, like nature, the past is a crucial and limited resource, is under threat and needs conserving.

2   New nation-states and indigenous communities seeking cultural identity. The passing of the old European colonial empires in the second half of the twentieth century created many new nation-states that are looking to the past for cultural origins on which to found their efforts at nation-building. Modernisation, with its rapid changes and bland global anonymity of consumerism, is often seen as a threat to traditional cultures. People are looking to history and the archaeological past for their authentic cultural roots. Since 1986 the World Archaeology Congress, an association of academic and professional archaeologists, has taken up this agenda of globalisation and indigenous archaeology.

3   Cultural tourism. Tourism is big business. Global travel is cheaper and easier than ever, and a favourite destination of many tourists is what is left of the past of their own or another culture.

These three factors combine in an overall celebration of the past in contemporary society. The key concept here is heritage. Some, like the cultural critic Robert Hewison (1987), have even called the present's fascination with the past, Public Archaeology included, a heritage 'industry'.

What is heritage? Heritage can include just about anything – from landscapes to collections, buildings and institutions, living traditions, even impressions and orientations. The United States Constitution, Native American spirituality, Stonehenge, traditional French cheese, a castle on the Rhine, all might be conceived as someone's heritage. UNESCO accredits some sites and regions as World Heritage Sites – places of exceptional value to humanity as a whole. The important thing about heritage is that it is about relationships with the past. Heritage is what the present values in the past, and the value of the past lies in its contribution to contemporary senses of worth and identity.

Some see heritage as a positive cherishing of the past: English Heritage is the name given to the state agency that oversees public archaeology in the UK. For others, heritage all too often lapses into inauthentic spectacle and entertainment. David Lowenthal, a prominent academic commentator on heritage, has argued that heritage is neither history nor archaeology, because it has no need to respect accuracy of fact and can simply deal in fantasy and invented tradition that distort history (tartan or plaid, for example, that mainstay of Scottish heritage and identity, was invented in the nineteenth century).

This debate around heritage is about values, the crucial issue in public archaeology. The conservation ethic is driven by value being attached to the remains of the past. Should this or that site be conserved? Is this more worthy of display than that? And – in the antiquities markets, legal or illicit – how much is this sculpture worth? All these questions of value are about what the past means to different people now.

And, of course, values frequently elicit dispute. The outrage expressed at the deliberate destruction in 2002 of the Bamiyan Buddhas by the Taliban regime in Afghanistan illustrates a radical conflict of values. Dispute about the value and significance of the past is the main component of the cultural politics that so characterises Public Archaeology. Repatriation of antiquities and reburial of remains are two particular cases of such dispute. As an example of the first, the Greek government wants the repatriation, the return to Greece, of the marble sculptures that adorned the Parthenon, the temple on the Acropolis in Athens – they have been in the British Museum in London since the nineteenth century. One argument is that the sculptures are of unique value to Greek heritage. Reburial, rather than academic scientific study, of Native American human remains is often sought in the United States, because religious and spiritual respect is valued over the contribution to knowledge that the study of the remains might deliver.

For many, like J. E. Tunbridge and Geoffrey Ashworth in their book *Dissonant Heritage* (1996), dispute is the characteristic feature of heritage and Cultural Resource Management. It is certainly the case that the possibility of a diversity or pluralism of views of the past is on the archaeological agenda pursued by post-processual/interpretive archaeology (*see* p. 207) and is a feature of Indigenous Archaeologies (*see* p. 146).

Dispute often arises because the past is treated as cultural property owned by some and not others (this is my property, not yours – my heritage and identity, not yours). This stresses a proprietorial relationship with that past that, by definition, excludes some. It is better to focus on different kinds of relationship, respecting different senses of value. So some archaeologists have challenged the view that their role is one of stewardship, protecting resources that are conceived as cultural property. Instead, they see the role of the public archaeologist as one of professional mediator between different interests in the past.

Within Public Archaeology as a professional field, key issues concern codes of conduct and ethical standards in dealing with clients. The Society for American Archaeology, the Institute of Field Archaeology in the UK, and the European Association of Archaeologists have all developed codes of professional conduct for their membership. Public Archaeology is all about consulting and negotiating with a diverse set of people and their interests in a world that extends far from the academic discipline – Public Archaeology is in this way a transdisciplinary space.

For many, the main issue facing contemporary Public Archaeology is that of the threat to the archaeological past posed by modernisation and building development, and by the looting of sites to feed the black market in antiquities. For example, looting of thousands of graves in the Greek Cyclades for marble figurines for the antiquities market has destroyed almost all of the archaeological evidence for these prehistoric societies. The global scale of destruction and loss is enormous. Great efforts are being made in Public Archaeology to raise people's awareness of this, to pass further protective legislation, and to pressure collectors and museums to condemn looting and the black market.

Further reading

Hewison, R. 1987. *The Heritage Industry: Britain in a Climate of Decline*. London: Methuen.
Lowenthal, D. 1996. *Possessed by the Past: The Heritage Crusade and the Spoils of History*. New York: Free Press.

McManamon, F. and Hatton, A. (eds) 2000. *Cultural Resource Management in Contemporary Society: Perspectives on Managing and Presenting the Past*. London: Routledge.

Tunbridge, J. E. and Ashworth, G. J. 1996. *Dissonant Heritage: The Management of the Past as a Resource in Conflict*. Chichester: Wiley.

MICHAEL SHANKS

SIMULATION

Simulation is one of those notoriously slippery concepts which many scholars use in a variety of different ways. Some use the term almost synonymously with the word 'model' – a 're-creation' of reality. Others restrict the meaning to being a dynamic, causal replicating, rule-based construct on a computer that produces testable results or visualisations that may be compared to observations.

The boundaries are fuzzy. Consider the range among the following – the toy plastic model plane on the shelf in the bedroom, the static model plane being flown by wire or remote control on the school grounds, the model plane being flown in a wind tunnel to simulate drag, the remotely controlled Predators that fly in military combat situations (Schmitt 2003), and the flight simulators that are used to train pilots. A similar range exists in archaeology – ranging from simulated tools made from modern materials, to replicated butchering of animals or planting crops, to archaeological theme parks such as Jorvik (*see* p. 110), to computerised migrations and voyages out of Africa and across the Pacific, to the use of artificial intelligence programs to simulate prehistoric thought patterns. This entry will emphasise the latter – the more rule-based and the more dynamic computer-assisted simulations.

The famous geneticist Luca Cavalli-Sforza wrote that one uses models when one cannot find an analytical solution, and one uses simulations when one cannot be sure of the model. In particular simulations are used when traditional techniques are unable to address the complexity of behaviour. This is particularly true for human behaviour (Zubrow 1981) where 'distributed agency [is] embedded within the complex material and symbolic contexts' (Read 1999: 1.13) and conclusions are based upon the fragmentary detritus of archaeological sites.

There are several aspects to this 'complexity claim'. One meaning is that the average researcher cannot at present provide adequate analyses for complex collective phenomena. Another is that the modelling of such social phenomena is a demonstrable impossibility.

Read has suggested that simulations in the anthropological disciplines are used in two ways (Read 1999). First, they are used to work out the consequences of processes already reasonably well modelled. An archaeological example is the simulation by Piazza and Pearthree evaluating whether Kirch's hypothesised process of 'down-the-line' migration is substantiated by empirical prehistoric observations c. 1500 BC in the southwestern Pacific (Piazza and Pearthree 1999). The second are simulations that attempt to clarify what might be appropriate processes – such as the role of chance in prehistoric population growth (Zubrow 2000) – or that provide a choice of processes, e.g. the simulations of coastal versus non-coastal migration during prehistory (Zubrow 2002a).

On the other hand, there are some significant reasons not to use simulations. Simulations are very labour intensive. They are particularly intensive during the development (building the model, programming the simulation, creating the testing or visualisation, and initialising the parameters). Thus, simulations are not a very efficient method of study for a single test or single problem. The more frequently one uses the same simulation to solve new or related problems, the more suitable it is as a technique. Finally, simulations as inductive 'discovery' devices are not very efficient (induction is the process of inferring from the specific to the general, and includes most forms of analogy). To be effective, they must be backed by the simulators' knowledge of an underlying theory.

In short, simulation should be used when it will provide insights into the archaeological phenomena being simulated and promises either useful prediction or, as in the case of most archaeology, useful 'retrodiction' (i.e. predicting or extrapolating into the past). It must show aspects of the prehistoric individual or society that could not be reached by more conventional techniques.

The history of simulation may be divided into three decade-long periods of more or less similar developments – spanning 1970 to the present. They are the Inaugural (1970–80), the Formative Period (1980–90) and the Regeneration (1990–present).

There are several general trends cross-cutting the decades. First, as computers became more accessible, more archaeologists used simulations for a greater variety of problems. Second, as popular digital computing languages became higher level and more specialised, and archaeologists have become more computer literate, the tendency to use computer scientists to design simulations has been reduced. The computer scientist has been replaced by the archaeologist-programmer who not only understands the workings of the prehistoric processes but designs the simulation and writes the programs. Third, as computers became more personal and computing languages became more removed from the machine language, archaeologists have moved from simulating broad-based societal processes in large-scale environments to focusing on the individual, and individual cognition, in more agent-based simulations.

During the 1970s initial efforts at simulating social phenomena were built around systems of interrelated equations and tended to be deterministic. Many of these early simulations related to general systems theory (*see* p. 259), game theory or equilibrium theory. Following ideas popularised by Jay Forrester and the Club of Rome, researchers took their inspiration from a wide range of fields such as the Lotka–Volterra mathematical model of inter-specific competition or from demographic and ecological models such as the carrying capacity simulation for the prehistoric southwest (Zubrow 1974). Others focused on settlement patterns (Thomas 1972; Chadwick 1978) and even upon traditional verbal descriptions. An example of the latter (Hosler *et al.* 1977) was a simulation of the collapse of the Classic Maya based on a verbal description developed by Willey and Shimkin. Early explorations of the more cognitive aspects of archaeology were introduced through decision theory (Johnson 1978). This period culminated with Jeremy Sabloff organising a School of American Research Seminar on Simulations in Archaeology in 1978 (published in 1981) (Sabloff 1981) and with Ian Hodder's 1978 book *Simulation Studies in Archaeology* (Hodder 1978).

Several major innovations took place in the 1980s in archaeological simulations. One was the introduction of probability theory and randomness in simulations. This was augmented by simulations using fractal geometry (Zubrow 1985) and advances in the study of dynamic systems popularised by James Gleick in his book *Chaos* (Gleick 1987; Porter and Gleick 1990).

From the 1990s to the present, simulation has been expanding in most fields. In archaeometry, it has continued unabated. Many single and double blind experiments are used with simulated and real data to test the accuracy of techniques such as optical thermoluminescence (Liritzis 1998). In mainstream archaeology there seemed to be a brief hesitation as the views of 'critical archaeology' and 'post-processual archaeology' (*see* p. 207) became central subjects. However, by the mid-1990s simulations were becoming important again as it was recognised that one could use artificial intelligence and agent-based simulation to attack problems of cognition and memory. Kohler and Gumerman (2000) and Sallach (2000) have provided a good summary of agent-based simulations, pointing out their application to a variety of social processes and the emergence of social institutions from agent strategies. Agent-based simulation draws upon the technology of a mixture of artificial intelligence and object-oriented programming. The agents have communication languages allowing them to communicate with each other. They interact by cooperating, negotiating, subordinating or competing. These agents correspond to individuals and are the components of human societies.

A few examples will suffice to represent what has now become a large number of studies. First, Zubrow's very primitive early attempt to simulate prehistoric families by creating prehistoric individual agents and using stable population models in CAMSIM. He traced individuals being born, growing up, marrying and dying, and then compiled the size of individual families for egos of various ages. He then compared these in the Upper Palaeolithic, Neolithic, Iron Age and Roman society (Zubrow 2002b). Far more impressive are Andre Costopoulos's study of the importance of memory capacity 'on the ability of hunting and gathering agents to adapt to given subsistence environments and resource landscapes' (Costopoulos 2001), showing that increasing the number of events used in decision-making does not increase the ability to adapt, and Kohler and his colleagues' simulations of planting decisions based on past harvests, area knowledge and assessing the need for possible relocation with alternative sets of rules in the Mesa Verde region of Colorado (USA) between AD 900 and 1300 (Kohler et al. 2000).

Simulations are frequently used in archaeology for education. Few better ways exist to teach students about the destructive and incomplete nature of archaeology than to have them 'virtually' survey an area and excavate a site. There is also a tradition of using simulation for virtual reconstructions of how an area or a site appeared before the destructive processes of time had a chance to destroy their composition.

One of the best-known and most commercial simulations is FUGAWILAND (Price and Gebauer 1997, 2002). Written by Price and his associates, published by McGraw Hill, it is a combination workbook and computer simulation that allows the student to conduct archaeological fieldwork and apply creative techniques. WINDIG-FREEWARE is a Windows archaeological site excavation simulation suitable for undergraduates and senior high students based on SYSGRAF. Another freeware program is SVGASMP that emphasises combining and simulating sampling strategies for survey and excavation. ARCDIG is designed to download a site and help create excavation plans.

In between the site excavation simulations and the virtual reconstructions is PALOMA WORLD – a virtual tour of a prehistoric Peruvian village that not only provides 'fly throughs' but allows one to excavate a portion of the site. Numerous virtual reconstructions are available. There are a variety of groups working on different reconstructions. Maurizo Forte at Rome (Barceló *et al.* 2000a, 2000b) is interested in the theoretical and substantive issues of the application of virtual reality to archaeology. The large Shape Group at Brown University is creating the virtual reality of Petra (Joukowsky *et al.* 2003), Vince Gaffney's group at Birmingham is recreating Roman Wroxeter (Gaffney *et al.* 2003) and Paley's group reconstructs Nimrud while working at Buffalo (Paley 2002) . These are but a few of the many virtual reality simulators that are springing up throughout the world. One issue is how to determine, in the virtual reality reconstruction, what is based upon the evidence, what is based upon connecting the 'archaeological dots', what is based upon ethnographic analogy, and what is based upon pure speculation.

The future of simulation is bright. The trends of increasing computing power, increasing literacy and increasing ability of archaeologists to use simulation to solve previously insoluble problems continue. As archaeological resources become physically more limited, more difficult to reach, more politically, legally and bureaucratically difficult to survey and excavate, simulation becomes an increasingly important method of studying, visualising and communicating archaeological data.

Specifically, one expects the recent explosion of agent-based simulations to play a greater role in archaeology as well as seeing more virtual realities as visualisations of prehistoric sites, landscapes and cultures improve.

Suggested reading

Costopoulos, A. 2001. Evaluating the Impact of Increasing Memory on Agent Behaviour: Adaptive Patterns in an Agent Based Simulation of Subsistence. *Journal of Artificial Societies and Social Simulation* 4 (4). Available at: http://www.soc.surrey.ac.uk/JASSS/4/4/7.html
An excellent example of sophisticated simulation being applied to behaviour relevant to archaeologists.

Gaffney, V., Buteux, S. *et al.* 2003. *Virtual Wroxeter Roman Fortress*. Available at http://www.arch-ant.bham.ac.uk/bufau/ research/bt/fv102w/fortress.htm

A virtual recreation of the Roman fortress.

Joukowsky, M. S. , Willis, A. *et al.* 2003. *The Great Temple Tour.* Brown University. Available at http://www.brown.edu/Departments/Anthropology/Petra/temple/temple.html

Journal of Artificial Societies and Social Simulation. Available at http://www.soc.surrey.ac.uk/JASSS.html

One of the best places to find new work and new ideas.

Kohler, T. A. and Gumerman, G. J. 2000. *Dynamics in Human and Primate Societies: Agent-Based Modeling of Social and Spatial Processes.* New York: Oxford University Press.

Good examples of modern agent-based simulation.

Price, T. D. and Gebauer, A. B. 2002. *Adventures in Fugawiland: A Computer Simulation in Archaeology.* Boston: McGraw-Hill.

A good example of how simulation is used in education

Read, D. W. 1999. Introduction. *Journal of Artificial Societies and Social Simulation* 2 (3). Special Issue on Computer Simulation in Anthropology. Available http://www.soc.surrey.ac.uk/JASSS/2/3/10.html

An excellent compendium of the state of simulation at the turn of the millennium.

Sabloff, J. A. 1981. *Simulations in Archaeology.* Albuquerque: University of New Mexico Press.

An early classic compendium.

Zubrow, E., with Robinson, J. 2000. Chance and the Human Population: Population Growth in the Mediterranean, pp. 133–44 in (J. Bintliff and K. Sbonias, eds) *Reconstructing Past Demographic Trends in Mediterranean Europe.* Oxford: Oxbow.

Further reading

Barceló, J. A., Forte, M. and Sanders, D. H. 2000a. *The Diversity of Archaeological Virtual Worlds.* Oxford: Archaeopress.
—— 2000b. *Virtual Reality in Archaeology.* Oxford: Archaeopress.
Chadwick, A. J. 1978. A Computer Simulation of Mycenean Settlement, pp. 47–57 in (I. Hodder, ed.) *Simulation Studies in Archaeology.* Cambridge: Cambridge University Press
Gleick, J. 1987. *Chaos: Making a New Science.* New York: Viking.
Hodder, I. (ed.) 1978. *Simulation Studies in Archaeology.* Cambridge: Cambridge University Press.
Hosler, D., Sabloff, J. and Runge, D. 1977. Simulation Model Development: A Case Study of the Classic Maya Collapse, pp. 552–90 in (N. Hammond, ed.) *Social Process in Maya Prehistory.* London: Academic Press.
Johnson, G. A. 1978. Information Sources and the Development of Decision-Making Organizations, pp. 87–112 in (C. L. Redman, ed.) *Social Archaeology: Beyond Subsistence and Dating.* New York: Academic Press.
Kohler, T. A., Kresl, J., Van West, C., Carr, E. and Wilshusen, R. 2000. Be There Then: A Modeling Approach to Settlement Determinants and Spatial Efficiency among Late Ancestral Pueblo Populations of the Mesa Verde Region, US Southwest, pp. 145–78 in (T. A. Kohler and G. J. Gumerman, eds)

Dynamics in Human and Primate Societies: Agent-Based Modeling of Social and Spatial Processes. New York: Oxford University Press.

Liritzis, I. 1998. *Third Millennium BC. The Revised Age of Two Hellenic Pyramidal Buildings with a New Nuclear Dating Method.* Available at http://geocities.com/Athens/Forum/8635/liritzis.html

Paley, S. M. 2002. *The Citadel Mound at Nimrud* (CD). Williamstown, Mass.: Learning Sites Inc. (See also http://www.learningsites.com/Framelayout01.htm)

Piazza, A. D. and Pearthree, E. 1999. The Spread of the 'Lapita People': A Demographic Simulation. *Journal of Artificial Societies and Social Simulation* 2 (3). Available at http://www.soc.surrey.ac.uk/JASSS/2/3/4.html

Porter, E. and Gleick, J. 1990. *Nature's Chaos.* New York: Viking.

Price, T. D. and Gebauer, A. B. 1997. *Adventures in Fugawiland: A Computer Simulation in Archaeology.* Mountain View, Calif.: Mayfield.

Sallach, D. L. 2000. Review of Dynamics in Human and Primate Societies: Agent-Based Modeling of Social and Spatial Processes. *Journal of Artificial Societies and Social Simulation* 4 (3). Available at http://www.soc.surrey.ac.uk/JASSS/2/3/contents.html

Schmitt, E. 2003. In the Skies Over Iraq, Silent Observers Become Futuristic Weapons. *New York Times* 18 April.

Thomas, D. H. 1972. A Computer Simulation Model of Great Basin Shoshonean Settlement Patterns, pp. 671–704 in (D. Clarke, ed.) *Models in Archaeology.* London: Methuen.

Zubrow, E. B. W. 1974. *Prehistoric Carrying Capacity, a Model.* Menlo Park, Calif.: Cummings.

—— 1981. Simulation as a Heuristic Device in Archaeology, pp. 143–88 in (J. Sabloff, ed.) *Simulations in Archaeology.* Santa Fe, New Mexico: School for American Research.

—— 1985. Fractals, Cultural Behavior, and Prehistory. *American Archeology* 5 (1): 63–77.

—— 2002a. Experimenting with Migration: Simulating Population Growth and Continental Migration, pp. 143–58 in (J. R. Mathieu, ed.) *Experimental Archaeology Replicating Past Objects, Behaviors, and Processes.* Oxford: Archaeopress.

—— 2002b. The Prehistoric Family at Haddenham: An Iron Age Example. Haddenham 3. Cambridge: McDonald Institute of Archaeological Research.

EZRA ZUBROW

SITE CATCHMENT ANALYSIS

Site catchment analysis (SCA) was first defined in 1970 by Claudio Vita-Finzi and Eric Higgs to refer to the analysis of archaeological sites in relation to their environmental surroundings. It provides a means of creating and testing hypotheses about prehistoric economies independently of the material remains recovered in excavation. The initial spur to its development was the investigation of agricultural origins, and the problem of reconstructing economies at sites where plant and animal remains are poorly preserved. The basic premise is that sites supposedly dependent on crop agriculture should be located close to cultivable soils, sites dependent on deer hunting close to suitable deer habitat, and so on. In order to define the area relevant to a given site, Vita-Finzi and Higgs used simple cost–benefit principles, supported by a variety of ethnographic and historical examples, to suggest that the maximum radius of daily exploitation for hunting and gathering sites should be 10 kilometres and, for the more labour-intensive activities of agriculture, 5 kilometres. Since local topography can impede movement across the landscape, they defined these radii in terms of walking time – two hours and one hour, respectively.

In the first formal application of the technique, students were despatched to carry out timed walks from a sample of Natufian and Neolithic sites in Israel and Palestine, making notes on topography, soils, vegetation and other environmental variables along the way. The resulting maps were used to reject the hypothesis of incipient agriculture in the Natufian period, because few of the Natufian sites were located close to suitable topography or soils, in marked contrast to the sites of later periods.

In 1972, Higgs and Vita-Finzi renamed the above technique Site Territorial Analysis (STA), the analysis of site exploitation territories (SETs), defined as the areas habitually used for daily subsistence from given locations. They limited the term SCA to the analysis of site catchments in the strict sense, defined as the areas in the surrounding landscape from which materials preserved in an archaeological deposit are derived. The two techniques are complementary in that STA works inwards from the surrounding landscape to the archaeological site, whereas SCA works outwards from the materials in an archaeological deposit to their nearest point of origin. STA is a theoretical exercise based on hypothetical suppositions about the likely maximum distance of daily travel and transport and the likely distribution of past subsistence resources. SCA is a more strongly empirical exercise dealing with the nearest most likely source of materials actually present in the archaeological deposit. Moreover, a site can have different sorts of catchments. In practice, the economic catchment may turn out to be smaller or larger than the hypothetical exploitation territory, or to comprise different-sized catchments for different food resources. We can also imagine other sorts of catchments – for example 'geological' catchments comprising sources of raw materials for making stone artefacts or ceramics.

Most early examples of SCA are in fact exercises in STA, and in this form they serve two purposes. First, they result in a more fine-grained examination of environmental variability in relation to archaeological sites. Earlier inferences about economic function relied on the environmental zones within which sites occur, disregarding the fact that it is often local variation that is of human interest – the oasis in the desert, for example – or on questionable assumptions about the function of artefacts or the completeness of archaeological food remains. Second, they stimulate new hypotheses about the likely economic practices carried out at individual sites, and suggest new lines of research and relevant test data. These in turn demand improved techniques of recovering faunal and floral remains from archaeological deposits, and more careful analysis of the differential processes by which such materials were collected, transported, discarded, incorporated in archaeological sediments and ultimately preserved or destroyed (*see* p. 121). In the ideal situation, the deductions drawn from STA – the off-site record – should be compared with the on-site record to see how far actual subsistence practices and site functions correspond to their environmental setting, leading to more subtle interpretations of the relationship between environment and economy. Sites in unexpected locations, or having distinctive archaeological features and catchments compared to other sites in similar locations, might indicate use for purposes other than subsistence – for defence, for the procurement of valuable raw materials, for the control of trade routes or markets, for social aggregation or for ceremonial and ritual.

These studies raise a number of questions, which have shaped subsequent directions of research. First, there is the accuracy of the time–distance factors used in defining SETs. Kent Flannery and his colleagues in their study of Mesoamerican early agriculture have identified the use of satellite camps to collect or partially process specific resources and transfer them back to the main residential base from distances well beyond the 10-kilometre limit. Strictly speaking, the satellites have their own SETs, but their effect is to extend the economic catchment of the residential base. Optimal foraging theory, which identifies the optimal relationship between the costs and benefits of different subsistence activities, has been used to define more precisely time–distance limits for different resources. Acorns are expensive to process but rich in calories, and it is worth carrying heavy loads long distances. Large animals are often butchered at the kill site to remove the waste parts of the carcass before carrying the meat back to camp, while small animals are carried back entire. Molluscs are easy to process but the high bulk of inedible shell can reduce the economical transport distance to figures well below the 5-kilometre threshold, resulting in temporary sites for the removal of shells or consumption of the meat while out in the field. Intensive cultivation may confine the effective radius of exploitation to 1 kilometre or less. Water is the least transportable resource and proximity to water supplies rather than proximity to the principal food sources may be a key determinant of site location in areas where water is limited.

This highlights a second issue, the assumption that use of a landscape is focused on discrete sites at the centre of their SETs, to which people return every night from daily subsistence activities. This concept stems from Central Place Theory, devised by geographers for the study of rural agriculture. While appropriate for abundant and immobile resources such as plant foods, which have to be brought back to a central point for processing and sharing, it is less appropriate for mobile resources. Derek Sturdy first demonstrated in 1972 that hunters of large herds prefer sites situated on the edge of extensive grazing basins circumscribed by topographic barriers. This allows the hunters to monitor and control movements of animals over large areas without causing them disturbance. The sites are thus asymmetrically located in relation to their principal resources, and control an extended territory that is much larger than the conventionally defined site exploitation territory. The concept is widely applicable to many Upper Palaeolithic sites in Europe, and is probably of utility in the study of all animal-based economies.

Another problem with the central place concept is that many archaeological sites are probably not residential bases, but temporary locations used more or less fleetingly for particular tasks. This leads to a different approach, in which the distribution of key resources is mapped on a regional scale, and then compared with the distribution of archaeological remains using visual or statistical techniques. Such an approach avoids preconceptions about the function of individual sites or locations and highlights patterns of selectivity in the choice of some locations and environmental resources in preference to others.

Then there is the question of how reliably we can reconstruct past environments from a study of present-day patterns. Climate and vegetation change, and soils and sediments erode from hill slopes and river valleys and are redeposited in lower valley basins or washed out to sea. Rivers can change course and wells and springs run dry. Even the topography of hills and valleys can change dramatically on the human time scale in areas of active tectonics. Palaeoenvironmental techniques such as analyses of lake and river sediments and pollen sequences are often conducted to study climate change, resulting in large-scale reconstructions rather than the local detail necessary for archaeological purposes. Here too the concept of catchment – the pollen catchment or the sediment catchment – has proved effective in adapting these techniques to finer-grained spatial reconstructions.

Finally, there is the question of how reliably we can extrapolate present-day plant and animal habitats to the past. Modern red deer are confined to marginal woodland or moor, and ibex and chamois to high-altitude crags, where they have been driven by competition with domestic stock. However, prehistoric deer covered a wider range of wooded and open conditions, while ibex and chamois were found in rough terrain at any altitude. Technological change has also altered the potential of soils. Those most fertile for modern agriculture are often heavy soils that would not have been workable with hand tools in the Early Neolithic, when lighter soils were preferred. Often it is site catchment and site territorial analyses applied to archaeological sites and materials that have helped to identify these changes in the behaviour and economic potential of environmental resources.

Suggested reading

Bailey, G. N. (ed.) 1997. *Klithi: Palaeolithic Settlement and Quaternary Landscapes in Northwest Greece*. Cambridge: McDonald Institute for Archaeological Research. Application of a regional approach including updated discussions of methodology, incorporation of large-scale climatic, vegetational and geological change, and discussions of animal behaviour, archaeological and environmental catchments, and tectonics.

Flannery, K. V. (ed.). 1976. *The Early MesoAmerican Village*. London and New York: Academic Press. Application and development of the method to early agricultural economies in a North American context, including examples of both STA and SCA, and the analysis of regional distributions as well as site-centred analysis.

Higgs, E. S. (ed.) 1972. *Papers in Economic Prehistory*. Cambridge: Cambridge University Press. A series of chapters on methodology including clarification of the distinction between SET and SCA (by Higgs and Vita-Finzi), definition of the extended territory concept (by Sturdy), and use of soils (by Webley).

Higgs, E. S. (ed.) 1975. *Palaeoeconomy*. Cambridge: Cambridge University Press. A series of regional case studies illustrating the application of STA to hunter-gatherer and agricultural economies in Europe.

Jarman, M. R., Bailey, G. N. and Jarman, H. N. 1982. *Early European Agriculture: Its Foundations and Development*. Cambridge: Cambridge University Press. An overview of methods and principles and a wide range of applications to European prehistory.

Roper, D. 1979. The Method and Theory of Site Catchment Analysis: A Review, pp. 119–40 in (M. B. Schiffer, ed.) *Advances in Archaeological Method and Theory 2*. New York and London: Academic Press.
A useful critique from an American point of view.

Vita-Finzi, C. and Higgs, E. S. 1970. Prehistoric Economy in the Mount Carmel Area of Palestine: Site Catchment Analysis. *Proceedings of the Prehistoric Society* 36: 1–37.
Provides the first formal definition and field application of the method in the context of the problem of agricultural origins.

Further reading

Bailey, G. N. and Davidson, I. 1983. Site Exploitation Territory and Topography: Two Case Studies from Palaeolithic Spain. *Journal of Archaeological Science* 10: 87–115.
Bettinger, R. L., Malhi, R. and McCarthy, H. 1997. Central Place Models of Acorn and Mussel Processing. *Journal of Archaeological Science* 24: 887–99.
Findlow, F. J. and Ericson, J. E. (eds) 1980. *Catchment Analysis: Essays on Prehistoric Resource Space*. Anthropology UCLA, 10. Los Angeles, CA: Department of Anthropology, University of California, Los Angeles.
Foley, R. 1977. Space and Energy: A Method for Analysing Habitat Value and Utilization in Relation to Archaeological Sites, pp. 163–87 in (D. L. Clarke, ed.) *Spatial Archaeology*. London and New York: Academic Press.
Metcalfe, D. and Barlow, K. R. 1992. A Model for Exploring the Optimal Trade-off between Field Processing and Transport. *American Anthropologist* 94: 340–56.
Vita-Finzi, C. 1977. *Archaeological Sites in their Setting*. London: Thames and Hudson.

GEOFF BAILEY

SOCIAL ARCHAEOLOGY

Over the past century several prominent figures in archaeology foregrounded the social in an attempt to redirect the discipline, including Flinders Petrie, V. Gordon Childe (*see* p 35), Grahame Clark, Colin Renfrew and Ian Hodder. Despite his culture historical position, Flinders Petrie's (1923: 1) insightful statement underscored the complex dimensions of social difference coupled with the interpreter's role in constructing society:

Society is a very complex structure, and therefore the study of it cannot be simple. In any country at one time there are many varieties of it in different classes, and probably the contemporary differences are as great as those of many centuries in any one class. In different lands under different climates, with different ancestries and different religions, and still more different modes of life, the diversity far exceeds our power of realisation ... It is not too much to say that the discoverer is the maker of society. Each step of discovery or invention reacts on the structure of social relations.

Processual or New Archaeologists (see p. 212) of the 1960s and 1970s were also interested in identifying social factors in the past, but were significantly less focused on the subjective nature of their interpretations and upon the social impacts of their research in contemporary settings. Colin Renfrew was among the earliest to use the term 'social archaeology', in his inaugural lecture as professor at the University of Southampton, entitled 'Social Archaeology', in 1973. This was followed by his *Approaches to Social Archaeology* (Renfrew 1984), which remains an important work on the topic. Renfrew argues that this shift towards social archaeology resulted from researching innovating societies in prehistoric Europe that were producing change and creating a different world: theories of diffusion were deemed insufficient. More recently he has acknowledged that social archaeology is characterised by issues of identity, specifically understanding the 'individual in society and how the individual becomes socialised, or what it means to be a person in a particular prehistoric community, or indeed in a contemporary community' (Renfrew 2001).

Taken at its broadest, social archaeology refers to the ways in which we conceptualise the relationships between ourselves and others, society and history, in both past and present contexts. Regarding materiality as central, it explores how we express ourselves through the things that we make and use, collect and discard, value or take for granted, and seek to be remembered by (Hall 2001). It involves an appreciation of the multiple entailments of our very being-in-the-world. A social archaeology conceptualised as an archaeology of social being can be located at the intersections of temporality, spatiality and materiality. To take these concepts as a focus of research is to explore the experiences of material life, the constitution of the object world and, concomitantly, their shaping of human experience (Meskell and Preucel 2004). The particular nature of social archaeology can be said to be twofold: one aspect underscores the importance of social factors in the constitution of ancient ways of life, the other recognises the social responsibilities and ramifications of archaeological practice in the experience of more recent and contemporary communities

(Meskell 2002a). Studying ancient constructions of difference such as gender (*see* p. 127) or ethnicity, or the ways in which notions of place or belonging are forged in the past are examples of the former. Analyses of nationalism and heritage or the impacts of colonialism or globalism in reference to archaeological materials and field practice might be instances of the latter.

Post-processual archaeology (*see* p. 207) is explicitly a social archaeology. Other ways of framing post-processualism include interpretive or contextual archaeologies. Starting in the early 1980s and continuing to the present, the work of Ian Hodder and the Cambridge school has provided the major impetus (Hodder 1982, 1984, 1989, 1990, 1991, 1992, 1999; Shanks and Tilley 1987a, 1987b; Tilley 1990, 1994). This work has encompassed major shifts in the subject matter, methodologies and wider responsibilities of archaeology in the past twenty years. An explicit focus on 'the social' in terms of identity, meaning and practice can certainly be seen as a positive transition in archaeology. It is an outcome of the discipline's growing engagement with social theory in fields as diverse as history, social anthropology, linguistics, sociology, human geography, literary theory and gender studies. While archaeology has always engaged with questions of temporality, under a social archaeology this has entailed a more theorised undertaking, whether in the form of monumentality, memory, diasporas or landscapes. Contemporary archaeology considers questions of time and identity in regard to lived and embodied experience, specifically as manifest in studies of rituality, mortuary customs, daily practice, household activities and human interaction with material culture. In terms of trends, social archaeology in the past twenty years has encompassed diverse theoretical positions including Marxism, behaviouralism, structuralism, post-structuralism, post-modernism, feminism, queer and masculinist theory.

Few can now deny the political entanglements of the archaeological past and contemporary narratives. More recently, a number of debates have been framed around the roles of archaeology in nationalism (Kohl and Fawcett 1995; Meskell 1998; Schmidt and Patterson 1995), heritage (Byrne 1991; Cleere 1989; Leone 2001; Meskell 2002b), indigenous issues (Dongoske, *et al.* 2000; Swidler *et al.* 1997; Watkins 2001), gender, feminism and sexuality (Franklin 2001; Gilchrist 1994, 1999; Joyce 1996, 2001; Meskell 1996, 1999; Meskell and Joyce 2003; Schmidt and Voss 2000) and postcolonialism (Gosden 1999, 2001; Shepherd 2003). These developments are leading to newer directions that coalesce around identity, indigenous theory, collaborative projects, new forms of narrative and media, tourism and intellectual property.

As a vehicle for these new directions the *Journal of Social Archaeology* was developed, first appearing in 2001. Here the term 'social archaeology' refers to a broad orientation within the discipline, rather than to any one theoretical position. Its rationale is to understand past societies in terms of their social contexts and lived experiences while, at the same time, to remain aware of how the knowledge of the past that we produce is used in the present.

Suggested reading

Gosden, C. 1999. *Anthropology and Archaeology: A Changing Relationship*. London: Routledge.

Hodder, I. 1991. *Reading the Past*. Cambridge: Cambridge University Press.

—— (ed.) 2001. *Archaeological Theory Today*. Oxford: Polity.

Journal of Social Archaeology (from 2001). Sage: London.

Meskell, L. M. 2002a. The Intersection of Identity and Politics in Archaeology. *Annual Review of Anthropology* 31: 279–301.

Meskell, L. M. and Preucel, R. (eds) 2004. *Companion to Social Archaeology*. Oxford: Blackwell.

Renfrew, C. 1984. *Approaches to Social Archaeology*. Cambridge: Harvard University Press.

Further reading

Byrne, D. 1991. Western Hegemony in Archaeological Heritage Management. *History and Anthropology* 5: 269–76.

Cleere, H. (ed.) 1989. *Archaeological Heritage Management in the Modern World*. London: Unwin Hyman.

Dongoske, K. E., Aldenderfer, M. and Doehner, K. (eds) 2000. *Working Together: Native American and Archaeologists*. Washington, DC: Society for American Archaeology.

Franklin, M. 2001. A Black Feminist-Inspired Archaeology. *Journal of Social Archaeology* 1: 108–25.

Gilchrist, R. 1994. *Gender and Material Culture: The Archaeology of Religious Women*. London: Routledge.

—— 1999. *Gender and Archaeology: Contesting the Past*. London: Routledge.

Gosden, C. 2001. Post-Colonial Archaeology: Issues of Culture, Identity and Knowledge, pp. 241–61 in (I. Hodder, ed.) *Archaeological Theory Today*. Cambridge: Polity Press.

Hall, M. 2001. Social Archaeology and the Theatres of Memory. *Journal of Social Archaeology* 1: 50–61.

Hodder, I. 1982. *Symbols in Action*. Cambridge: Cambridge University Press.

—— 1984. Archaeology in 1984. *Antiquity* 58: 25–32.

—— (ed.) 1989. *The Meanings of Things: Material Culture and Symbolic Expression.* London: HarperCollins.

—— 1990. *The Domestication of Europe.* Oxford: Blackwell.

—— 1992. *Theory and Practice in Archaeology.* London: Routledge.

—— 1999. *The Archaeological Process: An Introduction.* Oxford: Blackwell.

Joyce, R. A. 1996. The Construction of Gender in Classic Maya Monuments, pp. 167–95 in (R. P. Wright, ed.) *Gender and Archaeology.* Philadelphia: University of Pennsylvania Press.

—— 2001. *Gender and Power in Prehispanic Mesoamerica.* Austin: University of Texas Press.

Kohl, P. L. and Fawcett, C. (eds) 1995. *Nationalism, Politics and the Practice of Archaeology.* Cambridge: Cambridge University Press.

Leone, M. P. 2001. Creating Culture through Choosing Heritage. *Current Anthropology* 42: 582–4.

Meskell, L. M. 1996. The Somatisation of Archaeology: Institutions, Discourses, Corporeality. *Norwegian Archaeological Review* 29: 1–16.

—— (ed.) 1998. *Archaeology Under Fire: Nationalism, Politics and Heritage in the Eastern Mediterranean and Middle East.* London: Routledge.

—— 1999. *Archaeologies of Social Life: Age, Sex, Class etc. in Ancient Egypt.* Oxford: Blackwell.

—— 2002b. Negative Heritage and Past Mastering in Archaeology. *Anthropological Quarterly* 75: 557–74.

Meskell, L. M. and Joyce, R. A. 2003. *Embodied Lives: Figuring Ancient Maya and Egyptian Experience.* London: Routledge.

Petrie, W. M. F. 1923. *Social Life in Ancient Egypt.* Constable: London.

Renfrew, C. 2001. From Social to Cognitive Archaeology. An Interview with Colin Renfrew. *Journal of Social Archaeology* 1 (1): 13–34.

Schmidt, P. R. and Patterson, T. C. (eds) 1995. *Making Alternative Histories: The Practice of Archaeology and History in Non-Western Settings.* Santa Fe, New Mexico: School of American Research Press.

Schmidt, R. and Voss, B. (eds) 2000. *Archaeologies of Sexuality.* London: Routledge.

Shanks, M. and Tilley, C. 1987a. *Social Theory and Archaeology.* Cambridge: Polity Press.

—— 1987b. *Re-constructing Archaeology: Theory and Practice.* London: Routledge.

Shepherd, N. 2003. 'When the Hand that Holds the Trowel is Black'; Disciplinary Practices of Self-Representation and the Issue of 'Native' Labour in Archaeology. *Journal of Social Archaeology* 3 (3): 334–52.

Swidler, N., Dongoske, K. E., Anyon, R. and Downer, A. S. (eds) 1997. *Native Americans and Archaeologists: Stepping Stones to Common Ground.* Walnut Creek, Calif.: AltaMira Press.

Tilley, C. (ed.) 1990. *Reading Material Culture.* Oxford: Blackwell.

—— 1994. *A Phenomenology of Landscape: Places, Paths and Monuments*. Oxford: Berg.

Watkins, J. 2001. *Indigenous Archaeology*. Walnut Creek, Calif.: AltaMira Press.

LYNN MESKELL

THEORY OF SOCIAL PRACTICE

Basic questions posed by the social archaeologist concern social order, reproduction and social change. Why do some societies apparently stay the same for perhaps hundreds of years; why do others undergo rapid social change; why do others apparently undergo complete collapse? In their approach to these questions, most archaeologists have usually focused on broad structural, institutional and environmental factors. So the shift to an agricultural economy has been explained by environmental change. The emergence of cities has been explained, for example, in terms of the intensification of the agricultural economy, or in relation to institutionalised warfare. Trade in prestige goods is popularly invoked as a determining factor in the development of complex stratified society. Marxist archaeologists (*see* p. 165) often emphasise relationships between social classes in, for example, the early empires of the Near East. Processual archaeologists (*see* p. 212) usually talk about the past in terms of social systems. Structuralist archaeologists have explained the prehistoric paintings of animals and geometric motifs on cave walls as expressions of an underlying structure or grammar centred upon a distinction between male and female principles.

But, as one feminist critic put it, this leaves archaeology dealing in accounts of 'faceless blobs'. It is sometimes hard to see how and where real people, carrying out their daily lives, fit in these explanations of past societies. Do people act just as social structures and other determining forces have them act? Where do the social systems, structures and forces come from in the first place? Do people not have the power to act differently? We all have a sense of self and of varying degrees of freedom to act. But archaeology's long-term view of history and human culture makes it very clear that there are very strong regularities – people live in communities that direct, to a greater or lesser extent, our sense of self and our actions. This is the issue, the conundrum of social archaeology – how do broad social structures and historical forces connect with individual agency (*see* p. 3), the power of people to act?

The French social theorist Pierre Bourdieu (1930–2002) has had a great influence on Post-processual (*see* p. 207) and Interpretive Social Archaeology (*see* p. 235) with his ideas about the nature of social practice. He attempted to find a middle ground between accounts that emphasise forces such as environment or economy in determining the shape of history and social evolution, and accounts which focus upon the acts of great individuals, as found in much political history.

His concept of *habitus* (*see* p. 133) refers to commonsense attitudes and dispositions that direct people in their everyday life. Archaeologists have found it useful as a way of understanding how everyday routines and rituals, often very visible in the archaeological record, give an overall structure to society and history.

Bourdieu was a professor of sociology at the prestigious Collège de France and a left-wing activist. In a prolific career he conducted ethnography in Algeria, studied contemporary education, photography, art and aesthetic taste, the mass media, museums, and intellectuals. He is particularly known for his writing on social and cultural theory. Much of this applies directly to the basic conundrum of social archaeology just outlined.

In the late 1970s and 1980s post-processual archaeologists criticised Processual Social Archaeology for an overriding emphasis upon structures and systems binding people into particular behaviours. Bourdieu's theory of practice and concept of *habitus,* as well as Anthony Giddens's theory of structuration and the duality of structure, were important parts of a rethinking of archaeology's use of concepts like person, individual, society and social actor.

People know how to go about everyday life. People think, perceive and act without considering how and why. They intuitively know what to do and say, what to think. *Habitus* refers to the durable dispositions that are the heart of this intuitive skill. *Habitus* is durable because it is embedded in routines. Much of *habitus* is unsaid and much is of the body, learned through experience, encounter, imitation and encouragement; this is socialisation. It is about the habits, values and attitudes that mark sex and gender roles, the division of labour, class and status, morality and taste.

In this view people's actions are seen as opportunistic improvisations or performances based upon their commonsense knowledge of what is possible and appropriate. *Habitus* is thus the site of interplay between people and social structures or constraints, with each person operating within their own sense of the possible.

Habitus and its theory of practice mean that archaeologists should look closely at everyday routines. Gender (*see* p. 127), for example, is not something imposed on people so much as being embedded in what are considered as appropriate ways of behaving, dressing, relating to one another.

Pot style is regularly used by archaeologists as a way of identifying social groups such as cultures. The concept of *habitus* questions this. It means that identity is not something coded into artefact style and design, but is negotiated in everyday life. It is not that a certain style of dress or ornament means high status, with a system of rank determining what people do, but rather people wear this dress or that ornament because it is just what you do, and in so doing they create the distinctions of status that others recognise.

Prehistorians of northern Europe have been very successful in working with Bourdieu's ideas. John Barrett (1994) and Julian Thomas (1996) see these routines of social practice and *habitus* in the Neolithic monuments of Britain, in the coming and going of people in monumental landscapes, in everyday ritual practices relating to human and animal body parts, the design and use of ceramic vessels. The embodied nature of *habitus* directs attention to sensory experience such as the ceremonies that occurred in and around megalithic and henge monuments. This is the basis of Phenomenological Archaeology (*see* p. 20).

Roberta Gilchrist has studied medieval nunneries and interpreted the routines of their everyday life in relation to medieval concepts of gender and the social and cultural independence of nuns. Overall the theory of social practice is part of a new interest in the everyday that is found, for example, in Feminist (*see* p. 116) and Gender Archaeology.

Further reading

Barrett, J. 1994. *Fragments from Antiquity: An Archaeology of Social Life in Britain, 2900–1200 BC.* Oxford: Blackwell.
Interesting application of the ideas of Bourdieu and Giddens to the British Neolithic.

Bourdieu, P. 1998. *Practical Reason: On the Theory of Action.* Cambridge: Polity Press.
Fundamental text on the theory of social practice and the concept of *habitus*.

Giddens, A. 1984. *The Constitution of Society: Outline of the Theory of Structuration.* Cambridge: Blackwell Polity.
A sociological development of the theory of structuralisation.

Gilchrist, R. 1994. *Gender and Material Culture: The Archaeology of Religious Women*. London and New York: Routledge.
Interesting application of social and gender theory to the monastic communities of the Middle Ages of Britain and Europe.

Thomas, J. 1995. *Time, Culture and Identity: An Interpretive Archaeology*. London: Routledge.
Thoughtful discussion of theories of social practice, especially as applied to the British Neolithic.

MICHAEL SHANKS

PRINCIPLES OF STRATIGRAPHIC SUCCESSION

Stratigraphic succession is the foundation of relative dating in archaeology and is based on the principle that underlying objects or deposits must be older than those which cover them. The relative age determination technique, using the law of superposition and context, is at the heart of every single archaeological excavation, and almost every other dating technique. Stratigraphic succession, and the relative ordering of objects and strata in time, has been part of at least some archaeologists' methodology since the eighteenth century.

Two definitions of stratigraphy are commonly used: one from an archaeological perspective, the other from a slightly broader geoscientific perspective. Archaeological stratigraphy is defined as the study and interpretation of stratified deposits. The emphasis is on superposition and succession for the purpose of dating. In geosciences, stratigraphy is defined as

> the science dealing with the description of all rock bodies forming the Earth's crust – sedimentary, igneous, and metamorphic – and their organization into distinctive, useful, mappable units based on their inherent properties or attributes. Stratigraphic procedures in geosciences include the description, classification, naming, and correlation of these units for the purpose of establishing their relationship in space and their succession in time.

(Salvador 1994:137)

The difference between these two definitions is minor but significant. The archaeological definition does not include formally describing, naming, classifying or correlating the strata. Rather, it indicates the primary purpose of stratigraphy in archaeology as dating, and specifically superposition and context. The geoscientific definition focuses on the description of rocks, their classification, and especially the correlation of rock formation and fossils across time and space. The purpose of stratigraphy for geoscientists is establishing the relationship of strata in space and succession in time. For archaeologists the purpose is establishing time.

The reason for this dichotomy is in part historical and in part scalar. Archaeology has developed differently in Europe and the Americas, and is used differently by those who study very old periods (e.g. Palaeolithic and Paleoindian) and younger periods (e.g. early agriculturalists, urban settings of complex societies, classical areas and historic occupations). Also, the two different disciplines operate at different scales. Archaeologists do not correlate rock units from site to site, and often not from trench to trench. Archaeologists focus on temporal correlation within a site of less than one kilometre, and emphasise superposition rather than environmental reconstruction or correlation.

The beginnings of stratigraphy are traced clearly to concerns with fossils. The first observers of sequences of rocks were actually drawn to explaining the presence of marine shells in odd places, such as the high altitudes of the Alps and under the city of Rome. Nicholas Steno is credited with being the first stratigrapher, when he suggested that shell-bearing strata beneath ancient Rome must be older than the ancient city itself. These particles and shells must have been deposited particle by particle and layer by layer, one on top of another. Therefore, in a sequence of multiple layers, a lower one must be older than any overlying layers. This observation, which is common sense to us, was revolutionary in 1669.

The beginning of specifically archaeological stratigraphy starts when the naturalists who used Steno's principles started looking at primitive artefacts made by people. These scholars were using superposition to establish the antiquity of people as well as ordering in relative time all life in general. Archaeologists who collaborate with these naturalists and who established a discipline within archaeology are called prehistorians. They remained close to geologists and their development in the last hundred years follows the history of stratigraphy.

The stratigraphy of prehistorians requires that a single sequence of rock be divided into multiple sets of units. The units are constructed using different criteria such as lithology (how a rock looks), fossils, magnetism, weathering zones, or anything else that is useful for correlation. Each criterion is measured in the sequence of rocks, and the position of significant changes is noted by defining boundaries and where the boundaries fall. If they all overlap at one boundary in the sequence, then one interprets that location as a place of significant change. Prehistorians follow these procedures in excavating rockshelters and open-air sites throughout Europe, Asia and Africa.

At the same time, a large group of archaeologists studying urban centres came to the discipline from an entirely different methodological direction. They explored the connections between archaeology and historical texts, languages and classical period civilisations. The sites had walls, foundations, streets and inscriptions. The texts spoke greater volumes concerning age and temporal relationships than the artefacts in strata. The strata, therefore, could be ignored.

The first archaeologists to consider stratification of urban centres for purposes of dating were Kathleen Kenyon and Sir Mortimer Wheeler. Their contribution is that they excavated layer by layer. Wheeler, in his 1954 book *Archaeology from the Earth*, emphasises that good archaeologists have to know history, but also have to pay attention to useful information from sciences. 'The important thing is that the archaeologist must know his dates and how to use them: recorded dates where they are valid, and unwritten dates where geological or physical or chemical or botanical science can win them from the earth' (1954: 24).

Not until Edward Harris, in his book *Principles of Archaeological Stratigraphy* (1979), introduced a recording device referred to as the Harris Matrix did urban archaeologists take Wheeler's words to heart. Harris was frustrated by having only profile sections to reconstruct superpositional relationship of complex walls, floors and urban rebuilding. He invented the Harris Matrix, where each layer is drawn as a box. The placement of the boxes relative to each other corresponds to the superpositional relationship of their deposition. The matrix is, therefore, a record of the temporal superposition of all strata in the site.

The Harris Matrix revolutionised how both urban archaeologists and prehistorians reconstructed their sites. The archaeologists who have archival information such as references to kings' reigns do not use the matrix to date the sites relative to calendar years. They use the matrix to decipher small-scale temporal events that occur within the urban setting, such as building a certain road and remodelling part of a house.

In the Americas, much the same sort of dichotomy as the one in Europe developed between those archaeologists who studied the Ice Age and those who studied urban settings. Those archaeologists who focused on the oldest periods of prehistory stayed closely tied to the geosciences. Those who focused on the recent, complex, cultures relied on pottery, architecture, art and ethnography to date sites and correlate them across space.

Archaeologists searching for the first inhabitants of the North and South American continents were faced with the dilemma of using the sequence developed in Europe or devising their own. The first archaeologists used the crude morphology of objects to suggest the great antiquity, and their similarity to the forms found in the Lower Palaeolithic of Europe. This was replaced with the association of artefacts and Ice Age fossils. The discovery of fluted points (a projectile point with a flute or chip running up both faces of the blade) in association with extinct Ice Age animals allowed geologists and archaeologists to establish that people were in the Americas for thousands of years, and at least as long as the Palaeolithic periods of Europe.

Archaeologists who investigate complex societies in North America did not have texts or king lists to date their strata, nor did they have historic objects such as coins with dates stamped on their surface. These archaeologists were scrambling to figure out the antiquity of the North American inhabitants and from where the living Native Americans came. They embraced stratigraphy only when the new technique of seriation was discovered, a technique that could establish the antiquity and age of sites. Seriation uses the attributes of artefacts that changed slowly over time to cluster assemblages into time periods. Seriating artefacts according to slowly changing attributes allowed sites to be precisely dated using artefactual material collected from stratified or non-stratified contexts.

The most influential of these new American archaeologists who relied on seriation to date urban sites were Phillips, Ford and Griffin (1951: 240–1), who describe the new stratigraphy in their publication of excavations in the Lower Mississippi Valley.

> To many archaeologists, stratigraphy necessarily involves a situation in which materials can be segregated on the basis of distinct and separable soil zones. Such is fortunately not the case. It frequently happens, as we shall show, that a homogeneous deposit, without observable soil stratification, may be made to yield a stratigraphic record of the utmost

value. Obviously, such an unstratified deposit will have to be excavated by arbitrary levels, to which method the term 'metrical stratigraphy' has sometimes been applied in derogation, as opposed to 'natural stratigraphy' obtained by peeling stratified layers.

The emphasis on artefact-oriented stratigraphy did not change in the Americas until Schiffer (1987) preached that archaeologists had to consider the 'natural processes' that have an impact on artefacts as well as the cultural ones (*see* p. 121). Schiffer emphasised the history of the artefact in the ground, and referred to that history as formational processes. Most archaeologists now consider stratigraphy to include seriation (time) and context (formation processes).

Stratigraphic succession has been the backbone of dating in archaeology since the inception of the discipline. It has, however, developed along different historical pathways that influence what we think of it today.

Suggested readings

Browman, D. L. and Givens, D. R. 1996. Stratigraphic Excavation: The First 'New Archaeology'. *American Anthropologist* 98. 80–95.
The history of stratigraphic excavation is discussed in detail for both European and American archaeology, with a special emphasis on the difference between dating sites using stratigraphy and excavating sites using stratigraphy.

Harris, E. C. 1979. *Principles of Archaeological Stratigraphy.* London: Academic Press.
This book articulates the view of the Urban and Historical Archaeologists primarily working in European and Near Eastern settings. Harris's view of stratigraphy as a discipline separate from geoscientific stratigraphy is articulated, along with an introduction to the Harris Matrix.

Harris, E. C., Brown, M. R., III, and Brown, G. J. 1993. *Principles of Archaeological Stratigraphy.* London: Academic Press.
This edited collection provides the reader with examples of archaeological projects that successfully use the Harris Matrix to record the stratigraphy at sites.

O'Brien, M. J. and Lyman, R. L. 1999. *Seriation, Stratigraphy, and Index Fossils: The Backbone of Archaeological Dating.* New York: Kluwer Academic/Plenum.
The role of stratigraphy and seriation is explored in detail in this compilation of the most influential American Archaeology contributions to research on dating methods.

Schiffer, M. B. 1987. *Formation Processes of the Archaeological Record*. Albuquerque: University of New Mexico Press.
This book is a complete description of formation processes as defined by a behavioural archaeologist, including cultural and natural formation processes.

Stein, J. K. 1987. Deposits for Archaeologists, pp. 337–93 in (M. B. Schiffer, ed.) *Advances in Archaeological Method and Theory*, vol. 11. Orlando, Flor.: Academic Press.
Both archaeological and geoscientific stratigraphy is defined, with detailed descriptions of the various stratigraphy units, laws and principles as used by archaeologists.

Stein, J. K. 2000. Stratigraphy and Archaeological Dating, pp. 14–40 in (S. E. Nash. ed.) *It's About Time: A History of Archaeological Dating in North America*. Salt Lake City: University of Utah Press.
The history of stratigraphy as a dating method is traced for American Archaeology. The contributions and their implications are given in the context of a broad history of archaeological dating methods.

Further reading

Kenyon, K. M. 1952. *Beginning in Archaeology*. London: Phoenix House.
Phillips, P., Ford, J. A. and Griffin, J. B. 1951. *Archaeological Survey in the Lower Mississippi Valley, 1940–1947*, Papers of the Peabody Museum of Archeology and Ethnology No. 25. Cambridge, Mass.: Harvard University Press.
Pyddoke, E. 1961. *Stratification for the Archaeologist*. London: Phoenix House.
Rowe, J. H. 1961. Stratigraphy and Seriation. *American Antiquity* 26: 324–30.
Salvador, A. 1994. *International Stratigraphic Guide: A Guide to Stratigraphic Classification, Terminology, and Procedure*, 2nd edn. Boulder, Col.: Geological Society of America.
Steno, N. 1968. *The Prodromus of Nicolaus Steno's Dissertation Concerning a Solid Body Enclosed by Process of Nature within a Solid* (English version with introduction and explanatory notes by John Garrett Winter). New York: Hafner.
Wheeler, M. 1954. *Archaeology from the Earth*. London: Oxford University Press.

JULIE K. STEIN

SURVEY

One of the key problems archaeologists face is how to find the full range of surviving evidence for past human activity or habitation within a given area, and how to do so in an efficient and accurate manner. Sites must first be discovered before they can be explored in more detail (for instance, by excavation – *see* p. 106), but only a very small proportion of them take the form of great urban centres or remarkable monuments, such as Teotihuacán or Stonehenge. Most of the record of the human past is to be found in vast numbers of much less prominent sites, often very small and short-lived, as well as in a myriad of structures, features and artefacts scattered over land surfaces or buried under later deposits. Reconstructions of that past are seriously incomplete unless we take account of all types of archaeological resources spread across the landscape, and we can hardly begin to understand the economic, political or ideological roles of central sites without placing them in their wider context. Surface survey is the chief methodology for collecting information at the regional scale, and it allows archaeologists to formulate research questions at a level not available from work at one or a few sites alone (Ammerman 1981).

Pedestrian survey – also called fieldwalking or archaeological reconnaissance – refers to the careful search of the ground surface within a defined study area, usually by one or more teams of surveyors walking across it in a systematic manner (in some settings, inspection by four-wheel-drive vehicle or boat is more practical, if less thorough). Rather confusingly, 'site survey' can also refer to the procedure of using appropriate instruments to lay out a controlled grid of reference points over an individual site, in order to map its features (for which the term 'surveying' is preferable); where this is supplemented by controlled collection of artefacts, it is sometimes described as 'large-site survey' or 'urban survey'.[1] Ground survey depends on the willing feet and keen eyes of knowledgeable archaeologists, but this commonest technique for locating sites has been usefully extended by various remote-sensing technologies, including the use of space imagery and aerial photography, and numerous geophysical methods (such as ground-penetrating and side-scanning radar, resistivity surveys, magnetometer surveys, etc.). Advances in technology, including submersibles and other robotic devices, are now making it possible to conduct regional surveys of archaeological resources underwater, at levels of thoroughness and accuracy comparable to land-based surveys.

Searching for archaeological sites – whether specific named places (e.g. Homer's Troy), or potentially 'productive' sites suitable for excavation – is a practice with a very long history in the western world. Modern techniques of survey, however, had their beginnings in the river basin surveys of the pre-World War II era in the United

States, while Gordon Willey's Peruvian Virú Valley survey in the 1940s is frequently cited as the first project in which the understanding of regional settlement patterns constituted an explicit problem orientation.[2] Unsurprisingly, survey's success has been greatest in environments in which archaeological remains are well preserved, and steep terrain and dense vegetation cover do not pose serious logistical problems: consequently, it is in areas such as Mesopotamia, many parts of the Mediterranean, the coastal Andean region, highland Mesoamerica, and the American Southwest that the survey approach has been the most effective and influential. In several parts of the world, large-scale intensive survey was a distinctive area of growth during the 1970s and 1980s, in part as a consequence of the emphasis placed by New Archaeology (*see* p. 212) on the importance of problem orientation, a regional perspective, sampling, survey as an alternative to excavation, and the long-term perspective provided by settlement archaeology.

The boundaries of an area targeted for survey are generally determined by a problem, or series of problems. It can be selected primarily on geographic or environmental factors (an island, for instance, or a river valley), or on socio-economic and political considerations (such as the probable territory of a Greek city-state, or the sustaining area of a Mayan centre). Increasingly, it is cultural resource management (CRM) or 'rescue archaeology' concerns that dictate the shape and size of survey areas, but even hurriedly conducted surveys along pipeline, highway or transmission-line corridors are capable of yielding worthwhile data that shed light on broader questions.

A major issue in all surveys is that of the sample of the target region actually to be surveyed. During the 1970s and 1980s, there was considerable enthusiasm for schemes involving the survey of a statistically representative small sample of the study-region (see Judge *et al.* 1975), using quadrats or transects as the most common units. Subsequent studies showed the belief that such probabilistic schemes would acquire high-quality data at relatively low cost to be wishful thinking. On the one hand, there exist serious problems concerning the extrapolation of regional population parameters from non-normally distributed sample statistics. On the other hand, it has been increasingly realised that the quality and reliability of survey data are themselves powerfully affected by the circumstances of data collection – for example, the intensity at which each survey unit is examined; the impact of weather and light, and of fieldwalkers' fatigue and experience; and the disconcerting ability of archaeological remains to appear or disappear in response to seasonal and inter-annual fluctuations in rainfall, vegetation or crop cultivation. One response to such problems has been to urge repeated survey of the same area,[3] a proposal that in most circumstances is both impractical and prohibitively costly. Another is the recommendation that archaeologists follow what Fish and Kowalewski (1990) term 'full-coverage survey' – meaning the survey of the entirety of a continuous study area, although not its 100 per cent coverage (since, even in the case of 'high intensity' surveys where the archaeologists are separated by only 10–15 metres or less, the spacing between individual walkers is still sufficiently wide to leave much unexamined ground surface between them). It seems wisest to accept that no survey can be 'complete', and to settle for being as explicit as possible about the circumstances under which any particular project was conducted.

A classic paper by Schiffer *et al.* (1978) succinctly discusses several crucial variables that the archaeologist is largely powerless to control, but that greatly affect the outcome of any survey project: the abundance, spatial distribution and obtrusiveness of the archaeological phenomena within the region, and their relative visibility and accessibility. One thing that the archaeologist can control is intensity, best measured by the amount of time spent covering a given area, and thus the yield of information per unit of effort (few survey projects, unfortunately, keep accurate records of such things). How much time is needed for the adequate survey of any given region is strongly dependent on its occupational history (and, thus, the relative richness of its archaeological record), on geomorphological factors that may favour good preservation, and on whether artefacts can be collected during survey or must be studied and left in place (as some governmental permits may require).

Not all surveys adopt the 'site' as the basic unit of observation and data collection, since surface remains are found in so bewildering an array of forms – from substantial architecture associated with abundant artefacts, to small, diffuse, low-density scatters of pottery or chipped stone, and even single artefacts or features in isolation. Faced with the problem of defining precisely what a site is and where its boundaries should be drawn, some archaeologists (e.g. Ebert 1992) have preferred a 'non-site' approach, in which the individual artefact is the basic unit of record within the region. With the advent of GPS (Geographical Positioning Systems) as a fast and accurate way to record data in the field, and of GIS (Geographical Information Systems) as a means for plotting and manipulating this information, it has now become feasible to experiment with densities, boundaries and concentrations of artefacts as a means of representing settlement patterns and land use for various periods in the past.

It is intrinsic to survey as a methodology that its data generally span many eras of the past. An excavator can focus on exploring a site of very specific type and age (such as a Late Roman villa), but the surveyor may come across yesterday's rubbish one moment and a piece of Palaeolithic chipped stone the next, a circumstance that brings both disadvantages and benefits. Both because surface artefacts often occur in very large quantities and because they may be from many different periods, it is necessary for the survey archaeologist to become conversant with an unusually wide range of material culture in the study area, or else to bring in specialists to assist in determining the dates and functions of surface artefacts. On the other hand, the diachronic (i.e. multi-period) character of most survey evidence makes it particularly well suited for the study of change over extended periods, and the most successful projects have tended to be those in which landscape archaeology (*see* p. 156) has been the basis for writing 'long-term history'.

Notes

1 See, for instance, A. M. Snodgrass and J. L. Bintliff (1988) Mediterranean Survey and the City, *Antiquity* 62: 57–71, and (1991) Surveying Ancient Cities, *Scientific American* 264 (3): 88–93.

2 G. R. Willey (1953) *Prehistoric Settlement Patterns in the Virú Valley, Peru* (Bulletin 155), Washington, DC: Smithsonian Institution Bureau of American Ethnology; (1999) The Virú Valley Project and Settlement Archaeology: Some Reminiscences and Contemporary Comments, pp. 9–11 in (B. Billman and G. Feinman, eds) *Settlement Pattern Studies in the Americas: Fifty Years since Virú*, Washington, DC: Smithsonian Institution Press.

3 A. J. Ammerman and M. W. Feldman (1978) Replicated Collection of Site Surfaces, *American Antiquity* 43: 734–40.

Suggested reading

Adams, R. McC. 1981. *Heartland of Cities: Surveys of Ancient Settlement and Land Use on the Central Floodplain of the Euphrates*. Chicago: University of Chicago Press.

A remarkable study that presents very large amounts of information from surveys in Mesopotamia, and uses it to describe and explain the evolution of political organisation in the region.

Alcock, S. E. and Cherry, J. F. (eds) 2004. *Side-by-Side Survey: Comparative Regional Studies in the Mediterranean World*. Oxford: Oxbow.
Discussion of the problems and potential of comparing data from very different survey projects, and the value of combining them to help build pictures of the past at the macro-regional scale.

Ammerman, A. J. 1981. Surveys and Archaeological Research. *Annual Review of Anthropology* 10: 63–88.
Classic article that explains clearly why surveys are not simply the prelude to excavation, but provide information, available from no other source, relevant to crucial archaeological and anthropological research questions.

Given, M. and Knapp, A. B. (eds) 2003. *The Sydney Cyprus Survey Project: Social Approaches to Regional Archaeological Survey*. Los Angeles: The Cotsen Institute of Archaeology, University of California, Los Angeles.
A recently published final report of a high-intensity survey conducted in the foothills of the Troodos Mountains in Cyprus, exemplifying the current state of theory and method in regional fieldwork projects.

Manning, E. B. 2002. *Archaeological Survey. Manuals in Archaeological Method, Theory, and Technique*. New York: Kluwer Academic/Plenum Publishers.
The latest practical guide to the variety of approaches adopted in field survey (mainly in North America); particularly strong on sampling and statistical methods.

Plog, S., Plog, F. and Wait, W. 1978. Decision Making in Modern Surveys, pp. 383–421 in (M. B. Schiffer, ed.) *Advances in Archaeological Method and Theory*, vol. 1. New York: Academic Press.
Article that discusses how decisions about various practical matters affect the likelihood that a survey will be successful in accurately determining the range of archaeological phenomena within the project area.

Richards, J. C. 1990. *The Stonehenge Environs Project*. London: English Heritage.
A project undertaken to locate and record sites, monuments, burials and other archaeological remains in the area around Stonehenge illustrates how much the regional survey perspective can add to our understanding of an already very well-known monument.

Schiffer, M. B., Sullivan, A. P. and Klinger, T. C. 1978. The Design of Archaeological Surveys. *World Archaeology* 10: 1–28.
A very clear discussion of the interrelationships between the characteristics of archaeological phenomena, the data requirements of archaeological research problems, and the design of archaeological surveys.

Further reading

Cherry, J. F. 2003. Archaeology beyond the Site: Regional Survey and its Future, pp. 137–59 in (J. K. Papadopoulos and R. M. Leventhal, eds) *Theory and Practice* in *Mediterranean Archaeology: Old World and New World Perspectives.* Los Angeles: The Cotsen Institute of Archaeology at UCLA.

Ebert, J. I. 1992. *Distributional Archaeology.* Albuquerque: University of New Mexico Press.

Fish, S. K. and Kowalewski, S. A. (eds) 1990. *The Archaeology of Regions: The Case for Full-Coverage Survey.* Washington, DC: Smithsonian Institution Press.

Judge, W. J., Ebert, J. I. and Hitchcock, R. K. 1975. Sampling in Regional Archaeological Survey, pp. 82–123 in (J. W. Mueller, ed.) *Sampling in Archaeology.* Tucson: University of Arizona Press.

Renfrew, C. and Bahn, P. 2004. *Archaeology: Theories, Methods, and Practice,* 4th edn. London: Thames and Hudson (Chapter 3, 'Where?' Survey and Excavation of Sites and Features).

Sanders, W. T., Parsons, J. R. and Santley, R. S. 1979. *The Basin of Mexico: Ecological Processes in the Evolution of a Civilization.* New York: Academic Press.

Sullivan, A. P., III (ed.) 1998. *Surface Archaeology.* Albuquerque: University of New Mexico Press.

JOHN F. CHERRY

SYMBOLIC AND STRUCTURALIST ARCHAEOLOGY

The archaeology of symbolism has a long pedigree, even if research in this area was not always known by that name. For example, culture historical approaches focused on style and cultural variation that was often thought to relate to groups of people (Childe 1925). The styles of cultures 'represented' social or ethnic groups, and in this sense they were symbolic. The symbolism of an artefact is usually defined as the secondary meanings that go beyond primary (often functional) use. Thus an axe may be used to cut down a tree (the primary or 'sign' meaning of the axe) but its secondary meaning may refer to strength, or agricultural power, or the people that used it. Thus the axe can 'stand for' or represent the group – the axe symbolises the group. On the whole, however, culture historical approaches to symbolism focused most on the affiliations between regional styles and cultures without exploring secondary meanings very fully.

To some extent the situation changed in processual archaeology (*see* p. 212), although the focus on symbols primarily concerned how the symbols functioned to enhance adaptations of people to environments, For example, Wobst (1977) argued that larger groups would have more material symbolism because they needed symbols to handle the greater flow of information. So symbols were seen as a function of information exchange. The main interest of processual approaches to symbols concerned their functional aspects rather than their secondary meanings. Another important area of processual concern with symbols was the study of burial assemblages where the presence of prestige goods helped to identify individuals of higher status (Renfrew and Shennan 1982).

One of the limitations of such views is that symbolism is seen as compartmentalised and peripheral or secondary. But in fact it is difficult to identify any act or object that does not have symbolic meaning. It is also often difficult to argue that the functional meanings are always primary over the symbolic or representational. An alternative view is that everything is symbolic to some degree, or that symbolism is everywhere. According to this view, even the most mundane aspects of the archaeological record – such as the discard of refuse or the digging of pits – had a symbolic dimension which was important in structuring people's lives.

It can be argued, therefore, that material culture is always meaningfully constituted (Hodder 1982). One way of studying symbolic material culture is to treat it as a text – the material objects are made or placed in sites in a way comparable to the writing of words in order to say something, and they are organised in sets or sentences so that they have meaning. There are problems with the text metaphor, as will be noted below, but the comparison between objects and words allows the study of material culture to be drawn into the wider science of semiotics – the study of signs. One of the major contributors to semiotics was de Saussure, whose work strongly influenced Lévi-Strauss (1963) in his development of structuralism within anthropology, It is the de Saussure and Lévi-Strauss forms of structuralism that have had most impact in archaeology, although others, such as the semiotics of Pierce (Preucel and Bauer 2001) and space syntax (Hillier et al. 1976) have had some impact.

In archaeology, structuralism is often used to argue that objects can be seen as organised into systems of signs in order to have meaning. For example, objects are organised into 'paradigmatic' relations (i.e. the alternatives available such as the different types of brooch worn on the shoulders of skeletons in a cemetery), and into 'syntagmatic' sets (i.e. the groupings available such as the set of brooch, pin, pot and animal bone associated with female rather than male skeletons). Some studies examine the formal structure of such relationships between objects and focus on the arrangements of rooms within houses and the ordering of designs on pots. Study of such sets is described as formal or structural analysis and is best distinguished from structuralist analysis in the anthropological Lévi-Strauss sense. The latter posits that systems of signs are organised by underlying structures. These often have, though they may not, some binary form. Thus the organisation of space inside a settlement may be characterised by differences between clean and dirty areas, zones with or without burials, and the doors may face east (Campbell 2000; Parker Pearson 1996). In such cases we might say that clean is to dirty as burial is to non-burial as west is to east. Such statements can be written as clean:dirty::burial:non-burial::west:east. Or we might generalise further and argue that underlying all these oppositions is a culture:nature or male:female deep structure. Such studies have been widely applied in order to make sense of variability in the archaeological record, even if the final step of identifying unifying themes such as culture:nature is often eschewed as overly abstract and determining (McGhee 1977; Yentsch 1991).

There are several difficulties in the application of structuralist methods in archaeology. Perhaps the most significant is that material culture is in many ways quite unlike a spoken word or a written text. In particular, material culture meanings are rarely, if ever, entirely arbitrary. Thus any distinctive sound could have been chosen to represent 'tree' in English. The relation between signifier (the word 'tree') and signified (the concept of tree) is arbitrary. But when a pot represents cooking, or the house, or domestic life in general, the relationships between signifier and signified are not arbitrary – the real object, the pot, intrudes into the semiotic process. The meanings of a pot are tied up with the practical uses of a pot in daily life. Thus any patterning of pot use and pot style is likely to be tied up with labour relations, technologies and daily routines – all issues very far from language syntax and abstract binary codes (although language too can be seen as having important social and practical aspects – words are spoken to do something).

Much contemporary analysis of archaeological materials in terms of structures (organising principles) is less directly influenced by Lévi-

Strauss, and is more indebted to the 'practice theories' (which describe how daily life is socially organised) of Giddens (1979) and Bourdieu (1977). These latter authors make a link between structuralism and Marxism (see p. 165). Agency (see p. 3) and practice theories often identify 'structured deposition' (Richards and Thomas 1984) in artefact assemblages, and these are related to 'habitus' (structuring principles or dispositions in the practices of daily life). The habitus (see p. 133) is seen as more flexible and open to change than the underlying structures championed by structuralism, and as more engaged in social practice. Examples of studies that explore the habitus or structuring principles of daily life include work on historic pottery by Yentsch and Beaudry (2001), and on prehistoric burial and settlement (Barrett 1994; Thomas 1996).

As well as having an influence on agency and practice theories, structuralism has spawned a response termed post-structuralism (Bapty and Yates 1990), the main value of which has been in terms of critique. If systems of signs are seen as arbitrary (and we have seen some problems with this above), then the meaning of a sign can only be understood in relation to a total set of signs. And if all acts have a symbolic or sign dimension, then much of what we hold to be 'real' or 'true' can only be part of a system of signs. It becomes possible to critique any claim to truth or objective reality by showing that the claim is in fact based on an arbitrary system of signs. Such insight has led to fruitful critique (e.g. Olsen 1991; Thomas 1993), but such critiques have to contend with the logical conclusion that their own claims to 'truth' are themselves undermined.

Suggested reading

Bourdieu, P. 1977. *Outline of a Theory of Practice*. Cambridge: Cambridge University Press.
This is the main text that introduced practice theories.

Hodder, I. 1982. *Symbols in Action*. Cambridge: Cambridge University Press.
This provided ethnographic evidence for a critique of processualism and a move towards symbolic approaches in archaeology.

McGhee, R. 1977. Ivory for the Sea Woman: The Symbolic Attributes of a Prehistoric Technology. *Canadian Journal of Archaeology* 1: 141–59.
This is a very clear example of structuralist analysis in archaeology.

Parker Pearson, M. 1996. Food, Fertility and Front Doors: Houses in the First Millennium, pp. 117–32 in (T. Champion and J. R. Collis, eds) *The Iron Age in Britain and Ireland: Recent Trends.* Sheffield: Sheffield Academic Press.
This provides a good example of the application of practice theories in archaeology.

Richards, C. and Thomas, J. 1984. Ritual Activity and Structured Deposition in Later Neolithic Wessex, pp. 189–218 in (R. Bradley and J. Gardiner, eds) *Neolithic Studies: A Review of Some Current Research.* British Archaeological Reports British Series 133. Oxford: BAR.
This article introduced the idea of 'structured deposition' into British prehistory.

Wobst, M. 1977. Stylistic Behaviour and Information Exchange, pp 317–42 in (C. E. Cleland, ed.) *For the Director: Research Essays in Honor of James B. Griffen.* University of Michigan Museum of Anthropology, Anthropological Paper 61. Ann Arbor: University of Michigan Museum of Anthropology.
This is the classic application of a processual approach to symbolism.

Further reading

Bapty, I. and Yates, T. (eds) 1990. *Archaeology after Structuralism.* London: Routledge.

Barrett, J. 1994. *Fragments from Antiquity.* Oxford: Blackwell.

Bourdieu, P. 1977. *Outline of a Theory of Practice.* Cambridge: Cambridge University Press.

Campbell, E. 2000. The Raw, the Cooked and the Burnt: Interpretation of Food and Animals in the Hebridean Iron Age. *Archaeological Dialogues* 7: 185–98.

Childe, V. G. 1925. *The Dawn of European Civilization.* London: Kegan Paul.

Giddens, A. 1979. *Central Problems in Social Theory.* London: Macmillan.

Hillier, B., Leaman, A., Stansall, P. and Bedford, M. 1976. Space Syntax. *Environment and Planning* Series B3: 147–85.

Hodder, I. 1982. *Symbols in Action.* Cambridge: Cambridge University Press.

Lévi-Strauss, C. 1963. *Structural Anthropology.* New York: Basic Books.

Olsen, B. 1991. Metropolises and Satellites in Archaeology, pp. 211–24 in (R. Preucel ed.) *Processual and Postprocessual Archaeologies.* Southern Illinois University, Centre for Archaeological Investigations, Occasional Paper 10. Illinois: Southern Illinois University.

Preucel, R. W. and Bauer, A. A. 2001. Archaeological Pragmatics. *Norwegian Archaeological Review* 34 (2): 85–96.

Renfrew, C. and Shennan, S. (eds) 1982. *Ranking, Resource and Exchange.* Cambridge: Cambridge University Press.

Thomas, J. 1993. Discourse, Totalisation and 'the Neolithic', pp. 357–94 in (C. Tilley, ed.) *Interpretative Archaeology.* Oxford: Berg.

—— 1996. *Time, Culture and Identity.* London: Routledge.

Yentsch, A. 1991. The Symbolic Dimensions of Pottery: Sex-Related Attributes of English and Anglo-American Household Pots, pp. 192–230 in (R. H. McGuire and R. Paynter, eds) *The Archaeology of Inequality*. Oxford: Blackwell.

Yentsch, A. and Beaudry, M. 2001. American Material Culture in Mind, Thought, and Deed, pp. 214–40 in (I. Hodder, ed.) *Archaeological Theory Today*. Cambridge: Polity Press.

IAN HODDER

SYSTEMS THINKING

Systems thinking was one of the main influences upon the archaeological theory in the later half of the twentieth century, and remains influential in some respects today. The term 'systems thinking' is perhaps preferable to 'systems theory', since there is no such recognisable body of explicit theory, at least in archaeology, but rather a series of coherent approaches, drawn in part from other disciplines, which offer useful tools for thinking about past societies, their behaviour and the factors underlying their development.

A 'system' is a functioning whole that is composed of interrelated parts, and systems may be defined at different scales, from that of the cell or the single organism towards the smaller end, to the society or the nation-state or the world as a whole or indeed the solar system at the other. In archaeology we are usually looking at societies – groups of interacting human beings, in interaction also with their environment. Our interest is to understand better how such a system maintains itself successfully in the face of the changes it may encounter, and how it may itself develop and grow and undergo transformation into something different. The processes of change are not always easily predictable, and they need not be the direct result of human intentionality. For very often the actions of the individual or of the community have unintended consequences. Indeed, the sometimes counter-intuitive behaviour of complex systems is something which a coherent systems analysis seeks to address and sometimes to explain.

Systems thinking formed an integral part of the processual archaeology of the 1960s and 1970s (*see* p. 212), when Lewis Binford was arguing that a culture should be seen as a system composed of subsystems. Kent Flannery, in an influential article published in 1968,

'Archaeological Systems Theory and Early Mesoamerica', examined culture change during the transition from food-collecting to sedentary agriculture in this way. And in *The Emergence of Civilisation* in 1972, the transition to complex society in the Aegean Bronze Age was analysed using a systems framework. The approach was first given detailed and coherent expression by David L. Clarke in his *Analytical Archaeology* in 1968.

The approach came in for sustained criticism in the early days of 'post-processual' archaeology (*see* p. 207) on several grounds, notably that the role of the individual actor was overlooked or underplayed (*see* p. 3), and that societies and their members were represented as mindless automata. Advocates of the approach, while conceding that some of the analyses tended to represent societies simply as functioning ecosystems reacting rather automatically to environmental change, argued that these deficiencies were the result of shortcomings in the application of systems thinking rather than in the methods themselves.

It should be noted that the arguments for and against were not unlike those deployed with relation to Marxist archaeology (*see* p. 165). For there, a century earlier, Marx had set out to develop a framework for analysing the society as a whole in terms of the forces and relations of production. Later critics argued that the economic infrastructure was unduly privileged in that analysis over the symbolic and intellectual superstructure, where human beliefs and thoughts and aspirations came into play. Neo-Marxists denied the priority of the infrastructure over the superstructure, just as cognitive–processual archaeologists have more recently criticised the limitations of a functional–processual approach (*see* p. 41).

At least three major influences can be discerned in the development of systems thinking in archaeology. The first was the development of 'cybernetics', the study of control mechanisms which were and are a feature of most complex machines, and which came into their own with the development of electronics in the 1950s. The notion of system equilibrium or *homoeostasis* could be applied as much to human societies as to ecosystems, to living organisms as well as to functioning mechanisms. The notion of system input and system output led to the concept of *negative feedback*, where the output is monitored so that a marked change in output can be countered by a modification (in the opposite direction) to the input so as to keep the *system parameters* within the desired range, and so maintain an equilibrium or steady state. There are a few new items of terminology here, which some critics have regarded as jargon, but they permit real conceptual advances. The notion that the continuing progress or development of a system may be regarded as a *system trajectory*, which can be tracked and defined by monitoring the system parameters, opens the way to quantitative and indeed mathematical descriptions and treatments. These can be as detailed as the objectives of the analysis require.

The second influence was the study of ecology and the ecological approach to archaeology (*see* p. 79). The ecosystem approach to the living world was already well developed. Just as the island ecosystem could be analysed in terms of climate and predator/prey relationships, so cultural systems could be analysed in terms of such relationships, as anthropologists such as Rappaport had already begun to do. The third influence was the so-called 'General Systems Theory', developed by Ludwig von Bertalanffy, where patterns of growth (for instance exponential, or logistic) in a wide range of systems, including living systems, could be compared and analysed. The exponential growth pattern, involving rapid and increasing expansion, is widely seen for instance in the early stages of population development when individuals of a species colonise a new and favourable environment. The logistic growth pattern, when population growth gradually levels off to a constant maximum or 'carrying capacity', is seen in a wide range of cases when population numbers within a specific territory have achieved as high a level as the resources there can sustain. Clear analyses of this kind for instance permit the old and dangerous metaphor of the childhood, maturity and death of civilisations to be replaced by an explanation which could show in detail why human cultures do in some respects resemble living organisms, but differ in other identifiable ways.

The definition and the determination of the boundaries of the system are a matter for the choice of the analyst. Sometimes a specific region and its human population may be chosen, or a settlement and its hinterland, or a culture and its environment. A closed system is one with no interactions across its boundaries, and in practice human societies are open systems, where there are indeed inputs and exchanges of matter, energy and information. Likewise the division of a system into its component subsystems is a matter for the analyst. Sometimes it is convenient to define distinct subsystems for subsistence, technology, social structure, the symbolic or cognitive realm and for external trade, yet these subsystems intersect in every human individual, so that the distinctions are always somewhat arbitrary. Despite such difficulties, economists have used System Dynamics modelling to undertake a formal and quantitative analysis of the economies of individual nations, and most economic models today depend upon an analysis that is ultimately based upon systems thinking.

A good example of such an approach (although without any formal analysis in terms of equations of state) is offered by Kent Flannery's analysis of the transition to agriculture in Mesoamerica in terms of the human exploitation of different food resources, with respect to changing human population densities and, where appropriate, changing ecological conditions. He criticises the earlier view that the transition to agriculture was occasioned by the 'discovery' that planted seed would sprout. As he puts it, the use of such a model:

> does not attribute cultural evolution to 'discoveries', 'inventions', 'experiments', or 'genius' but instead enables us to treat prehistoric cultures as systems. It stimulates inquiry into mechanisms that counteract change or amplify it, which ultimately tell us something about the nature of adaptation. More importantly it allows us to view change not as something arising *de novo* but in terms of quite minor deviations in one small part of a previously existing system, which once set in motion can expand greatly because of positive feedback.

> (Flannery 1968: 80)

It should be noted that a systems approach has sometimes been criticised, wrongly, as regarding all major innovations and changes as *exogenous*, that is to say as responses to changes originating outside the system. That might be the case if we were considering only the effects of negative feedback, straining always to maintain the pre-existing equilibrium. But a good systems analysis should be able to deal also with *endogenous* change – originating within the boundaries of the system. It must allow for the possibility of innovation, and for the ways in which *positive feedback* can, in some circumstances, amplify small changes which have taken place. It is in this way that *morphogenesis* can occur – significant transformations in the system – changes in system state which are indeed internally generated. The emergence of complex society can be analysed in such terms, as Flannery set out to show in another influential article 'The Cultural Evolution of Civilisations' (1972).

Systems thinking has generally been applied at what one may term the macro level – to the behaviour of entire communities and societies. But the significant innovations which often lie at the root of sustained growth and change (of morphogenesis) often originate at the micro level, with the individual. Moreover, the acceptance of innovations is a matter of choice, which operates at a cognitive level. Choice and cognition can be made part of a systems analysis, but they do not often form part of an ecosystem approach, which has to be modified to take note of symbolic and cognitive factors. That, I think, is one reason why the systems approach, while very useful for studying the behaviour of complex systems, has proved less satisfactory in the analysis of long-term change. It is, however, particularly well suited to formal analysis of the kind which most simulation studies require (*see* p. 224). The increasing sophistication of computational methods is likely in the future to lead to developments in the systems approach, allowing effective modelling even where very many relevant variables interact. But problems are still likely to arise when cognitive considerations (including symbolic or religious factors) have to be taken into account. These currently seem much more difficult to predict, particularly over the long term. The archaeologist has not yet found ways of modelling such factors. Until we do, the current limitations by which systems thinking is restricted will not effectively be transcended.

Suggested reading

Ashby, W. R. 1956. *An Introduction of Cybernetics*. London: Methuen.
Early general outline of systems thinking.

Clarke, D. L. 1968. *Analytical Archaeology*. London: Methuen
Early discussion of systems thinking in archaeology.

Flannery, K. V. 1968. Archaeological Systems Theory and Early Mesoamerica, pp. 67–87 in (B. J. Meggers, ed.) *Anthropological Archaeology in the Americas*. Washington, DC: Anthropological Society of America.
The first case study in archaeology using systems thinking.

Flannery, K. V. 1972. The Cultural Evolution of Civilizations. *Annual Review of Ecology and Systematics* 3: 399 – 426.
Discussion of the origin of complex societies in a systemic framework.

Renfrew, C. 1972. *The Emergence of Civilisation, the Cyclades and the Aegean in the Third Millennium BC.* London: Methuen.
Early application of systems thinking to the problem of state origins.

Sabloff, J. A. (ed.) 1978. *Simulations in Archaeology.* Albuquerque: University of New Mexico Press.
Volume of papers with several applications of the systems approach.

Further reading

Bertalanffy, L. von, 1950. An Outline of General System Theory. *British Journal of the Philosophy of Science* 1: 134–65.
Renfrew, C. and Cooke, K. L. (eds) 1979. *Transformations: Mathematical Approaches to Culture Change.* New York: Academic Press.
Waddington, C. H. 1977. *Tools for Thought.* St Albans: Paladin.

COLIN RENFREW

THE THREE AGES

By the eighteenth century, in the course of the intellectual movement known as the European Enlightenment, there had arisen a firm belief in the idea of human progress, and in particular of technological progress. In earlier times, prehistoric stone tools had been interpreted in very fanciful ways, such as elf-shot or thunderbolts. But the sixteenth-century scholar Michel Mercati, who undertook an inventory of the Vatican's collections, decided that the 'thunderbolts' and flint arrowheads in it had been made by humans, and in a time before iron existed.

It was only in the late seventeenth century that such ideas began to be widely accepted. In part this was through scientific deduction – such as the work of German antiquarian A. Rhode who made experimental replicas of early stone tools to reconstruct their manufacturing techniques, one of the earliest examples of experimental archaeology (*see* p. 110); and in part it was also through the discovery and study of 'primitive' peoples in far-off lands who still used tools of stone. In 1723, Antoine de Jussieu specifically compared the 'thunderbolts' in European collections with stone axes from Canada and the Caribbean. Like Mercati he attributed the European specimens to a remote period when iron was unknown.

These pioneering scholars were not, however, the first to entertain such notions. They were drawing in large measure on classical literature, and especially the writings of Lucretius, a Roman poet of the first century BC, whose masterpiece, the poem *De Rerum Natura* (On the Nature of Things) contains a passage on the probable sequence of human technologies, from stone to bronze to iron. As quoted by Mercati, it says:

> The earliest tools were the hands, nails and teeth, as well as stones, pieces of wood, flames and fire as soon as they were known. Later the properties of iron and bronze were discovered, but bronze came first, the use of iron not being known until later.

Even before Lucretius – but doubtless unknown to the European scholars in question – a Chinese philosopher of the Eastern Zhou period (c. 770–221 BC) had put forward a similar scheme in the following poem:

> In the age of Xuan Yuan, Shen Nong, and He Xu, weapons were made of stones, for cutting trees and building houses, and were buried with the dead ... In the age of Huang Di, weapons were made of jade, for cutting trees, building houses, and digging the ground ... and were buried with the dead. In the age of Yu, weapons were made of bronze, for building canals and houses ... At the present time, weapons are made of iron.

Mercati's manuscript was not published until 1717, by which time other scholars had reached the same conclusion quite independently, and were openly speculating about a sequence of stone, bronze and iron ages. But even then, the notion was very slow to gain general acceptance, and it was not until the reorganisation of the Danish National Museum in the early nineteenth century that what became known as the 'Three Age System' was established as the cornerstone of prehistoric chronology in Europe.

As a direct result of a theft, in 1802, of prehistoric gold drinking horns from the antiquities room of the Danish royal palace, a committee decided to establish a national collection of Danish antiquities, but by 1816 its size had grown so large that a professional curator was needed for it. The man chosen was Christian Jurgensen Thomsen, the wealthy son of a Copenhagen merchant. His first task was to organise the material for public display. Not surprisingly, in view of its growing acceptance through the eighteenth century, he chose to use the Three Age System to classify the objects – he arranged them according to the material used for their cutting tools: i.e. the earliest stage was that of stone tools, the second stage was tools of bronze, and the third and most recent had tools of iron.

The great importance of Thomsen, however, was that he took this notion further, by looking at associations. In other words, he looked at artefacts not as isolated objects, but in relation to what was found with them. He thus discovered that pottery was made during all three ages, but glass vessels only existed in the Iron Age. This approach enabled him to arrange not only the cutting tools but all the finds in the collection into these three ages.

Thomsen presented each phase in its own displays, and then proceeded to extend the scheme beyond the museum to the field monuments of Denmark. For example, he discovered that the Stone Age tended to have burials in stone chambers, whereas cremations were only found in the Bronze and Iron Ages. But, being a cautious man, he did not rush his new chronology and principle of association into print – in fact it was only in 1836 that he published an account of his work in his *Guide to Northern Archaeology*, a book which had tremendous influence and was quickly translated into various European languages.

Thomsen's version of the Three Age System became, and remains, the very basis of European prehistoric chronology. It made it possible for the first time to bring order where there had previously been chaos – to place objects into sequence, and to group them according to the period to which they belonged. Obviously, it did not provide any precise dates – archaeologists had to await the advent of absolute dating methods for that (*see* p. 64) – but it nevertheless provided a basic chronological dimension. The scheme was rapidly adopted in museums across Europe, and was soon given internal subdivisions, and polished and fine-tuned, to account for innumerable local variations.

For example, even within Thomsen's lifetime, his scheme was outgrown, with new archaeological problems leading to new refinements. One mystery was the so-called 'kitchen middens', great rubbish heaps of shells along the Danish coast. They were clearly the remains of countless meals from some remote period, but their age was unknown. The man who found the answer was Jens Jacob Worsaae, who had been a volunteer helper at Thomsen's museum in the late 1830s. On excavating one of the shell mounds in 1851, Worsaae realised that the Stone Age could be subdivided into an Early and a Late Stone Age in Denmark. It was the early sites, such as the shell middens, which had roughly shaped, chipped stone tools, while the later Stone Age sites had better formed stone tools, which were often smoothed and polished, and also pottery, which was absent in the earlier phase.

What Worsaae had lighted upon was the distinction we now draw between the 'Mesolithic' (Middle Stone Age) and the 'Neolithic' (New Stone Age), although he did not use these terms himself. The word 'neolithic' (from the Greek *neo*, 'new', and *lithos*, 'stone') was coined in 1865 by the British archaeologist Sir John Lubbock, and became the standard term for those early societies which made pottery, raised crops and livestock, and used polished stone tools. Before this, in Lubbock's scheme, was the 'Palaeolithic' (Old Stone Age), the period of the ice ages, the 'cave dwellers' and flaked flint tools. Worsaae's Mesolithic was an intervening phase.

As new discoveries were accumulated and archaeological knowledge increased, many further subdivisions of the Stone, Bronze and Iron Ages were proposed – some were accepted, some fiercely debated, and others quietly dropped. Inevitably, chronological schemes, based on typology (the classification of artefacts into different types), produced ever more detailed and complex refinements. But the Three Age System remains the foundation stone of this entire edifice.

Suggested reading

Bahn, P. G. (ed.) 1996. *The Cambridge Illustrated History of Archaeology.* Cambridge: Cambridge University Press.
Well-illustrated survey of the global history of archaeology.

Daniel, G. E. 1967. *The Origins and Growth of Archaeology.* Harmondsworth: Pelican.
Invaluable annotated collection of quotations from original sources important to the history of archaeology.

Daniel, G. E. 1975. *150 Years of Archaeology.* London: Duckworth.
Excellent history of archaeology by its foremost specialist.

Daniel, G. E. and Renfrew, C. 1988. *The Idea of Prehistory.* Edinburgh: Edinburgh University Press.
Extremely useful survey which places emphasis on the history of ideas in archaeology, rather than discoveries.

Gräslund, B. 1987. *The Birth of Prehistoric Chronology. Dating Methods and Dating Systems in Nineteenth-century Scandinavian Archaeology.* Cambridge: Cambridge University Press.
Detailed account of the development and application of Thomsen's Three Age System,

Klindt-Jensen, O. 1975. *A History of Scandinavian Archaeology.* London: Thames and Hudson.
Useful account of Thomsen's work and that of subsequent noteworthy Scandinavian archaeologists

Thomsen, C. J. 1848. *A Guide to Northern Archaeology.* London.
Thomsen's original application of his approach to the archaeological record.

Further reading

Grayson, D. K. 1983. *The Establishment of Human Antiquity.* New York: Academic Press.
Schnapp, A. 1996. *Discovering the Past.* London: British Museum Press.
Trigger, B. G. 1989. *A History of Archaeological Thought.* Cambridge: Cambridge University Press.
Van Riper, A. B. 1993. *Men among the Mammoths, Victorian Science and the Discovery of Human Prehistory.* Chicago: Chicago University Press.

PAUL BAHN

CONCEPTS OF TIME

The expanded time depth of human history made available by archaeological methods of study and dating has been seen by many archaeologists as a virtue. Gordon Childe (*see* p. 35) and Grahame Clark, for example, two of the twentieth century's greatest prehistorians, saw prehistory as a means of highlighting the grand themes and directional trends of human development, unclouded by the small-scale detail of individual biographies and historical records. Eric Higgs, in his development of the Palaeoeconomic approach (an emphasis on the study of prehistoric economies as a major directive force in long-term human development), saw archaeology as providing a record of what works in the long run and evidence of underlying continuities in human behaviour imposed by economic survival and competition. Many others have seen archaeology as a source of evidence for a belief in an almost infinite human capacity to generate cultural variety and cultural change. Contrasts between concepts of *change, direction, continuity* and *variability* have continued to provide an underlying tension in archaeological theory and interpretation. In 1981, Geoff Bailey, Lewis Binford and Rob Foley separately published papers emphasising the low resolution of archaeological deposits, seeing in that characteristic an opportunity to investigate a different scale of phenomena, rather than a limitation, thereby highlighting *time scale* and *time resolution* as additional key concepts in the archaeological vocabulary. From these early insights, broadly four themes have emerged, and can be grouped under the label of 'time perspectivism'.

The first theme is an investigation of the ways in which the seemingly fragmentary, poorly dated and biased nature of material remains can be turned to advantage to create a different conception of human history. The key here is the perception that all material records are palimpsests − that is, mixtures or aggregations of events or phenomena, in which much of the original information has been removed, so that the palimpsest cannot be resolved, or perhaps only partially so, into its individual constituent parts. This is obviously the case with archaeological deposits, which are palimpsests of individual surfaces on which materials have been repeatedly disturbed, displaced or modified by subsequent use (*see* p. 121), but it applies more generally and at all scales of analysis, from individual artefacts and monuments to archaeological sites in their wider landscape setting (*see* p. 156).

Take a 'closed find', for example, such as a shipwreck, a burial chamber or the room of a house, where all the materials are found together because they are constituents of a single episode of activity or deposition. We might consider these to be 'moments in time', but these too have some of the characteristics of a palimpsest, in particular a loss of temporal resolution. Laurent Olivier has demonstrated this effect in his analysis of the Late Hallstatt 'princely' grave of Hochdorf in southern Germany, an earth-covered burial chamber of the sixth century BC. Some of the objects in the archaeological funerary assemblage belonged to the deceased during his lifetime, others were introduced between his death and his installation in the chamber, and yet others were introduced at the moment when the chamber was sealed. Some objects were altered during the man's lifetime, others after his death, and many by subsequent physical and chemical processes in the ground and by archaeological investigation and restoration. The archaeological funerary assemblage as a whole thus represents a series of different 'temporalities' (objects of different ages) that cannot be resolved into a single contemporaneous event except at a resolution of several hundred years or more.

Even an individual artefact acquires what we can describe as a palimpsest of different uses and meanings during the course of its trajectory from the original moment of manufacture to its current resting place in the ground, a museum, a textbook or an intellectual discourse. In fact, all material environments are palimpsests, mixing together materials of different ages, durability, states of preservation and meaning, including the modern built environment in which we conduct our everyday lives, and the wider physical landscape with its palimpsest of many different types and scales of geological processes. From this, it follows that we need to analyse the structural properties of these records in terms of their temporal scale, duration and resolution if we are to understand what sorts of questions we can explore with them. Moreover, material records in different parts of the archaeological sequence may differ radically in terms of scale and resolution, encouraging the pursuit of different questions using different methods of investigation.

The second theme focuses on the sorts of phenomena that are brought into focus by large-scale palimpsests, and hence on processes that may operate on longer time scales. Here the emphasis is on how an expanded time perspective alters our own concepts of time and our perception of the relationship between larger-scale and smaller-scale factors, and the cause and effect relations between them. The starting point here is the recognition that an 'event' is in fact an integration of processes operating on different time scales and that different scales of observation bring into focus different sorts of 'events' or phenomena, such that our understanding of causation may differ, depending on the scale of observation. This is in part about the ways in which we perceive the relationship between longer-term and shorter-term processes and in part about the ways those processes operate, to some extent, independently of our perception.

Consider as an example the badlands erosion that has affected mountain landscapes in the Mediterranean region. According to conventional wisdom, this erosion is the result of increased human impact in recent millennia associated with expanding agricultural economies – deep ploughing of fragile hill soils, tree felling and overgrazing of domestic livestock. In northwest Greece, domestic goats are typically associated with hill slopes stripped bare of vegetation and soil, and are blamed for the destruction. An expanded time perspective, however, reveals that erosion has a much longer history, and is largely the result of an underlying tectonic instability, coupled with climatic and vegetational change, that has resulted in massive erosion over the past million years and more, besides which the human impact of the postglacial period seems quite tame. On the shorter time scale of millennia, goat herding appears to be the cause of the recent erosion. On a longer time scale, goat herding appears rather to be the result of erosion, an economic adaptation to an existing landscape that cannot be profitably used in any other way. Moreover, expanding our spatial perspective shows that erosion in one part of the landscape results in re-deposition of soil elsewhere, often concentrated in lowland basins that provide fertile conditions for crop agriculture. This example shows how changing time scale and time perspective alters our understanding of cause-and-effect relationships. What appears negative at one scale of observation has positive effects at another. Such examples have profound implications for modern policies of conservation and land management.

A third theme is an investigation of the time concepts held by past people, how they experienced time and their own position in relation to past, present and future, and how those concepts affected their thinking and behaviour. Time in this sense may be experienced in different ways by different people and by different societies, and these experiences are intimately bound up with social tradition and how people locate themselves in relation to the past. This approach to time draws heavily on social theory and has stimulated the most extensive archaeological literature. Richard Bradley provides a succinct illustration of this approach, showing how enduring monuments and changing traditions of material culture are linked with social memory and used to create a sense of continuity during periods of social and political change. On a longer time scale, Grahame Clark has charted how an expanded consciousness of time and space has characterised the major turning points in human development.

The final theme is the philosophical issue of how we define the differences between past, present and future. If the world we inhabit is a composite of processes of varying time scale and of palimpsests that mix together elements of past, present and future, then there can be no absolute or objective means of determining the temporal boundaries of 'the present', only a present of varying duration. This *durational present* extends both backwards and forwards from our present point of view in time, and may be hours to days for the newspaper journalist, weeks to years for the politician, decades to lifetimes for the ethnographic observer, centuries to millennia for the historian of written documents, and millennia to millions of years for the prehistoric archaeologist. The 'past' and the 'future' are thus arbitrarily defined concepts, which we use to dismiss phenomena that we believe to be beyond our powers of observation or control, or irrelevant to our interests. Yet ours is a material universe – a huge and complicated palimpsest that blurs the boundaries between past, present and future – full of durable objects and processes acting on them that not only link us with the deep time that extends far behind us, but also encourage us to project our thinking forwards into an indefinitely long future.

Suggested reading

Bailey, G. N. 1981. Concepts, Time-Scales and Explanations in Economic Prehistory, pp. 97–117 in (A. Sheridan and G. Bailey, eds) *Economic Archaeology*. British Archaeological Reports International Series 96. Oxford: BAR.

—— 1983. Concepts of Time in Quaternary Prehistory. *Annual Review of Anthropology* 12: 165–92.

—— 1987. Breaking the Time Barrier. *Archaeological Review from Cambridge* 6: 5–20.

These three papers form a set that first defined the concept of time perspectivism, explored its empirical underpinnings and theoretical and methodological consequences, and challenged the prevailing convention that knowledge of the present and especially social theories created to explain observations of modern societies are the key to interpretation of the past.

Bailey, G. N. (ed.) 1997. *Klithi: Palaeolithic Settlement and Quaternary Landscapes in Northwest Greece*. 2 vols. Cambridge: McDonald Institute for Archaeological Research.

Provides detailed field examples of the analysis of scale and resolution in palimpsests ranging from tectonic history to modern perceptions of landscape change, and from intra-site variation in Palaeolithic rockshelters to inter-site variations at a regional scale.

Binford, L. R. 1981. Behavioral Archaeology and the 'Pompeii Premise'. *Journal of Anthropological Research* 37: 195–208.

A characteristically polemical piece that attacks the search for high resolution datasets, and challenges archaeologists to deal with the chief characteristic of the archaeological record as a massive palimpsest referring to a different level of organisation not visible to the contemporary observer but uniquely accessible to archaeological investigation.

Bradley, R. 2002. *The Past in Prehistoric Societies*. London and New York: Routledge.

An elegant analysis of the 'past in the past', of how we can examine the ways in which prehistoric people used their material environment to construct a sense of time, drawing on a wide range of examples from Neolithic and later periods in

Europe. The most recent of several books dealing with social theories of time in archaeology.

Foley, R. A. 1981. A Model of Regional Archaeological Structure. *Proceedings of the Prehistoric Society* 47: 1–17.
Highlights the palimpsest nature of the long-term archaeological record and the need to develop appropriate scales of analysis and interpretation. Notable, like the Bailey and Binford papers of the same date, for the long delay in following up the initial concepts with a fully worked out archaeological case study, and for the fact that it was written from the perspective of dealing with Palaeolithic datasets.

Murray, T. 1997. Dynamic Modelling and New Social Theory of the Mid- to Long Term, pp. 449–63 in (S. Van der Leeuw and J. McGlade, eds) *Time, Process and Structured Transformation in Archaeology*. London and New York: Routledge.
Articulates the challenge of dealing with the distinctive structural properties of the archaeological record, especially of the Pleistocene, in terms of their scale and resolving power in relation to commonsense preconceptions of human behaviour, and highlights the need to develop distinctive social theories of the long term.

Olivier, L. 1999. The Hochdorf 'Princely' Grave and the Question of the Nature of Archaeological Funerary Assemblages, pp. 109–38 in (T. Murray, ed.) *Time and Archaeology*. London and New York: Routledge.
Provides an illuminating analysis of the range of temporalities inherent in a closed assemblage, and explores their capacity to subvert the conventional classification and periodisation of Iron Age material culture.

Stern, N. 1993. The Structure of the Lower Pleistocene Archaeological Record. *Current Anthropology* 34: 201–25.
One of the first attempts to put into practice thinking about low-resolution datasets and 'time-averaged' archaeological deposits. Also interesting for the range of comments it elicited in *Current Anthropology*'s commentary section.

Further reading

Bradley, R. (ed.) 1993. Conceptions of Time and Ancient Society. *World Archaeology* 25: 152–74.
Clark, G. 1992. *Space, Time and Man*. Cambridge: Cambridge University Press.
Gosden, C. 1994. *Social Being and Time*. Oxford: Blackwell.
Knapp, A. B. (ed.) 1992. *Archaeology, Annales, and Ethnohistory*. Cambridge: Cambridge University Press.
Murray, T. (ed.) 1999. *Time and Archaeology*. London and New York: Routledge.
Rossignol J. and Wandsnider, L. (eds) 1992. *Space, Time, and Archaeological Landscapes*. New York: Plenum.
Thomas, J. 1996. *Time, Culture and Identity*. London and New York: Routledge.
Van der Leeuw, S. and McGlade, J. (eds) 1997. *Time, Process and Structured Transformation in Archaeology*. London and New York: Routledge.

GEOFF BAILEY

UNIFORMITARIANISM

'Uniformitarianism', a complex set of ideas associated with British geologist Charles Lyell, was built upon the accumulated investigations of some notable predecessors. The term 'uniformitarian' itself, like that of 'catastrophist', was actually coined in 1832 by William Whewell, the English philosopher of science, in a review of Lyell's second volume.

Until the second half of the eighteenth century, in Europe, the Earth and humankind were thought to be as old as each other – and this was not very old, according to Archbishop Ussher (*see* p. 65). This notion was the orthodox view of the world of scholarship, and even Isaac Newton confirmed that the bishop had the age more or less correct. But in March 1785, the new ideas of Scottish gentleman farmer and geologist James Hutton were presented to the Royal Society of Edinburgh: 'The purpose of this dissertation is to form some estimate with regard to the time the globe of this Earth has existed, as a world maintaining plants and animals.' His view was that the Earth had existed for a very long time, longer than people or scripture could measure.

Hutton's theory, which was eventually published in three volumes in the 1790s, was that the planet was in a state of continuous change. Continents were always being eroded and renewed by processes still visible today; these processes had operated in the same way in the past, and would be repeated in the future. Soil was washed down to the sea, consolidated into rock, and then uplifted by the tremendous force of subterranean heat. These cycles of renewal and decay occurred in indefinite time 'so that, with respect to human observation, this world has neither a beginning nor an end'. So Hutton burst the boundaries, and contributed the notion of 'deep time' to human thought: as he put it, 'Time ... is to nature endless and as nothing.' But his purpose was not to question religion – far from it; he was a deeply religious man, who believed that 'the globe of this Earth is evidently made for man' by God. He wanted to reinforce religion, not as scripture, but as what was known as 'deism' or 'natural religion', and he referred to his rock specimens as 'bibles all wrote by God's own finger'.

Hutton travelled widely in Britain, observing the rock formations and speculating on how they came about, but his theory arose primarily through wondering about soil – i.e. since soil is so necessary for the growth of plants and hence for human life, and since it comes from the erosion and destruction of solid land, how can one explain that the sediments have not all been washed into the sea? There must be a 'concept of repair', a restorative force to replenish the soil supply, and so he set out to find it, finally attributing it to the Earth's internal fire which consolidates and uplifts sediments. Thus he eventually deduced that the geological mechanisms in operation today are the same as those that determined how rocks behaved in the past. He could not assign a precise age to the world, but he knew that the rock formations must have taken more than a few thousand years to be formed.

The important point to grasp is that Hutton's system, his 'world machine', was cyclical – a cycle of erosion (the only stage we can observe directly today), deposition, consolidation and uplift. It was dynamic and endlessly recurring, but moved nowhere. And his work was a landmark in inferring unobservable past processes from their results preserved in rocks.

Some decades later, Paul Tournal's researches (see p. 9) also proved a crucial turning point at which the concept of an historical antediluvian period was transformed into the idea of prehistory. So the defenders of 'antediluvian man' inevitably became the 'enemies' of the Bible and religion: according to the British art critic John Ruskin, stricken with religious doubt, it was the geologists and 'those dreadful hammers' which drowned out 'every cadence of the Bible verses'. However, the debate should not be seen in such black-and-white terms, since some clerics, like MacEnery (see p. 9) recognised the archaeological evidence, whereas many geologists still believed in the universal floods described by classical authors. It was Tournal who came to see the disappearance of extinct animals as being due not to catastrophes but to the same gradual processes of change that can be seen today. Hence, in explaining the past by today's laws, both he and Hutton anticipated the more famous work of the British geologist Charles Lyell.

Lyell had been a pupil of Buckland's (see p. 9) at Oxford, and he proposed in his hugely influential book *Principles of Geology* (1830–3) that all past geological processes were the same as those of the present; that they spanned an immensely long period; and that there was thus no need to believe in supernatural catastrophes like Noah's Flood to explain the fossil and stratigraphic record. His arguments were presented so forcefully that he transformed the intellectual climate of his time. Traditional 'catastrophism' (see p. 20) largely gave way to the doctrine of 'uniformitarianism' – i.e. the idea that if the geological processes operating in the past and present are uniform, then the surface of the Earth must have been shaped by sedimentation and erosion over huge spans of time. This rendered Ussher's date for the creation of the world (*see* p. 65) absolute nonsense, and Buckland was led to change his mind about the contemporaneity of humans and fossil animals.

In a way, however, uniformitarianism depended more on faith than had catastrophism, because the geological record does seem to record catastrophes – rocks are fractured and contorted, whole faunas suddenly disappear – so that the catastrophists were basing themselves on empirical observation, whereas the uniformitarians had to apply their imaginations to the evidence, argue that the geological record was extremely imperfect, and use reason to infer what cannot be seen – gradual change was assumed to lie in the missing transitions. To cite Lyell's classic example: if Vesuvius erupted again, and buried a modern Italian town above Pompeii, would the abrupt transition from Latin to Italian, or from clay tablets to computers, record a true jump, or simply two millennia of missing data? Obviously, simple observation cannot always adequately account for a complex and imperfect world.

Lyell's concept of uniformity actually had four very different components:

- First, that natural laws are constant (uniform) in space and time; so the past is not capricious, and everything has a natural cause, with no need of theological intrusion.
- Second, we must invoke current, observable processes that operate to mould the Earth's surface in order to explain past events (uniformity of process through time). Only present processes can be observed. (But while Lyell believed that present processes were sufficient to explain the past, catastrophists thought that, while present processes should always be preferred, some past events still required explanation by faster processes. We may be quite ignorant of some past phenomena.)
- Third, geological change is slow, gradual and steady, not cataclysmic (uniformity of rate).
- And fourth, the Earth has been fundamentally the same since its formation (uniformity of configuration) – once it had settled down after its initial formation, there had been no global catastrophes. Obviously, this claim was erroneous – why, then, were dinosaurs extinct? – and it led Lyell to propose, contrary to all evidence, that mammals would be found in the earliest fossil beds, that mass extinctions in the geological record were not abrupt but actually extended over millions of years, and that dinosaurs would return as

the cycle turned. Yet, of course, he had to accept the arrival of humans as a discontinuity in our planet's history.

In short, some of Lyell's proposals were sound and a great contribution; but others were too rigid or false, so that modern geology actually represents a mixture of his uniformitarianism and of scientific catastrophism, a combination of both observation and inference.

Lyell's work had a tremendous influence on the work of British biologists like Charles Darwin, Alfred Wallace and Thomas Huxley, and on the very concept of evolution (*see* p. 70). As with geology, biology turned from being constrained by a biblical seven-day creation to the vista of an immensely long past. The crucial key was time – the vast age of the Earth provided ample time to produce all observed results, however spectacular, through the simple accumulation of small changes over immense periods.

It is ironic that Lyell, the apostle of geological uniformitarianism, in 1832 still believed that man had been created by the 'special and independent attention of God', and maintained that belief for another twenty years. And, like Buckland before him, he refused to admit geological proofs from excavations made in caves. But his views were dramatically changed after his visit in 1859 to Boucher de Perthes' excavations in France (*see* p. 10), while a tour of British and French archaeological sites two years later only served to confirm his belief that stone tools did indeed regularly occur deeply stratified alongside the bones of extinct animals.

It should be noted that uniformitarianism remains fundamental to archaeology, because one of the basic assumptions that always needs to be made is that the behaviour and tolerances of plant and animal species were the same in the past as in the present, and hence knowable; and exactly the same applies to early humans – if we could not assume that their physical needs, their tolerances and their behavioural responses were the same in the past, and hence predictable, archaeology would simply be impossible.

Suggested reading

Bahn, P. G. (ed.) 1996. *The Cambridge Illustrated History of Archaeology*. Cambridge: Cambridge University Press.
Well-illustrated survey of the global history of archaeology.

Baxter, S. 2003. *Revolutions in the Earth: James Hutton and the True Age of the World.* London: Weidenfeld and Nicolson.
Excellent recent study of Hutton's life and work.

Hutton, J. 1795. *Theory of the Earth, with Proofs and Illustrations.* Edinburgh: William Creech.
Hutton's original publication of his theory.

Lyell, C. 1830–3. *Principles of Geology, Being an Attempt to Explain the Former Changes of the Earth's Surface by Reference to Causes Now in Operation* (3 vols). London: John Murray.
Lyell's enormously influential presentation of his theories.

Repcheck, J. 2003. *The Man Who Found Time: James Hutton and the Discovery of the Earth's Antiquity.* New York: Simon and Schuster.
A more lightweight recent study of Hutton's life and work.

Van Riper, A. B. 1993. *Men among the Mammoths, Victorian Science and the Discovery of Human Prehistory.* Chicago: Chicago University Press.
An account of the interactions of the major figures and their theories in the nineteenth century.

Further reading

Daniel, G. E. 1967. *The Origins and Growth of Archaeology.* Harmondsworth: Pelican.
—— 1975. *150 Years of Archaeology.* London: Duckworth.
Daniel, G. E. and Renfrew, C. 1988. *The Idea of Prehistory.* Edinburgh: Edinburgh University Press.
Gould, S. J. 1980. Uniformity and Catastrophe, pp. 147–52 in (S. J. Gould) *Ever Since Darwin. Reflections in Natural History.* Harmondsworth: Pelican.
—— 1983. Hutton's Purpose, pp. 79–93 in (S. J. Gould) *Hen's Teeth and Horse's Toes. Further Reflections in Natural History.* Harmondsworth: Penguin.
—— 2001. Lyell's Pillars of Wisdom, pp. 147–68 in (S. J. Gould) *The Lying Stones of Marrakech. Penultimate Reflections in Natural History.* London: Vintage.

PAUL BAHN

INDEX

Abu-Lughod, J.L. 166
acorns 232
Adams, R.McC 55
'affirmative' postmodernists, possibility of saying something about the world 92–3
Afghanistan, destruction of Bamiyan Buddhas 222; lapis lazuli and 32
Africa, computerised migrations and voyages out of 224; cranial capacity after humans disseminated out of 178–9; discovery of Taung child 72; (east) and controversy over dating volcanic sediments 67–8; human populations came to encompass variation 179–80; more species of hominids that predate *Homo erectus* 73
African Eve/mitochrondrial mother 17–18
agency theory in archaeology, core elements 3–5; social evolution inadequate to explain diversity in human societies 194–5
agent-based modelling, elite social control models and 53
agent-based simulation, artificial intelligence and object-oriented programming 227
Agorsah, K. 100
air photography 156
Algaze, G., *The Uruk World System* 167
Alvarez, Walter 21
amber, infra-red spectroscopy 32
America, attempts to discover other genders 130; basic tools 154; wheel and wagon never invented in 155

American Midwest, PPI and 200
American processualist tradition, ambitious political actors and 3
Americas, Ice Age and urban settings 246
Ammerman, A.J. 249
analytical methods, physics and chemistry 34
Anatolia (modern Turkey), analysis of obsidian 33
ancient history and prehistory, centre, periphery and semi-periphery 166
Andrews, G. 210
animals, large butchered at kill site to remove waste parts 232
Antarctica, location of Atlantis 22
Anthony, David 78
anthropological archaeologists, holistic archaeology and 141
anthropological literature, debates whether dividual and individual selves form two ends of continuum 188
anthropology, participant observation 203
Anthropus neanderthalensis (later *Homo neanderthalensis*), first named hominid taxon 71
Antiquity, British journal responsive to gender-related papers (1990s) 130
Antiquity of Man xii
Anyon, R. 209
ARCDIG 228
archaeoastronomers, astronomical explanation to human actions 12
archaeoastronomy 11–15

archaeogenetics xii, 16–19

Archaeologia (journal of Society of Antiquaries) 8

archaeological agenda, diversity or pluralism of views of the past 223

archaeological dating, methods used for nuclear research 68

archaeological evidence, oral histories and 150

archaeological formation processes , 121–5

archaeological method, Complex Systems perspective and flaw in 185

archaeological sites, pottery, metalwork and stone survive in 95

archaeological stratigraphy, study and interpretation of stratified deposits 243; tended to emphasise sequence 86

archaeological theory xi, xii

archaeologists, chronological framework 66; collaborate with naturalists called prehistorians 244–5; 'collapse' societies 54; computer simulations 225–6; concerned with nature of human mind 171; contribute to debates on mental modularity 173; dilemma of searching for inhabitants of North and South Americas 246; distinguish experiential learning from experimental archaeology 141–2; ecological models during (1960s) using scientific methods 141; explored connection between archaeology and historical texts and 245; gender as element of personal identity 131; influence of concept of semi-periphery 167; interactions prior to PPI 197; non-cultural or environmental processes 124; origin and evolution of governments 101; the past and 93; past culture-environment interactions 213; pot style as way of identifying social groups 242; pottery as harvested mud 85; power relations and social organisation 195; problem of how states form 102; question of past if people had not identified themselves

as individuals 189; 'reading the landscape' 156; religion fell inside domain of palaeopsychology 47; reuse of vessels can add or remove chemical residues 124; 'ritual' to describe material which might be religious 46; sampling strategies to draw conclusions about cultural system 215; some prefer non-site approach to survey 251; stratigraphy to include seriation (time) and context (formation processes) 247; tended to avoid term 'religion' except living religions 45–6; term 'cultural evolution' and 49; thinking about landscape 157–8; work for public as well as academic interests 220

archaeology, agent-based simulations and 228; aspects of society documents did not record 140; Childe moved towards Marxist interpretation of (1930s) 36; cognitive 41–4; complex undertaking xiii; of cult and religion 45–8; de Saussure and Lévi-Strauss forms of structuralism and 255; definition of characterisation in 31; developed differently in Europe and the Americas 244; frontiers of dating methods in 69; landscape and 204; long relationship with materialism 163; measurements but little to say about material qualities 202–3; motivated by phenomenological and interpretive approaches 168; non-linear processes and 182–5; post-processual research and sceptical stances 93; radioactive decay in dating further revolutionised (1970s) 67; relation between cultural identity 169; role in nationalism 237; source of belief in human capacity to generate cultural variety 269; structuralism argues that objects can be seen as organised into systems of signs that have meaning 256; talks about the unobservable – past cultural systems 209; trade and exchange 32; uniformitarianism fundamental to 277

archaeology of childhood 131
Archaeology of Gender, The (1991) xii, 129
'archaeology of personhood' 186, 188
archaeology of religion, holistic approach recently 48
archaeology of sexuality 131
archaeometry, simulation in 226
Aristotle, conflict and collapse of society 55
Arrow, K. 183
Arthur, Brian 182
artifacts, altered by archaeological formation process 121–2; archaeologists' view of 90; bodies in Middle and late Bronze Age treated as 189; investigator studies group to answer specific question 123–4; moved by glaciers and human action 86
artificial intelligence programs, used to simulate prehistoric thought patterns 224
Ashworth, Geoffrey 222
Asiatic Mode of production 38
astronomical relationships, 'statistical' type of approach 15
Atlantis 22
Atran, S. 173
Aubrey, John 46
Australian *Women in Archaeology* conferences 129
australopithecines, only known from southern Africa till (1959) 72
Australopithecus robustus 72–3
autistic children, lack a 'theory of mind' module 172
Avebury 46, 51–2
axes, Acheulean handaxes 25–6; comparison of European, Canadian and Caribbean 264; distribution maps for finds of stone 34; Europe and America 154; Lower Palaeolithic handaxes (Hoxne in Suffolk) 8; trade of British Neolithic stone axes and 32

Babylon, site evaluation by Claudius Rich 108
Bahn, P. xiii

Bailey, Geoff, *time scale* and time resolution 269
Bamiyan Buddhas 222
bands 51, 164, 191
Bapty, I. xii, 257
Baringo, Hodder's work in 100
Barker, Philip, excavating at Wroxeter and Hen Domen 107
Barkow, J.H. 172
Baron-Cohen, S. 172
Barrett, J. 4, 208, 210, 242, 257
Bauer, A.A. 255
Beaudry, M. 257
behaviour and tolerances of plant and animal species, same in past as in present 277
behavioural archaeologists, historical nature of archaeological record 123
behavioural archaeology programme 123
Berkeley, Bishop George 91–2
Bertalanffy, L. von 261
Bible, the, ornamented with gold leaf to show value of Word of God 140
Biddle, Martin, excavating at Winchester 107
Binford, L.R., xi; 'Archaeology as Anthropology' 213; a culture seen as system of subsystems 259–60; ethnoarchaeology and 99–100; 'giving meaning to the archaeological record' 217; key points of agenda for New Archaeology 214; 'New Archaeology' and 83; problems with processual archaeology 216; religion a factor to be considered 46–7; research among living peoples (ethnoarchaeology) 123; sites as parts of burial systems 106; time scale and time resolution 269; universal laws of culture and 186, 214
Binford, S.R. xi
biology, species identification of exotic species 34
biostratigraphy, centre of palaeoanthology 65
Bleed, P. 28
body, expressive of values in ways it moves 136; funerary archaeology and 135

body, the, principal physical locus of experience 6
Book of Genesis, scholars and Earth's formation 8
Boone Conference (1992) 129
Boucher de Perthes, Jacques 10; Lyell's visit to (1859) 277
Bourdieu, P. 4–5, 133, 135–6, 208, 241–2, 257
Boxgrove, English Lower Palaeolithic site and development of voles 65
Bradley, B. 26
Bradley, R. 204, 271
Braithwaite, Richard Bevan xi
Britain, archaeology allied with anthropology 193; beads of faience from Bronze Age 32; indigenous archaeology 149; open area excavation (1960s) 107; post-processual archaeology 208; PPI 200; Working Group on human remains in museums and universities 148
Britain and America, individual approach to biological data 87; study of social organisation has broadened 194
Britain and Scandinavia, impact of post-procesual critique 207
British 'Rescue' movement, idea of total excavation 107
Bronze Age Near East, baton of technology to prehistoric Europe 50
Bronze Age onwards, distances by networks of exchange expanded 77
Bronze and Iron Ages, cremations found 266
Bruck, J. 189
Buckland, William 9, 275–6
Burgess, Ernest 83
Busby, C.
Butser (Hampshire), experimental archaeology 111, 113–14
Butterworth, B. 172
Butzer, K. 55
Byrne, D. 237

Calusa Indian society of Florida, urbanised 165
Cambridge school 237
Campbell, E. 256

CAMSIM 227
Canada (Chacmool Conference (1989)) 129
Carruthers, P., cognitive function of language 174; 'inner speech' conveys information between modules 172
Carver, M., 'Field Research Procedure' 108; *recovery levels* monitor intensities of digging required 109
cataclymic collision between extraterrestrial object and Earth, massive extinction and 21
catastrophist archaeology 20–23
Cavalli-Sforza, Luca 224; *History and Geography of Human Genes* 18
Çatal Hüyük 119
Celtic and Viking settlers, more difficult to trace 78
Central Place Theory, geographers for study of rural agriculture 233
Chacoan society (US Southwest), collapse twelfth century AD 55
Chad, *Shalanthropus tchadensis* (2002) and dates 7 million years ago 73
Chadwick, A.J. 226
chaîne opératoire 25–9, 42, 96
change, from within as well as from outside 183
changing time scale and time perspective, cause-and-effect relationships 271
characterisation and exchange theory 31–5
Chase-Dunn, C.K. 167–8
Chavín de Huantar (Peru in first millennium BC), Lanzón or Great image 161
Cherry, J.F. 197
Chicago School of Human Ecology 82–3
chiefdom-level societies, depend on agricultural intensification 192–3
chiefdoms 51, 102, 164, 191–2, 194
Childe, Gordon, chronological foundation stone 66; concepts of time and 268; diffusionism and 67; Marxist by persuasion 50; revolutions 35–9; social archaeology 235; technical change impeded by social

hierarchy except European Bronze Age 165; wrote on Neolithic and urban revolutions about cultural and social issues 38, 81, 255; *Dawn of European Civilization, The* 36, 75; *Man Makes Himself (1936)* 36, 50; *New Light on the most Ancient East (1934)* 36; *Piecing Together the Past* 35; *Piecing Together the Past* xi; *Prehistory of European Society, The (1958b)* 38; *What Happened in History (1942)* 37–8

China 102, 138, 165, 168

Chinese philosopher (Eastern Zhou period), poem 265

Chomsky, Noam, humans born with language acquisition device 173

Christian era, autonomous individual and 188–9

Christy, Henry 65

Claassen, Cheryl 129

Clark, G. 81, 235, 268, 271

Clarke, D.L., xi; *Analytical Archaeology* (1968) 260

Clelow, C. 95

Clements, Frederick 80–81

Club of Rome 226

cognitive archaeologist 41–3, 171

'cognitive fluidity' 173

cognitive processual archaeology, post-processual and interpretive archaeology 210

Cohn, N. 65

Cold War, research into radioactivity and 67

Cole, G.D.H., *What Marx Really Meant (1934)* 36

Coles, Henry Chandler 80

Coles, John, *Archaeology by Experiment* 111

collapse 54–7

Collingwood, R.G. xi, 41

Coltheart, M. 172

commonsense view of reality, attack since rise of modern science 90

community approaches, living community and death assemblage 88

Complex Systems 182–5

complex woodlands, cycle nutrients and water in effective manner 82

complexity 54, 56

'complexity claim' 224–5

'complexity' scale, complex societies more valued than simple ones 52

computational methods, development of systems approach and 263

'concept of repair', restorative force to replenish soil supply 275

concepts of time 268–72

conflict, price of social life and cannot explain collapse 56

Conkey, Margaret 129, 209

context, definition 107

contextual archaeology, social organisation and status differences 144

Contract Archaeology 220

Cooke, K.L. 182

copper, sources 34

core traditions, cultural attributes linked together in time and space 62

correction ('calibration') curves, convert 14C dates 68–9

Cosmides, Leda 172–3

cosmological principles, location, design and orientation of houses, temples and tombs 13

Costopoulos, A. 227

'covenantal archaeology', agreements between archaeologists and local people 149

Cowgill, George, method at Mexican city of Teotihuacán 108

Crawford, O.G.S 156, 158

cremations 266

Croce, Benedetto 41

'cult', connotations of marginal 'freakish' and occasional 45

cultural ecology 83

cultural evolution 49–53; changing distributions of cultural attributes 59; cognitivist or Darwinian perspective 168; no preordained direction 53

cultural formation processes, use and reuse activities 124

cultural packages, different sizes 62

cultural politics, politicisation of archaeology and 169

cultural resource management (CRM) or rescue archaeology 220, 250

Cummings, V. 204
Cunliffe, Barry, 'levels of Publication' 109
Cuvier, Georges 8–10; mammoths become extinct and new forms come into existence 65
cybernetic system model 82
cybernetics, feature of most complex machines 261

Dakota village, ethnographic accounts of girl's relationship to her awl 119
Daniel, G.E. xi, 64
Danish National Museum in early nineteenth century, 'Three Age System' 266
'dark ages' in archaeology/systems collapse 54–7
Darwin, Charles 134, 277; descent trees and 18; *Descent of Man, The: and Selection in Relation to Sex* 71; *On the Origin of Species* 10, 70–71, 79, 85
Darwinian archaeology 49, 58–62, 168
Darwinian evolution xii
David, Nicholas 98
Davidson, I. 173
Dawkins, Richard, 'meme' as cultural equivalent of genes 59
de Jussieu, Antoine 264
de Saussure, influenced Lévi-Strauss 255
debris 121
decadence, changing morals cause collapse 56
deep time, chronological information form of animal bones 65
deer, prehistoric covered wider range of wooded and open conditions 234
Denmark 110–11, 113–14, 131, 267
Descartes, René 188; *Meditations* 92
descent of man, the 70–4
Dibble, H. 26
diet breadth model, best return for given amount of effort 60
diffusion 75–6
directional schemes for evolution of society 49, 52

directional trade, preferential access and 34
discard and abandonment behaviours, specialisation and 122
disequilibrium, ecology that has made significant contribution to archaeological ideas 83–4
Dissonant Heritage (1996) 222
distribution maps, extent and intensity in distribution of goods and 31
Dmanisi (Georgia) 179
DNA 16, 18–19, 43, 69, 73, 148
Dobres, M.-A. 210
documents, part of material culture 140; tax records and field surveys 157
domestic institutions, social change and 52–3
Donald, Merlin, development of speech and 42–3
Donnan, C. 95
Donnelley, I., *Atlantis: The Antediluvian World (1881)* 23
Dordogne region, stone axes both polished and flaked (chipped) 26
Dorset cursus, walk along and description 204
Druids 46, 138
'duality of structure' 4–5
Dubois, Eugene, finds in Java (1891–2) 71–2
Dunnell, R.C. 26
durational present, extends backwards and forwards 271–2

Earle, T. 192, 194
Early Holocene mismatches between temperature-sensitive insects and trees, post-glacial warming 87
Earth and humankind, thought to be as old as each other 274
East Africa, potassium-argon decay caused controversy (1970s) 67–8
ecofacts, not artifacts 85
ecofacts, serve as proxy for something else 86–7
ecological archaeology 79–84
ecological pyramid, substantial dissipation of energy at each feeding step 81

ecologists, movement of energy and 81
ecology, and ecological approach to archaeology 261; key concepts within had crystallised (1920s) 80
ecosystem concept 80–82
ecosystem models, equilibrium as the 'natural' state 83
Edmonds, M. 204, 210
Eggert, M.K.H. xii
Egypt, low Nile floods and collapse of Old Kingdom 55; writing and 138
Ehrenberg, Margaret, Women in Prehistory 129
Ekholm-Friedman, model of Kongo kingdom 166
Electron Spin Resonance 68
elf-shots or thunderbolts 264
Eliade, Mircea 48
embodied human experiences, central to phenomenological approach 205
energy, non-renewable resource 51, 82
energy transfer, took place during food consumption 81
engagement theory, symbol and reality co-exist in a 'hypostatic (indivisible) relationship 161
Engels, Friedrich 50
Engelstad, Erica 117
Engendering Archaeology: Women in Prehistory 129
English Heritage (UK) 220, 222
English Industrial Revolution, Childe and 37
Enlightenment, philosophy of eighteenth century 49–50
environment 79–80, 85
environmental archaeologists, study beetles to research climate or urban living conditions 86
environmental archaeology 85–9
'environmental of evolutionary adaptedness' for the human mind 173
epistemological debate, political influence on questions 118
epistemology 89–93
equifinality, definition 34
erosion, underlying tectonic instability and 271
Esper, Johann Friedrich 8
Ethiopia, Ardipithecus ramidus (1994)

73; Australopithecus afarensis (Lucy skeleton 1974) 73; Herto site discovery of modern humans (2002) 74; Homo specimens 72
ethnoarchaeology 95–100
ethnography 95,143
ethnohistory, data from used in direct historical approach 143
Eurasia in third millennium BC, period of social and economic expansion 78
Europe 168; Archaeological Heritage Management 220; basic tools such as pottery or axes invented 154; Beaker burials and La Tène complexes 200; directionality from Anatolia towards Britain and north-western Europe 18; (medieval) Dark Ages known from burials 57; (medieval) origins of humanity and the Bible 7; (medieval) saints' relics sought to promote cults 138; prehistoric and PPI 200; schnitt (slice) method of excavation 107; Upper Palaeolithic sites and hunting sites 233
European aristocracy, study of classical art and 138
European Association of Archaeologists 223
European Enlightenment, idea of human progress 264
European megalithic tombs, what it feel like to move around inside 204
European peat bogs, botanists and Nature that mirrored progress within Culture 80
Europeans, Creation as described in the Bible 138
evaluation, before excavation starts 108
'Eve theory' 178
'event', integration of processes operating on different time scales 270
evolution 50–51, 164, 186
evolution of social complexity and the state 101–4
Evolutionary ecology 83
evolutionary processes, inheritance, mutation, selection and drift 59
excavation, design relies on evaluation and is multi-vocal 108

excavation records, multi-level and multi-media 109

exchange, new levels of production and forms of specialisation 198

experimental archaeology 110–14

experiments 113–14

extraterrestrial collisions, craters scattered across our planet and 21

family tree, operating over the millennia 17

Fawcett, C. 237

feedback between culture and biology, rate of culture appears to accelerate 174

feeding relationship between predator and prey, dynamic modelling and 81

feminist archaeology xii, 116–20, 209–10

feminist critic, archaeology dealing in accounts of 'faceless blobs' 240

feminist documents, found on the web as hypertext and virtual sites 120

Feminist and Gender Archaeology, theory of social practice and 240

fieldwalking 156

fieldwork, gendered aspect of 119

first named hominid taxon, *Anthropus neanderthalensis* (later *Homo neanderthalensis*) 71

First Peoples, bones taken without consultation or permission 148; debate on cultural heritage 150

Fish, S.K. 251

Flag Fen (Peterborough), timbers under conservation and analysis 150

Flannery, K.V. 39, 143; analysis of transition to agriculture in Mesoamerica and 262; 'Archaeological Systems Theory and Early Mesoamerica' (1968) 260; contested notion that religion, ritual or art epiphenomenal 142; ecosystem thinking 83; excavated cave site of Guila Naquitz 191–2; holistic archaeology 141; human societies depended upon ritual activities 142; processual or 'New' archaeology 106; satellite camps in study of

Mesoamerican early agriculture 232; *Early Mesoamerican Village* 144; *Emergence of Civilisation* (1972) 260; 'Cultural Evolution of Civilisations, The' 263

Flem-Ath, Rand 22

Flem-Ath, Rose 22

Fodor, Jerry, *Modularity of Mind, The (1983)* 171

Foley, Rob 83, 269

Ford, J.A. 246–7

formation processes, research organised in terms of object histories 123, 125n.1

Formative Period simulations (1980–90) 225

Forrester, Jay 226

Fossils 8, 67, 72, 179

Foster, Max, invention of the context (1972) 107

Foucault, M. 4

foundationalism, attempts to identify what justifies a belief and 91–2

Fowler, C., notions of dividual and 'partible' personhood 189, 204

France, (Aude region), marks of cutting tools on bones of 'lost species' 9; cave paintings 43; cultural technology sociological and anthropological from (1930s) 26–7; Lyell's visit to Boucher de Perthes' excavations 277; Marxist anthropology (1960s and 1970s) 166; (northern) Abbeville region of Picardy, stone tools and bones 10; tradition of the body and *chaînes opératoires* 100

Frank, A.G. 166, 168

Frankenstein, S. 166

Franklin, M. 237

Fraser, S. 204

Frere, John 8, 10

Fried, M., influenced by Marx 193

Friedman, J. 166

FUGAWILAND simulation 227

full-coverage survey 251

funeral, meanings of 4

Gaffney, V., Roman Wroxeter with group at Birmingham 228

Gaillenreuth Cave (Bayreuth in German Jura), human bones and 8
Gathercole, P. 36, 38
Gebauer, A.B. 227
Geographical Positioning Systems (GPS), way to record data in field 251
Gell-Mann, M. 182, 185
Gender 130, 132, 241–2
gender archaeology 116–17,128–32
Gender in Archaeology Conference, biennial 129
gender in prehistoric archaeology, (1970s) in Europe, the Americas and Australia 128–9
gender relations, element in dynamics of communities 187
gender and sex, relationship drawn from social sciences 130
Gendered Past: A Critical Bibliography of Gender in Archaeology 129
General Systems Theory 261
genes promoted by natural selection, disperse because they bring advantages 177
Genesis, scholars and Earth's formation 8
genetics, bottleneck 179; (modular), mutation rate problem of 19
geographic variation, reflects population size expansions 178
Geographical Information Systems (GIS), plotting information 251–2
geological catchments, sources of raw materials 231
geoscience stratigraphy, science dealing with description of all rock bodies forming Earth's crust 243–4
Germany (1991), Netzwerk der Archaeologishe Arbeitende Frauen 129
Germany and Central Europe, community approach to biological data 87
Gero, Joan 119, 129, 209
Gibraltar, Neanderthal skull found (1848) 9
Giddens, A. 4–5, 135, 195, 208, 241, 257
Gilchrist, R. 117, 237; Gender and Archaeology, Contesting the Past (1999) 130; studied medieval nunneries 242

Gills, B.K. 166, 168
glass vessels, existed only in Iron Age 266
Gleick, J., Chaos 226
Goddess movement, arguments use archaeological data 117
Godelier 166
Godwin, Harry and Mary (palynologists), collaboration with archaeologist Graham Clarke 81
gold, difficult to find sources 34
golden age, Greek and Roman idea of decline from 49
Gosden, C. 237
Gosselain, O.P., potters of southern Cameroon using chaîne opèratoire 96
Gould, R. 95
Great Sphinx (Giza in Egypt), Egyptologists date to 2500 BC 23
Greece, domestic goats and hill slopes bare of vegetation and soil 271; post-Mycenaean, Dark Ages known from burials 57
Greek city-state, PPI in action 198–9
Greek Cyclades, looting of graves has destroyed evidence for prehistoric societies 223
Greek farmers, stars to identify times for ploughing and harvesting 13
Greek government, repatriation of marble sculptures and 222
Greek polis 102
Greek ship, construction of full-scale ancient experiment 113
Green, S. 39
Griffin, J.B. 246, 248
ground survey, remote-sensing technologies and 249
group-oriented chiefdoms, southern Britain responsible for henge monuments 194
Gumerman, G.J. 53, 183, 185, 227
Gunn, J. 186

habitus xii, 4, 27, 133–7, 241–2, 257
Haeckel, Ernst, hypothetical human evolutionary sequence 71; term Oecologie (1866) 79

Hall, M. 236
Hall, T.D. 167–8
Hancock, G. 23
Handbook of the South American Indians 164
Hapgood, Charles 22
Harris, David 83
Harris, E.C., contexts on diagram (matrix) 107; Principles of Archaeological Stratigraphy (1979) 245
Harris, M. 163
Harris Matrix 245
Hawkes, Christopher, 'ladder of inference' 46
Hawkins, Gerald, Stonehenge Decoded 11
Hedeager, L., Scandinavia in the Roman Age 167–8
Hegmon, M. 210; 'processual-plus' 131–2
Heidegger, M. 202
Helms, Mary 77
Hempel, Carl xi
Hendon, J. 131
heritage 221–2
hermeneutic, fitting of pieces of information 209
Hesiod's works, Greek farmers of eighth century BC 13
Hewison, R 221
Higgs, Eric 83, 230–31; development of Palaeoeconomic approach 268–9
Hill, J.N. 186
Hillier, B., space syntax 255
Historic archaeologists, written material and 128
historical archaeology, co-exists with documentary history 137–40
Hodder, I. xii, 188–9, 207–10; 'domestication of Europe' 47, 100; 'ecological functionalism' and 187; interpretation on site and 108; material culture always meaningfully constituted 255; on-site 'reflexivity' and 109; question of scale 187; social archaeology 235, 237; Simulation Studies in Archaeology (1978) 226
holistic archaeology 141–3, 145
Holmes, William Henry 26

homeostasis, could be applied to human societies as well as ecosystems 260
Homo erectus, contemporaneous with robust australopithecines 73; originated in Africa about 1.8 million years ago 71
Homo habilis (handy man) 72
Homo sapiens neanderthalensis, Homo sapiens sapiens and 17
Homo sapiens sapiens and Homo erectus, operated by 'mimesis' 43
Hosler, D. 226
human action, fluctuations of components such as elm 88
human agency, set of cultural practices 134
human body, starting point for knowledge of the world 203
human communities 80–81,194
human culture, inheritance mechanism is social learning 59
human ecology, concept of two distinct pathways in 81
human evolution, debate between Multiregional and Out-of-Africa theories 73
human occupation, pre-Clovis in New World and 122
human perception, fusion of all the senses 205
humans, based on Dubois theorists argue they evolved in Far East 72; can only study things as they experience them 205; evolved from australopithecine ancestor in Africa 178–9; experience themselves as embodied entities 188; fundamentally disequilibrium species 84; interact with each other and hence inventions and innovations 155; mental modules for reading, writing and playing chess 172; much diversity among 73, 85; not seen as dupes – they had agency 208; populations descent from multiple antecedents 178; see in species-specific way 91; selection more complex than among other animals 59–60; variation greater within populations than between them 178

hunter-gatherer societies, roles arising from age and sex 54

hunters of large herds, preferred sites 233

hunting-and-gathering, supposed to generate band society 165

Husserl, E.G.A. 202–3

Hutchins, R.M. 22

Hutton, James, planet in a state of continuous change 274–6; *Theory of the Earth* (1795) 20

Huxley, Thomas Henry 277; *Evidence as to Man's Place in Nature* 70

ibex and chamois, rough terrain at any altitude 234

ideas in relative and absolute dating 64–9

Inaugural period simulations (1970–80) 225

India 168; persons who conceive their bodies as 'permeable' 188; republican form of Vedic Period states in Ganges area 102

indigenous Americans, expansion of prairie and 81

indigenous archaeologies, xii; contracts between archaeologists and local people 150; critique of positivism 209; definition 146; problems of definition 149

indigenous cosmologies, relationships involving celestial objects and 14

individual, theories about 5

individualising chiefdoms, Mycenaean polities (1500BC) 194

individualism, valorisation of individual after French Revolution 189

Indus Valley and northwest India, state development 102

industrial societies, social roles 54

innovation and invention 59, 151–5, 262–3

Institute of Field Archaeology (UK) 223

International Code of Zoological Nomenclature, naming of new taxa and 71

internet and virtual realities, feminist archaeologists and 119

interpretation, reserved till sequence has been put together 107–8; to-and-fro between data and theory 209

interpretive archaeologists, effort of active empathy 41

interpretive archaeology 209–10

interpretive or contextual archaeologies, post-processualism and 237

invention 151–3, 155

Ireland, PPI and 200

Irish potato famine, society did not collapse 56

iron technology, stopped south of Scandinavia 154

irrigation systems 165

Isaac, Glynn 83

Isle of Man, Neolithic mortuary practices 189

isotopic analysis, information on past genealogies and diets 148

Java, *Homo erectus* 74; Ngandong fossils 72

Johnson, A. 194

Johnson, G.A. 226

Johnson, M 208; *Archaeological Theory, an Introduction* xii

Jones, A. 205

Jordan, P. 23

Jorvik archaeological theme park 224

Jouannet, François 26

Joukowsky, M.S. 228

Journal of Social Archaeology (2001) 238

Joyce, R.A. 119, 210, 237

Judge, W.J. 250

Kant, Immanuel, on what makes a person human 188

Karmiloff-Smith, A. 172, 174

Kauffman, Stuart 182

Keating, D. 205

Keen, Jake, Ancient Technology Centre (southern England) 113

Keller, C. 29

Keller, J.D. 29

Kennewick man or 'the Ancient One', legal battles over 148

Kent's Cavern (southwest England), flint tools with bones of extinct fauna 9

Kenya, Nariokotome youth discovered (1984) 73; *Orrorin tugenensis* (2001) and dates to 6 million years ago 73
Kenyon, K.M. 245
key ideas in excavation 106–9
kilogram weight, embodies the thing signified 161
Kluth, R. 146
knowledge, justified true belief 91
Kohl, P. 237; trading entities in ancient Mesopotamia 167
Kohler, T.A. 53, 183, 185, 227
Kowalewski, S.A. 251
Krakatoa eruption (South Pacific), no political collapse 56
Kramer, C. 98
Kristiansen, K., work on European Bronze Age 168
Kusimba, C. 100

landscape 29, 156–8, 204, 233, 252
landscape archaeology 156, 210, 252
'Lara Croft Tomb Raider' (computer game) 221
large-site survey or urban survey 249, 252n.1
Lartet, Edouard (French scholar) 10, 65
Late Hallstatt 'princely' grave of Hochdorf (southern Germany) 269–70
lead isotope analysis, characterisation for lead, silver or copper 34
Leakey, Louis and Mary 72
Lemonnier, Pierre 27–8, 98, 154
Leone, M. 207
Leroi-Gourhan, André, *Le Geste et la parole (1964)* 27; *L'Homme et la matière (1943–6)* 27
Leslie, A. 173
Lévi-Strauss, C. 255–7
Levy, J.E. 131
Levy, T.E. 38–9
Libby, Willard 67
Liège, animals and human bones with archaic features 9
limit cycle, stable state of oscillation 184
Liritzis, I. 226
Locke, John 91

logistic equation 82–3
long-lasting difference between regions, population isolation 177
long-term history, archaeology and 6
long-term social transformation, global dynamics and 167
Lotka, Alfred 81
Lotka-Volterra mathematical model 226
Lowenthal, D., on heritage 222
Lubbock, Sir John, word 'Neolithic' and 267; *Prehistoric Times (1865)* 66
Lucas, Gavin, interpretation on site and 108
Lucretius, poem *De Rerum Natura* (On the nature of Things) 265
Lukes, S. 189
Lyell, Charles 20–21; four different components of uniformity 276–7; geological deposits must represent tens of millennia 65; mixture of uniformitarianism and scientific catastrophism 277; uniformitarianism and 274; *Geological Evidence of the Antiquity of Man* 10; *Principles of Geology* (1830–3) 275–6
Lyman, R.L. 62

MacEnery, John 9, 275
McGhee, R. 256
McGlade, J. 183, 185
MacGregor, G. 205
McNairn, B. 36, 39, 66
Madeleine, La, Ice Age portable art 10
Mafa speakers around Mokolo, spiral with linked series of rooms 98–9
Maiden Castle 106
man, antiquity of 7–10
'Man the Hunter' model, 'Woman the Gatherer' and 128
Mandara Archaeological Project 98–9
Marcus, J. 141, 143
Marsh, G.P., *Man's Role in Changing the Face of the Earth (1864)* 85
Marx, K. idea of praxis 4
Marxism 165, 169, 260
Marxist archaeologists, relationships between social classes (Near East) 240

Marxist materialism xii, 27, 50, 160
'massive modularity' thesis 172
material culture, access to non-elite majority of society 140
material culture studies 6
material engagement approach towards study of past societies 159–60
material engagement and materialisation 159–62
material engagement theory 161
material records, perception that all are palimpsests 269–70
materialisation, way human societies use aspects of material world to give expression to symbolic concepts 160–61
materialism, determination of techno-ecological factors 163, 166, 168
materialism, Marxism and archaeology 163–9
mathematical models, fall-off curves and 34
Mauss, Marcel 27, 96
May, Sir Robert (ecologist) 83, 182
Maya, (Classic) 54–5, 131, 226
Maya 'Dresden Codex' 12
Maya region, PPI and 200
Mayanists, archaeoastronomy and 12
median-joining network methods, mutational pathways and 19
Mediterranean region, badlands erosion 270–71
Meggers, Betty 164
Meillassoux, C 166
Meltzer, D.J. 26
mental modularity 171–4
Mercati, Michel, thunderbolts and flint arrowheads made by humans 264–5
Merleau-Ponty, M. 202
Meskell, L.M. 187–8, 210, 236–7
Mesoamericanists 12 13
Mesolithic Lepenski Vir site (Balkans) 165
Mesolithic (Middle Stone Age) and Neolithic (New Stone Age) 267
Mesolithic and Palaeolithic studies, emphasis on ecological adaptation 81
Mesopotamia, city-states 23; discussion of trading entities in ancient 167;

salinisation of fields 55; (Uruk Period) import of raw materials into cities 104; writing invented 138
metals 33–4, 95, 131
Mexico, (western), complex societies 167
Middle East 168
Middle Palaeolithic Cave Bear Cults, over-interpretation of evidence 47
middle-range theory 217
migrations 75, 78
Miles, D. 150
Miller, D. 207–8
mind/body dichotomy 135
Minoan collapse, eruption of Thera and 56
Mississippian chiefdoms, mounds of 192
Mithen, S. 173–4, 210
modern techniques of survey 249–50
modularity, extended to central systems 172
molluscs 232–3
molluscs and insects, resilient in face of devastation 88–9
Moore, H. 95
Morgan, L.H., sequence from savagery to barbarism to civilisation 21, 50
motor habits 186
multiregional evolution 176–80
multiregional model, natural selection and 177
multivocality, post processual claim and 119
Munnell, K. 146–7
Museology or Museum Studies, research into museums as cultural institutions 220
museums, visitor experience and 219–20
Myres, J.L., Dawn of History, The 36
mystical factors, collapse of society and 55

Nagaoka, L., exploitation of seals and moas 61
Napoleon's expedition to Egypt, Rosetta Stone (1799) and 138
National Parks Service (United States) 220

Native American Graves and protection and Repatriation Act (NAGPRA 1990) 147–8

natural catastrophes, course of human history and 21

natural communities, path of succession to climax 80

natural selection, idea of optimisation 60

naturalists, using Steno' principles started looking at primitive artifacts 244

nature/culture 134–5

Neanderthal (1856), bones discovered at 9

Neanderthal hominid, ancient DNA from bones of 17

Neanderthals 71, 74, 173

Near East, Egyptian king lists basis of chronological reconstructions 66

negative feedback, where output is monitored so that change can be countered 260–1, 262

Nelson, S.M., *Gender in Archaeology, Analysing Power and Prestige* 130

Neo-Marxists, denied priority of infrastructure over superstructure 260

neo-Pagans and Druids, objected to excavations at Seahenge on Holme-next-the-Sea 149

Neolithic axes 26

Neolithic and Bronze Age Britain, astronomical and calendrical knowledge 12

Neolithic economy, resisted by Late Mesolithic society (Ertebølle Culture) 154

Neolithic religions, priests and priestesses and 47

New archaeologists, particularities of human experience of little interest 186; sites as parts of buried systems 106

New Archaeology or processual archaeology xi, 41, 46, 212; anthropological theme of cultural ecology and 83; environmental archaeology and 85; influence of Leslie White 164

New Guinea Highlands, *chaíne opératoire* 98

Newton, Isaac 274

nineteenth-century geology, landscape as slow process of change 157

Nineveh, excavation by Layard 139

Noble, W. 173

non-site approach, individual artifact is basic unit of record 251

North America 26, 246

North American academic circles, feminist archaeology and 117

northern Europe, prehistorians and Bourdieu's ideas 242

Northwest Coast Indians, society quite stratified 165

Norway, KAN (*Kvinner in Archaeologi*, Women in Archaeology) 130; 'Were They All Men?' 129

notions of the person xii, 186–9

Nunamiut, the, Binford's work among 100

Oakley, Kenneth 67

object history 123

O'Brien, M. 62

observatory, used to describe astronomically aligned monuments 12

obsidian, characteristics important for characterisation study 33

Oldowan technology among austropithecines, mental modules 174

Olduvai Gorge (Tanzania), hominid fossil 72

Olivier, L. 269–70

Olmec in Mesoamerica, massive sculpted stone heads and chiefdom 192

Olsen, B. 257

optical thermoluminescence, single and double blind experiments 226

optimal diet, what would lead to change in? 61

optimal foraging theory, used to define time-distance limits 232

oral histories, archaeological evidence and 150

organic analogies, collapse of society and 55–6

organisation of societies, including chiefdoms 191–5

Overton Down (Wiltshire), experimental archaeology (1960s) 110–12

palaeoanthropogists, Neanderthals and 71
palaeoenvironmental techniques, climate change and 233–4
Palaeolithic and Neolithic periods, defined by Lubbock 66
Palaeolithic (Old Stone Age), ice ages, cave dwellers and flaked flint tools 267
Palaeolithic period, numerical and calendrical notations may have been recorded 139
Paley, S.M., Nimrud reconstruction while working at Buffalo 228
PALOMA WORLD, virtual tour of prehistoric Peruvian village 228
Papua New Guinea, slash-and-burn agriculture 28; Wola of Southern Highlands of 96–7
Park, Robert 83
Parker Pearson, M. 256
past and future, arbitrarily defined concepts 272
Patterson, T.C. 166, 237
Paviland Cave (south Wales), excavation of male burial 9
Pearthree, E. 225
peasant rebellions, collapse of society and 55
pedestrian survey (fieldwalking or archaeological reconnaissance) 249
Peer Polity Interaction see PPI
Per Polity Interaction and Socio-Political Change (1986) 197
Peretz, I. 172
Peru, Chav'n de Huantar 161; PALOMA WORLD, virtual tour of prehistoric village 228; Virú Valley survey (1940s) 250, 252n.2
Petrie, W M F 235–6
phenomenological archaeology 201–6; habitus and 242
phenomenology xii, 201–2
phenomenon, entity (thing or event), that presents itself to a subject 201
Philippines 165
Phillips, P. 247

philosophical issue, differences between past, present and future 271–2
phylogenetic methods, analysis to arrange data into tree diagram (dendrogram) 18
Picard, Casimir 26
Pierce, 256
Piggott, S. 46, 67
Pikirayi, I. 149
Piltdown fossils 67
Pinker, Steven 172–3
Pithecanthropus erectus (erect ape man) 71
Pitt-Rivers, General xi
Pizza, A.D. 225
Plato, on collapse of society 55; Timaeus and Critas 22
Pleistocene human evolution, species replacements and 178
Polanyi, Karl, substantivist approach 35
pollen analysis (1916) 80–81, 85
pollen catchment, finer-grained spatial reconstructions and 234
pollen falling into a bog, determined by single measure 107
Polybius, conflict and collapse of society 55
Pomeroy, Sarah, Goddesses, Whores, Wives and Slaves (1975) 128
Popper, Karl 42, 112
population growth (prehistoric), role of chance 225
population mixing, widespread evolution of common features 177
populations living in desert conditions 184
Porter, E. 226
post processual claim, multivocality and 119
post-Hittite Anatolia, almost no archaeological record 57
post processual archaeologists 144–5, 208, 241
post-processual/interpretive archaeology xi–xii, 4, 207–11; archaeoastronomy and 13; archaeologists and views outside academia 149; based on critiques of processual archaeology in (1980s) 209; critique dealt with

meaning or symbolism and 207; explicitly a social archaeology 237; gender fits well with methods and aims of 131; interpretive tradition (1980s and 1990s) 41; need to return to history 208; neglected religion in favour of 'ritual' 47; particular persons and their biographies 187; response to failings of processual archaeology 207; twenty-first century is used in two ways 210
post-processualists 99
postmodernists as group, reject 'standard' epistemological concerns 93
pot, intrudes into the semiotic process 257
pottery 62, 85, 95–6, 108, 154, 266
power 3, 6
PPI 196–200
prehistory 78, 139, 268
prehistory and historic archaeology, mental modularity and 174
prestige goods 166
Preucel, R.W. 236, 255
Price, T.D. 229
Prigogine, I. 182
principles of stratigraphic succession xii, 243–7
processual archaeologists 215–17, 236, 240
processual archaeology 212–17; cultural change should be principal goal 212–13, 255; functional aspect of symbols 255; has been less interested in gender 131; hypothetico-deductive positivism from Hempel 208; new research into archaeological formation processes 122; systems thinking an integral part (1960s and 1970s) 259–60; United States and 210, 213
processual/post-processual archaeology 75, 211
processual/post-processual split, American scholars and 5
production, always socially organised 166
proprietorial relationship with the past, excludes some 223

proxies, best are those that have narrow ecological range or niche 87
public archaeology 219–23
public archaeology/museology/conservation/heritage 219–23

quasi-periodic, two or more attractors differ 184

radioactive decay, requires understanding of U-Series and Electron Spin Resonance 68
radioactive decay detected (1905) 66
radiocarbon clock, natural production of 14C alters ticking of 68
radiocarbon dating (1949) xi
radiocarbon dating by Accelerator Mass Spectrometry (AMS) 68
Rappaport, R. 83, 142, 261
Read, D.W. 224–5
recognising processes, artifact assemblage and 124
Redman, Charles, Qsar es-Seghir excavation 107
Regeneration period simulation (1990-present) 225
'regional continuities', anatomical distinctions 176–7
Reid, J.J. 123
'Reindeer age', identified by Gabriel de Mortillet 65
religion 45, 47
religious dimension, social relationships and intelligent use of *things* 161
Renaissance, the 157, 188
Renfrew, C. xiii, 39, 210; archeological record of Late Neolithic Wessex of Avebury and Stonehenge 51–2; cognitive processual archaeology 210; consideration of religion in four main categories 47; effect of absolute dating techniques 66; on Greek city-states 199; 'group-oriented' and 'individualising' chiefdoms' 194; 'How many people belong to the society?' 193; monuments and other features symbolise group's presence in territory 192; non-linear change 182; peer polity interaction 76; post-collapse

societies and 57; prestige goods in burials and status 255; social archaeology 235; 'symbolic entrainment' 198; 'Trade as Action at a Distance' 197; *An Island Polity (1982)* 197; *Approaches to Social Archaeology* (1984) 23

Renfrew, C. and Cherry, *Peer Polity Interaction and Socio-Political Change (1986)* 197

repeated survey of same area, to counter fluctuations in data 251, 252n.3

resilient social system, can adapt to wide range of changes 184

resources, ranked in terms of returns they produce 60–61

restoration, Babylonian king (sixth century BC) 138

Reynolds, P.J. 113

Rhode, A. 264

Rhodes, Cecil 149

Rice, P. 96

Richards, C. 204, 257

ritual, as problematical term 46

ritual discard 125

Robb, J. 210

Roman Empire, collapse in fifth century AD 54

Romantic movement, aesthetic appreciation of landscapes 157

Roskams, Steve, records deposit context by context 107

Rowlands, M. 39, 166, 168

Ruelle, David 182

Ruskin, John, on defenders of 'antediluvian man' 275

Sabloff, J.A., School of American Research Seminar on Simulations in Archaeology (1978) 226

Sahlins, M. 4, 192, 208

Sallach, D.L. 227

Salvador, A. 243

salvation, Christian idea of movement towards 49

samples 106

Samuels, R. 172

Sangiran (Indonesia), fossil remains show colonisation as early as when human line emerged 179

sapient paradox 43, 162

Sartre, J.-P. 202

Sauer, Carl Ortwin 83

Sawer, M. 38

SCA 230–32

Scandinavia, layer surfaces (open area excavation) 107

Scarre, C. 204

sceptical arguments, reframe epistemology to bridge the gap 92

sceptical postmodernists, 'reality' is linguistic convention 92

Schiffer, M.B. 123, 247, 251

Schlanger, N. 26–7, 29

Schmerling, Philippe-Charles (Dutch doctor) 9

Schmidt, P.R. 237

Schmidt, R. 237

Schmitt, E. 224

Schoch, R. 23

scholars, ancient cooking activities 124

sea travel by pre-sapiens hominids, questions about communication 43

Seahenge on Holme-next-the-Sea (Norfolk), controversy about 149

Searle, John 44, 93, 161; *Construction of Social Reality, The* 92

Second World War, absolute dating techniques, rewriting of European prehistory 66–7

sediment catchment, finer-grained spatial reconstructions and 234

seeds of plants eaten on a site, extracted by sieving single pit 107

semiotics 27

seriation 61–2, 246–7

Service, Elman 51, 103, 191, 193–4

SETs 231–3

settlement, space within clean and dirty areas and 256

settlement pattern archaeology 104

settlement pattern studies 217

sex, biological differences between men and women 130

Shag River Mouth (New Zealand), use of sea and land resources 61

Shanks, Michael 47, 207, 237

Shape Group (Brown University), virtual reality of Petra 228

Shennan, S.J. 62, 255

Shepherd, N. 237
Sherratt, A. 38–9, 75–6, 168
Siberia (1908), 'Tunguska bolide' 21
sign, meaning can only be understood in relation to total set of signs 257
signifier and signified, relationship between arbitrary 256
Silbury Hill 64
Sillitoe, Paul 96–7; *Made in Niugini (1988)* 97–8
simulations 224–8
single context recording 108
site catchment analysis *see* SCA
site exploitation territories *see* SETs
site survey 249
Site Territorial Analysis *see* STA
sites, must be discovered before they can be explored 249
sky phenomena 14
social archaeologist, social order, reproduction and social change 240
social archaeology 235–8
'social complexity' 102, 104
social Darwinist competition 50
'social differentiation', degrees of economic privilege 102
societies, survive by changing 183
Society of American Archaeology 223
Sorenson, M.L.S., *Gender Archaeology (1999)* 130
Soviet archaeologists, denied existence of AMP 38
Spain, cave paintings 43; Rhesus Negative blood group in Basque country 17–18
Spanish chroniclers, ethnohistorical data and 12
spatial models for trade and exchange 34
Spector, Janet 129; *What This Awl Means (1993)* 119
speech, controversial question of development 42
Spelke, E.S. 173
Spencer, Herbert 85
Spencer-Wood, Suzanne, historic archaeology meeting (1986) on gender 128
Sperber, D., mental mobile integrating output from other modules 172

Sri Lankan experiments, hillside iron-smelting furnaces and 112
STA 231–2
staircase model of cultural change 182
stars, long-distance navigation and 13
'state', the 102, 142
states 51, 102–3, 191, 193
Stein, G. 167
Steno, N., first stratigrapher 244
Stensen, Niels 8
Steward, Julian (American) 50, 83, 163–4, 165
Stone Age 266–7
Stonehenge 11, 46, 51–2, 138, 249; 'bluestones' Prescelly Mountains (South Wales) 31; chiefdom and 192
strange attractors, predictions impossible 184
Strathern, M., Melanesians are 'dividuals' 188
stratigraphic principle, fossils in geological layers and 8
stratigraphic succession, foundation of relative dating in archaeology 243
stratigraphy 86, 243–4
stratigraphy of prehistorians, single sequence of rock divided into multiple set of units 244–5
strontium isotope analysis on bones, whether person has moved 77
structural archaeology xii
structuralism 27, 256–7
structuralist archaeologists, prehistoric paintings and geometric motifs on cave walls 240
structure, four successively complex social types 51
students, timed walks from Natufian and Neolithic sites in Israel and Palestine 231
Stukeley, William 46, 64, 138
Sturdy, D. 233
style and workmanship, recognition of Olmec mask or Egyptian sculpture 32
surface survey, methodology for information at regional scale 249
survey 249–52
survey data, affected by circumstance of data collection 251

sustainable biomass 81–2
Sutton Hoo (English site), evaluation lasted three years 108
SVGASMP, emphasises combining and simulation strategies for survey and excavation 227–8
swidden (slash-and-burn) agriculture 164
Swiss lakes, dry summers (1860s) lowered water levels 85
symbolic material culture, treat as a text 255
symbolic and structuralist archaeology 255–7
symbolism 208, 254
symbols, function of information exchange 255
Syria, collapse of Tell Leilan 55
system, functioning whole composed of interrelated parts 259
systems approach, criticised as exogenous 262
systems thinking 259–63

Tainter, J.A. 56–7
Tanner, Nancy 128
Tansley, Arthur 80–82
taphonomic studies, insight into human action 88
taphonomy, laws of burial 122
Taung child (1924), *Australopithecus africanus* 72
Taylor, W.W. 213
technological change, altered the potential of soils 234
Teotihuacán monument 249
theorising diffusion and population movements 77–8
theory of natural selection, human evolution and 70
theory of social practice 240–42
theory of structuration xii, 135, 241
thinking and problem-solving, distinctly unmodular 171
Thom, Alexander 12
Thom, René, 'Theory of Complex Systems' 182
Thomas, J.S. 189, 202–3, 226, 242, 257
Thomsen, Christian Jürgensen (Danish museum curator) 21, 46, 265–7; *Guide to Northern Archaeology* 266

Three Age System (stone, bronze and iron) xii, 46, 64, 264–7
Tilley, C., xii; 47, 189, 202–3, 205, 207–10, 237
Time Team, Seahenge on Holme-next-the-Sea and 149–50
Tooby, John 172–3
tools 9–10, 174, 264–5, 267
topography, scholars of sixteenth to eighteenth centuries and 157
Tournal, Paul 9, 275
trace element analysis 32–4
trade in metals, problem that there can be many possible sources 33–4
trading empires, colonies and diaspora populations 167
traditional catastrophism, doctrine of 'uniformitarianism' 275–6
transdisciplinary discussions, archaeologists, anthropologists, political scientists and sociologists 168
travels and interaction, universal features of all societies 77
tree ring dating (1930s) 66–7
tribes 51, 164, 191–2, 194
Trigger, B.G. 36, 38–9, 52, 67, 208
Tringham, R. 39, 119, 210
Troy, excavation by Schliemann 139
Tsembaga Maring (New Guinea) 83
Tunbridge, J.E. 222
Turner, V. 208
twentieth-century ecologists, treatment of group units and environment 79–80
'Two Spirits', known ethnographically in America 130
Tylor, Edward. 45; *Reaches into the Early History of Mankind and the Development of Civilization* 21

UK, Theoretical Archaeology Group 129
UNESCO, role in promoting the conservation of remains of the past 220, 222
uniformitarianism 20, 87, 274–7
uniformitarians, had to apply imagination to the evidence 276
United States 208, 210, 213, 220, 222, 249–50

DISCARD

Upper Palaeolithic hunter-gatherers, property relationships limited 162

Upper Palaeolithic seafaring, characterisation study and 34

urban archaeology, elite zones and 104

urban revolution, Childe on complexity of 37

Ussher, Archbishop, chronology of human history and 7–8, 65, 138, 274, 276

validation, rests on testability not upon authority 42

Valley of Oaxaca (Mexico), ethnography data and 143; Flannery excavated cave site of Guila Naquitz 191–2; Marcus/Flannery 143

value-led excavation, reconciles ethical and academic concerns 109

van der Leeuw, S.E. 183, 185

Veit, V. xii

Vita-Finzi, Claudio 230–31

Volterra, Vito 81

Von Post, Lennart 80–81

Voss, B. 237

Walker, W.H. 125

Wallace, Alfred Russell 70, 277

war chariot 152

warfare, intensifies production and favours hierarchical institutions 198

water, least transportable resource 233

Watkins, J. 237

Watson, A. 205

weeds, resilient in face of soil disruption 88

Western City, explaining in ecological terms 83

Wheeler, Sir Mortimer 67, 106, 245; *Archaeology from the Earth* xi, 245

White, Leslie 50–51, 163–4, 186, 214

white marble, not easy to distinguish between different quarries 33

Whiten, A. 174

Wilkinson, J.R. 62

Willey, G. 226, 250, 252n.2

WINDIG-FREEWARE, simulation based on SYSGRAF 227

Wittfogel, Karl 165

Wobst, M. 208, 255

World Heritage Sites 222

World System approach, archaeological cases and 35

Worsaae, Jens Jacob 46, 267

writing 138, 172, 174

Wylie, Alison 117–18, 129, 209

Y chromosome 17–18

Yates, T. xii, 257

Yentsch, A. 256–7

Zapotec civilisation 143

Zihlman, Adrienne 128

Zimmerman, L. 149

Zinjanthropus boisei (now *Australopithecus boisei*) 72

Zooarchaeologists 122

Zubrow, E. 224–7